Maritime Law Evolving

To mark the 30th anniversary of the Institute of Maritime Law at Southampton University, current and former maritime law researchers came together to discuss the evolution of this fascinating area of law in the last 30 years and to stimulate discussion on its possible future. Their papers, edited by Professor Malcolm Clarke under the title Maritime Law Evolving, provide a series of thought-provoking essays on the most controversial and topical issues which have occupied maritime law researchers in the last three decades and which will continue to be at the heart of this ever-evolving discipline in the foreseeable future. The resulting work cuts across disciplines, spanning developments in areas as diverse as the management of the oceans and the evolution of the carriage and insurance sides of shipping law, including the ever increasing influence of the European legislator in matters of conflict of laws and enforcement.

Maritime Law Evolving

Thirty Years at Southampton

Edited by Malcolm Clarke

·HART·
PUBLISHING

OXFORD AND PORTLAND, OREGON
2013

Published in the United Kingdom by Hart Publishing Ltd
16C Worcester Place, Oxford, OX1 2JW
Telephone: +44 (0)1865 517530
Fax: +44 (0)1865 510710
E-mail: mail@hartpub.co.uk
Website: http://www.hartpub.co.uk

Published in North America (US and Canada) by
Hart Publishing
c/o International Specialized Book Services
920 NE 58th Avenue, Suite 300
Portland, OR 97213-3786
USA
Tel: +1 503 287 3093 or toll-free: (1) 800 944 6190
Fax: +1 503 280 8832
E-mail: orders@isbs.com
Website: http://www.isbs.com

British Library Cataloguing in Publication Data
Data Available

ISBN: 978-1-84946-399-7

Typeset by Criteria International
Printed and bound in Great Britain by
TJ International Ltd, Padstow, Cornwall

MIX
Paper from
responsible sources
FSC® C013056

To Emeritus Professor John F. Wilson

Preface

Maritime Law Evolving: Thirty Years at Southampton is an apposite but seemingly surprising title for this book. It is apposite in its accuracy, reflecting the content of a collection of peer reviewed essays which covers a wide range of mostly maritime law topics. The title is surprising at first sight in that the publication of the book marks the achievements of the past – the past 30 years – in which members of the Institute of Maritime Law, a prominent part of the Faculty of Law in the University of Southampton, have crossed the world with the message of maritime law to those (many) willing to listen and learn. Of these some have been motivated to come to the Institute to learn more.

Having worked with members of the Institute on various projects in the past, it has been no surprise to me that it has been an instructive process to read and in minor respects edit this collection of their scholarship.

Malcolm Clarke
St John's College
Cambridge
April 2013

Table of Contents

3. Developments in Marine Insurance, Jurisdiction and Enforcement

List of Contributors

Regina Asariotis
Senior Legal Affairs Officer, United Nations Conference on Trade and Development
(UNCTAD), Geneva
A Barrister of England and Wales

Prof Yvonne Baatz
A Solicitor of the Senior Courts of England and Wales
Professor of Maritime Law, Institute of Maritime Law, University of Southampton

Prof Malcolm Forster
Principal Consultant, former Partner, Freshfields Bruckhaus Deringer LLP
A Solicitor of the Senior Courts of England and Wales

Prof Nick Gaskell
Professor of Maritime and Commercial Law, Marine and Shipping Law Unit
(MASLU), TC Beirne School of Law, University of Queensland
Barrister, Quadrant Chambers, London

Johanna Hjalmarsson
Informa Law Senior Research Fellow in Maritime and Commercial Law, Institute
of Maritime Law, University of Southampton

Jennifer Lavelle
Post-Graduate Researcher in Law, University of Southampton
Tutor in Law, University of Southampton

Filippo Lorenzon
A Solicitor of the Senior Courts of England and Wales
Avvocato in Venezia (Italy)
Senior Lecturer in Maritime and Commercial Law
Director, Institute of Maritime Law, University of Southampton
Consultant, Campbell Johnston Clarke LLP, London

Dr Melis Özdel
Lecturer in Maritime Law, University College London (UCL)

Alexander Sandiforth
A Solicitor of the Senior Courts of England and Wales
Associate, Reed Smith LLP

Dr Andrew Serdy
A Solicitor of the Supreme Court of New South Wales
Reader in Public International Law, Institute of Maritime Law, University of Southampton

Richard Shaw
Senior Research Fellow, Institute of Maritime Law, University of Southampton

Prof Mikis Tsimplis
Professor of Oceanography and Maritime Law, Institute of Maritime Law, University of Southampton

Table of Cases

Table of Legislation

Directives

Statutory Instruments

United States

Introduction

Maritime Law Evolving: Thirty Years at Southampton is a collection of peer-reviewed papers written by present and past members of the Institute of Maritime Law at the Southampton Law School on the occasion of the thirtieth anniversary of the Institute.

The purpose of the exercise is to celebrate three decades of maritime law scholarship at Southampton; and what better way to celebrate legal research than more legal research spanning all areas of maritime law? Every contributor to this book has played (and in most cases still plays) a crucial role in the Institute's past and current success.

Each piece in this collection has a dual purpose: to look back to the development of the law during the last three decades with the unique perspective of a close active observer and to look forward to the direction which that development may take. As one may expect, every piece has its own identity, style and approach: some have looked at one case and its impact while others have focused on a convention or a particular issue. But all pieces are firmly about development, movement forward, *evolution*. The overall result is an insightful, thought-provoking and dynamic picture of the evolution of the maritime law and a unique vision of its future challenges and direction.

Maritime Law Evolving is about celebrating the ground-breaking vision of our founders David Jackson, John Wilson and Robert Grime, the tireless work of our many members and the extraordinary achievements of thirty years of passion and commitment to the development of maritime law. Thirty years. And what extraordinary years of change, challenges and achievements these have been! The world we are living in today is a brand new one where passengers and cargo ships, platforms and off-shore vessels are plying a sea swimming with a new and complicated network of norms, regulations and international best practices. And a lot more change is coming… The Institute has devoted three decades of its existence to contribute to these developments with research and its dissemination to many generations of doctoral and masters students and delegates at their professional training events.

It may be worth at this stage to say a word about the cover of this book: SeaTrade, a piece of contemporary art by Frank Worthington, the winner of a competition held at the Winchester School of Art for a piece which represents our 30 years of law reform. Contemporary art is a very personal matter but if you see international maritime trade as the cause and effect of a network of contracts, hard and soft laws and customs as I do, SeaTrade is a very striking visual representation of the work performed at the Institute.

In the last three decades the Institute has seen many storms, lost members of its crew to the waves of life and recruited new ones from near and distant shores. Aged 30, the Institute continues to grow in numbers, commitments and influence into the world of shipping and commodities and to offer food for thought to the maritime professions. *Maritime Law Evolving: Thirty Years at Southampton* is intended to provoke further reactions, opinions and discussion and further the impact of the research made in Southampton.

This work would not have been possible without the patience and encouragement of Prof. Malcolm Clarke who has kindly agreed to edit this work and arrange the review of all papers. We are also grateful to friends and colleagues at the Institute of Maritime Law at the Southampton Law School for their unconditional continuous support and encouragement. We mention in particular Debo Awofeso and Tobi Seriki at the IML for their patience, accuracy and efficiency and Rachel Turner and Tom Adams at Hart Publishing for their remarkable patience and the excellent quality on the production side.

Filippo Lorenzon
Director, Institute of Maritime Law
April 2013

Part 1

Developments in the Management of the Oceans

1

*Somali Piracy – An Affront to International Law?**[1]

MALCOLM FORSTER

I. INTRODUCTION

WHEN THE INSTITUTE of Maritime Law was founded in 1982, the ancient tradition of piracy might have been expected to be a thing of the past. In that very year, however, the draftsmen of United Nations Convention on the Law of the Sea (UNCLOS), which was seen as recasting and modernising the international legal regime of hydrospace, felt themselves unable to dispense with a proscription of piracy, itself cast in terms which were almost exactly identical to those which had appeared in its predecessor, the Geneva Convention, quarter of a century before.[2] That 1958 definition[3] itself largely codified the pre-existing customary law, so the lineage of the UNCLOS provision testifies to both the longevity and the resilience of the custom of piracy.

In the thirty years since 1982, there have been several important changes in the circumstances surrounding this age-old custom of the sea. Of these, among the most influential, have been the association of the venerable institution of piracy with the recent phenomenon of the 'failed state', the linkage (or lack of it) between piracy and terrorism and the impact of human rights concerns on the readiness of States to take robust action (or, on occasion, any action to speak of) against pirates.

---

* This chapter describes the position as at July 2012.
[1] 'Piracy off the Somali coast is an affront to the rule of international law'. *per* the Rt.Hon. William Hague PC, MP, UK Secretary of State for Foreign Affairs, *A New Effort to Help Somalia,* speaking at Chatham House on 8 February 2012
[2] UNCLOS, art 101 and text at footnotes below.
[3] Geneva Convention on the High Seas 1958, art 15.

II. IS PIRACY A NATURAL CONSEQUENCE OF THE RECENT HISTORY OF SOMALIA?

Somalia[4] owes its existence to the withdrawal of the colonial power from British Somalialand in 1960, a withdrawal ostensibly co-ordinated with that of Italy from its neighbouring territory of Italian Somalialand. The subsequent political history of the newly-formed country has been unfortunate. The oppressive regime of Mohammed Said Barre, which seized power in 1969, condemned the country to three decades of authoritarianism and human rights abuse. Following the collapse of that regime in early 1991, there was some fear that the country might disintegrate, with the region of Somalialand, in the north-west asserting its ambitions for independence. The north-eastern provinces, which form the true 'Horn of Africa' and which are collectively known as Puntland, subsequently established themselves as an autonomous, self-governing region, but one which does not at present aspire to statehood. After a false start in 2000, a national government, the Transitional Federal Government (TFG), was established in 2004, to a large extent as a result of international involvement.

The seas surrounding the Arabian peninsula have long been the haunt of pirates, but the modern era of piracy off the Somali coast is said to have begun in the early 1990s, allegedly in desperation caused by the systematic over-fishing of the Somali stocks by foreign fishing fleets. This state of affairs is said to have prompted the dispossessed fisherman to 'police' the fishing grounds, demanding payments from foreign vessels in the form of a fishing 'tax', demands which were soon reinforced by resort to small arms.[5] In 2008, pirates attacked about 120 vessels and the industry was calculated to be worth about $100 million.[6] The tempo continues to quicken, with no fewer than 97 attacks taking place in the first quarter of 2011.[7] Whatever may have been the origin of Somali piracy, in its modern form it is clearly no longer a substitute for fishing, but highly organised maritime crime, with few of the current target vessels being fishing trawlers, but rather commercial traffic.[8] There is evidence that the pirates themselves are financed by investors, both within Somalia and elsewhere, who receive 'dividends' from the ransom payments and other proceeds of piracy.[9]

---

[4] Although Somali piracy is the most topical, the practice is truly international, with significant pockets of pirate activity in South-East Asia (especially Indonesia) and off the West African coast – see the 'live' piracy incident maps on the website of the International Maritime Bureau at www.icc-ccs.org/piracy-reporting-centre/imb-live-piracy-map.

[5] See 'Piracy At Sea', *New York Times*, 14 February 2012.

[6] *Ibid.*

[7] House of Commons, Select Committee on Foreign Affairs, 10th Report of Session 2010–2012, *Piracy of the Coast of Somalia* [hereinafter Select Committee, 10th Report], at para 2. The Committee also noted the possibility of 'copy-cat' attacks in the Gulf of Guinea being inspired by events off Somalia. There is some fear also that increased naval patrols off Somalia have driven pirates 'into the Arabian Sea and beyond', see *Best Management Practices for Protection Against Somalia Based Piracy*, 4th version (*infra*), at para 2.1.

[8] Select Committee, 10th Report, at para 5, quoting the evidence of the Head of the Defence Crisis Management Centre (MoD). Witnesses before the Select Committee attributed the recent increase in the use of violence by pirates also to 'an increasing degree of criminality' – see para 13. As many as 62 seafarers have been killed in attacks, above at para 17.

[9] *Ibid,* at para 7; see the evidence of Captain Reindorp, RN.

The typical method of operation favoured by the pirates is to approach the target vessel in relatively small skiffs driven by high-performance outboard motors and to scale the ship's side using grappling lines and boarding ladders.[10] The crew is then often held hostage and a ransom demanded. Despite official disapproval, but understandably, these ransoms are often paid. They are thought typically to amount to $1–2 million.[11] The economic impact, of course, is much wider:–

> Lawlessness in Somalia is ... a threat to international shipping. 23,000 ships transit through (*sic*) the Gulf of Aden each year, a vital artery of the global economy. Nearly one trillion dollars of trade to and from Europe alone travelled through the Gulf last year.[12]

Latterly, in a disturbing new development, pirates have begun to use captured vessels as sea-going mother-ships, thus transforming the thitherto essentially coastal-based piracy into a 'blue water' operation.

As a result of the patrols by the international flotilla, the epicentre of piracy has moved into the almost entirely lawless regions in the south and east of the country. At about the same time, there appeared an apparent connection between piracy and terrorism, perhaps involving *al-Qaeda*. Also of concern is the possible relationship between the pirates and *al Shabab*, a local Islamicist group with an appalling record of human rights abuses, including the engagement of child soldiers.[13] The House of Commons Select Committee on Foreign Affairs, however, recently received 'no direct evidence of a link between piracy and terrorism'.[14]

Somalia is a party to UNCLOS[15] and a Member State of the International Maritime Organisation (IMO). It adopts the modern standard territorial sea of 12 nautical miles and claims a 200-mile exclusive economic zone (EEZ).

III. WHAT DOES INTERNATIONAL LAW REGARD AS PIRACY?

The question of what amounts to piracy is one which some domestic courts have approached with caution. In a leading English case,[16] the then Lord Chancellor warned that:–

---

[10] *Ibid,* at para 9. Note that Captain Reindorp, RN points out that pirates have become very adaptable and may use other techniques, but the method described in the text is very common.

[11] In its evidence to the Select Committee, the Baltic Exchange calculated the cost of ransoms to the insurance industry at $350 million a year – Select Committee, 10th Report, at para 19. Piracy has doubled the premiums payable by vessels passing through areas subject to piracy – *ibid* at para 22, citing the evidence of Lloyd's.

[12] The Rt.Hon. William Hague, above.

[13] Human Rights Watch, in February 2012, accused Al Sabaab of recruitment of child soldiers, rape and forced marriage of children, etc. It also accuses the TFG of employing child soldiers – see www.hrw.org/news/2012/02/21/somalia-warring-parties-put-children-grave-risk.

[14] Select Committee, 10th Report, at para 16, citing the Head of Counter-Terrorism and UK Operational Policy at the MoD.

[15] Somalia ratified the Convention on 29 July, 1989.

[16] *In re Piracy Jure Gentium,* [1934] AC 586 , [1934] 3 All ER 506, at p 514, per Lord Sankey L.C. A couple of sentences earlier, His Lordship made clear that 'their Lordships do not themselves propose to hazard a definition of piracy'.

A careful examination of the subject shows a gradual widening of the earlier definition of piracy to bring it from time to time more in consonance with situations either not thought of or not in existence when the older jurisconsults were expressing their opinions.

The international law definition of piracy is presently contained in Article 101, UNCLOS, as

  (a) any illegal acts of violence or detention, or any act of depredation, committed for private ends by the crew or the passengers of a private ship or a private aircraft, and directed:
    (i) on the high seas, against another ship or aircraft, or against persons or property on board such ship or aircraft;
    (ii) against a ship, aircraft, persons or property in a place outside the jurisdiction of any State;
  (b) any act of voluntary participation in the operation of a ship or of an aircraft with knowledge of facts making it a pirate ship or aircraft;
  (c) any act of inciting or of intentionally facilitating an act described in subparagraph (a) or (b).

A number of issues stem from this definition.

First, Article 101 appears in that Part of UNCLOS which deals with the legal regime of the High Seas and this is reflected in the geographical scope of the Article. Thus, it would seem that, if the actions proscribed by the article were to be committed in the territorial waters of a State, these would not amount to piracy, unless the domestic law of that State[17] so characterises it. This presents very real problems in some parts of the world, eg in the South-East Asian region, almost all 'pirate' attacks take place within territorial seas.[18] Such attacks are classified by the International Maritime Organisation (IMO) as armed robbery against ships.[19] The International Maritime Bureau[20] has attempted to paper over this crack in international law by promoting a more inclusive definition of piracy, which is

an act of boarding (or attempted boarding) with the intent to commit theft or any other crime and with the intent or capability to use force in furtherance of that act.

Secondly, as is widely recognised, the Convention regards piracy as essentially a private enterprise operation. For the most part, this presents few practical difficulties, as most pirate attacks are undertaken for material gain, but, if an attack were to be motivated by other impulses (eg terrorism[21]), it would fall outside the definition in UNCLOS.[22]

---

[17] Or the laws of another State apply because that State's piracy laws assert jurisdiction on the basis of active or passive nationality.

[18] Most States now claim territorial seas of 12 nautical miles in accordance with Part II of UNCLOS.

[19] Also an unsatisfactory definition, as it resurrects the *true* issue in point in *In re Piracy Jure Gentium* (ie is actual robbery an essential element in piracy, a question answered in the negative by the Privy Council in that case).

[20] A specialist division of the International Chamber of Commerce established originally to deal with maritime fraud, but which has since developed a significant anti-piracy capability.

[21] Such as the hijacking of the *SS. Achille Lauro* in 1985. The *Achille Lauro* and the *City of Poros* (a Greek inter-island ferry attacked by Abu Nidal gunmen in 1988) may not be, on this definition, the victims of pirates, as the gunmen boarded the vessels prior to engaging in the acts of violence, their 'boarding' being, at the time is was undertaken, *arguably* legitimate.

[22] But would be covered by the definition contained in Art 3, Convention for the Suppression of

One of the important difficulties in implementing anti-piracy activities is that, in many States, the domestic law of the State do not criminalise the activities of pirates *until an attack has actually been undertaken or attempted*. While this conclusion might be drawn from the drafting of Article 101, it is more difficult to defend in the light of the definition of 'pirate ship' in Article 103, which provides that:–

> A ship ... is to be considered a pirate ship ... if *it is intended by the persons in dominant control* to be used for the purpose of committing one of the acts referred to in Article 101.[23]

It would seem clear enough that the Convention therefore imposes on States an obligation to 'repress' the activities of such a vessel, even though it has not yet embarked on an attack, provided that there is clear evidence of intention to engage in an activity proscribed under Article 101. Thus, there would seem to be clear authority for a naval patrol vessel to take action against a skiff found at sea carrying boarding ladders, grappling irons, etc (let alone weapons[24]).

IV. RESPONSE OF THE INTERNATIONAL COMMUNITY TO PIRACY IN SOMALIA

A. Dealing with the Problem – The Shipping Industry and the International Maritime Organisation

i. The International Maritime Organisation

IMO, as the United Nations agency specially responsible for securing the safety of navigation, has been engaged in anti-piracy activities since late in the last century. Initially, it was principally engaged in raising awareness and capacity-building, together with technical assistance missions in affected areas. It then moved into developing regional response organisations to combat piracy, its first success being the establishment in 1994 of the Regional Cooperation Agreement on Combating Piracy and Armed Robbery against ships in Asia (RECAAP), which includes an intelligence-sharing function.

When the situation in Somali waters deteriorated, the success of RECAAP prompted IMO to convene in January 2009 a meeting of states in the region to try to produce a similar response. The result of the meeting was the Djibouti Code of Conduct concerning the Repression of Piracy[25] and Armed Robbery against

Unlawful Acts of Violence Against the Safety of Maritime Navigation, as to which see below. Note, however, that some authorities take the view that any act of violence *without the sanction or endorsement of a State* is a private act and thus piracy – see D Guilfoyle, 'Piracy off Somalia: UN Security Council Resolution 1816 and IMO Regional Counter-Piracy Efforts' (2008) 57 ICLQ 690 (2008). See also *In re Piracy Jure Gentium* and the authorities there cited.

[23] Emphasis added.
[24] It was suggested to the Select Committee that the possession of weapons might not be enough to indicate piratical intent, as Somali fishermen might colourably claim that the weapons were kept in order to provide defence against pirates. The question, though, is one of fact and degree, and the presence of boarding gear in addition might be more difficult to explain away.
[25] The Code uses Art 101, UNCLOS definition.

Ships in the Western Indian Ocean and the Gulf of Aden (the Djibouti Code). The Code also calls upon States which sign up to it[26] to share intelligence about pirate activities and provides for a network of national focal points and information centres to facilitate this process. They are also urged to co-operate in 'arresting, investigating and prosecuting persons who have committed piracy or who are reasonably suspected' of having done so, seizing pirate ships and rescuing ships, people and property which have been 'subject to piracy'.[27] There are also extensive co-operation and mutual assistance provisions.

The Djibouti Code, however, while representing a welcome commitment by States in the region to finding, for themselves, a solution to the piracy problem, is couched in the most tentative of terms. Thus, a participating State merely declares that 'to the fullest possible extent [it] intends to cooperate' in the achievement of the desired result.[28] Furthermore, Article 15 bluntly declares that:–

> Nothing in this Code of Conduct is intended to (a) create or establish a legally binding agreement.

In April 2010, IMO established a Project Implementation Unit to assist States to meet their aspirations under the Djibouti Code, which has received something in the order of $14 million to assist in implementing the aspirations of the signatory States.

IMO is also the sponsoring organisation for the Convention on the Suppression of Unlawful Acts Against the Safety of Maritime Navigation (the SUA Convention). Initially conceived as a weapon in the struggle against terrorism, the treaty is cast in terms broad enough to be applicable in the case of piracy. The Convention provides that:–

> Any person commits an offence if that person unlawfully and intentionally:
> (a) seizes or exercises control over a ship by force or threat thereof or any other form of intimidation; or
> (b) performs an act of violence against a person on board a ship if that act is likely to endanger the safe navigation of that ship; or ...
> (g) injures or kills any person, in connection with the commission or the attempted commission of any of the offences set forth in subparagraphs (a) to (f).[29]

States Parties are obliged to exercise jurisdiction over offences of this description committed on board ships flying its own flag, or within its territory (including territorial waters) or when the offence is committed by its own nationals[30] and they may do so in other circumstances, eg when the victims of the offence include one or more of its nationals.[31] In any case, States Parties are obliged, if an alleged offender is found

---

[26] States which signed the Code of Conduct at the Djibouti meeting were Djibouti, Ethiopia, Kenya, Madagascar, Maldives, Seychelles, Somalia, Tanzania and Yemen. It has subsequently been signed by Comoros, Egypt, Eritrea, Jordan, Oman, the United Arab Emirates, Sudan and Saudi Arabia.

[27] Art 4(3)(a)–(c).

[28] For example, in relation to the core anti-piracy tasks in Art 4(3).

[29] Art 3.

[30] Art 6(1).

[31] Art 6(2)

within their jurisdiction, either to extradite the offender to a State having jurisdiction or to conduct a *bona fide* prosecution themselves.[32] The Convention entered into force on 1st March 1992 and has over 150 States Parties, but these do not include Somalia. A number of other States in the region, however, have become parties.[33]

Under the Djibouti Code of Conduct three Information Sharing Centres have been established, in Dar es Salaam, Tanzania, in Mombasa, Kenya and in Sana'a, Yemen. The three Centres became operational during the first half of 2011 and have since actively collected and disseminated piracy-related information.

ii. Industry Initiatives

The shipping industry has adopted an extensive set of recommendations, known as Best Management Practices (BMP),[34] for reducing the risk of pirate attack in the Somali region. These have been endorsed by the International Maritime Organisation (IMO).[35]

Despite the prevalence of piracy, the Maritime Safety Committee found it necessary as late as May 2011 to adopt a Resolution urging the adoption of Best Management Practices and *as a minimum* ensuring that masters have up-to-date information about conditions in the High Risk Area,[36] that they register with the security centres and 'effectively implement all recommended preventive, evasive and defensive measures'.[37]

The approved Best Management Practices for avoiding pirate attack focus on a number of aspects of ship management. Masters are advised that:–

> one of the most effective ways to defeat a pirate attack is by using speed to try to outrun the attackers and/or make it difficult to board.

There have been no recorded instances of pirates boarding a ship travelling at 18 knots or faster, so vessels are advised to maintain this speed or their full sea speed, if that is greater, while passing through the High Risk Area.[38] Similarly, while a high freeboard will not in itself guarantee defence against attack, experience shows that freeboard heights of 8 metres and above give a vessel 'a much greater chance of successfully escaping' attack.[39] In view of the limitations on the effective use of skiffs, pirates also rarely attack in sea state 3[40] or higher. A particular reason for paying attention to

---

[32] Arts 10–15.

[33] Including Djibouti, Kenya, Tanzania, Seychelles and Mauritius.

[34] International Chamber of Shipping, *et al, Best Management Practices for Protection Against Somalia Based Piracy*, 4th Version [hereinafter BMP4].

[35] Most recently, in Maritime Safety Committee Circular MSC 1/1339, 14 September 2011, in relation to BPM4.

[36] For the purpose of BMP, the High Risk Area is an area bounded by Suez and the Strait of Hormuz to the North, 10°S and 78°E.

[37] Resolution MSC 324(89), see MSC 89/25/Add.4, Annex 29, operative paragraph 1.

[38] BMP4, para 3.4. Masters are also instructed to increase speed as early as possible after sighting a suspicious vessel, in order to make its approach more difficult.

[39] *Ibid,* para 3.3.

[40] Wave heights of 0.5 to 1.25 metres; see the definitions adopted by the World Meteorological Organisation at www.wmo.int/pages/index-en.html. Note, however, that the use of mother-ships of

speed and manoeuvring is to counter the tendency of pirates to fire at the bridge of the vessel under attack[41] in order to force it to stop; for this reason, shipowners are advised to consider some form of 'ballistic protection' for crew on the bridge.[42] The bridge should also be protected by metal screens over the windows, layers of chain-link fencing to repel rocket-propelled grenades and by strict controls over access.[43] Access to the decks of the vessel should be impeded by the use of physical barriers, such as razor wire or water, foam or seam hoses.[44] Close circuit television and adequate levels of deck lighting are also recommended.[45] There are further recommendations about the advisability of providing safe muster points to which non-essential crew can retreat in the case of a pirate attack or even a 'citadel', defined as a designated pre-planned area purpose built into the ship where, in the event of imminent boarding by pirates, all crew will seek protection and which is designed and constructed to resist 'a determined pirate trying to gain entry for a fixed period of time'.[46]

Perhaps most important of all is the necessity of reporting to the two monitoring centres which provide the mechanism for liaison with the international naval forces operating off Somalia. These are the UK Maritime Trade (UKMTO) in Dubai, which should be the first point of contact for ships in the region, as it provides a day-to-day interface between masters and the naval forces deployed. Transiting vessels should send regular reports to UKMTO on entering the High Risk Area, daily while in transit through it and finally on leaving it.[47] In addition, the vessel should be in contact with the Maritime Security Centre – Horn of Africa (MSCHOA), which is the planning and co-ordination Centre for EU Naval forces (EUNAVFOR).[48] The MSCHOA website[49] contains up to the minute information on conditions in the High Risk Area and it organises group transits[50] through the International Recommended Transit Corridor (IRTC). Details of these transits (and of the 'national convoys' organised by some countries) are to be found on the MSCHOA website.[51]

The most controversial and problematic response for the shipowner is the provision of armed[52] security personnel aboard the vessel.[53] If they are to be

---

greater size means that the pirates can remain on station in more adverse conditions, although the skiffs used for the attacks themselves remain sensitive to higher sea states – see BMP4 at para 4.2.

[41] Pirates commonly use small arms and rocket-propelled grenades – BMP4, at para 4.3.

[42] *Ibid*, para 2.2.

[43] *Ibid*, paras 8.2, 8.3.

[44] *Ibid*, paras 8.5, 8.6.

[45] *Ibid*, paras 8.8, 8.9. Attacks during the hours of darkness are relatively uncommon – see para 4.5.

[46] *Ibid*, para 8.13. A safe muster point is an area, preferably low down in the ship, which can provide ballistic resistance to small arms and RPG fire for a short period of time.

[47] *Ibid*, para 5.1.1.

[48] *Ibid*, para 5.1.2.

[49] At www.mschoa.org ; see also the NATO Shipping Centre website at www.shipping.NATO.int.

[50] Details of these transits (and of the 'national convoys' organised by some countries) are to found on the MSCHOA website.

[51] See also the worldwide piracy incident reporting system operated by the International Maritime Bureau Piracy reporting Centre. See www.icc-ccs.org/piracy-reporting-centre/live-piracy-report.

[52] The use of experienced, competent but *unarmed* security personnel, while categorised as a matter for the shipowner to consider as an element in its anti-piracy risk assessment, is endorsed by BMP4 as a potentially 'valuable addition to BMP' – BMP4 at para 8.14.

[53] Note that it is not *per se* unlawful for a merchant ship to carry arms – see *Several Dutch Schuyts* (1805) 6 C.Rob.48; *The Panama* [1900] U.S.325, but a merchant ship can not lawfully assume the

carried, the compilers of BMP4 express a clear preference for them to be drawn from dedicated military service personnel, known as Military Vessel Protection Detachments. If non-military armed personnel are on board, this fact must be communicated in the vessel's reports to UKMTO and MSCHOA.[54] IMO has published guidance for shipowners in the selection and deployment of private marine security contractors,[55] which stresses that the principle of the ship's master remaining in overall command must be respected and stipulates for careful control of firearms and precise rules of engagement.[56] It insists that the primary purpose of carrying armed private marine security contractors is to ensure the safety of those on the vessel and that the contractors should be required to adopt a graduated scale of response to a potential pirate attack; all reasonable steps should be taken to avoid the use of force. Furthermore,

> If force is used, it should be in a manner consistent with applicable law. In no case should the use of force exceed what is strictly necessary, and in all cases should be proportionate to the threat and appropriate to the situation.

Contractors are to ensure

> that their personnel not use firearms against persons except in self-defence or defence of others against the imminent threat of death or serious injury, or to prevent the perpetration of a particularly serious crime involving grave threat to life.[57]

IMO accompanied this guidance to shipowners with a set of recommendations to flag States,[58] which, while stressing that the use of armed private marine security contractors is a matter for those States, advised that the States should bear in mind the possibility that the presence of armed personnel may escalate the level of violence[59] and should have in place a policy on whether or not the use of such personnel would be authorized and, if so, under what conditions.[60] The UK, which thitherto had set its face against the presence of armed security contractors on British-flagged ships[61] has availed itself of the invitation to promote such a policy[62]

---

functions of a warship, eg in seizing a pirate ship under Article 105 UNCLOS – see *The Curlew* (1812).

[54] *Ibid*, para 8.15. Among other reasons, it is important that naval personnel called to respond to a pirate attack are aware that they are armed personnel on board in addition to any pirates.

[55] In MSC Circ.1/1405, issued on 23 May 2011.

[56] *Ibid*, para 3.3.

[57] *Ibid*, para 3.5.

[58] *Interim Recommendations For Flag States Regarding The Use Of Privately Contracted Armed Security Personnel On Board Ships In The High Risk Area*, MSC.1/Circ.1406, 23 May 2011.

[59] *Ibid*, Annexe, para 3.

[60] *Ibid*, Annexe, para 5.

[61] Select Committee, 10th Report at para 26. The Select Committee concluded that the UK Government had failed to respond quickly enough to the need for armed protection, describing the case for carrying armed security personnel as 'compelling' – at para 31

[62] In Department of Transport, *Interim Guidance to UK Flagged Shipping on the Use of Armed Guards to Defend Against the Threat of Piracy in Exceptional Circumstances*, November 2011. See also *Guidance to UK Flagged Shipping on Measures to Counter Piracy, Armed Robbery and Other Acts of Violence Against Merchant Shipping*, also issued in November 2011.

and has indicated that it will only contemplate the use of armed private marine security contractors in the following exceptional circumstances:–

- Where the ship is transiting the High Risk Area;
- In circumstances in which latest BMP are being employed, but (in the opinion of the shipowner and master) are inadequate to protect the ship against acts of piracy; and
- The use of such personnel is assessed as contributing to the reduction of risk to the lives and well-being of those on board.

The UK insists on a nominated security team leader who reports to the master. The policy further states that:–

> Lethal force can generally only be used in the context of self defence or defence of others. The decision to use lethal force must lie with the person using force where they believe there to be a risk to human life. Neither the Master nor the security team leader can command a member of the security team against that person's own judgement to use lethal force or to not use lethal force.[63]

The carrying of armed personnel on ships likely to be the targets of piracy is not without risk for the personnel involved themselves.[64] The UK guidance points out:–

> Having and complying with rules of use of force may serve to reduce the risk of armed guards acting unlawfully. However in the event that criminal charges (e.g. of grievous bodily harm, manslaughter or murder) are brought to court, proving that one acted within the agreed rules would not in itself serve as a defence. It would be for the court to decide whether the force used in the particular case was necessary.[65]

The House of Commons Select Committee was rather critical of the Government's somewhat Olympian detachment in providing this 'guidance':–

> The Government should not offload responsibility onto ship owners to deal with the most difficult aspects of handling private armed guards.....We conclude that the guidance on the use of force, particularly lethal force, is very limited and there is little to help a master make a judgement on where force can be used. The Government must provide clearer direction on what is permissible and what is not. Guidance over the use of potentially lethal force should not be left to private companies to agree upon. We recommend that the change of policy be accompanied by clear, detailed and unambiguous guidance on the legal use of force for private armed guards defending a vessel under attack. This guidance should be consistent with the rules that would govern the use of force by members of the UK armed forces in similar circumstances, and should include:

---

[63] *Ibid*, para 5.6.

[64] Even if the armed personnel are members of the armed forces. In February 2012, a Spanish newspaper reported a jurisdictional dispute between India and Italy after two Indian fishermen were allegedly killed by Italian soldiers aboard an oil tanker, when they failed to obey signals from the Italian vessel – see 'Dos militares italianos juzgados en la India por el homicidio de dos pescadores', *El Mundo*, 20 February 2012.

[65] *Ibid*, para 8.6. Note that the court in question may not be in the UK, but perhaps the court of the *locus in quo* or the courts of the State of which the victim was a national. The Select Committee highlighted this possibility and recommended that the Government take steps to avoid possible extradition to States where the accused may not face a fair trial – 10th Report at para 36.

- the circumstances in which private armed security guards faced with a clear threat of violence may respond with force, including lethal force, where proportionate and necessary, and
- examples of a 'graduated response' to an attack, including confirmation that nothing in UK law or the CPS guidance requires a victim of pirate attack to await an aggressor's first blow before acting in self-defence.[66]

In reality, most shipowners would much prefer to carry military personnel from the Military Vessel Protection Detachments,[67] as provided by several other countries such as France, Spain, Italy and Israel, but the British Government is unwilling to do so routinely at present, partly because of 'overstretch' in the Armed Forces.[68] Acknowledging this constraint, the House of Common Select Committee recommended that some thought be given to having the shipping industry contributing to the cost of Military Vessel Protection Detachments, which it saw as a 'very attractive option'.[69]

This concern over the particular question of armed personnel, however, should not detract from the general effectiveness of the measures adopted by the shipping industry. In the majority of cases, ships adopting approved Best Management Practices have succeeded in repelling attacks by pirates.[70] The Chief of Staff of EUNAVFOR also recently pointed out that the success of BPM may have a strategic effect beyond the safety of individual vessels:–

> The final mile towards an attack on a merchant vessel needs to be crossed in the open, in manoeuvrable and fast skiffs. Denying pirates this capability by disrupting skiffs, pirates cannot press home their attack and have to return back to their beaches. And returning to the beach, maybe repeatedly, without weapons and other equipment investors have paid for to get a big return, must come at a cost for those failed pirates.[71]

B. Dealing with the Problem – The United Nations

Article 100, UNCLOS imposes on all States a duty to:–

> … cooperate to the fullest possible extent in the repression of piracy on the high seas or in any other place outside the jurisdiction of any State.

As mentioned above, this broad obligation is elaborated for States Parties to the SUA Convention by the more detailed obligations to take action against, arrest, prosecute and/or extradite pirates. Similarly, for States in the region, the Djibouti Code recognises some form of responsibility in similar vein.

---

[66] Select Committee, 10th Report at para 37.
[67] Select Committee, 10th Report at para 25.
[68] *Ibid* The Select Committee heard that Germany, the Netherlands and Norway were also contemplating the use of Military Vessel Protection Detachments.
[69] *Ibid.*
[70] *Ibid,* para 2.6. The Select Committee commended the maritime industry's work on BPM and the consequent reduction in the vulnerability of ships to attack – see 10th Report at para 24.
[71] *Per* Captain P Haslam in a press briefing on 20th February 2012, available at www.eunavfor.eu.

The existence of these obligations and instrument, however, has palpably failed to ameliorate the situation off Somalia. In 2008, the UN became alarmed at the impact of piracy on relief vessels carrying shipments of food, medical supplies and other materials to Somalia, cargoes which *ex hypothesi* presented a marketable attraction to pirates. These World Food Programme ships were, at the request of the UN Secretary-General supplied with naval support from several Member States.

The UN Security Council had already concerned itself with several aspects of the breakdown in civil government in Somalia[72] and in June 2008 it addressed itself particularly to the situation in the offshore zone, including Somali territorial waters. The Security Council noted the lack of capacity to control pirates on the part of the Transitional Federal Government and referred to requests from that Government to the UN Secretary-General for help in that regard. The Council adopted Resolution 1816(2008) which uncontroversially urged all States to co-operate with one another and with IMO to share information about piracy and to render assistance 'in accordance with the relevant international law' to vessels threatened or under attack by pirates;[73] more remarkably, however, it included a provision under which the States co-operating with the TFG (essentially the States which were providing informal naval protection to shipping in the region) were empowered to:–

(a) Enter the territorial waters of Somalia for the purpose of repressing acts of piracy and armed robbery at sea, in a manner consistent with such action permitted on the high seas with respect to piracy under relevant international law; and

(b) Use, within the territorial waters of Somalia, in a manner consistent with action permitted on the high seas with respect to piracy under relevant international law, all necessary means to repress acts of piracy and armed robbery.[74]

This resolution, like all subsequent ones relating to piracy off Somalia, was made under Chapter VII of the United Nations Charter, under which the Security Council, if it considers that other steps would be inadequate to address a threat to international peace and security, may authorise military action to achieve that end.[75] This is relevance of the magic words 'all necessary means' contained in the text of the Resolution.

---

[72] See, eg the arms embargo imposed by Security Council Resolution 733(1992).

[73] SC Res 1816(2008), para 3. Strictly, this injunction may be thought redundant in view of the duty to collaborate in the repression of piracy contained in Article 100, UNCLOS. The particular difficulty to be addressed, however, was the habit of pirates of retreating into Somali territorial waters, when under pressure from patrolling vessels.

[74] SC Res 1816(2008), para 7. Note that, in view of the draconian nature of this provision (which clearly impinged severely on the sovereignty of Somalia), the Resolution expressly stated that shall not affect the rights or obligations or responsibilities of Member States under international law, including any rights or obligations under the Convention, with respect to any other situation, and underscores in particular that it shall 'not be considered as establishing customary international law, and affirms further that this authorization has been provided only following receipt of the letter from the Permanent Representative of the Somalia Republic to the United Nations to the President of the Security Council dated 27 February 2008 (S/2008/XXX) conveying the consent of the TFG' – *ibid*, para 9. The authorisation was originally for six months, subsequently renewed – see, eg SC Res 1846(2008), at para 10, SC Res 1897(2009), para 7, SC Res 1950(2010), para 7, etc.

[75] UN Charter, Art 42.

The first international naval force to appear was EUNAVFOR,[76] conducting Operation Atlanta. The remit of Operation Atlanta has been extended by the European Council until December 2012 and has the following objectives:

- protect vessels of the World Food Programme, humanitarian aid and African Union Mission in Somalia (AMISOM) shipping;
- help deter, prevent and repress acts of piracy and armed robbery;
- protect vulnerable shipping;
- also monitor fishing activities off the coast of Somalia.

Operation Atlanta is a multi-national force,[77] commanded by a Rear-Admiral in the Royal Navy[78] and its remit has been extended by the European Council until December 2012.

There is also a NATO operation, Ocean Shield, which is also responsible for counter-piracy operations in the region. This grew out of an earlier mission (Allied Provider) which was specifically directed to the protection of World Food Programme ships. It draws its vessels and personnel from a wider range of States than EUNAVFOR, including several from the Indian Ocean region, and is presently commanded by a Rear-Admiral in the Pakistan Navy.

Finally, Combined Task Force 151 is an international anti-piracy force made up of vessels and personnel from 25 nations. It is directed from the coalition Combined Forces Base in Bahrain.

Naval activity in the region is constant and 'naval forces maintain a high concentration of assets in the IRTC that can respond quickly to distress calls'.[79]

The multiplicity of naval task forces engaged in anti-piracy operations off Somalia has led to some criticism,[80] but the House of Commons Select Committee concluded:–

> that a unified command structure, while it may be the ideal, is of a lower priority than securing the widest possible international participation in counter-piracy operations in the Indian Ocean and the Gulf of Aden, and the maximum number of assets patrolling the waters.[81]

There is some concern that the effectiveness of the naval response off Somalia has had the effect of dispersing pirate activity (supported by larger mother-ships) into the wider Indian Ocean, where it is impossible to maintain a similar intensity of

---

[76] EUNAVFOR is remarkable for being the first naval task force ever set up by the European Union.

[77] The force has included vessels from Belgium, Bulgaria, Cyprus, Czech Republic, Finland, France, Germany, Greece, Hungary, Italy, Ireland, Luxembourg, Malta, The Netherlands, Poland, Portugal, Romania, Slovenia, Spain, Sweden, United Kingdom (also hosting the EU NAVFOR Operational Headquarters), Lithuania, Latvia as well as non-EU countries such as Croatia, Montenegro, Norway, Switzerland, and Ukraine. At the time of writing, the most recent vessel to join the force was ESPS Infanta Elena, a corvette of the Spanish Navy. Details of the force and its activities can be found at www.eunavfor.eu.

[78] His Deputy is a Rear-Admiral from the Federal German Navy.

[79] See Select Committee, 10th Report, at para 50. The Committee heard that the IRTC had ensured that there had not been a successful pirate attack in the Gulf of Aden since September 2008.

[80] *Ibid*, at para 45 and the evidence there cited.

[81] *Ibid*, at para 47.

naval presence. In view of the harsh fact that a greater number of warships is likely to be forthcoming,[82] the Select Committee was forced to conclude that the naval operation, although successful in the IRTC, 'have so far been unable to make the oceans safe from Somali piracy' and to propose alternative means of spotting pirate vessels, eg by satellite technology.

There has been some criticism, especially in the UK, of the lack of firm enforcement action taken against pirates in Somali waters. This criticism has come from, among others, victims of piracy who have been taken hostage and who have felt that their ordeal could have been alleviated if the naval vessels in the area had acted more positively, even if doing so enhanced the chances of the hostages being harmed.[83] The Royal Navy's preferred approach is to stand off and monitor developments, with the laudable of aim of avoiding any escalation of the threat to hostages, but the navies of other States have been rather more forceful in their approach, in some cases using commandoes to recover control of the target vessel.[84] The Select Committee concluded on this point that:–

> the cautious approach to military operations when hostages are involved is appropriate and agree that protecting the safety of hostages is paramount. However, if the use of violence against hostages continues to increase this may change the balance of risk in favour of military intervention in the future.[85]
>
> There remains, nonetheless, some dissatisfaction with the current UK enforcement policy merely to 'deter and disrupt' pirate operations (sometimes mischievously referred to as 'catch and release'. While the current climate of opinion has proceeded a long way from the view of Lord Stowell that 'With pirates, there is no state of peace. They are the enemies of every country and at all times.'[86]

Pirates are, in a proper case, clearly legitimate targets of lethal force. Modern opinion would probably not accept the equation of pirates with combatants on the battlefield and thus subject only to the constraints imposed by international humanitarian law. Indeed, most, if not all, of the States whose navies are engaged in anti-piracy operations off Somalia are parties to one or more of the international instrument for the protection of human rights. Indeed, it may be that an imperfect understanding of the obligation imposed by those instruments has obscured the position as to what is a permissible response to an armed attack (or perhaps, more properly, resistance to attempted enforcement) by pirates. Nonetheless, it remains entirely legitimate for naval enforcement personnel to resort to lethal force in such a case. It is to be expected that lesser forms of intervention (warning shots, etc.) would be employed first, but there is no ground for insisting on their use if an armed response is reasonably to be anticipated.

---

[82] The Select Committee heard that no fewer than 83 warships would be required to ensure response times of 30 minutes throughout the Indian Ocean – *ibid* at para 52.

[83] Select Committee, 10th Report, citing the evidence of Paul and Rachel Chandler, whose yacht was hijacked by pirates with naval forces in sight.

[84] eg the recapture of the South Korean flagged *Samho Jewelry* by South Korean special forces.

[85] Select Committee, 10th Report, para 54. The time for a review of this policy may come more quickly than supposed, as recent incidents have indicated that pirates are more inclined to use violence against hostages (eg the amputation of limbs) in order to ensure that ransom payments are forthcoming.

[86] In *The Le Louis* (1817) 2. Dods 210, at 214.

Pursuant to Security Council Resolution 1851(2008), the international community has formed the Contact Group on Piracy off the Coast of Somalia. The Contact Group has established four Working Groups. The first of these (chaired by the UK) deals with improving the co-ordination of naval operations and criminal justice and maritime capacity building in the States of the region, in close co-operation with IMO, as part of the effort to implement the Djibouti Code. Another Working Group, chaired by Denmark, is charged with setting up and supporting judicial frameworks for the arrest, detention and prosecution of suspect pirates. Another working group, under the chairmanship of the USA and collaborating particularly closely with IMO, is charged with stimulating commercial shipping self-awareness and self-defence. A final group, chaired by Egypt, addresses the financing of piracy and has established a Trust Fund to support international action against piracy, in particular, the costs linked to prosecution and imprisonment.

V. BRINGING PIRATES TO JUSTICE – WHAT IS THE PROBLEM?

The members of the House of Common Select Committee on Foreign Affairs were somewhat taken aback to be told that nine out of every ten pirates apprehended were released without trial.[87] This apparently shocking statistic was explained by a number of factors. It was pointed out that, especially since the *locus in quo* of pirate attacks has increasingly been situated further from the coast than formerly, taking pirates to shore facilities in the region may take five or six days (during which time, of course, the ship which has made the capture is off-station, thereby increasing the potential exposure of other vessels).[88] Furthermore, any jurisdiction to which alleged pirates are taken for trial would be bound to consider the charges of piracy as extremely grave ones and, therefore, the more that jurisdiction relies upon the rule of law, the higher the evidentiary burden to be overcome by the prosecutor. That being so, it may be difficult in many cases to gather a sufficiently heavy weight of evidence to ensure a conviction, not least because crucial witnesses (such as the master and crew of the target ship) may be reluctant to undertake a long and tedious journey from their home country, which they have regained to the State which has taken jurisdiction.[89] Also, the Select Committee as told that pirates in the region are becoming much more sophisticated in their understanding of the demands of successful prosecution.

---

[87] Select Committee, 10th Report, at para 74.

[88] Select Committee, 10th Report, at para 77, *per* Captain Reindorp RN. Although not mentioned in evidence before the Select Committee, human rights jurisprudence would suggest that pirates held on board a warship are under the 'control' of the flag State. For a recent case on very similar facts, see the decision of the Grand Chamber of the European Court of Human Rights in *Hirsi Jamaa and others v Italy*, 23 February 2012 (Somali 'boat-people' fleeing from Libya were in the 'continuous and exclusive *de jure and de facto* control of the Italian authorities' while on board Italian warships. As most modern warships do not have cells, pirates may be held in less secure conditions than are desirable or, if they were to be closely confined in non-bespoke accommodation, they may be able to mount a human rights claim, at least of nuisance value.

[89] It is perhaps unworthy to suggest that the attraction of transfer agreements with jurisdictions such as Seychelles or Mauritius may have the result of diminishing this reluctance!

For example, it is now common for the pirates, on the approach of a patrol vessel, to jettison incriminating material such as weapons, boarding gear, etc,[90] so that, even if the forum State has in place a criminal offence which reflects the terms of Article 103 UNCLOS, it is not unreasonable for the naval commander to question whether a prosecution is likely to proceed in the absence of tangible evidence of such equipment in the possession of the accused when apprehended.[91]

Be that as it may, the Select Committee reacted with some scepticism to the case for the defence of current practice:–

> gathering evidence to secure a successful prosecution for piracy is challenging. However, not all claims made by the Government about the difficulty in securing evidence were wholly convincing: when pirates are observed in boats with guns, ladders and even hostages, it beggars belief that they cannot be prosecuted, assuming that states have the necessary laws in place and the will to do so. We urge the Government to pursue alternative means of securing suitable evidence (such as photos or video recordings of pirates with equipment, and supplying witness testimony by videolink). We urge the Government to engage with regional states to agree consistent and attainable rules on evidence required for a piracy prosecution.[92]

Finding a State which is prepared to try pirates captured off Somalia has not always been easy. Although UNCLOS imposes an international law obligation binding on every State to collaborate in the repression of piracy,[93] the Convention only provides that a State *may* (not *shall*) seize pirate ships and arrest the pirates. Similarly, States seizing pirates are merely empowered, not obliged, to try them in their courts.[94] In principle, there should be no difficulty in asserting jurisdiction.[95] The traditional view of the crime of piracy is that any and every State can prosecute pirates:–

> With regard to crimes as defined by international law, that law has no means of trying or punishing them. The recognition of them as constituting crimes and the trial and punishment of the criminals are left to the municipal law of each country, But whereas according to international law the criminal jurisdiction of municipal law is ordinarily restricted to crimes committed on its terra firma or territorial waters or its own ships, and to crimes by its own nationals wherever committed, it is also recognised as extending to piracy committed on the high seas by any national on any ship, because a person guilty of such piracy has placed himself beyond the protection of any State. He is no longer a national, but *hostis humani generis* and as such he is justiciable by any State anywhere. Grotius (1583–1645)) *De Jure Belli et Pacis*, vol 2, cap 20, s 40.[96]

---

[90] It is, of course, undeniable that, even in these cases, there is a 'deter and disrupt' effect, as referred to *supra*.

[91] Select Committee, 10th Report, at paras 78–80 and the evidence there referred to. Note that this difficulty is usually presented only where the pirates have not been taken in the course of an attack or while on a target vessel. In the latter category of cases, it is unusual for the alleged perpetrators to be released – *ibid* at para 74.

[92] *Ibid,* at para 81.

[93] In Art 100.

[94] Art 105, UNCLOS. Note that only warships or other public ships clearly marked as such may carry out such seizure – Art 107 UNCLOS.

[95] *Pace* the existence of adequate domestic law conferring jurisdiction on the local courts.

[96] *In re Piracy Jure Gentium*, at p 507, *per* Lord Sankey L.C.

This view of piracy was not confined to the common law world. The description of a pirate as *hostis humani generis* was also recognised by civilian writers.[97] In practice, however, it is not so simple. Trying pirates remains a matter for national courts, as none of the obvious international tribunals has had jurisdiction for piracy, even on the high seas and even where accompanied by brutality or murder. Neither the International Tribunal for the Law of the Sea (established by UNCLOS) nor the International Criminal Court have jurisdiction over piracy. In view of this lacuna, the UN Secretary-General's Special Adviser on piracy[98] proposed that a special tribunal should be established in Arusha, Tanzania,[99] which would operate as an extra-territorial Somali court, but this suggestion attracted a good deal of criticism, both as to its practicality[100] and the expense involved. The Select Committee agreed that this form of extra-territorial court was not to be supported.

Indeed, the idea of such a special court refuses to go away. In its most recent Resolution on Somali piracy, the Security Council decided:–

> to continue its consideration, as a matter of urgency, without prejudice to any further steps to ensure that pirates are held accountable, of the establishment of specialized anti-piracy courts in Somalia and other States in the region with substantial international participation and/or support, and [requested] that the Secretary-General, in conjunction with UNODC and UNDP, further consult with Somalia and regional States willing to establish such anti-piracy courts on the kind of international assistance, including the provision of international personnel, that would be required to help make such courts operational; the procedural arrangements required for transfer of apprehended pirates and related evidence; the projected case capacity of such courts; and the projected timeline and costs for such courts, and to provide to the Council in the light of such consultations within 90 days detailed implementation proposals for the establishment of such courts, as appropriate.[101]

The UN Secretary-General's most recent Report on Somali piracy concluded that, if the various recommendations made in it to assist the States in the region most likely to assist were carried out:–

> in two years, Somalia, Kenya, Seychelles, Mauritius and the United Republic of Tanzania collectively could conduct a maximum of 125 piracy prosecutions per year in accordance with international standards, involving up to 1,250 suspects. This would be a very significant contribution to combating piracy off the coast of Somalia, and would be greater than the total number of suspects prosecuted globally to date.[102]

---

[97] Eg Molloy, *De Jure Maritimi et Navali*, cited by Lord Sankey in *In re Piracy Jure Gentium* at p 508.

[98] Jack Lang, the former Foreign Minister of France.

[99] The idea was that the Court would be accommodated in the premises of the International Criminal Tribunal for Rwanda.

[100] There were doubts, eg, about the compatibility of the proposal with the Somali Constitution and about the adequacy of the domestic Somali law on piracy which the Court would presumably have to apply.

[101] SC Resolution 2015(2011), 24 October 2011, at para 16. The Resolution also called for a workable and effective Somali domestic law on piracy – *ibid* at para 7.

[102] The Report of the Secretary-General on specialised anti-piracy courts in Somalia and other States in the region, S. 2012/50, 20 January 2012, at para 124.

States are reluctant to mount expensive and potentially complex trials (and, indeed, to provide prison accommodation for the lengthy sentences which are to be expected in piracy convictions). It may also be that some States are reluctant to accept convicted pirates in prisons on their territory for fear that, when their sentences have been served, the pirates may seek to avoid deportation back to Somalia (or elsewhere) on the grounds that they would be in danger of death if they were to be repatriated, a course of action which would therefore be contrary to the international human rights obligations undertaken by the imprisoning State.

Some States in the region, particularly Kenya, have in the past undertaken to try pirates taken off Somalia, but Kenya has subsequently refused to do so as a general commitment, but only on a case-by-case basis. It is thought that this change of heart is due to the unforeseen volume of cases brought before the Kenyan courts. No fewer than 143 prosecutions have taken place in Kenya, only Puntland (with 290 cases and about 240 convictions) has conducted more trials.[103]

The United Kingdom convened an international conference on Somalia in London in late February 2012, attended by 55 States and international organisations. The conference dealt with the whole gamut of issues relating to Somalia, but it naturally addressed piracy and, in particular, the importance of solving the jurisdiction problem. The Final Communiqué included the following statement:–

> There will be no impunity for piracy. We called for greater development of judicial capacity to prosecute and detain those behind piracy both in Somalia and in the wider region and recognised the need to strengthen capacity in regional states. We welcomed new arrangements, which enable some states and naval operations to transfer suspected pirates captured at sea for trial by partners across the Indian Ocean region, and if convicted, to transfer them to prisons in Puntland and Somaliland which meet international standards. We noted the intention to consider further the possibility of creating courts in Somalia specialised in dealing with piracy.

The conference also made some progress on the matter of transfer agreements, as the United Kingdom and Tanzania signed a Memorandum of Understanding allowing the Royal Navy to transfer suspected pirates to Tanzania for prosecution. The Foreign Secretary also signed a statement of intent with Mauritius by which the parties committed themselves to conclude a similar Memorandum by early June. The UK said it would continue to work with other states in the region to secure similar agreements. Somaliland signed an agreement with the Seychelles to transfer pirates convicted there to prisons in Somaliland – the first transfer of 19 convicted pirates is likely to take place by the end of March. Puntland also agreed to the transfer of convicted pirates from prisons in the region to prisons in Puntland as from August.

---

[103] Select Committee, 10th Report, at para 104. Convictions were obtained in 50 of these cases. In Yemen, all 120 prosecutions resulted in convictions – *ibid.*

VI. THE STORY CONTINUES...

While it is clear that the problem of Somali piracy is now receiving a degree of attention in the international community commensurate with its importance, it is hard to disagree with the rather gloomy conclusion of the Select Committee that:–

> for too long there has been a noticeable gap between ... rhetoric and ... action. Despite nine UN Security Council resolutions and three multinational naval operations, the counter-piracy policy has had limited impact.[104]

It must also be the case, as emphasised in the Final Communiqué of the London Conference that the solution to piracy off the Somali coast lies in the resolutions of the problems within Somalia itself. Sadly, despite the obvious international goodwill towards that end, the melancholy truth is that it seems as remote as ever, as does the opportunity to write *Finis* to the long and dismal story of the Somali pirates.

---

[104] *Ibid*, at para 154.

2

Changing Perspectives on the High Seas Freedom of Navigation?

ANDREW SERDY

IN THE 30 YEARS' existence of the United Nations Convention on the Law of the Sea (UNCLOS)[1] – and, coincidentally, of the Institute of Maritime Law – there has been no doubt about the status as customary international law of the freedom of navigation on the high seas found in Article 87 of UNCLOS:

> 1. The high seas are open to all States, whether coastal or land-locked. Freedom of the high seas is exercised under the conditions laid down by this Convention and by other rules of international law. It comprises, *inter alia*, both for coastal and land-locked States: (a) freedom of navigation;…

This text is virtually identical to Article 2 of the 1958 High Seas Convention,[2] the second paragraph of whose preamble affirms 'the following provisions as generally declaratory of established principles of international law'. Unaltered too is the nature of the high seas, laid down thus in Article 89 of UNCLOS: 'No State may validly purport to subject any part of the high seas to its sovereignty.'[3] Thus the only thing that significantly changed thanks to UNCLOS was the spatial extent of the high seas, now reduced by the exclusive economic zone (EEZ) which can extend up to 200 nautical miles from the territorial sea baseline (Article 57), but even that is deceptive, because in the EEZ the freedom of navigation, though subject to the new jurisdiction that the coastal State now has, still applies: Article 58(1). Hence the freedom of navigation begins at the outer limit of the territorial sea, now fixed at a maximum of 12 nautical miles from the baseline (Article 3).

There are two ways of looking at the high seas. One is the historical perspective (once upon a time, what we now call the high seas was all there was – descended from the public law of the Roman Empire first stated by Marcianus (as recorded in Justinian's Digest) as 'the sea and its coasts are common to all men' (*communis*

---

[1] Montego Bay, 10 December 1982; 1833 United Nations Treaty Series (hereinafter UNTS) 3.
[2] Convention on the High Seas, Geneva, 29 April 1958; 450 UNTS 11.
[3] The equivalent in the High Seas Convention, *supra* n 2, is in the first sentence of Art 2.

omnium naturali jure).[4] On this view, everything that has happened since, including the general recognition of zones of national sovereignty and jurisdiction beginning with the territorial sea[5] through to the most recent zones (the EEZ and archipelagic waters), is a process of gradual whittling away of the high seas, to be resisted as much for sentimental reasons as because of fears of expansion of coastal State jurisdiction, as illustrated by a remark attributed to President Reagan: 'We're policed and patrolled on land and there is so much regulation that I kind of thought that when you go out on the high seas you can do as you want'.[6] This leaves the freedom of navigation as the default setting; in so far as it is not abolished or qualified by other positive law, it continues to apply.

The other view (preferred by the author) is dictated by modern pragmatism, starting from the position that the law exists to serve human beings, who after all are land-dwelling creatures unable to survive beyond a short period in the ocean, though make use of it they certainly do. This attitude is encapsulated by the pithy phrase 'The land dominates the sea', enunciated by a chamber of the International Court of Justice (ICJ) in the Gulf of Maine case.[7] It is also consistent with the negative definition of the high seas in modern times: in both the High Seas Convention[8] and Article 86 of UNCLOS[9] it is defined as what is left over after all the other zones encompassing the water column (internal waters and territorial sea in the older treaty; these plus archipelagic waters and the EEZ in UNCLOS) are accounted for.

Even supporters of the first view do not normally insist that the freedom of navigation is absolute. This would have precluded not only any willingness of States to conclude the various International Maritime Organization (IMO) conventions dealing with the safety of navigation and the avoidance of collisions that place limited constraints on navigation,[10] and deprived that organisation of much of its *raison d'être*, but also the requirement in paragraph 2 of Article 87 that the exercise

---

[4] PT Fenn Jr, 'Justinian and the Freedom of the Sea', (1925) 19 *American Journal of International Law* 716 at 716 and original sources there cited.

[5] Though this postdates Grotius, to whom the modern doctrine of freedom of navigation is attributed, he was willing to concede that the impossibility of occupation of the sea, on which he based his reasoning, did not extend to certain narrow bodies of water in the immediate vicinity of the coast such as bays or straits: H Grotius, *The Freedom of the Seas Or the Right Which Belongs to the Dutch to Take Part in the East Indian Trade* (translated by R van Deman Magoffin) (New York: Carnegie Endowment for International Peace, 1916) at 31 and 37.

[6] L Cannon, 'Public Perception Seems Split in Its Perception of Reagan', *The Washington Post*, 12 July 1982 at 3; the remark was made at the 29 June 1982 meeting of the National Security Council at which the decision that the US would not sign UNCLOS was taken.

[7] *Delimitation of the Maritime Boundary in the Gulf of Maine Area (Canada/United States of America)*, Judgment, ICJ Reports 1984, p 246 at 312 (para 157).

[8] *Supra* n 2, Art 1.

[9] *Supra* n 1, Art 86.

[10] The most prominent examples are the International Convention on Load Lines (London, 5 April 1966), 640 UNTS 133; the International Convention on Tonnage Measurement of Ships (London, 23 June 1969), 1291 UNTS 3; the International Convention Relating to Intervention on the High Seas in the case of Oil Pollution Casualties (Brussels, 29 November 1969), 970 UNTS 211; the Convention on the International Regulations for Preventing Collisions at Sea (London, 20 October 1972), 1050 UNTS 16; the International Convention for the Safety of Life at Sea (London, 1 November 1974), 1184 UNTS 3; and the International Convention on Maritime Search and Rescue (Hamburg, 27 April 1979), 1456 UNTS 221.

of any of the freedoms of the high seas, navigation included, must take place with due regard for the exercise by other States and their nationals of the same or a different freedom.[11]

Unlike the freedom of fishing, which is now heavily qualified in UNCLOS Article 87(1)(e) by cross-reference to the many rules of Articles 116–120 because the old assumption of inexhaustibility of fish stocks has long since been shown to be untrue, and a fish caught by X is not available for catching by Y, freedom of navigation endures largely unscathed because there is normally no scarcity of the only 'commodity' on which it depends – ocean space. In most parts of the ocean beyond the territorial sea there is more than enough room to accommodate the comings and goings of all the ships making use of the freedom of navigation, but certain areas are subject to congestion and the risk that two ships will (inadvertently) seek to occupy the same space at the same time, ie collide. On this view, the survival of the high seas at all is principally due to the fact that it has not yet been affected by the modern trend of economic efficiency which dictates that scarcities and the problems they cause on each part of the world's surface, ocean as well as land, are best managed if there is a single identifiable owner responsible for its regulatory upkeep, which in most contexts leads to rights of a proprietary or quasi-proprietary nature. The high seas' character as a commons remains unchallenged only because managing the ocean becomes ever more costly the farther out to sea one goes, so that beyond a certain point the cost of good management is likely to exceed the economic benefit derivable from exclusive jurisdiction. Because law, no less than nature, abhors a vacuum, some system of law must be found to govern human activities on the high seas, and this is the purpose served by the rule of exclusive jurisdiction of the flag State on the high seas found in both UNCLOS[12] and before it the High Seas Convention.[13] In other words, the high seas are likely to be with us for a very long time to come, and as long as this is so, the flag-State rule, or something like it, would need to be invented if it did not already exist.

Most of the time, therefore, these two ways of looking at the high seas can co-exist because they do not lead to any practical difference in outcomes – the observer standing on dry land looking out to sea, or the mariner viewing from mid-ocean the steady encroachment of coastal State jurisdiction on the common domain.

---

[11] The exact wording is 'These freedoms shall be exercised by all States with due regard for the interests of other States in their exercise of the freedom of the high seas...', the equivalent phrase in the last sentence of Art 2 of the High Seas Convention, *supra* n 2, was the slightly weaker 'reasonable regard'. D Anderson, 'Freedoms of the High Seas in the Modern Law of the Sea', in D Freestone, R Barnes and DM Ong (eds), *The Law of the Sea: Progress and Prospects* (Oxford University Press, 2006), 327 at 332 denies that there is any difference in meaning between the two phrases, but if that is the case it is not clear why the negotiators of UNCLOS thought fit to change the wording. The author has usually been able to convince his students otherwise by drawing their attention to the signs placed at several points on the perimeter of the University of Southampton's Highfield campus, enjoining cyclists to proceed with 'due regard for the safety of pedestrians', and inviting them to consider whether as pedestrians they would feel safer if 'due' were to be changed to 'reasonable'.

[12] *Supra* n 1, Art 92(1).

[13] *Supra* n 2, Art 6(1).

Occasionally, however, questions arise that lead to different answers depending on the perspective from which one starts, as illustrated by two recent cases in which the high seas freedom of navigation was invoked on behalf of ships not actually on the high seas at the time.

I. ABSOLUTISM LOOKING FROM SEA TO LAND – *SELLERS V MARITIME SAFETY INSPECTOR*[14]

The earlier of the two cases, this was a successful further appeal by Sellers against the dismissal by Morris J in the New Zealand High Court of a first appeal against his conviction in the District Court for leaving the port of Opua without having a radio and emergency locator beacon on board the *Nimbus*, the Maltese-registered cutter of which he was the master. Doing so was in breach of s 21(1) of the Maritime Transport Act 1994 (NZ), which as far as material is in the following terms:

> No master of a pleasure craft shall permit that pleasure craft to depart from any port in New Zealand for any place outside New Zealand unless…(b) The Director is satisfied that the pleasure craft and its safety equipment are adequate for the voyage[.]

The Director of the Maritime Safety Authority, an office created under s. 439(1) of the Act, had published a guideline specifying that, for the safety equipment of any pleasure craft to be considered adequate for the purposes of s. 21(1)(b), it would have to include at a minimum a radio and emergency locator beacon;[15] in evidence he stated that its rationale was as an attempt to make search and rescue efforts more effective.[16] Sellers objected on philosophical-cum-religious grounds to the requirement to carry emergency equipment.[17] The prosecution took place after the *Nimbus* returned to the same port several months later. Counsel for Sellers argued that his conviction infringed the flag State's freedom of navigation on the high seas, thus rendering it invalid, as the Act, properly interpreted, could not conflict with New Zealand's international legal obligations. That is, the Act should be read down so as to be consistent with those obligations.

The judgment of the Court of Appeal was delivered by Keith J (now Judge Keith of the ICJ), who noted that the Act was in part intended to give effect to UNCLOS[18] (although the Act did not incorporate UNCLOS into New Zealand law, hence its applicability as an unincorporated treaty was due to the fact that the relevant provisions codified customary international law, which is treated as part of the common law). Despite correctly stating the position under Article 92 of UNCLOS that the 'state of nationality of a ship (the flag state) has exclusive jurisdiction over

---

[14] [1999] 2 NZLR 44.

[15] *Ibid*, at 46.

[16] *Ibid*, at 48–49.

[17] *Ibid*, at 46.

[18] *Ibid*, at 57. UNCLOS was not, however, among the conventions declared for the purposes of s 5(b) of the Act under the Maritime Transport Act (Conventions) Order 1994 (NZ) (SR 1994/273), cl 2 and Schedule.

the ship when it is on the high seas',[19] and observing that s.21(1) created an offence that was committed within (or at the moment of departure from) New Zealand's internal waters,[20] the Court thereafter proceeded to treat this as being equivalent to the wider notion of exclusive jurisdiction over a ship *in relation to* the high seas. Although Article 87 was not actually mentioned by the Court, the freedom of navigation it embodies was, in the finding that

> [t]he effect, if not the purpose, of the provision [i.e. s.21(1)(b)] is to place requirements on the exercise of the freedom to navigate on the high seas by reference to the adequacy of the ship, her crew and her equipment for the voyage(…).[21]

It concluded that under international law a port State

> has no general power to unilaterally impose its own requirements on foreign ships relating to their construction, their safety and other equipment and their crewing if the requirements are to have effect on the high seas. Any requirements cannot go beyond those generally accepted, especially in the maritime conventions and regulations; we were referred to no generally accepted requirements relating to the equipment particularly in issue in this case so far as pleasure craft were concerned.[22]

The Court also relied on Article 21, paragraph 2 of UNCLOS, which restricts in the same way the rights of coastal States to prescribe laws on the construction, design, equipment and manning of ships passing through their territorial sea in the exercise of the right of innocent passage.[23] It may be conceded that had the *Nimbus* merely been passing through New Zealand's territorial sea on the way to a New Zealand port (or not intending to enter a port), it could not have been stopped, and Sellers could have not been prosecuted, for not having the prescribed safety equipment on board, without violating the flag State's right of innocent passage.[24] Similarly, an offence of entering the territorial sea (from either the seaward or landward side) without such equipment would be contrary to UNCLOS. But the *Nimbus* was not stopped, and that is not where the offence was committed. It is significant that UNCLOS makes no parallel provision for internal waters including ports;[25] rather, the assumption underlying the general reference in UNCLOS Article 25, paragraph 2 to conditions that States can impose on the entry of foreign ships into their ports,[26] and the specific reference to anti-pollution conditions in Article 211,

---

[19] *Ibid*, at 46–47.

[20] *Ibid*, at 48.

[21] *Ibid*.

[22] *Ibid*, at 57.

[23] *Ibid*, at 54.

[24] By analogy with the hot pursuit exception to the flag State rule in UNCLOS Art 111, however, a pursuit for the offence in question, begun and maintained under the right conditions, could culminate in stopping the *Nimbus* in the territorial sea on the way out – though not on the way back in some months later.

[25] Ports are taken to be internal waters because they lie landward of the baseline from which the breadth of the territorial sea is measured (UNCLOS, *supra* n 1, Art 8(1)), the outermost permanent harbour works forming part of the baseline (*ibid*, Art 11).

[26] The *locus classicus* in this respect is the statement of the ICJ in *Military and Paramilitary Activities in and against Nicaragua (Nicaragua v United States of America), Merits, Judgment*, ICJ Reports 1986, p 14 at 111 (para 213): 'It is … by virtue of its sovereignty that the coastal State may regulate access to its ports'.

paragraph 3, is that port States can exclude those ships not satisfying the conditions (as long as they have not taken on other treaty obligations requiring them to admit certain ships, for example those of a particular nationality). This extends on the drafting principle *expressio unius est exclusio alterius* to rules on the construction, design, equipment and manning of ships: the restrictions on the coastal State's legislative powers apply in the territorial sea but not in its ports, and in return for permission to enter the port, foreign ships may need to submit voluntarily to rules affecting their conduct in the territorial sea, and indeed on the high seas, to which they could not otherwise be subject. Were it otherwise, the United States would not have been able, long before the IMO moved to phase out single-hulled tankers,[27] to close its ports to them in the Oil Pollution Act of 1990 (by establishing double hull requirements both for new and existing tankers in order to be allowed to continue operating to and from US ports beyond given dates).[28]

Given the references in the Maritime Transport Act to compliance with and implementation of international maritime conventions to which New Zealand is party, the Court stressed that s 21 of the Act, whose purpose is to assist the Maritime Safety Authority in carrying out its search and rescue obligations under the IMO Search and Rescue Convention,[29] had to be understood and interpreted in the light of how international law limited the regulatory jurisdiction of port States. In order for the powers of the Director not to exceed what was permitted by international law, the Court held that those powers must be 'read as subject to the relevant rules of international law' and the restrictions they placed on port States' powers.[30] It said that 'national law in this area has been essentially governed by and derived from international law with the consequence that national law is to be read, if at all possible, consistently with the related international law'.[31] The Director of Maritime Safety was therefore required to exercise his powers consistently with the jurisdictional limitations imposed at the relevant time by international law, which did not permit New Zealand to exercise jurisdiction over foreign-flagged vessels[32] (though they might in future evolve in that direction, much as the shrinking scope of State immunity was broadening coastal States' jurisdiction in other ways without any legislative amendment taking place[33]). In other words, under s 21 the Director was confined to doing no more than 'ensure compliance with accepted international standards and rules, to the extent that they allow that judgment to be made by a

---

[27] See Regulation 13F of Annex I to the International Convention for the Prevention of Pollution from Ships (London, 2 November 1973; 1340 UNTS 61), inserted by Resolution MEPC.52(32) adopted on 6 March 1992 and in force since 6 July 1993, reproduced at 1733 UNTS 385.

[28] 46 USC s 3703a, inserted by s 4115 of the Act (PL 101-380). See also *Patterson v Bark Eudora* (1903) 190 US 169 at 178, where the US Supreme Court said *per* Brewer J that 'the implied consent to permit [foreign merchant vessels] to enter our harbors may be withdrawn, and if this implied consent may be wholly withdrawn, it may be extended upon such terms and conditions as the government sees fit to impose'.

[29] *Supra* n 10 (last item).

[30] *Sellers v Maritime Safety Inspector, supra* n 14, at 59.

[31] *Ibid*, at 62.

[32] *Ibid*.

[33] *Ibid*, at 61.

coastal state.[34] So interpreted, s.21 did not authorise the Director to require foreign-flagged pleasure craft to carry specific equipment, leading the Court to quash the conviction and sentence.

As one commentator states,

> [t]he net effect of the Court's gloss – as international law currently stands and as far as foreign-flagged yachts are concerned – is to erase s 21 from the statute book. The Director of Maritime Safety cannot require foreign yachts to carry even basic safety equipment while they are within New Zealand's search and rescue area. This result cannot be reconciled with the plain wording of s 21, which, although of general scope, does not seem to be particularly ambiguous or unclear.[35]

Now there is nothing unusual in courts in common law jurisdictions construing statutes in accordance with what they conceive to be the broad purpose of the treaty to which the statute gives effect in domestic law, as the House of Lords has done in the United Kingdom in *The Jade; The Eschersheim* in relation to s.1 of the Administration of Justice Act 1956, giving effect to the International Convention relating to the Arrest of Seagoing Ships:[36]

> As the Act was passed to enable Her Majesty's Government to give effect to the obligations in international law which it would assume on ratifying the Convention to which it was a signatory, the rule of statutory construction laid down in *Salomon* v *Customs and Excise Commissioners* [1967] 2 Q.B. 116 and *Post Office* v *Estuary Radio Ltd.* [1968] 2 Q.B. 740 is applicable. If there be any difference between the language of the statutory provision and that of the corresponding provision of the Convention, the statutory language should be construed in the same sense as that of the Convention if the words of the statute are reasonably capable of bearing that meaning.[37]

But, it is submitted, there was no need for the Court of Appeal to read down the Maritime Transport Act in the way it did, for the simple reason that there was no conflict with the international law of the sea. Such conflict as the Court believed existed could only come about from the conviction of Sellers interfering with the right of Malta as the flag State of the *Nimbus* to have it return to the high seas.

The Court declined to read down the territorial scope of the Act to exclude the high seas and innocent passage in the territorial sea, on the basis that the words 'for the voyage', as defined elsewhere in the Act, clearly applied to a voyage to a port outside New Zealand.[38] But it was unnecessary to do so at all, since the act with which Sellers was charged was not committed either on the high seas or in the territorial sea. Indeed, the Court would not have perceived any need to read down the Act had

---

[34] *Ibid*, at 62.

[35] P Myburgh, 'Shipping Law', [1999] *New Zealand Law Review* 387 at 398.

[36] Brussels, 10 May 1952; 439 UNTS 193.

[37] *Owners of the motor vessel Erkowit v Owners of the ship Jade; Owners of cargo lately laden on board the motor vessel Erkowit v Owners of the ship Eschersheim* [1976] 1 All ER 920 at 924 per Lord Diplock.

[38] *Sellers v Maritime Safety Inspector, supra* n 14, at 60; the Court also considered and rejected two other possible interpretations that would avoid the Director's powers in s 21 conflicting with international law: exclusion of foreign pleasure craft from the scope of the section, or limitation of the section's spatial application so as not to extend to the high seas: at 59–60.

it not 'read it up' in the first place, on the unsatisfactory basis that what the Act in reality sought to do was to require all pleasure craft departing New Zealand to have a radio and emergency locator beacon in the part of the ocean where New Zealand under the Search and Rescue Convention[39] would have the responsibility to rescue them should they encounter trouble. Yet, while this may well have been the New Zealand authorities' desired outcome, it does not explain why the Act did not simply impose such an obligation if that were so. Of course, it is obvious that to subject a specified area of the high seas to legislation directly applicable to foreign craft in this way would have exceeded New Zealand's jurisdiction at international law – but the Act did not do this even indirectly. What the parliamentary draftsmen appear to have tried to do instead is to use the full extent of that permissible jurisdiction in order to achieve a result as close as possible to the assumed desideratum, while still falling some way short of it. That is, the master of any foreign craft lacking the prescribed equipment on arrival in a New Zealand port would need to purchase it in order to leave; the authorities could then rely on the inertia of most mariners, having made that investment, to make the most of it by keeping the equipment on board even after the obligation to do so had ceased. The Court of Appeal fails to give any credit for this restraint in electing to read the Act as though Parliament was not merely motivated by but actually intending to enact the inferred jurisdiction-exceeding policy – but this makes sense only if Sellers could have been prosecuted even if he had had the required equipment at the moment of leaving port and thereafter, his religious objections outweighing his inertia, jettisoned it. That, however, does not seem possible, given how the Act is drafted. The offence of which Sellers was convicted was completed in New Zealand's internal waters – or, more precisely, at the boundary between internal waters and the territorial sea, the point beyond which Parliament appears to have intended that he would be beyond the reach of the Act, in order not to infringe against the prohibition in UNCLOS Article 21, paragraph 2 on legislating on equipment to be carried by ships in the territorial sea other than so as to enact international standards.[40] Hence, it can be deduced that what motivated the Court in the way it applied Article 92 must have been the (mis)apprehension that convicting the master of a foreign-flagged vessel would wrongfully interfere with the vessel's return to the high seas where it would enjoy its flag State's freedom of navigation. In other words, the Court unnecessarily subordinated the right of New Zealand as the port State *within its own port* to that of the flag State in regaining access to the high seas.[41]

---

[39] *Supra* n 10 (last item).

[40] *Supra*, text at n 23.

[41] The oddness of this result may be gauged by asking whether a New Zealand court would now refuse to apply against a foreign ship a statute criminalising entry into a New Zealand port of any ship that had engaged in specified behaviour on the high seas, on the same ground that the statute was 'really' regulating conduct on the high seas outside New Zealand's jurisdiction at international law. The answer is not obvious, as unlike the *Sellers* case situation, where a ship in port wishing to return to the high seas cannot do so except by leaving port and thus exposing its master to s 21 of the Maritime Transport Act 1994 and its equivalent for other craft, nothing compels a ship on the high seas to enter a New Zealand port (except distress, but in that event a customary law right to enter port exists and it may be assumed

Curiously, there is no mention in the judgment of the nationality of Sellers himself. If he were a New Zealand national, New Zealand would have criminal jurisdiction over him at international law even if the Court's reasoning based on the *Nimbus* being a foreign vessel were correct, as Article 90, unlike its Article 116 equivalent on the freedom of fishing, mentions only States and not natural persons of their nationality: 'Every State, whether coastal or landlocked, has the right to sail ships flying its flag on the high seas'. But he does seem at least to have been based in New Zealand, as it was only on his return to the same port after an absence of some months that he was charged with the offence committed by leaving it without the prescribed equipment.

The decision has not met with universal approbation,[42] yet, although it is sometimes treated as an aberration,[43] until recently there was no contrary authority on the central point under discussion. This is possibly because, despite there being no paucity of examples of ships and their masters being subjected to penal and administrative proceedings in foreign ports (most notoriously the master of the *Prestige* in Spain, whose case went as far as a Grand Chamber of the European Court of Human Rights[44]) – these usually involve a sinking, grounding, collision or some other misadventure, meaning that the ship concerned is in no fit state to resume its voyage, so that even the most imaginative of counsel would be unlikely to think of raising the denial of high seas freedoms as a defence.[45] Of the relatively

that the New Zealand authorities would not prosecute), and a ship voluntarily present in a foreign port subjects itself to the legal system of the port State. If the answer is yes, New Zealand is needlessly limiting, if not depriving itself of, its power to impose conditions on entry into its ports assumed by UNCLOS Art 25(2) – see *supra*, text at nn 26 and 27 – and of the policy leverage this brings with it. But if the answer is no, it creates a distinction, incongruous in navigational terms, between entering and leaving a port.

[42] The most thoughtful defence of it is by D Devine, 'Port State Jurisdiction: A Judicial Contribution from New Zealand', (2000) 24 *Marine Policy* 215 at 218, but it is ultimately unconvincing because it relies on a contrived distinction between *ex post facto* and *a priori* jurisdiction not known to international law, asserting that the former is permitted, to punish wrongdoing after the event, but not the latter, seeking to prevent undesirable occurrence X by banning Y which can lead to it or requiring Z which may prevent it, since X may never actually happen. This is equivalent to a distinction between legislating directly and indirectly to achieve a given end. It may be noted that formally a criminal conviction is always after the event – in this case, the relevant event was leaving port without the prescribed equipment.

[43] H Ringbom, 'Global Problem–Regional Solution? International Law Reflections on an EU CO$_2$ Emissions Trading Scheme for Ships' (2011) 26 *International Journal of Marine and Coastal Law* 613 at 622 calls it 'rare'; EJ Molenaar, 'Port State Jurisdiction: Toward Comprehensive, Mandatory and Global Coverage', (2007) 38 *Ocean Development & International Law* 225 at 231–232 describes the reasoning as 'flawed', in part because it assumes a right of foreign ships to enter ports that does not exist.

[44] *Mangouras v Spain*, Application No. 12050/04 (2012) 54 EHRR 25; in 2012 the Gladstone Magistrates Court convicted the master and chief officer of the *Shen Neng 1* which ran aground on Douglas Shoal off that Queensland port in April 2010, sentencing them to a A$25,000 fine and three months' imprisonment respectively: http://www.abc.net.au/news/2012-11-14/captain-fined-25k-over-shen-neng-oil-spill/4370828 (accessed on 25 February 2013).

[45] The Master and Second Officer of the *MV Rena*, which struck Astrolabe Reef off Tauranga in October 2011, were charged under the Resource Management Act 1991(NZ) and the Maritime Transport Act 1994 (NZ), as well as the Crimes Act 1961 (NZ): T Leander, 'Rena master and second officer accused of altering ship records', *Lloyd's List*, 22 December 2011, 2. Both pleaded guilty to all charges against them (see J Morton, 'Rena captain jailed for 7 months', http://www.nzherald.co.nz/nz/news/article.

few precedents cited to or by the Court of Appeal, in none of them were the facts on all fours with those of this case in denying the port State's jurisdiction over a ship in or leaving port. Most are of no assistance in supporting the Court's decision because they deal with acts of outright interference with a ship while it was on the high seas, which is clearly and uncontroversially impermissible.

The Court first discussed[46] the well-known *Lotus* case, in which a narrow majority of the Permanent Court of International Justice found that there was nothing in the customary international law rules on jurisdiction to prevent Turkey from prosecuting in its port the responsible officer of a French ship for involuntary manslaughter of several persons on board a Turkish ship as a result of a collision between the two on the high seas.[47] It laid emphasis on the overturning of this outcome in Article 1 of the International Convention for the Unification of Certain Rules relating to Penal Jurisdiction in Matters of Collision or Other Incidents of Navigation[48] and subsequently also in Article 97(1) of UNCLOS and Article 11(1) of the High Seas Convention, which restrict prosecutions of mariners in this situation to the flag State of the ship aboard which they are serving or, except in the first-named convention above, the mariner's own State of nationality. It is submitted, however, that this is beside the point, for the basis of Turkey's criminal jurisdiction in that case was essentially quasi-territorial: less the presence in a Turkish port of the individual charged than the assimilation of death caused by a collision on the high seas between ships flagged to States A and B to the situation much used as an illustration by textbook writers of a person in State A who shoots a gun across the border into State B, killing a person there. (Lest this be perceived as overly contrived, mention may be made of the *Enrica Lexie* incident of February 2012, an incipient dispute between Italy and India over the killing of two crewmembers aboard an Indian fishing vessel on the high seas. The deceased were shot from an Italian-flagged merchant ship by an Italian naval detachment posted on board to protect it from piracy, who suspected the vessel of piratical intentions.[49]) Only one element of the *actus reus* of the offence need have taken place in a State for that State to have jurisdiction over the crime, so where different elements occur in both States A and B, at international law both can legitimately try the person for the crime. The equation of the ships to the territory of the flag States no longer

cfm?c_id=1&objectid=10808468 (accessed on 25 February 2013)), forgoing the opportunity to move the Tauranga District Court to dismiss the charges on the basis that it was bound to follow the Court of Appeal in *Sellers* by reading down the Acts in question, no doubt because it would have been simple to distinguish the earlier case as the ship, having broken in two, was unable to continue its voyage.

[46] *Sellers v Maritime Safety Inspector, supra* n 14, at 49–51.
[47] *The Case of the SS Lotus (France v Turkey)* (1927), PCIJ Reports Series A, No 10.
[48] Brussels, 10 May 1952; 439 UNTS 233.
[49] In early May 2012 the ship itself was released from detention pursuant to the order of the Supreme Court of India in *MT Enrica Lexie & Anor v Doramma & Ors*, Civil Appeal No. 4167/2012, but the same court confirmed in January 2013 that two Italian marines charged with the killings would be tried in an Indian federal court, where they and Italy would be able to argue that the courts of Italy, not of India, should have jurisdiction to try them: see D Mahapatra, 'Kerala can't try Italian naval guards', http://timesofindia.indiatimes.com/india/Kerala-cant-try-Italian-naval-guards-Supreme-Court/articleshow/18081014.cms (accessed on 25 February 2013).

represents the law, but is not necessary to support the analogy – when the collision takes place on the high seas, the ships are still places where the law of States A and B respectively apply, the event of the collision bringing them momentarily into a situation of adjacency as in the case of the cross-border shooting. In other words, the better view is that the *Lotus* was correctly decided according to the law as it then stood, and the subsequent reversal in the three conventions to which the Court of Appeal draws attention was motivated by policy considerations rather than a belief that the decision was wrong, even though, as a result of the preamble to the High Seas Convention, the treaty rule now also represents the position at customary international law. In changing the rule specifically for collisions, however, States cannot be taken to have circumscribed *sub silentio* at the same time the general jurisdiction of coastal States in their ports, and the original rule would, it is submitted, still apply to the *Enrica Lexie* incident.

The only case cited in *Sellers v Maritime Safety Inspector* that on the facts was remotely similar to the latter, as the ship was in port, was the United States Supreme Court decision of *Lauritzen v Larsen*[50] where the Court rejected a claim of the respondent, a Danish sailor aboard a Danish ship who had suffered personal injury in the Cuban port of Havana, by reading down a statute that on its face applied to 'any seaman who shall suffer personal injury in the course of his employment'. That result falls far short, however, of compelling the Court of Appeal's finding. Firstly, as the claim was in tort, the rules applicable are those of private international law, concerning which, on most analyses, public international law leaves States free to follow their own rules; the rules on jurisdiction in public international law cover criminal matters and on some views public civil matters such as competition law also,[51] with only a small minority of writers adopting the stance that all civil claims, and thus private international law itself, are subject to those rules.[52] Secondly, even on the minority view, the tort in question had been committed outside the United States by one alien against another, and thus had no nexus with the United States,[53] whereas Sellers's offence was committed within waters assimilated to New Zealand territory.

In more recent times, *Sellers v Maritime Safety Inspector* was unsuccessfully relied on by the plaintiffs in *Air Transport Association of America v Secretary of State for Energy and Climate Change*,[54] referred to the European Court of Justice

---

[50] (1953) 345 US 571.

[51] See, eg M Shaw, *International Law*, 6th edn (Cambridge University Press, 2008), at 652. This opens the way to the well-known phenomenon of forum-shopping, which may be undesirable but is not contrary to international law. For example United States courts have jurisdiction over civil claims arising out of collisions on the high seas, even where neither ship is US-flagged: *The Belgenland* (1885) 114 US 355.

[52] The best-known exponent of this latter view is FA Mann, 'The Doctrine of Jurisdiction in International Law' (1964) 111 *Recueil des Cours de l'Académie de Droit International* 1.

[53] The fact that the respondent's contract of employment had been made in New York did not constitute such a nexus, as this was a claim not in contract but in tort, and in any event the proper law of the contract was Danish law: *Lauritzen v Larsen, supra* n 50, at 588.

[54] Case C-366/10, *Air Transport Association of America, American Airlines Inc, Continental Airlines Inc, United Airlines Inc v Secretary of State for Energy and Climate Change* [2012] 2 CMLR 4.

for a preliminary ruling under Article 267 of the Treaty on the Functioning of the European Union[55] by Ouseley J in the High Court.[56] This was an attempt to overturn the Aviation Greenhouse Gas Emissions Trading Scheme Regulations 2009,[57] the United Kingdom legislation implementing European Union Directive 2008/101,[58] which extended the EU's greenhouse gas emissions trading scheme in Directive 2003/87[59] to operators of aircraft arriving in or departing from EU airports. One of the grounds argued was that subjecting such flights to an obligation to make indirect payments (via the surrender of allowances purchased, calculated on the entirety of the flight, including the overflight of other States' territory and the high seas) amounted to a denial of the State of registration's freedom of overflight of the high seas guaranteed by customary international law (and UNCLOS Article 87(1)(b), though that was not pleaded, presumably because the plaintiffs' aircraft were registered in the United States, not party to UNCLOS).

The Grand Chamber of the European Court of Justice held that the application of the Directive to foreign aircraft

> founded on the fact that those aircraft perform a flight which departs from or arrives at an aerodrome situated in the territory of one of the Member States...does not infringe the principle of territoriality or the sovereignty which the third States from or to which such flights are performed have over the airspace above their territory, since those aircraft are physically in the territory of one of the Member States of the European Union and are thus subject on that basis to the unlimited jurisdiction of the European Union.[60]

A fortiori, its application to such aircraft overflying the high seas did not 'affect the principle of freedom to fly over the high seas since an aircraft flying over the high seas is not subject, in so far as it does so, to the allowance trading scheme.'[61] Rather, it was only the voluntary presence of the aircraft within the territory of a Member State as a consequence of its operator scheduling a commercial flight arriving at or departing from an airport in that territory that rendered it subject to the requirement to (purchase and) surrender allowances. No rule of custom therefore prevented the EU from calculating the amount of allowances to be surrendered on the fuel consumed during the whole flight, as opposed to only the portion in or over EU Member States' territory and airspace.[62]

[55] See the Treaty of Lisbon amending the Treaty on European Union and the Treaty Establishing the European Community (Lisbon, 13 December 2007), Official Journal C 306, 17 December 2007, Art 5(1) and Annex.

[56] [2010] EWHC 1554 (Admin).

[57] SI 2009/2301.

[58] Directive 2008/101/EC of the European Parliament and of the Council of 19 November 2008 amending Directive 2003/87/EC so as to include aviation activities in the scheme for greenhouse gas emission allowance trading within the Community, Official Journal L 008, 13 January 2009, p 3.

[59] Directive 2003/87/EC of the European Parliament and of the Council of 13 October 2003 establishing a scheme for greenhouse gas emission allowance trading within the Community and amending Council Directive 96/61/EC, Official Journal L 275, 25 October 2003, p 32.

[60] Case C-366/10, *supra* n 54, at 162 (para 125).

[61] *Ibid*, at para 126.

[62] *Ibid*, at 162–63 (paras 127 and 130).

This ruling was in line with the opinion of Advocate-General Kokott,[63] who had earlier also argued, taking as an example the fact that many States taxed their nationals' worldwide income, that it was 'by no means unusual for a State...to take into account in the exercise of its sovereignty circumstances that occur or have occurred outside its territorial jurisdiction'.[64] While there was thus no objection in principle to the extraterritorial operation of States' laws, the Directive did not in fact have extraterritorial effect:

> Admittedly, it is undoubtedly true that, to some extent, *account is thus taken of events* that take place over the high seas... This might indirectly give airlines an incentive to conduct themselves in a particular way when flying over the high seas..., in particular to consume as little fuel as possible and expel as few greenhouse gases as possible. However, there is no concrete *rule* regarding their conduct within airspace outside the European Union.[65]

Sellers v Maritime Safety Inspector was not referred to in the judgment, having received short shrift from Advocate-General Kokott. While she chose not to take direct issue with that case, dismissing it instead as not relevant to aircraft,[66] the analogy from the freedom of navigation to the freedom of overflight is a close one, hence, had she found the Court of Appeal's reasoning at all persuasive, it would have been a simple matter for her to apply the analogy.

II. RELATIVISM LOOKING FROM LAND TO SEA – THE M/V LOUISA

It was not until 2010 that a shipping case was brought that offers an opportunity to reinstate what is, or ought to be, the orthodoxy in this regard. That case, between Saint Vincent and the Grenadines and Spain, is before the International Tribunal for the Law of the Sea (ITLOS)[67] and has already been the subject of an application for provisional measures under Article 290 of UNCLOS, which ITLOS declined to order.[68] It concerns the prolonged detention in a Spanish port of the Vincentian-flagged ship the *M/V Louisa* and its (US-flagged) tender for allegedly illegally removing underwater cultural heritage objects from Spain's territorial sea, where it was licensed to explore for oil. A decision on the merits is likely during 2013, considering that the

---

[63] Available online at: http://curia.europa.eu/juris/document/document.jsf?docid=110742&pageIndex=0&doclang=en&mode=lst&dir=&occ=first&cid=659109 (accessed on 25 February 2013), [2012] 2 CMLR 4 at 121–22 (paras 149, 152–53 and 155).

[64] *Ibid*, at 121 (para 148).

[65] *Ibid*, at para 147.

[66] *Ibid*, at 119 (para 131 and footnote 126).

[67] This is because both Saint Vincent and the Grenadines and Spain have made declarations under Art 287 of UNCLOS, on 22 November 2010 and 19 July 2002 respectively, electing ITLOS as their preferred forum for settling disputes about the interpretation and application of that treaty: see the figure '1' against both States in the ITLOS column on the dispute settlement webpage of the UN Secretariat's Division for Ocean Affairs and the Law of the Sea, available at http://www.un.org/Depts/los/settlement_of_disputes/choice_procedure.htm (accessed on 25 February 2013).

[68] *M/V 'Louisa' (Saint Vincent and the Grenadines v Kingdom of Spain), Provisional Measures, Order of 23 December 2010*, ITLOS Reports 2008–2010, p 58.

hearing took place in October 2012.[69] The applicant's case appears so weak, however,[70] that even at this advanced stage in the process it would not be surprising if the litigation were to be settled or abandoned before judgment is delivered. Of the five articles of UNCLOS it alleges Spain to have breached,[71] the facts emerging from the application instituting proceedings[72] do not support even plausible arguments that four of them have been breached,[73] and any non-compliance with the fifth, Article 87, is possible only on the assumption in *Sellers v Maritime Safety Inspector* that the freedom of navigation of ships on the high seas is absolute, taking precedence even over the sovereign powers of a port State within its internal waters and territorial sea. It is confirmed by the Request for Provisional Measures, which reserves the full particulars of the alleged breach of Article 87 to the memorial to be filed, but states that 'provisional measures are appropriate based on Respondent's failure to allow the Louisa to enjoy its rightful freedom of navigation and scientific research'.[74]

Should the *M/V Louisa case* not proceed all the way to a decision on the merits, it is the pronouncements in the provisional measures phase of the case that will have to serve as elucidation on the spatial scope of the freedom of navigation. For these purposes, that phase is notable not for the majority decision,[75] which did not discuss it, but rather for the four dissenting opinions, those of Judges Wolfrum, Cot, Golitsyn and Treves.

The decision of the majority was that 'the circumstances, as they now present themselves to the Tribunal, are not such as to require the exercise of its powers to prescribe provisional measures under article 290, paragraph 1, of the Convention',[76] but it was not this conclusion with which the four judges disagreed – as it is clear from their dissenting opinions that none of them would have awarded provisional measures to Saint Vincent and the Grenadines – but the reasoning of the majority. For in order even to reach the question of whether the circumstances warranted provisional measures, the majority must first have found that ITLOS had jurisdiction to grant those measures, which depended on it being satisfied that *prima facie* it would have jurisdiction over the merits of the case.

---

[69] *M/V 'Louisa' (Saint Vincent and the Grenadines v Kingdom of Spain), Order of 4 July 2012* (ITLOS Order 2012/1), available at: http://www.itlos.org/fileadmin/itlos/documents/cases/case_no_18_merits/Ord_1-2012_04_07_12_E.pdf (accessed on 25 February 2013).

[70] Accord R Churchill, 'Dispute Settlement under the UN Convention on the Law of the Sea: Survey for 2010', (2011) 26 *International Journal of Marine and Coastal Law* 495 who at 505 describes the application as 'poorly argued'.

[71] Arts 73, 87, 226, 245 and 303.

[72] See: http://www.itlos.org/fileadmin/itlos/documents/cases/case_no_18_merits/SVG_Application _Instituting_final_112310.pdf (accessed on 25 February 2013).

[73] This was among the reasons that Judge Treves gave for coming to the view that ITLOS 'manifestly' lacked jurisdiction to entertain these claims: *M/V 'Louisa' (Saint Vincent and the Grenadines v Kingdom of Spain), Provisional Measures, Dissenting Opinion of Judge Treves*, ITLOS Reports 2008–2010, p 87, at 92 (para 15).

[74] See: http://www.itlos.org/fileadmin/itlos/documents/cases/case_no_18_prov_meas/Request_for _the_prescription_of_provisional_measures.pdf (accessed on 25 February 2013), at 22 (para 62). Scientific research is another of the freedoms of the high seas: UNCLOS Art 87(1)(f).

[75] *Supra* n 68.

[76] *Ibid*, at 70–71 (para 83(1)).

Judge Wolfrum made plain the fundamental flaw in the applicant State's submission:

> As far as article 87 of the Convention is concerned…[e]vidently the Applicant takes the position that the arrest and detention of the M/V 'Louisa' constitutes an infringement on the freedom of navigation. In my view this approach is not sustainable considering the situation of the vessel which was arrested, as the Applicant stated, when docked in a port of the Respondent for some time with no intention of sailing. It is hard to imagine how the arrest of a vessel in port in the course of national criminal proceedings can be construed as violating the freedom of navigation on the high seas. To take this argument to the extreme it would, in fact, mean that the principle of the freedom of navigation would render vessels immune from criminal prosecution since any arrest of a vessel, under which ground whatsoever, would violate the flag State's right to enjoy the freedom of navigation. This leads me to the conclusion that on the facts provided by the Applicant article 87 of the Convention does not form a plausible basis for a claim of the Applicant.[77]

Judge Cot for his part ridiculed the conclusion to which the *reductio ad absurdum* led him:

> [L]'existence d'une liberté fondamentale n'interdit pas l'exercice des pouvoirs de police et de justice par l'Etat côtier sur son propre territoire. Un tel raisonnement conduirait à considérer que le Premier Amendement à la Constitution des Etats-Unis, qui garantit le droit de réunion, interdirait l'interpellation à Chicago dans les années dix-neuf cent trente d'un suspect soupçonné de trafic illicite de boissons alcooliques au motif que celui-ci comptait se rendre à une réunion pacifique organisée à propos de la législation sur la prohibition.[78]

Not much less forthright was Judge Golitsyn:

> Article 87 of the Convention…does not imply that action taken by the authorities of a coastal State, in accordance with its laws and regulations, against a foreign vessel owing to that vessel's involvement in alleged violations of those laws and regulations in the internal or territorial waters of that State, constitutes infringement of the right of States Parties to the Convention to exercise freedom of navigation on the high seas.[79]

Judge Treves did not need to decide this point because in his view no dispute under UNCLOS existed at all,[80] but agreed nonetheless with Judges Wolfrum and Golitsyn, adding that:

---

[77] *M/V 'Louisa' (Saint Vincent and the Grenadines v Kingdom of Spain), Provisional Measures, Dissenting Opinion of Judge Wolfrum,* ITLOS Reports 2008–2010, p 78, at 83–84 (para 22).
[78] *M/V 'Louisa' (Saint Vincent and the Grenadines v Kingdom of Spain), Provisional Measures, Dissenting Opinion of Judge Cot,* ITLOS Reports 2008–2010, p 93, at 97 (para 21). The official English translation renders this as:
> [T]he existence of a basic freedom does not prohibit the coastal State from exercising the powers of its police and judiciary in its own territory. It is as if the First Amendment of the United States Constitution, which guarantees the right of assembly, had prevented the police from arresting a gentleman suspected of bootlegging in 1930s Chicago because he was going to attend a peaceful meeting on prohibition.
[79] *M/V 'Louisa' (Saint Vincent and the Grenadines v Kingdom of Spain), Provisional Measures, Dissenting Opinion of Judge Golitsyn,* ITLOS Reports 2008–2010, p 100, at 104 (para 19).
[80] Dissenting Opinion of Judge Treves, *supra* n 73, at 87–89 (paras 2–8).

Jurisdiction on the basis of article 87 of that instrument [UNCLOS] seems to me, in the circumstances of the case, *prima facie* unfounded. I cannot, however, exclude the possibility that, upon attentive examination at a further phase of the case, the Tribunal might find in it a basis for its jurisdiction *ratione materiae*.[81]

The issue in the provisional measures hearing was not whether Spain's detention of the *Louisa* constituted a breach of Article 87 of UNCLOS; that will be decided in the merits phase. Rather, the jurisdictional hurdle that an applicant must surmount is to show that jurisdiction exists *prima facie*, in the words of Article 290, paragraph 1:

> If a dispute has been duly submitted to a court or tribunal which considers that *prima facie* it has jurisdiction under this Part [XV, on dispute settlement generally]..., the court or tribunal may prescribe any provisional measures which it considers appropriate under the circumstances to preserve the respective rights of the parties to the dispute or to prevent serious harm to the marine environment, pending the final decision.

That is, the elements which the applicant must cumulatively prove in order for ITLOS to be properly seised of the merits of the dispute need to be at least arguably present, and there must be no obvious countervailing factor which would negative any of these. This, as Judge Paik observes, is hardly a formidable obstacle:

> [W]hile the provisions invoked by the Applicant as the legal basis of its claims do not appear to be manifestly related to the facts of the case, the Tribunal does not need to ascertain, at this stage, whether the allegation made by the Applicant are 'sufficiently' arguable or plausible. The threshold of *prima facie* jurisdiction is rather low in the sense that all that is needed, at this stage, is to establish that the Tribunal 'might' have jurisdiction over the merits. As long as the Tribunal finds that the Applicant has made an arguable or plausible case for jurisdiction on the merits, the requirement of *prima facie* jurisdiction should be considered to have been met. On the face of it, at least one provision invoked by the Applicant in its request, Article 87 of the Convention, may provide a basis for an arguable case on the merits, in light of the Respondent's unreasonably long period of detention of the vessel without rendering an indictment or taking any of the necessary judicial procedures. Thus, it appears *prima facie* that 'a dispute concerning the interpretation or application of the Convention' existed between the parties on the date the Application was filed.[82]

In the form that its argument on Article 87 will have to take, a breach of the right of Saint Vincent and the Grenadines to freedom of navigation on the high seas for its ship the *Louisa* is not merely a consequence of, or otherwise dependent on, breach of some other provision of UNCLOS (such as Article 73, 226, 245 or 303 as claimed) or of another obligation having its origin elsewhere in international law (say the right of the owners under human rights law to have the Spanish authorities' allegations against their ships brought to trial without undue delay). To the contrary, even if there has been no breach by Spain of any other obligation, it is

---

[81] *Ibid*, at 92 (para 15).
[82] *M/V 'Louisa' (Saint Vincent and the Grenadines v Kingdom of Spain), Provisional Measures, Separate Opinion of Judge Paik*, ITLOS Reports 2008–2010, p 72 at 73–74 (para 7).

possible – at least on the reasoning underlying *Sellers v Maritime Safety Inspector* – for Article 87 to be breached independently of these, indeed the detention by Spain of the *Louisa* may in all other respects be lawful, and is rendered unlawful simply because of the effect it has in depriving that ship of the opportunity to exercise its flag State's freedom of navigation on the high seas.

On this basis, it is submitted that the majority decision is to be preferred, as ITLOS has jurisdiction over the Article 87 element of the dispute not just *prima facie* but definitively, inasmuch as it turns on which of the two views of the freedom of navigation on the high seas in that article is ultimately found to be correct. This is irrespective of the fact that one of those views has much more to commend it than the other; as long as the weaker view is still arguable, as it is, this conclusion holds. Hence it is all the more significant that three of the four judges who penned dissenting opinions (Judge Treves being the exception, in view of the second sentence of the extract quoted above) would have denied ITLOS even *prima facie* jurisdiction, as they are implicitly saying that the *Sellers* position is not merely wrong, it is not even plausible. It is clear, therefore, that when the merits of this case are argued, Saint Vincent and the Grenadines has little hope of convincing four of the 21 ITLOS judges that Spain has contravened Article 87 of UNCLOS, even though in theory there is still room for all but Judge Cot to change their minds. This could conceivably happen on the ground that the Article 87 point fell outside the *ratio* of their dissents because they also found some logically anterior basis on which to deny the relief sought: this is true not only of Judge Treves,[83] but equally of Judges Wolfrum and Golitsyn, who would both have denied provisional measures for lack of fulfilment of the Article 283 condition to exchange views on the settlement of the dispute.[84]

Judge Cot might well have taken his colourful comparison further, as the absurd consequences that he highlights also arise closer to home in the law of the sea. Similar reasoning to *Sellers* would mean in addition that no fishing vessel could ever be detained for violating a coastal State's fisheries laws in waters under its sovereignty or jurisdiction, as that would interfere with its freedom of fishing on the high seas in UNCLOS Article 87(1)(e). The inherent improbability of that is underlined not only by the mere existence of the prompt release procedure of Article 292 for vessels detained for fisheries and pollution offences, which would then be unnecessary, but also the right to fish is expressed as applying to nationals in Article 116, which includes but is not limited to fishing vessels. That in turn

---

[83] *Supra*, text at n 80.

[84] Judge Wolfrum said that the way the majority had applied Art 283, accepting a *Note verbale* threatening proceedings as amounting to the required exchange of views, 'renders it meaningless': Dissenting Opinion of Judge Wolfrum, *supra* n 77, at 85 (para 28). Judge Golitsyn gave similar reasons for coming to the same conclusion: Dissenting Opinion of Judge Golitsyn, *supra* n 79, at 101–02 (paras 7–9). Both appeared to treat Art 283 as a prior procedural step, not going to jurisdiction in the same way as would a manifest agreement by the parties to use some other dispute settlement mechanism entailing compulsory procedures leading to binding decisions (Art 282), or not to use the Part XV procedures at all (Art 281): Dissenting Opinion of Judge Wolfrum, *supra* n 77, at 85–86 (paras 27–29); Dissenting Opinion of Judge Golitsyn, *supra* n 79, at 100 (para 3).

would mean that States could never arrest and detain foreign nationals for offences committed even within their land territory, because that would prevent them from exercising their right to fish on the high seas, even if they had never engaged in fishing before or were doing so aboard another State's vessel. It is no answer to say that the right extends only to those who make their living from fishing; why should fisherfolk alone be immune from the criminal laws of all States but their own? There exists an entire branch of public international law on the immunities enjoyed by States and the officials and diplomats who represent them, and the modern trend is that commercial activity in general has ceased to be subject to immunity,[85] with a specific denial of immunity for commercial shipping operated by States,[86] so *Sellers* reasoning would in practice perversely give an immunity to private persons engaged in an economic activity that not even the State itself would enjoy if it chose to engage in it.

Despite the unmeritorious nature of the case it has brought, therefore, Saint Vincent and the Grenadines may unwittingly be doing the law of the sea a service if it pursues its case to the end. Should it do so, the likelier and more welcome result, as indicated above, would be that ITLOS finds no infringement of the freedom of navigation on the high seas that it claims on behalf of the *M/V Louisa*, putting paid to the notion that the freedom overrides even the territorial sovereignty of States over foreign ships that are voluntarily present in their ports. Were the applicant's argument based on UNCLOS Article 87 to succeed, however, the law of the sea might find itself at the start of another swing of the pendulum back towards the original all-encompassing and absolute nature of the freedom of the seas. Would States willingly absorb this blow to their regulatory powers? To the present author that seems difficult to conceive and, while it once took 25 years and a subsequent treaty to overturn a decision of an international court on a related matter (the *Lotus case* above[87]), now there are faster ways, such as the annual General Assembly debate on Oceans and the Law of the Sea, in which they could make their dissatisfaction known, even if there was insufficient consensus for this to be reflected in the subsequent resolution. Meanwhile an unexpected side-effect would be that potentially a new defence for shipowners and seafarers charged with

---

[85] The United Nations Convention on Jurisdictional Immunities of States and Their Property, adopted by the UN General Assembly on 2 December 2004, not yet in force (see General Assembly resolution 59/38, Annex, reproduced at (2005) 44 *International Legal Materials* 803) provides in Art 10(1) that:

> If a State engages in a commercial transaction with a foreign natural or juridical person and, by virtue of the applicable rules of private international law, differences relating to the commercial transaction fall within the jurisdiction of a court of another State, the State cannot invoke immunity from that jurisdiction in a proceeding arising out of that commercial transaction.

In the United Kingdom, s 3(1)(a) of the State Immunity Act 1978 is in like vein.

[86] Art 16(1) of the United Nations Convention on Jurisdictional Immunities of States and Their Property, *supra* n 85, is in the following terms:

> Unless otherwise agreed between the States concerned, a State which owns or operates a ship cannot invoke immunity from jurisdiction before a court of another State which is otherwise competent in a proceeding which relates to the operation of that ship if, at the time the cause of action arose, the ship was used for other than government non-commercial purposes.

See also State Immunity Act 1978, s 10.

[87] *Supra* n 47 and surrounding text.

offences arising out of shipwreck or pollution incidents would become available, at least in situations where the ship is still not beyond repair and thus has some hope of exercising its flag State's freedom of navigation on the high seas.[88] The consequences of that could keep the Institute of Maritime Law busy well beyond its 40th anniversary.

---

[88] Although this may not currently be true of the *Louisa*, that is alleged to be the result of lack of maintenance during its prolonged detention – see Request for Prescription of Provisional Measures, *supra* n 74, at 7 (paras 23 and 25) – and the cost of restoring its seaworthiness is presumably part of the damages claimed.

3

Pollution of the Sea by Hazardous and Noxious Substances – Is a Workable International Convention on Compensation an Impossible Dream?

RICHARD SHAW

'MAY YOU LIVE in interesting times!' Thus runs the adage attributed to a Chinese Philosopher, although its exact origin remains a matter of doubt. The phrase has been described as a Chinese curse, but may also be applied to the times during which the Institute of Maritime Law has developed within the School of Law at the University of Southampton. Certainly in the field of legal rules governing compensation for oil pollution of the sea the times have been interesting and fruitful. The development of a Convention on pollution by harmful chemicals has been more frustrating.

I. INTRODUCTION

The grounding of the super tanker *'Torrey Canyon'* off Cornwall in March 1967 led to pollution of the coasts of England and France on a scale that had never been seen before, and it quickly became apparent that the existing rules of national and international law were incapable of providing adequate compensation to the victims. With commendable alacrity the member states of the International Maritime Organization ('IMO' then called IMCO), developed and adopted the 1969 International Convention on Civil Liability for Oil Pollution Damage (the CLC Convention), and, shortly afterwards, the 1971 International Convention on the Establishment of an International Fund for Compensation for Oil Pollution Damage (the 1971 Fund Convention).

These two conventions, which have evolved steadily over the years since they were initially adopted, have provided prompt and fair compensation to victims of oil pollution incidents resulting from spills of oil carried in bulk by sea. The size of the claims arising from such incidents, and the ships carrying such cargoes, have grown enormously, but the member states of these conventions, and the bodies which administer them, have adapted them to the changing world.[1]

Pollution of the sea is not caused solely by oil cargoes. Chemicals and bulk solid cargoes such as coal and fertilizers have the capacity to cause massive pollution damage. Indeed one of the largest man-made non-nuclear explosions occurred in Texas City USA in 1947 when the vessel *'Grandcamp'* loading a cargo of ammonium nitrate exploded with the loss of over 550 lives and massive damage to property ashore. There have been other instances of such disasters.

It was not surprising therefore that following the entry into force of the CLC and Fund Conventions in the mid-1970s,[2] the member states of the IMO started to look into the possibility of a parallel legal regime governing liability and compensation for damage caused in connection with the carriage by sea of dangerous cargoes. Despite the considerable efforts of many governments and individuals since then, no international regime to compensate victims of disasters involving such cargoes has yet entered into force.

A Convention on this subject was adopted in 1996 by a Diplomatic Conference of the IMO, but has failed to attract the necessary ratifications. Following a study initially developed in Canada, with a view to identifying the particular reasons for this failure and to develop an instrument to address those issues, a Protocol to the 1996 HNS Convention was adopted by a Diplomatic Conference in April 2010, and it is hoped that the entry into force of a convention setting up an international regime of compensation of the victims of pollution from such substances may be in sight.

The purpose of this paper is to review the evolution of the HNS Convention over the last 30 years, to comment on the reasons for its slow development, and to look forward to the working of such a system of compensation in the light of experience gained with the oil pollution compensation regime.

II. AFTER THE 'TORREY CANYON'

In the late 1960s the oil industry was dominated by seven major oil companies,[3] who also owned a substantial proportion of the world's tanker tonnage. When it became apparent after the *'Torrey Canyon'* disaster that the legal regime then in place, which enabled a shipowner to limit his liability to a figure based on the tonnage of the ship involved, was manifestly insufficient to meet the claims of the victims of oil pollution, the pressure to develop a means of providing reasonable compensation for those victims became irresistible. The major claimants against the owners of the *'Torrey Canyon'* were the British and French Governments.

[1] As at 1 February 2012 127 states has ratified or acceded to the 1992 CLC Convention, and 109 states had ratified or acceded to the 1992 Fund Convention. 27 States have also ratified or acceded to the 2003 Supplementary Fund Protocol, which provides a total compensation of 750 million SDR (approximately USD 1,102.7 million) to victims of pollution from tanker accidents.
[2] The CLC Convention on 19 June 1975 and the 1971 Fund Convention on 16 October 1978.
[3] Known as 'the Seven Sisters'.

Supported by the Protection and Indemnity Associations ('P&I Clubs') which insured almost all tanker owners for such liabilities, the shipping industry developed what became the 1969 CLC Convention, which provided four principal elements:

1. Strict liability on the owner of the carrying ship for oil pollution damage caused by persistent oil carried by sea, with a very small number of defences;
2. Limited liability at a level significantly higher than the limits then available under the existing international conventions, and separate from the limitation funds provided for under those conventions;
3. Compulsory oil pollution liability insurance;
4. Direct action against the shipowner's liability insurer.

It was envisaged that an additional fund contributed to by the owners of the oil cargoes carried by sea, would provide additional compensation in cases (expected to be few in number) where the CLC liability was insufficient to cover all claims.

This fund was to be administered by an international organisation governed by a separate convention, but in the interim the oil companies set up an agreement whereby the claims in excess of the CLC Fund were met by a body known as 'CRISTAL'.[4]

Discussions commenced in the mid-1970s at the IMO on the possibility of putting in place a comparable legal regime to cover compensation for pollution damage caused by non-oil cargoes.[5] There was general support from the governments of the IMO member states and after extensive negotiations, a draft International Convention[6] was submitted to a Diplomatic Conference in London in 1984. However the conference was not able to agree on several important issues, and ended with no agreed instrument.

The failure of the 1984 Conference was a major disappointment to the IMO, which had hoped that a regime built on the principles of the 1969 and 1971 Conventions relating to oil pollution would be achievable. Much has been written on the reasons for the failure, and this is not the place to rehearse all the arguments, but underlying the reports is a clear message that the chemical industry has far more participants than oil, and that, unlike the oil industry, there was no concerted resolve on the part of that industry to establish a compensation regime. There was likewise no consensus on how the burden of such a regime should be shared between ship owning and chemical cargo trading interests. Further there was debate over possible linkage between the international rules governing a shipowner's right

---

[4] Contract Regarding a Supplement to Tanker Liability of Oil Pollution – an oil industry scheme to supplement the interim arrangements provided by the P&I Clubs pending the entry into force of the 1971 Fund Convention. This provided a clear demonstration of the ability of the oil industry to act in concert when necessary.

[5] For a detailed description of the debates during the period between 1978 and 1994 see the article by Nicholas Gaskell, then Professor of Maritime Law at the University of Southampton, in H Tiberg, P Wetterstein and A Beijer, *Book of Essays in Honour of Hugo Tiberg* (Stockholm, Juristforlaget, 1996) and the sources there cited.

[6] The International Convention on Liability and Compensation for Damage in Connection With the Carriage of Hazardous and Noxious Substances By Sea ('the HNS Convention').

to limitation of liability generally with potential liabilities under an HNS damage compensation scheme.

III. AFTER THE FAILURE OF THE 1984 CONFERENCE

The 1984 Diplomatic Conference was not in fact a complete failure, for it succeeded in adopting the texts of two protocols which brought the 1969 CLC Convention and the 1971 Fund Convention up to date. These protocols, apart from significantly increasing the amount of compensation available, both from the shipowners and the Fund, made important changes to clarify matters such as claims for damage to the environment, the scope of application and the persons potentially liable for oil pollution damage.

Considerable diplomatic efforts were made to persuade the USA, which was not a member state of the 1969 and 1971 Conventions, to adhere to the 1984 Protocols. Unfortunately the grounding of the tanker 'Amoco Cadiz' off Alaska in 1989 changed the climate of political opinion in the United States, and the USA still remains outside the International Oil Pollution Compensation regime.

Sadly the time and effort spent on attempting to bring the USA into the scheme caused work on developing improvements to the HNS compensation regime to be delayed. Work continued in correspondence groups dealing with particular topics, and a Group of Technical Experts ('GTE') was formed to formulate guidelines for the guidance of national delegations. In 1993 a target date for a new Diplomatic Conference was adopted, namely spring 1996, but the Chairman of the Legal Committee emphasised to delegates that considerable further work was needed if agreement was to be reached on matters of important principle which were as yet unresolved.

A significant step forward took place in March 1994, when a joint paper was submitted by Australia, Canada and Norway, which became known as the 'ACN paper', based on proposals of the GTE. This proposed that a second tier fund should be created, similar to that applicable to oil pollution, which would be constituted from contributions from receivers of HNS cargoes. This would have a limited number of separate accounts (a proposal initially introduced by Japan) applying to specific categories of cargo which had distinct risk profiles, such as oil, LNG[7] and LPG.[8]

Coal was also included in the proposed list of separate accounts, but this was later removed during the 1996 Diplomatic Conference.

The IMO Legal Committee agreed during the March 1994 session that even if the HNS Compensation regime were to adopt the two-tier structure of the oil pollution regime, this could be embodied in a single instrument.

The 72nd session (held in March 1995) of the IMO Legal Committee accepted the Chairman's proposal that the HNS Convention was ready for a Diplomatic

---

[7] Liquified natural gas – principally methane.
[8] Liquified petroleum gas – principally propane and butane.

Conference, but as Professor Gaskell perceptively observed at the time '...*a neutral observer might have concluded that more work was still needed on a number of issues, such as linkage*.'[9] Subsequent events proved him right.

IV. THE 1996 DIPLOMATIC CONFERENCE

This was a three-week long affair, of which two weeks were set aside for the HNS Convention and one week for the proposed protocol revising the 1976 International Convention on Limited Liability for Marine Claims ('LLMC'). These may at first seem strange bedfellows, but it must be borne in mind that an important issue in the HNS debate (referred to by Professor Gaskell in the work cited above) was the question of 'linkage'. This term, much referred to in the discussions, was shorthand for the wish on the part of the shipowners and their liability insurers that payments to victims of HNS pollution should be treated within the ambit of claims generally against a ship and her owner. The oil pollution regime, with its 'stand-alone fund' was, they said, a special arrangement, and not a precedent for further such arrangements. They also wished to confine the concept of strict liability and direct action, which effectively meant an anticipatory guarantee by the P&I Clubs of liability for such claims, within the narrow limits of oil pollution.[10]

The debates were long and difficult, and a number of changes were made to the text submitted by the Legal Committee. Among them was the removal of coal, woodchips and fishmeal from the category of Hazardous and Noxious Substances. It was accepted by the GTE that these commodities were capable of spontaneous combustion when shipped in bulk, but it was equally accepted that the risks were relatively small.

It was also accepted by the conference that the substantial tonnages of these commodities which are carried by sea would distort the fair sharing of the burden of the levies to the HNS Fund when compared with inflammable commodities such as chemicals, fertilizer and solvents. It was also accepted that it was not practical to create special categories for each of these cargoes, and that they should be excluded from the ambit of the HNS Convention.

A more technical change concerned LNG. The states importing such cargoes in bulk argued that since the LNG markets are largely governed by long-term contracts, many concluded at government level, the burden of making contributions to the HNS fund should be borne by the 'title holder' to the cargo. This was accepted by delegates to the conference, most of whom had no practical knowledge of these specialist markets, but this provision proved to be one of those requiring modification by the 2010 Protocol.

The 'linkage' debate was finally resolved by creating 'stand-alone' funds independent of those applicable to oil pollution claims and of LLMC limitation funds generally.

At the end of the conference the text of the 1996 HNS Convention was adopted, and hopes were high that States would move swiftly to ratify it, but those proved over optimistic. The European Union agreed in principle that its Member States should ratify this convention, but a number of technical obstacles have prevented this from happening.

V. EVENTS SINCE THE 1996 DIPLOMATIC CONFERENCE

A. In the Period 1996–2007

In the years since 1996 progress in ratification of this Convention has been regrettably slow. To date only nine States have deposited instruments of ratification, and the majority of those States have not provided the statistical data on quantities of HNS imported by them which is necessary for the Secretariat to assess whether cargo tonnages sufficient to meet the entry into force provisions and to calculate the initial call for funds had been imported into those States. The European Union is encouraging its member States to ratify this Convention and many of them are well on the way to doing so.

There was however an evident reluctance on the part of the governments of several large HNS importing states to burden their chemical industry with the financial contributions involved until they could be sure that the other 'serious players' would also ratify. The IOPC Funds have agreed that their Secretariat will undertake the administrative tasks necessary to get the HNS Fund into operation.

By 2007 concerns were growing that there was little sign of progress towards entry into force of the HNS Convention, and that a serious attempt should be made to advance matters. To facilitate this, a Focus Group, under the chairmanship of Alfred Popp of Canada, was formed in 2008.

The mandate of this Focus Group was to examine the underlying causes of the issues which have been identified as inhibiting the entry into force of the HNS Convention, to examine any issues of an administrative nature which would facilitate the operation of the Convention, and to identify and develop legally binding solutions to these issues in the form of a draft protocol to the Convention.

B. IOPC Fund March 2008

In March 2008 the Focus Group reported to the IOPC Fund that the three principal areas of concern were:

1.   Contributions from packaged cargo;
2.   Contributories to the LNG Fund; and
3.   Non-reporting of contributing tonnage of HNS.

Following this meeting a correspondence group of the IOPC Fund prepared the text of a draft protocol addressing these issues, and this work received widespread support. However this text had to be approved by the IMO Legal Committee and Assembly before it could be submitted to a Diplomatic Conference.

C. Legal Committee October 2008

The principal task of the October 2008 Legal Committee meeting was the adoption of the text of a draft protocol to the 1996 HNS Convention. At this meeting a developed text was presented to the IMO Legal Committee for the first time.

An unusual feature of the previous discussions in the IOPC Fund was that HNS was not strictly the concern of the IOPC Fund, which deals with compensation of pollution by persistent oil. However the similarity between the two conventions and the fact that the IOPC Fund Secretariat had already been tasked with administering the HNS Fund meant that the delegates attending IOPC Fund meetings were well informed of the potential problems and were better able to develop practical solutions.

Some delegations to the Legal Committee seemed to be unaware of these facts, and strong protests were voiced that the draft protocol seemed to be being rushed through without proper consideration. That was certainly not the intention of the sponsoring states,[11] but eventually it became necessary for all concerned to accept that, to allow time to meet these concerns, a Diplomatic Conference to adopt this protocol would not be held before 2010.

The four principal areas of concern were:

1. Packaged HNS goods;
2. Contributions to the LNG account;
3. Non-submission of contributing cargo reports;
4. Definition of 'hazardous and noxious substances'.

1. Packaged HNS goods

Article 1(5) of the HNS Convention contains a broad definition of HNS cargoes including solids, liquids and gases. The final paragraph covers solid HNS cargoes which are subject to the IMDG Code[12] when carried in packaged form. In practice this means containerised cargo.

The structure of the HNS Convention, based as it is on the CLC and Fund Conventions applying to oil pollution damage, establishes a two-tier compensation framework, with the shipowners (and their P&I Clubs) paying claims up to the limit of the first tier, and a fund contributed to by cargo interests paying claims

---

[11] Including Australia, Belgium, Canada, Denmark, France, Germany, Japan, Malaysia, the Netherlands, Norway, Sweden, and the United Kingdom.
[12] International Maritime Dangerous Goods Code published by the IMO.

in excess of that limit.[13] The operation of the fund requires member states to report all relevant cargoes imported into their territory above certain thresholds. The administrative burden of reporting HNS cargoes imported in containers in relatively small quantities (but which may cumulatively exceed the relevant threshold) is very considerable indeed, and detailed studies by the major importers of such cargoes have indicated that this is impractical.

The focus group draft therefore proposed that packaged HNS cargoes should not be reported, and should not be included in the calculations of contributing cargo on the basis of which contributions to the HNS Fund will be levied. Victims of an HNS casualty, even when caused by packaged goods, will still be compensated. This is a revolutionary, but practical, proposal. To meet the concern that the receivers of bulk HNS cargoes may be obliged to make greater contributions to the HNS Fund to make up for the lack of contribution from packaged goods, it was agreed by the shipowners' representatives and the International Group of P&I Clubs that the shipowners' contribution to the first tier will be increased. The exact amount of the increase will be fixed by the Diplomatic Conference to adopt the protocol.

2. LNG Cargoes

The present state of the gas industry today was not foreseeable in 1996. The quantities of gas shipped by sea have increased dramatically in recent years, and the development of gas fields notably in Nigeria, Indonesia and Qatar has led to the building of a large number of new ships to carry both Liquified Petroleum Gas ('LPG') and Liquified Natural Gas ('LNG').[14]

When the HNS Convention was adopted in 1996, the transport of LNG was almost entirely in the hands of governmental organisations and the major energy companies, due to the enormous capital costs required for the construction of the necessary gas liquefaction plants and the sophisticated ships to carry this product.[15] When the HNS Convention was under consideration at the 1996 Diplomatic Conference, the delegates were informed that it would be simpler for the contributions to the HNS fund to be made by the 'title holder' to the cargo immediately prior to discharge, and an appropriate wording was adopted in article 19 (1)(b).

However further study has revealed that this arrangement could give rise to considerable difficulty, particularly when the title holder in question is resident in a State which is not a party to the Convention. Moreover a number of gas producing countries, notably Algeria, protested that this imposed an unreasonable burden on them which was inconsistent with the overall structure of the IOPC and HNS Conventions, which were based on funds contributed to by the receivers rather than the exporters of the cargoes in question.

---

[13] Up to a maximum of 250 million SDR.
[14] LPG is principally propane and LNG methane.
[15] LNG is transported at a temperature of minus 169 degrees C.

The Focus Group encountered very considerable difficulty in finding a solution to this problem despite the good intentions of all concerned. The differences between the positions adopted by various States were of a political, economic and policy nature, and not just a matter of drafting. At the June 2008 meeting of the IOPC Funds it was agreed that the Malaysian delegation would coordinate an informal correspondence group during the summer to attempt to resolve the problem, and this led to the presentation to the Legal Committee of a paper[16] containing revised wording. This provided that the duty to report on receipts of LNG, and to make contributions to the HNS Fund, should lie with the physical receiver, but that the Convention (as amended by the protocol) should allow the parties to an LNG contract the flexibility to determine by agreement the person liable to make contributions to the LNG fund.

To cover the possibility of non-payment by a title holder liable under such an agreement who is resident in a State not party to the HNS Convention and Protocol, in such a case the Fund will be able to invoice the receiver of the cargo in question for the appropriate contribution.

The delegates to the Legal Committee approved the proposed provisions, although some expressed difficulty in understanding the intricacies of the proposed arrangements. It seems that these had been worked out with the close cooperation of the gas exporting and importing industries as well as the governments concerned, and demonstrated how the IMO and its associated body the IOPC Fund can solve difficult technical and legal problems.

3. Non-submission of Contributing Cargo Reports

The functioning of the HNS Fund and of its predecessor, the IOPC Fund, requires the reporting by member states of the quantities of the relevant cargo imported by their ports and terminals during the preceding year, in order to apportion the burden of the financial contributions to the fund. The IOPC Fund has a proud record of collection of such contributions, which has enabled it to make prompt payments to the victims of major oil pollution incidents.

However it has encountered persistent problems with some member States in collecting the statistical data of the tonnages of relevant cargoes imported by receivers in those States. In theory no apportionment of any distribution of funds to victims of pollution can be made until all member States have submitted their oil reports for the year in question. In practice the system has been made to work, partly because the quantities of unreported cargoes are relatively small, and partly by making, in the case of some states, estimates based on statistics for previous years.[17]

---

[16] LEG94/4/1. A further paper LEG94/4/2 was put in by the IOPC Fund suggesting minor improvements to the draft text.

[17] The oil industry is no longer dominated by the 'Seven Sisters', but is still a coherent body. No doubt the major contributing oil companies will be aware of any large imports of oil which a member State had failed to declare. This is less likely with HNS cargoes.

Considerable concern has however been expressed at the failure of the IOPC Fund system to solve this problem,[18] and when the Supplementary Fund Protocol was adopted in 2003 a provision was included[19] which enables the Fund to withhold payment of compensation for pollution damage in a state party which has not complied with its reporting obligations.

The HNS Convention contains no such provision, but it was the view of many governments that a provision to this effect should be included in the Protocol. An eloquent demonstration of the need for such a provision was in fact, confirmed by the Director of Legal Affairs of the IMO,[20] that of the 13 States which had deposited instruments of ratification of the HNS Convention, only 2 had submitted data on the relevant quantities of contributing cargo as required by Article 43. Article 46 of the HNS Convention provides that the Convention will enter into force 18 months after consents to be bound have been expressed by at least 12 States, including four States each with at least 2 million units of gross tonnage, and instruments of ratification have been deposited (with the IMO) accompanied by details of at least 40 million tonnes of cargo contributing to the general account. Without the relevant information it is simply impossible for the ratifying states, or the IMO, to establish whether or not the required tonnage level has been reached.

Despite the persuasiveness of these arguments, there was a marked reluctance by some delegations to accept the need for the proposed provision, which they perceived as being draconian in nature. The delegate of Cyprus in particular, suggested that the IMO secretariat would in such circumstances be 'judge, jury, and executioner'.

Such remarks represented the views of a very small minority however, and at the end of the debate on this topic the Chairman concluded that the Legal Committee had reached agreement on the need for some sanction to ensure that States complied with their obligation to report tonnages of contributing cargo. The proposed clauses in the draft protocol to give effect to this were approved. As a gesture to those States whose delegations claimed that they did not fully understand the proposal, a resolution was adopted urging that further technical cooperation and assistance in capacity-building should be offered to such States.

4. Drafting Matters

Several drafting points in the proposed protocol were discussed. The most difficult concerned the wording of Article 1(5)(vii), which contains a reference to both Appendix B of the Code of Safe Practice for Solid Bulk Cargoes as amended and the IMDG Code. It was explained by several delegates who had been present at the 1996 Diplomatic Conference that the purpose of this paragraph was to ensure that certain bulk cargoes which can be hazardous in certain limited circumstances,

[18] See the papers submitted by the Audit Body to the October 2007 and March 2008 Fund meetings.
[19] Art 15.
[20] The depositary of ratifications of the HNS Convention.

notably coal, fishmeal and woodchips, should not be included in the definition of Hazardous and Noxious Substances to which the HNS Convention will apply.

The fact that the words 'as amended' do not appear after the mention of the IMDG Code indicated, they said, that this was a reference to the 1996 edition of the IMDG Code, and not to any subsequently amended version. This led to a frantic search for a copy of the 1996 edition of this document, both by the IMO staff and also by several delegations.[21]

Much discussion on the margins of the meeting failed to produce a solution to this problem, and it was left to the IMO Secretariat to try to develop a drafting solution which achieved the objective of which there was no real doubt.

5. Concluding Debates

As the meeting drew to its close on Thursday 23 October there was still uncertainty as to the future of the Draft Protocol. A majority of States favoured an early Diplomatic Conference in 2009 to adopt the Protocol and hopefully to ensure early entry into force of the amended HNS Convention. However there was a significant, but vocal, minority who accepted the need for the Convention to enter into force but argued for more time to study the implications of the changes brought about by the Protocol. Notable among these were Cyprus and China.

The debates in the IMO Legal Committee are usually good mannered and concentrate on genuine efforts to find solutions to the problem in hand. Sadly this was not always the case at this meeting, where positions based on politics rather than law became apparent. Finally Dr Balkin, Legal Affairs Director of the IMO, put forward a carefully worded compromise proposal, which was quickly approved by almost all present.

The principal points were:

1. All delegates recognised that the HNS Convention should enter into force as soon as possible.
2. Many delegations recognised that the only way for the 1996 HNS Convention to enter into force is by the adoption of a Protocol;
3. We had an in-depth consideration of many provisions of the Draft Protocol;
4. There was agreement on most, if not all, of the provisions of the Protocol;
5. Many delegations wanted to see a clean text and if possible a consolidated text;
6. It was the view of the Legal Committee that the Protocol should be adopted as soon as possible, and the Committee requested the Council to schedule a Diplomatic Conference in 2010.

The Chairman concluded that there was not a sufficient consensus to advise the IMO Council to fix a Diplomatic Conference in 2009, but that if the Legal

---

[21] A copy of the 1997 edition of the IMDG Code was located in the library of the University of Southampton, Institute of Maritime Law. A copy of the 1996 edition has now been published on the IMO website.

Committee meeting scheduled for April 2009 could approve the text of the Protocol and hopefully of a consolidated text of the HNS Convention, it should be possible to fix a Diplomatic Conference for a date in 2010.

D. Legal Committee March–April 2009

The text of a Protocol to the HNS Convention was therefore laid before the March–April meeting of the IMO Legal Committee. At the conclusion of the meeting the Legal Committee approved the text of the Draft Protocol and recommended that it should be submitted to a Diplomatic Conference as soon as possible, hopefully in the spring of 2010. There was surprisingly little debate on most of the substantive provisions.

The only one which caused some concern was the definition of 'Hazardous and Noxious Substances' in Article 1 paragraph 5 of the HNS Convention, as amended by Article 3 of the Protocol. There was no dispute among the delegates to the 2009 meeting that those cargoes should be excluded from the ambit of the HNS Convention, but there was a divergence of views as to how this could best be achieved.

An example of the technical and drafting problems encountered can be seen from a comparison of the proposed revised wording of paragraph 5(a)(vii) of Article 1, as set out in Article 3 of the Protocol, with the equivalent paragraph in the 1996 Convention. The original 1996 wording refers to 'solid bulk materials possessing chemical hazards covered by Appendix B of the Code of Safe Practice for Solid Bulk Cargoes, as amended...' The copy of the Draft Protocol prepared by the IMO Secretariat in January 2009[22] refers to the 2004 version of the Code of Safe Practice for Solid Bulk Cargoes, which contains no Appendices.

Moreover, in December 2008 the Maritime Safety Committee of the IMO adopted the International Maritime Solid Bulk Cargoes (IMSBC) Code which became mandatory on 1 January 2011, and replaced the Code of Safe Practice for Solid Bulk Cargoes. A working paper prepared by the Secretariat in March 2009[23] suggested amendments to paragraph 5(a)(vii) to cover this.

This evolution demonstrates the ability of the IMO Conventions to adapt to changing practices in the shipping industry, but also the difficulty of drafting suitable wording which can be understood and applied by seagoing personnel and maritime administrations alike.

The Head of the Cargoes Section of the Maritime Safety Division of the IMO gave an explanation of the position, and suggested a simplified wording which would include all solid bulk materials possessing chemical hazards covered by the IMSBC Code as amended, to the extent that these substances are also covered by the IMDG Code as amended when carried in packaged form, but with the specific exclusion of coal, woodchips and fishmeal. However this was not accepted by the delegates to the Legal Committee.

---

[22] Document LEG95/3.
[23] Document LEG95/WP.1.

The wording of the Protocol as adopted by the Legal Committee remained as set out in the original document[24] LEG95/3 including a reference to the version of the IMDG Code in effect in 1996. It seems regrettable that the HNS Convention as amended by the Protocol, when (or if) they enter into force, will contain a reference to a Code which is nearly 20 years old, but it is to be hoped that the *travaux preparatoires* of the HNS Convention and its Protocol will assist those who have to give effect to them.

After the lengthy debate on this provision, the substantive provisions of the HNS Protocol concerning packaged HNS goods, contributions to the LNG account and non-submission of contributing cargo reports were adopted without further discussion.

VI. THE 2010 DIPLOMATIC CONFERENCE

The International Convention on Liability and Compensation for Damage in Connection with the Carriage of Hazardous and Noxious Substances by Sea was adopted by a Diplomatic Conference in 1996 but has not yet entered into force. The Convention, modelled on the comparable instruments dealing with oil pollution, is long and complicated, but that has not proved the stumbling block.

As described in our previous reports on this subject,[25] a 'Focus Group' set up by the International Oil Pollution Compensation Funds (IOPC Funds) identified the principal reasons for the failure of the 1996 HNS Convention to attract the necessary number of ratifications by states for entry into force, and the work of this Focus Group led to the preparation of a Draft Protocol to amend the original 1996 Convention text. The Draft Protocol was refined at the last two meetings of the IMO Legal Committee, and the text, substantially unamended, was adopted by the Plenary Session of the Diplomatic Conference on 30 April 2010.

Consensus was achieved on all outstanding points, thanks in no small measure to the patient chairmanship in the Committee of the Whole of Alfred Popp QC of Canada.

VII. THE IMPORTANT CHANGES TO THE 1996 HNS CONVENTION

The four principal areas of concern identified by the focus group were: contributions by the receivers of packaged HNS goods, contributions to the LNG account, non-submission of contributing cargo reports and the definition of 'hazardous and noxious substances'.

---

[24] Document LEG95/3.
[25] See the short article R Shaw 'Hazardous and Noxious Substances – Is the End in Sight?' [2009] *Lloyd's Maritime and Commercial Law Quarterly* 289.

A. Packaged HNS Goods

Article 1(5) of the HNS Convention contains a broad definition of HNS cargoes including solids, liquids and gases. The final paragraph covers solid HNS cargoes which are subject to the International Maritime Solid Bulk Cargoes Code, as amended, to the extent that such substances are also subject to the IMDG Code[26] when carried in packaged form. In practice this means containerised cargo.

The structure of the HNS Convention, based as it is on the CLC and Fund Conventions applying to oil pollution damage, establishes a two-tier compensation framework, with the shipowners (and their P&I Clubs) paying claims up to the limit of the first tier, and a fund contributed to by cargo interests paying claims in excess of that limit[27] in proportion to the quantities of HNS material received in each member state after carriage by sea. This requires all member states to report all relevant cargoes received in their territory above certain thresholds. The administrative burden of reporting HNS cargoes transported in containers in relatively small quantities (but which may cumulatively exceed the relevant threshold) is very considerable indeed. Studies by the major importers of such cargoes have indicated that the burden of collecting this information far exceeds the benefits conferred.

The draft protocol therefore proposed that packaged HNS cargoes should not be reported, and should not be included in the calculations of contributing cargo on the basis of which contributions to the HNS Fund will be levied. Victims of an HNS casualty, even where it is caused by packaged HNS goods, would still be compensated. This was a revolutionary, but practical, proposal. To meet the concern that the receivers of bulk HNS cargoes might be obliged to make greater contributions to the HNS Fund to make up for the lack of contribution from packaged goods, it was agreed by the shipowners' representatives and the International Group of P&I Clubs that the limits of liability for ships carrying packaged HNS cargoes, and thus the shipowners' contribution to the first tier, would be increased.

This was the most significant matter decided by the Diplomatic Conference. Numerous suggestions were put forward for the level of increase, the major flag states arguing, predictably, for no increase at all or for a maximum of 5 per cent, while major cargo importing states argued for an increase of up to 50 per cent. The Chairman conducted discreet discussions in the margins of the Conference during the overnight adjournment between the sessions on Monday and Tuesday, and after lunch on Tuesday 27 April he announced that his sense of the meeting was that consensus could be achieved at a level of 15 per cent. One or two of the delegates which had argued for a higher level expressed disappointment, but all delegates present supported the Chairman's recommendation. The IMO spirit of consensus had again showed how effective it is.

---

[26] International Maritime Dangerous Goods Code published by the IMO.
[27] Up to a maximum of 250 million SDR.

B. LNG Cargoes

As previously mentioned,[28] the state of the gas industry today was not foreseeable in 1996. The quantities of gas shipped by sea have increased dramatically in recent years, and the development of gas fields notably in Nigeria, Indonesia and Qatar has led to the building of a large number of new ships to carry both Liquified Petroleum Gas ('LPG') and Liquified Natural Gas ('LNG').

When the HNS Convention was adopted in 1996, the transport of LNG was almost entirely in the hands of governmental organisations and the major energy companies, due to the enormous capital costs involved. When the HNS Convention was under consideration at the 1996 Diplomatic Conference, the delegates were informed by the representatives of the gas industry that it would be simpler for the contributions to the HNS fund to be made by the 'title holder' of the cargo immediately prior to discharge, and an appropriate wording was adopted in Article 19 (1)(b) of the 1996 text.

However further study has revealed that this arrangement would give rise to considerable difficulty, particularly when the title holder in question is resident in a State which is not a party to the Convention.

The wording set out in Article 11 of the Protocol amends Article 19 of the 1996 HNS Convention.[29] This provides that the duty to report receipts of LNG, and to make contributions to the HNS Fund, should lie with the physical receiver, but that the Convention (as amended by the Protocol) should allow the parties to an LNG contract the flexibility to determine by agreement the person liable to make contributions to the LNG fund, provided that the receiver has informed its government that such an agreement exists.

If a title holder liable under such an agreement fails to make payment of any contribution due from them, the receiver of the cargo in question will be liable to pay the outstanding contribution.[30]

This amendment raised significant difficulties, but the compromise wording developed by the delegation of Malaysia and its correspondence group was worked out with the close cooperation of the gas exporting and importing industries as well as the governments concerned, and this led to its unanimous acceptance by the Diplomatic Conference.

C. Non-submission of Contributing Cargo Reports

The functioning of the HNS Fund, like the IOPC Fund, requires the reporting by member States of the quantities of the relevant cargo received in their ports

---

[28] See above, at p 50.

[29] Developed by the group led by the delegation of Malaysia.

[30] The draft of this Article prepared by the correspondence group uses the words 'remaining contribution', and this led to a debate in the Drafting Committee. The English-speaking delegates suggested that 'outstanding' or 'unpaid' was more appropriate, but such was the delicacy of the negotiations in the correspondence group over this Article that the Drafting Committee decided not to interfere.

and terminals during the preceding year, in order to apportion the burden of the financial contributions to the fund. The IOPC Funds have a proud record of collection of such contributions, which has enabled it to make prompt payments to the victims of oil pollution incidents.

However it has encountered persistent problems with a small number of member States in collecting the statistical data of the tonnages of relevant cargoes received in those States.

Concern has been expressed at meetings of the IOPC Funds' governing bodies at the failure of the IOPC Fund system to solve this problem,[31] and when the Supplementary Fund Protocol was adopted in 2003 a provision was included[32] which obliges that Fund to withhold payment of compensation for pollution damage in a state party which has not complied with its reporting obligations.

The 1996 HNS Convention contains no such provision, but it was the view of many governments that a provision to this effect should be included in the Protocol. An eloquent demonstration of the need for such a provision is the fact, confirmed by the Director of Legal Affairs of the IMO,[33] that of the 13 States which have deposited instruments of ratification of the 1996 HNS Convention, only 2 have submitted data on the relevant quantities of contributing cargo as required by Article 43. Article 46 of the HNS Convention provides that the Convention will enter into force 18 months after consents to be bound have been expressed by at least 12 States, including four States each with at least 2 million units of gross tonnage, and instruments of ratification have been deposited (with the IMO) accompanied by particulars of the quantities of contributing cargo to show that the total has reached the required 40 million tonnes of contributing cargo other than oil, LNG and LPG. Without the relevant information it is simply impossible for the ratifying states, or for the IMO, to establish whether or not the required tonnage level of contributing cargo has been reached.

At previous meetings of the IMO Legal Committee, certain states had expressed reluctance to accept such a provision, but at the Diplomatic Conference the provision of the protocol adding such a provision to the amended HNS Convention was adopted unopposed. A Resolution was also adopted which urges the IMO and member states to provide technical assistance to states requiring support when considering whether they should ratify the Protocol and the amended HNS Convention.

D. Definition of HNS

Mention has already been made of the definition of HNS cargoes carried in packaged form in Article 3.1.5(a)(vii). This refers to the 1996 IMDG Code without the words 'as amended'. A proposal was put forward to the Committee of the Whole

---

[31] See the papers submitted by the Audit Body to the October 2007 and March 2008 IOPCF meetings.
[32] Article 15.
[33] The depositary of ratifications of the HNS Convention.

by a group of states led by the Bahamas to adopt an amended wording which would refer to the current version of the IMDG Code rather than to the one in force 14 years ago. The arguments against referring to an instrument which is 14 years old are self-evident, but these arguments were reinforced by an observation that no-one had been able to locate a copy of the IMDG Code in force in 1996. The reasons for including a reference to the 1996 IMDG Code were essentially political,[34] but it was accepted by all delegations at the Diplomatic Conference that the categories of packaged cargo to which the HNS Convention will apply should not be extended. The Bahamas proposal was not adopted by the Conference.

Members of the IMO staff present during the Conference were able to assure delegates that they did indeed have a copy of the 1996 IMDG Code, and the IMO Secretariat and the Secretariat of the HNS Fund have subsequently arranged for a copy of this document to be accessible on their websites. This should be accessible by a ship's master or chief officer faced with doubts over a particular cargo.[35]

Some concern was expressed that it will not be possible to add new hazardous and noxious substances carried in packaged form to the list in the 1996 IMDG Code, nor substances such as direct reduced iron (c) whose dangerous qualities have become known since 1996.[36] The definition in the HNS Convention, as amended by the Protocol, cannot be changed.

E. Tacit Acceptance Procedure

The 1996 text contains in Article 48, provisions for the amendment of the limits of liability of the shipowner and the HNS Fund by a simplified procedure which is also to be found in the 1992 Conventions and the 2003 Protocol on Compensation for Oil Pollution Damage. That procedure has already been invoked to increase the compensation limits in the 1992 CLC and Fund Conventions. It is known as the 'Tacit Acceptance Procedure'.[37]

However certain States have argued that, valuable as the tacit acceptance procedure is, the time limits and limitations on the amount and frequency at which those Convention limits can be amended make the procedure too slow to ensure that the Conventions are brought quickly up to date. The 2003 Supplementary Fund Protocol contains an amended wording compared with its predecessors,

---

[34] The purpose of this paragraph was to ensure that certain bulk cargoes which can be hazardous in certain limited circumstances, notably coal, fishmeal and woodchips, should not be included in the definition of Hazardous and Noxious Substances to which the HNS Convention will apply. The final position adopted by the 2010 Diplomatic Conference is that coal and woodchips are excluded altogether, while certain categories of fishmeal will remain subject to the HNS regime. See document LEG.COM.17/7.

[35] An authoritative summary of the substances which are subject to the HNS Convention as amended may now be found on the 'HNS Finder' section of the HNS website *www.hnsconvention.org* which is maintained by the IOPC Fund Secretariat.

[36] The Marshall Island flag vessel 'YTHAN' sank in 2004 after an explosion while laden with this cargo. See *Primetrade AG v Ythan Limited* [2005] EWHC 2399.

[37] It is often referred to as the 'Tacit Amendment Procedure'.

with shorter time intervals, and a smaller number of States who can initiate the amendment procedure.

A proposal was made at the HNS Protocol Diplomatic Conference that the number of states required to initiate the tacit acceptance procedure and the shorter intervals specified in the Supplementary Fund Protocol should also be adopted in the HNS Protocol. A significant number of States, including all the members of the EU together with Canada, Australia and New Zealand, argued in favour of this, but at the end of a lively debate the Chairman concluded that there was not a sufficient consensus to adopt this proposal.

VIII. ENTRY INTO FORCE OF THE HNS PROTOCOL AND THE 2010 HNS CONVENTION

Article 18 of the HNS Protocol provides that the (1996) Convention and the 2010 Protocol shall, as between the parties to the Protocol, be read and interpreted as one single instrument.[38] It goes on to state that Articles 1 to 44 of the Convention as amended by the Protocol and the Annexes thereto, together with the final clauses in Articles 20 to 29 of the Protocol shall *mutatis mutandis* constitute and be called the International Convention on Liability and Compensation for Damage in Connection with the Carriage of Hazardous and Noxious Substances by Sea, 2010 (the 2010 HNS Convention).

States ratifying the Protocol will therefore, after the requirements for its entry into force have been satisfied,[39] automatically become parties to the 2010 HNS Convention. Those requirements are aligned with Article 46 of the 1996 Convention text. Article 20, paragraph 8 of the Protocol provides that a State which has consented to be bound by the 1996 Convention shall be deemed to have withdrawn its consent on the date on which it signed or deposited an instrument of ratification, acceptance approval or accession to the 2010 Protocol. This should, it is hoped, avoid a situation which has been encountered with a small number of States who have become parties to the 1992 IOPC Fund Convention without having denounced the 1969 CLC and 1971 Fund Conventions.[40]

IX. CONCLUSIONS

It is inevitable that many governments will pause for reflection before ratifying this long and complicated international instrument. However it is devoutly to be hoped that the efforts by many distinguished international law specialists to modify the original 1996 text, intended to meet the concerns of governments and

---

[38] A consolidated text is published by IMO at http://www.imo.org/OurWork/Legal/HNS/Documents/HNS%20Consolidated%20text.pdf.

[39] In accordance with Article 21.

[40] By 31 October 2011 eight States, namely Denmark, Canada, France, Germany, Greece, the Netherlands, Norway and Turkey had signed the 2010 HNS Convention.

industry alike, will result in early ratification by a sufficient number of States (with the appropriate tonnage of ships and receipts of the set quantity of HNS cargo) for the 2010 HNS Convention to enter into force. Only then will the victims of a major HNS incident be sure of prompt and adequate compensation for the damage suffered by them.

The IOPC Fund Secretariat has already done a great deal of work in developing a web-based 'catalogue' of HNS substances listing those to which the provisions of the 2010 Convention apply and those to which it does not.[41] That will be of great value to the ships' officers who will be responsible for making the Convention work. Before ratifying, however, States will need to ensure that they have in place the necessary infrastructure to report the tonnages of each category of HNS imported into their territory, and to supply the tonnages of such cargoes imported in the years preceding the deposit of instruments of ratification. That will be no mean task.

The oil pollution compensation system has worked surprisingly well for the last 35 years, and many of the lessons learned during that period have been brought to bear by the IOPC Fund Secretariat, and by others such as the Focus Group chaired by Alfred Popp QC, in developing solutions to potential problems with the HNS regime. As this paper has attempted to demonstrate, the subject is a complex one and the casualties involving these cargoes are mercifully rare, but the potential harm which can be done to human life and the marine environment by hazardous and noxious substances certainly justifies the effort.

[41] See n 35 above.

4

Compensation for Offshore Pollution: Ships and Platforms

NICHOLAS GASKELL*

I. INTRODUCTION: 30 YEARS OF CHANGE

THE LAST 30 years have seen many significant developments in the law and practice relating to marine pollution liabilities.[1] In 1982 the international regime applicable for oil tanker disasters was that agreed following the *Torrey Canyon* disaster in 1967. In particular, the IOPC Fund Convention 1971[2] had been in force for four years, and some 13 incidents had been notified to it.[3] Even then, three features about the international system were evident, namely: a tendency to react to maritime disasters; disagreement as to who should pay compensation; and debates over the appropriate levels of limitation of liability.

It is a feature of human affairs that the focus tends to become more concentrated after a particular disaster rather than before it. The 'disaster reaction syndrome' can be seen in many instances following the *Torrey Canyon*.[4] Media interest is intense, if not long lasting, and that engenders political action. Legal action may take the form of court cases to resolve the latest disaster, followed by calls for legislative activity. Such activity may start at a national level, but it is soon realised that coordinated international action may be best. It takes time to produce an international

---

* This chapter is a revised and extended version of a paper originally presented at the International Commercial Law, Litigation and Arbitration Conference, Sydney 2011 and published as 'Compensation for Offshore Pollution from Ships: Problems and Solutions' in N Perram and K Lindgren (eds), *International Commercial Law, Litigation and Arbitration* (Sydney: Ross Parsons Centre for Commercial Corporate and Taxation Law, University of Sydney, 2011).

[1] Some of the background is explained in N Gaskell, C Forrest, 'Marine Pollution Damage in Australia: Implementing the Bunker Oil Convention 2001 and the Supplementary Fund Protocol 2003' (2008) 27 *University of Queensland Law Journal* 103, eg at 104–07 (Gaskell and Forrest).

[2] The International Convention on Civil Liability for Oil Pollution Damage (CLC) 1969 entered into force 19 June 1975. The International Convention on the Establishment of an International Fund for Compensation for Oil Pollution Damage (IOPC Fund) 1971 entered into force 16 October 1978.

[3] See *Incidents Involving the IOPC Funds 2011*, (IOPC Funds 2012), 76.

[4] eg, the *Braer* in Scotland in 1993, the *Erika* in France in 1999, and the *Prestige* in 2002 in Spain. The claims in these cases have been very high, eg over €1 billion for the *Prestige*, although the sums deemed admissible (€573 million) are far less than this, and those actually paid so far even less, see *Incidents Involving the IOPC Funds 2011*, 14.

convention: there are stages of debate about the need for action; several years of drafting text; usually the need for some sort of diplomatic conference; and then the long wait to achieve the necessary number of international ratifications to bring the convention into force. The final stage also has to be coordinated with national legislative action to give effect to that convention. In the long wait for entry into force there may be attempts to produce voluntary international schemes, or interim national legislation. Legal responses may concentrate on regulatory changes, using traditional public law mechanisms such as the criminal law. There will usually also be a need to consider issues of compensation, using private law approaches or remedies, eg damages. This chapter concentrates on these compensation issues.

The sinking of the *Amoco Cadiz* in 1978 led to pressure for substantial increases in limits of liability and resulted first in increases to the CLC 1969/FUND 1971 limits, and in the agreement of the 1984 Protocols to the CLC and Fund Convention. These Protocols never entered into force, largely because of disagreement as to who would contribute to the IOPC Fund, although they were effectively reproduced in the 1992 CLC and Fund Convention. The current regime for oil tankers is governed by a combination of three instruments: the CLC 1992, the Fund Convention 1992 and the Supplementary Fund 2003.[5]

One consequence of the reaction to *Torrey Canyon* has been that, instead of a single liability regime, there has been a piecemeal accumulation of regimes to deal with particular problems as they arise (or as is allowed by the timetables and budgets of international organisations). Thus, there is one regime for pollution from oil tankers, another for the pollution by the fuel (bunkers) of ordinary merchant ships (other than oil tankers), and a separate convention on the carriage of hazardous and noxious substances (HNS) other than oil. There are also separate regimes for the wrecks of ships (and their contents) and the transportation of wastes.[6] There are uneasy overlaps between the various conventions themselves[7] and with other instruments; as will be seen, it is sometimes unclear how far the regimes apply to the offshore sector. Through the use of boilerplate text, it has been possible to standardise certain legal solutions, although this means that it becomes difficult to modernise provisions in the latest convention[8] without revisiting the earlier ones (which may have different parties and amendment regimes). A central and continuing issue has been the traditional ability of shipowners to limit their liabilities under stand-alone provisions.[9]

---

[5] International Convention on Civil Liability for Oil Pollution Damage 1992; the International Convention on the Establishment of an International Fund for Compensation for Oil Pollution Damage 1992, and the Supplementary Fund Protocol 2003. There are 110 States Parties to the CLC and Fund 1992 (http://www.iopcfund.org/92members.htm).

[6] The International Convention on the Removal of Wrecks 2007, and the Protocol to the Basel Convention on the Control of Transboundary Movements of Hazardous Wastes and their Disposal 1989.

[7] Thus, the HNS Convention does not apply to nuclear material, which in theory is regulated by conventions putting liabilities on the operators of nuclear facilities.

[8] eg to insert a specific terrorism defence to reflect difficulties in obtaining insurance cover, or to adopt a more up to date definition of 'pollution damage' to reflect developments in environment reinstatement.

[9] N Gaskell, 'The Bunker Pollution Convention 2001 and limitation of liability' (2009) 15 *Journal of International Maritime Law* 477–94.

In the last three years, attention has been focused on oil spills not from ships, but from offshore platforms and structures. The *Deepwater Horizon* blow out from the Macondo well in the Gulf of Mexico on 20 April 2010 has received much attention.[10] Less well known is the *Montara* oil spill[11] from the *West Atlas* rig off North West Australia on 21 August 2009.[12] These incidents provide the opportunity for a review of how the lessons of the last 30 years concerning pollution from ships can inform the debate about how to provide a satisfactory compensation regime for pollution from offshore oil and gas facilities, including platforms and wells. They also raise questions about the traditional boundaries of maritime law, eg how far it can or should apply to activities at sea not directly involving ships.

II. EXISTING INTERNATIONAL MODELS FOR POLLUTION COMPENSATION INVOLVING SHIPS

A. Introduction

Since 1967, the international community has had to grapple with a series of legal and practical problems in providing compensation to victims of oil pollution at sea. It may be helpful to identify the basic solutions that have been adopted in respect of ships so that there is a context for discussing blowouts from oil rigs.

As noted, the international community has not produced a single all-encompassing convention providing for liability for pollution, from whatever origin (eg from ships, land, or seabed wells), or from whatever type of pollutant (eg oil, chemicals, nuclear material). It may be that if we were starting again, we would try to produce a generalised regime.[13] Perhaps in the long term it may be possible to consolidate all the disparate regimes, but in 1967 it was recognised that urgent solutions were needed for a newly recognised problem – oil tankers capable of carrying bulk cargo in previously unimagined tonnages. Moreover, the drafting had to be done by a new international body,[14] trying to devise new principles in 'uncharted legal waters', but in the context of existing maritime laws.[15] It is a tribute to those early drafters that the essential scheme that was produced between 1969–1971 is still applicable today. It was inevitable that relatively quick solutions to an immediate problem meant that there had to be compromises; once made it has proved difficult to change the structure of the solutions adopted.

---

[10] *Deep Water: The Gulf Oil Disaster and the Future of Offshore Drilling*, Report to the President, National Commission on the BP Deepwater Horizon Oil Spill and Offshore Drilling, January 2011, (http://www.oilspillcommission.gov/sites/default/files/documents/DEEPWATER_ReporttothePresident_FINAL.pdf). Martin Davies, 'Liability Issues Raised by the Deepwater Horizon Blowout' (2011) 25 *Australia and New Zealand Maritime Law Journal* 35.

[11] *Report of the Montara Commission of Inquiry*, June 2010, 24 November 2010 (http://www.montarainquiry.gov.au/).

[12] See M White, 'Offshore Oil and Gas Catastrophes: Montara Spill and Australian Oil and Gas Regulatory Laws' in Lindgren and Perram, above, 125.

[13] Such as the EU Directive on Environmental Liability 2004/35/CE.

[14] The Legal Committee of IMCO (later IMO, the International Maritime Organisation).

[15] Especially those dealing with limitation of liability.

Despite these comments, there has been a remarkable degree of success in the international system devised at the IMO, and (with the notable exception of the US) significant uniformity of rules. Amongst the main problems which have been grappled with are the following: who is liable; the pollutants covered; the basis of liability and defences; limitation of liability; insurance; jurisdiction and recognition of judgments.

B. Oil Tankers

i. *The CLC and Fund Regime*

The regime for oil tankers is set out in the CLC 1992, Fund Convention 1992 and the Supplementary Fund Protocol 2003.

The CLC provides for strict liability[16] with very limited defences[17] for oil[18] pollution damage.[19] Liability is 'channelled' to the registered shipowner only; claims cannot be brought against others such as salvors, pilots, crew members, or charterers. This restriction is justified because there is a compulsory insurance requirement for shipowner of tankers carrying more than 2,000t of oil cargo; importantly, there is a right of direct action against the insurer.

These insurance provisions were perhaps the most significant innovation made in 1969, in particular to deal with the single ship company whose only asset is now sunk (as with the *Torrey Canyon*). Moreover, there is a particular feature of marine liability insurance which is vital to ensure in practice that any insurance cover is real, and not simply a piece of paper issued by a straw company. For around 150 years most shipowners have insured their party liabilities not with commercial property underwriters[20] but have mutualised their risks through Protection and Indemnity (P&I) 'Clubs'. There are now some 13 principal underwriting member clubs of the International Group of P&I Clubs,[21] which provide cover for risks such as pollution and cargo damage. The International Group is a major force in

---

[16] This was a radical solution when adopted, but is now accepted as the norm for environmental liabilities.

[17] Including war, 'exceptional, inevitable and irresistible' natural phenomena (eg tsunamis); deliberate harm by third parties (eg most terrorist activities); wrongful acts of governments in maintaining navigational aids (eg buoys). There is a time bar of three years from the damage (with a maximum of six years from the incident).

[18] Whether the cargo or bunkers of an oil tanker. Non-persistent oils, such as gasoline, light diesel oil, kerosene are not covered.

[19] The definition of damage covers contamination, preventive measures (including 'threat removal' measures taken after an incident but before a spill), and reinstatement of the environment. Broadly, the definition covers most reasonable clean-up measures taken by States and individuals, and financial losses (including lost profit from impairment of the environment). There have been criticisms about how far the definition covers the costs of conducting assessments of natural resource or ecological damage (*cf Montara Report*, p 291).

[20] Thus, the marine market, eg at Lloyd's, provides cover for hull and cargo, but not usually for environmental liabilities.

[21] http://www.igpandi.org/.

international trade, although largely unknown to the public; its members are said to cover about 90 per cent of the world's ocean-going tonnage, and the reinsurance of the Group cover has been one of the world's largest reinsurance contracts. It is the Clubs that, in the main,[22] issue the insurance certificates that allow ocean going ships to enter coastal ports. Rights of action given by local or national legislation would often be practically worthless without the Clubs standing behind most shipowners.[23] It is said to be unheard of for a Group member to fail to honour a judgment. The presence of the Clubs is a major dynamic in the willingness of States to agree an international regime where potential defendants speak with one voice. Moreover, this is reinforced when combined with the CLC system of recognition of judgments in States Parties.

A particular feature of the tanker regime was the recognition that it was arguably unfair for all pollution liability to be on the shipowner,[24] and that shipowners might not have the resources to pay for a major pollution catastrophe. To answer the question 'who is the polluter who should pay?', it was decided that cargo interests (broadly the oil companies)[25] should contribute. But how was this to be done? A liability could have been imposed on the individual owner of the cargo concerned, but this would not really provide the necessary level of resources. So it was decided to create a two tier system of liability; the first tier being provided by the CLC system of shipowner liability, and the second tier of liability being met by a legal entity (the 'IOPC Fund').[26] This body would be financed by post-accident levies (in effect, taxes) imposed on *all* oil importers in States party to the system. There were doubts about whether this system would work in practice, but it has operated extremely well; virtually all bills are paid promptly. And even when there are major claims, the loss is so spread across the industry (and therefore the public at large) as to be almost unnoticeable. Thus, the annual levy due on 1 March 2012 to meet payable claims was £43.5m amounting to only £0.0290893 per tonne of oil imported.[27]

The IOPC Fund system has also been surprisingly successful in handling claims. Claims may be brought in any contracting State suffering damage within its EEZ, and there is compulsory mutual recognition of judgments. Not only is there

---

[22] The maritime liability conventions with compulsory insurance provisions do allow for the recognition of certificates issued by other insurers in state parties. This may itself present problems. Thus, a State must rely on other State parties to apply appropriate solvency requirements on their insurers. Further, members of the International Group may provide additional benefits to States, for instance through the STOPIA agreement, as shown in the *Volgoneft 139* incident in 2007 (*Incidents Involving the IOPC Funds 2011*, 27); and see II.B.ii.

[23] Ships can sink, or sail away from waters where damage is caused. For such reasons maritime law has long developed special remedies such as the *action in rem* (with a right of arrest), and maritime liens. In many ways the introduction of compulsory insurance and direct action against shipowners is a more modern and effective way of dealing with the security problems for which maritime liens were developed.

[24] The shipowner might be liable without fault, and the real cause of harm is the cargo.

[25] The oil majors have largely pulled out from being tanker owners and prefer to charter in tonnage from independent owners.

[26] More properly the International Oil Pollution Compensation Fund.

[27] http://www.iopcfund.org/npdf/genE.pdf. The maximum deferred levy for that year (to meet claims not finalised) was £5.5m.

cooperation by the IOPC Fund with the Clubs in dealing with claimants, but the IOPC Fund has developed great expertise in identifying and classifying admissible claims.[28] It is a body set up by States to *pay* claims, not a defensively minded insurer. The IOPC Fund has also handled some of the largest multiple claims in the world, eg 28,882 after the *Hebei Spirit* incident in 2007.[29] Yet, a system devised to provide States with protection against high clean-up costs has developed into one which is meant to provide economic recompense to individuals and companies, eg engaged in fishing and tourism. Indeed, the level of economic claims has now grown so as to dwarf clean-up and reinstatement costs; that in turn has put pressure on the funds available.

ii. The Limitation Conundrum: Pollution Claims

If there is an offshore catastrophe, should there be any financial limit available to potential defendants? When members of the public read about BP making available compensation in the order of $20 billion after *Deepwater Horizon*, it might be easy for them to assume that almost unlimited sums will easily be available for disasters off their coasts. But BP is massively dependent on the US for commercial reasons, whatever its legal liability. The US was fortunate in a sense that it was Exxon which was involved in the *Exxon Valdez* disaster in Alaska in 1989. Political and national factors may also be involved. France was lucky that it was Total which was interested in the cargo in the *Erika* disaster off Brittany in 1999.[30] Australia was relieved that it was BHP Transport which was the demise charterer of the *Iron Baron* which grounded in 1995.[31]

The CLC/Fund system was a compromise, both between the shipping and oil industries themselves, but also for both of them with the international community. One of the components was that the shipowners would be able to limit their liabilities under the first tier; another was that the IOPC Fund would have a second tier limit (the total liability being aggregated).

The idea that shipowners can limit their liabilities is longstanding, regarded as essential by the shipping industry and P&I Clubs, but nevertheless controversial. That there should be an overall limit for the IOPC Fund's liability is more understandable, as it is effectively funded by an international tax, but the continuing question has been the level at which to set the limits. Experience has shown that the limits become out of date through the effects of inflation, but also because

---

[28] See, eg the *IOPC Claims Manual* which reflects over 30 years of dealing with both normal and unusual, or difficult, claims. These vary, eg whether an inland hotel can claim for lost profits from tourists deterred by coastal pollution; or how to deal reasonably with subsistence fishers who may have no documentation to show what income has been lost; or where claims are greatly exaggerated. The experience available can greatly speed the processing of complex claims.

[29] See *Incidents Involving the IOPC Funds 2011*, 35, and details of the other 35 major incidents under the 1992 Fund, and the 107 under the 1971 Fund, documented therein.

[30] Total agreed to pay the French State €153.9 an amount awarded by a criminal court, taking into account sums already received from the IOPC Fund: (*Incidents Involving the IOPC Funds 2011*, 49).

[31] Giving rise to a loss of 4,325t of bunker fuel, and costs estimated at AU$30m (Gaskell and Forrest, pp 110–12).

environmental and economic loss claims have increased dramatically. The idea of a fund adequate to deal with localised clean-up has been supplanted by a desire to compensate whole industries affected over hundreds of kilometres. The scale of the *Erika* and *Prestige* disasters on tourist and fishing industries along the whole eastern Atlantic coast was immense. We have seen the real and imagined scale of losses claimed as a result of *Deepwater Horizon*. In Australia, a major tanker disaster off the Great Barrier Reef would have potentially huge financial implications for tourism and fishing.

These catastrophes exceed the normal bounds of what we might expect could be dealt with by a tort based compensation system; they are on the scale of great natural disasters like the 2011 floods in Queensland, or the 2009 storms in France (prior to *Erika*). The level of compensation required is immense, of a kind requiring a national response, but sometimes of international scale. Apart from the 'good fortune' of having a deep pocketed BP, can a national or international system produce an effective financial response, or must we accept that (as with floods and fires), some loss will lie where it falls?

The sums available for compensation under the CLC/Fund system have been progressively increased. After *Erika* and *Prestige*, the third tier 'Supplementary Fund' was created. In the context of the European experience the sums shown in Table 1 are only just about adequate – but they are securely available to claimants.

Table 1: CLC and Fund System Limits

1992 CLC Shipowner Limits [since 2003]
Minimum shipowner liability: 4.51 million sdr [about **£4.4 million**][32] then 631 sdr [about **£620**] per ton of ship's tonnage up to **Maximum**: 89.77 million sdr [about **£88 million**]
1992 Fund Convention Limits [since 2003]
Maximum: 203 million sdr [about **£200 million**]
Supplementary Fund Protocol 2003
Maximum: 750 million sdr [about **£737 million**]

The oil industry was concerned that the creation of the third tier (financed solely by those importing oil into Supplementary Fund States) had altered the industry balance between themselves and the shipowners. The Clubs then came up with two agreements STOPIA[33] and TOPIA[34] under which that balance was to be redressed,

---

[32] The sdr is the special drawing right of the IMF. Figures in this paper have taken on 1 June 2012 when 1 sdr = £0.983101: see, International Monetary Fund (IMF), http://www.imf.org. Note that the rates change daily.

[33] Small Tanker Oil Pollution Indemnification Agreement. Gaskell and Forrest pp 123–25.

[34] Tanker Oil Pollution Indemnification Agreement.

in particular by accepting minimum shipowner liabilities (eg for small tankers) of 20 million sdr (about £20 million). These agreements do not put any more money on the table. What they do illustrate is that potential defendants may sometimes accept obligations to the world at large[35] in circumstances where for whatever reason it is not possible to produce an international convention. At the very least these 'voluntary' schemes may offer interim protection to States where there are obstacles to national or international legislation. This may be relevant to the debate about compensation for oil rig catastrophes.

iii. Evaluation of the Oil Tanker Regime

Internationally the CLC/Fund system has been a success in achieving international equity[36] and also uniformity; as at 1 July 2012 there were 106 State parties to both the CLC and Fund,[37] and 28 States party to the Supplementary Fund Protocol 2003. The big omission is the US which went its own way after *Exxon Valdez* and enacted its own Oil Pollution Act 1990. Its system means that it does not directly contribute to pollution claims in other States caused by ships en route to the US,[38] but it has managed to preserve certain US state laws providing for unlimited liability.[39] While I am an admirer of the international system, one must always ask dispassionately whether or not there is an alternative. What would happen if a developed state, such as Australia, took a unilateralist approach like the US? Could it create unlimited liabilities? In reality, states trying to operate outside of the IOPC system will have great difficulties in enforcing such liabilities. Shipowners will only maintain P&I cover to the CLC limits and the Fund Convention will not be applicable. It may be that special insurance arrangements can only be made for big players like the US and China.

iv. Ships and Offshore Platforms

The CLC and Fund system only applies to 'ships' as defined, ie oil tankers. It does not apply to liabilities arising from the blow out of oil and gas wells, or explosions on oil rigs or platforms. Rigs, including *West Atlas* and *Deepwater Horizon*, are not 'constructed or adapted for the carriage of oil in bulk'. The reason is partly historical, because the CLC/Fund system was designed to deal with the *carriage* of oil on ships

---

[35] In my view, these schemes operate in the form of a classic *Carlill* unilateral contract, as did TOVALOP and CRISTAL (see III.B.iv, below).

[36] Small developing States contribute little or nothing to the IOPC Fund as they import relatively little oil; major importers of oil in the developed world pay for the pollution caused by the transport of oil to their industries. It is astonishing that through this system Japan alone would contribute (on 2009 figures) 15.57% of IOPC Fund liabilities around the world (Australia's figure was 1.95%), and 21.66% of any 2003 Supplementary Fund (Australia 2.72%): *IOPC Fund Annual Report 2010*. The contributions would be radically different if the US and China were part of the Fund systems.

[37] 110 by 4 May 2013. A further 19 States (20 by 2013) are party to the CLC alone.

[38] China is not party to the Fund Convention either, but it is party to the CLC 1992.

[39] Insurance is not provided directly by the Clubs for the US oil trade, but the viability of the US system of certificates of financial responsibility (COFRs) has not been tested in a series of major incidents.

at a time when offshore drilling did not have the importance it does today. The Clubs have traditionally only provided cover for ships, eg vessels involved in the carriage of cargo. With the advent of mobile offshore units (MOUs), including jack-up and semi-submersible rigs, the Clubs have offered limited 'ship-like' cover to their members. Thus, the Gard Club's 2012 Rules cover crew liabilities and repatriation, collisions with other vessels and wreck removal. There is a policy limit of US$100m for losses arising 'out of any one event', but the Club specifically excludes cover for pollution from the well being drilled or worked, or from production operations (eg seepage or uncontrolled flows), or of any damage to the well itself.[40]

The offshore industry has developed a whole series of floating units to receive, process and store resources extracted from the sea-bed. There has been considerable uncertainty about whether FPSOs (Floating Production Storage and Offloading vessels) or FSOs (Floating Storage and Offloading units) are 'ships' within the CLC/Fund system. Some of these units may be converted tankers with the appearance of, and history of being, ships; others are purpose built and with no resemblance to ships. Resolution of this issue depends on whether FPSOs fall within the complex definition of ship in Article 1 of the CLC and is largely beyond this chapter. The view taken within the Assembly of the IOPC Fund since 1999 was that FPSOs are not CLC/Fund 'ships' when they are semi-permanently moored at a well head, but are when actually in transit with oil cargoes.[41] A more recent legal opinion[42] commissioned by the Funds has broadly confirmed this view, emphasising the importance of carriage of cargoes to the application of the liability provisions in the CLC/Fund system.[43] The result of such reasoning is that the main international system for compensating for oil pollution would not be applicable to spills from units that could contain very large quantities of oil.[44] It is important to note that this

---

[40] See Gard, *Rules 2012*, Rules for Mobile Offshore Units, r 30–33 (pp 153–54).

[41] In 1998, the IOPC 1992 Assembly took the view that FSUs and FPSOs did not normally fall within the scope of application of the 1992 Conventions, but that it was possible that some structures of this type might fall within the scope of these Conventions in particular circumstances, see 92FUND/A/ES.3/21, 1 May 1998 and the Director's Note 92FUND/A/ES.3/ 17, 16 April 1998. In 1999, the 4th Session of the Assembly approved a Working Group Report to the same effect, see 92FUND/A.4/32, 22 October 1999.

[42] By Professor Lowe QC, see IOPC/OCT11/4/4, 14 September 2011, Annex I.

[43] The opinion was noted by the Assembly of the Fund at its 16th Session in October 2011 (see IOPC/OCT11/11/1, 28 October 2011, para 4.4 *et seq*). It also agreed (para 4.4.36) to establish a Working Group to consider some of the implications of proposals put to it by the IOPC Director (in para 7 of IOPC/OCT11/4/4), eg whether to confirm the view that FSOs are not 'ships', or to recognise a presumption that a year is a reasonable time beyond which a vessel is regarded as permanently or semi-permanently at anchor.

[44] The CLC/Fund would be equally inapplicable to FLNG (Floating Liquefied Natural Gas) vessels which may store and process LNG (not a hydrocarbon substance within the CLC/Fund). LNG would be covered by the HNS Convention, see II.D below, but similar questions would arise as to their characterisation as ships. However, Art 1(1) of the HNS Convention has a wider definition of 'ship', namely 'any seagoing vessel and seaborne craft, of any type whatsoever'. Even though the latter part of this definition might more easily apply to some of the wide variety of FPSOs and FSOs, liability under Art 7 still has to be 'in connection with their [ie HNS substances] *carriage* by sea.' Given that the CLC/Fund and HNS conventions were broadly trying to achieve the same aim, but in relation to different substances, it is unlikely that it was intended that they should produce a different result in relation to storage units. Still, it would be open to a national court to take a broad interpretation of 'in connection with…carriage'.

conclusion of the IOPC Fund on the applicability of its own convention would not be binding on the courts of member States.[45] If such units are *not* within the CLC/Fund system, then it would be necessary to consider how far ordinary principles of liability (and limitation) would then apply to such units.[46]

C. Bunker Pollution from Ships

i. Liability Position

The 1992 CLC/Fund system applies its strict liability regime to pollution from the bunkers of oil tankers when they are carrying oil and in some circumstances when they are carrying bunkers on a ballast voyage.[47] There was no special liability regime for the bunkers of all the other ships operating in the world, eg container ships, passenger ships and bulk carriers – all of whose fuel could cause considerable pollution damage. The bulk carrier *Pacific Adventurer* spilled a relatively tiny amount of oil (270 tonnes) off the Queensland coast in Australia in 2009, but this alone gave rise to claims for over Au$30 million. Partly because of such uncertainty, some States, including Australia, enacted interim legislation[48] – with varying degrees of effectiveness.

However, by March 2001, the IMO agreed the *International Convention on Civil Liability for Bunker Oil Pollution Damage* (the Bunker Pollution Convention) 2001 which entered into force on 21 November 2008. The Convention creates strict liability, on the CLC model, of the 'shipowner'. But 'shipowner' is here defined to include charterers and operators. This is because there is no second tier 'fund' (as with the IOPC Fund 1992). The registered shipowner (only) must have compulsory insurance for ships over 1000 gt. There is direct action against the insurer, and mutual recognition of judgments. The Bunker Pollution Convention affects huge numbers of ships and requires most which trade worldwide to have certificates; these certification requirements have been quite burdensome for States Parties.

ii. The Limitation Conundrum: Bunker Pollution

The main defect of the Bunker Pollution Convention is that it has no stand-alone limitation of liability provisions. This means that the ordinary regime of shipowners' limitation of liability may apply. In the UK the applicable convention

---

[45] Thus, in 2006 the Greek Supreme Court held that a converted tanker (the *Slops*) used as a port-based waste oil reception facility was a ship for the purposes of the CLC and Fund (*IOPC Annual Report 2006*, 94).

[46] Here the operators of such units might find they face a different problem; there may well be liability for negligence, but no limit of liability if the unit is not a ship.

[47] There is some uncertainty about whether bunkers in OBO's and combination carriers (eg including all parcel tankers and product carriers) are covered under the CLC/Fund. These would now need to be covered under the Bunker Pollution Convention.

[48] See, eg the Protection of the Sea (Civil Liability) Act 1981 (Cth) ss 20–22A, and state legislation, such as the Transport Operations (Marine Pollution) Act (TOMPA) 1995 (Qld), ss 115, 132F.

is the *Convention on Limitation of Liability for Maritime Claims* (LLMC) 1976, as amended by a Protocol of 1996.[49] This legislation is now directly relevant to bunker claims. It is not possible here to examine all the difficulties presented by this unhappy linkage of two conventions that are not precisely compatible.[50] Although there may be some State pollution prevention claims which may be without limit of liability, eg for bunker claims that involve 'cargo removal' costs, it seems that all economic loss claims will be limitable. The point here is that such claims will not have access to the whole of the normal limitation fund. In the event of a major casualty with many claimants, eg including cargo loss and collision damage, the fund would have to be shared rateably between the claimants. Table 2, below, shows some examples of the total sums available for ships of different sizes. For most small spills the sums may be enough; for larger spills they are already inadequate.

Table 2: LLMC 1996 Property Limits

Ship Size	LLMC 1996 SDR limit[51]	£ limit[52]
2,000 gt	1,000,000 sdr	£983,101
5,000 gt	2,200.000 sdr	£2,162,822
10,000 gt	4,200,000 sdr	£4,129,024
80,000 gt	26,200,000 sdr	£25,757,246

A key feature of the LLMC limitation provisions is that it makes the appropriate limitation amounts application for 'each distinct occasion' on which liabilities may arise.[53] Prior to the tonnage limitation system in the LLMC and its predecessor 1957 Convention,[54] the limiting event was the voyage. This meant that if there were two collisions in a voyage (eg on leaving Southampton and on arrival in Brisbane), there was only one limit. In effect, the LLMC was negotiated on the basis that in these circumstances there could be two limits; each would be a 'distinct occasion'. That is clear enough, but is it possible to sub-divide a single casualty, so as to find separate acts of causative negligence giving rise to more than one 'occasion'?[55] The effect might be to create several limits of liability out of what might appear to a commercial person as a single incident.

---

[49] Enacted in the Merchant Shipping Act 1995 Sch 7.

[50] See Gaskell 'The Bunker Pollution Convention 2001 and limitation of liability' (2009) 15 *Journal of International Maritime Law* 477.

[51] The figures show the sdr limits under Art 6(1)(b) of the LLMC 1996. These are limits applicable for claims 'other than for loss of life or personal injury'. Into this category fall *all* the 'other' claims, including most bunker pollution claims as well as all other property claims. See further generally, N Gaskell, 'Appendix 17: Limitation of Liability and Division of Loss' in Simon Gault (ed), *Marsden on Collisions at Sea*, 13th edn (London: Sweet & Maxwell, 2003), 828.

[52] Calculations made on the basis of a conversion rate of 1 June 2012, as in previous examples.

[53] The CLC Art V(1) makes the limits available 'in respect of any one incident'.

[54] Both based on the British Merchant Shipping Act 1894.

[55] I touched on this in *Marsden, above*, pp 858–64.

In a case of some international importance, *Strong Wise Limited v Esso Australia Resources Pty Ltd,*[56] Rares J decided that in certain circumstances it is indeed possible to take such an approach. The decision is meticulously reasoned[57] but, unless it is treated as a rather special case on its own facts, it could at a stroke prove a way for claimants in effect to multiply the limits available to them. From a claimants' perspective, one might say 'so what?' This would no doubt cause concern amongst the boards of the International Group of P&I Clubs; but apart from their discomfort, it could be said that an unduly wide application of the decision might rather undermine the highly sensitive and delicate international negotiations which take place periodically at the IMO to increase limits. There are many arguments against limitation of liability, but the ability of the Clubs to provide widespread cover is of great advantage to the international community. Their reliance on limitation may be overdone, but widespread attempts to circumvent it may ultimately have unintended consequences on the availability of insurance cover.[58]

iii. Pacific Adventurer and Moves to Increase LLMC Limits

On 9 March 2009, the Hong Kong registered container ship *Pacific Adventurer* (18,391 gt) was near Brisbane when she lost 31 containers overboard in very heavy seas.[59] The containers holed two of the ship's bunker tanks, and about 270 tonnes of fuel oil leaked into the sea, polluting 38 miles of Queensland's coastline. Clean-up operations from this fairly simple bunker incident took until 19 June.

The *Pacific Adventurer* incident occurred before the entry into force for Australia of the Bunker Pollution Convention. Claims for compensation therefore fell under the pre-existing law, requiring a complex enquiry into how far national federal or state law applied. It is these sorts of complications that international conventions can help to solve. The federal clean-up costs were recoverable under statutory provisions which were a limited precursor to the Bunker Pollution Convention,[60] while Queensland legislation[61] gave its Government the right to claim discharge expenses from the owner or master. Individual claimants could claim under the same legislation[62] for loss of or damage to their property, and costs or expenses in preventing or mitigating such loss or damage (including to the property of others). While this provision covered the clean-up expenses of voluntary organisations, it did not appear to extend to the economic loss claims of those from the fishing and tourism industries where their own property was not damaged. If that is right then,

[56] [2010] FCA 240, [2010] 2 Lloyd's Rep 555.
[57] For that reason, perhaps, as well as commercial reasons, the decision has not been appealed.
[58] As would attempts to make it easy to 'break limitation', using the test found in the LLMC Art 4 and other IMO liability conventions based on intentional or reckless conduct on the part of the defendant.
[59] See *Independent investigation into the loss of containers from the Hong Kong registered container ship Pacific Adventurer off Cape Moreton, Queensland 11 March 2009*, ATSB Transport Safety Report, Marine Occurrence Investigation No. 263 Final (2011).
[60] *Protection of the Sea (Civil Liability) Act 1981* (Cth) ss 20–22A. See Gaskell and Forrest p 144.
[61] TOMPA s 115.
[62] TOMPA 1995 s 132F.

for example, claims for reduced income as a result of bans on fishing might need to be brought under the common law. It is now clear that the Bunker Pollution Convention would give extensive rights to such economic loss claimants.

In any event, in September 2009 the shipowners, Swire, established in the Federal Court an LLMC 1996 limitation fund of about Au$17.5 million (including interest).[63] The various claims were said to amount to some Au$30 million, but in August 2009 a settlement was announced between the Queensland Government and Swire whereby the latter would bring the amounts available up to Au$25 million. It might be observed that Swire is a large reputable organisation. It could presumably have chosen to stand on its limitation rights. Nevertheless, it is significant that in the settlement the Queensland and Australian Governments agreed to defer their claims (eg for clean-up) in favour of non-government claims. This is similar to the approach in the *Braer* and the *Erika*, taken by the British and French governments, when limits of liability were likely to affect individual claimants (ie potential voters!). It is paradoxical that such action (taken no doubt mainly for domestic political reasons) has produced a very different priority to that created by those who originally devised the marine pollution compensation regimes. For, 'environmental' claims, represented by State clean-up costs, are now being postponed to private commercial interests.[64]

In the wake of the *Pacific Adventurer*, where claims exceeded the LLMC 1996 limits, Australia pressed at the IMO for an increase in the those limits using the LLMC's (relatively) rapid amendment procedure.[65] Although at the IMO Legal Committee in April 2011, there was 'wide agreement on the need to review the limits',[66] there was obviously going to be less agreement on the extent of those limits. The Australian proposal,[67] backed by a detailed report by KPMG, would have used the maximum increase allowed under the LLMC 1996, ie 6 per cent pa compounded.[68] The main opposition to using the maximum increase came from Japan,[69] which proposed a more 'modest' increase on the basis that there had been inflation at 45 per cent between 1996–2010. The methodology adopted by Japan in calculating inflation (and its transparency) was the basis of strong criticism from Australia.[70] Nevertheless, the IMO Legal Committee on 19 April 2012, decided to adopt the Japanese proposal adjusted to 2012, which gave an

---

[63] See 'Pacific Adventurer Private Sector Claims Process', http://www.pacificadventurer.com.au/claims.pdf. Note that the claimants were fortunate that the ship had not been involved in a collision or sinking (eg with third party property and cargo claims, along with injury or death claims). These claims would also to varying degrees have shared in the limitation fund (see II.C.ii above).

[64] It is noticeable that the Queensland Government involved itself in providing information about the claims process, including referring claimants specifically to the guidance in the IOPC Fund *Claims Manual* (by way of non-binding guidance as to the type of claims that might be recoverable).

[65] See IMO LEG 98/7, 16 February 2011, building on an earlier document submitted at the 97th Session in 2010.

[66] See Report of the Legal Committee on the work of its 98th Session, LEG 98/14, 18 April 2011, para 7.5.

[67] LEG 99/4, 11 October 2011, submitted with 19 other States.

[68] ie a 147% increase.

[69] LEG 99/4/1, 10 February 2012.

[70] Report of the Legal Committee on the work of its 99th Session, LEG 99/14, 24 April 2012, Annex 3.

increase of 51 per cent.[71] These increases in limits will only come into force in April 2015.

The irony for Australia is that even with the limits increased by 51 per cent, the limit of liability for the *Pacific Adventurer* is now *lower* than it was in 2009.[72] The reason is that in the period between 2009–12, the Australian dollar has increased in value dramatically. Such radical currency movements cannot fully be taken into account by an international system, but given that these limits may take another 20 years before they can be revised, it remains to be seen whether States will regard them as sufficient, particularly when it is borne in mind that the limits must also be shared with other claimants.

Like the UK, Australia has been a strong supporter of limitation of liability (eg in strict liability systems), and of international uniformity. For States such as Australia, unhappy with the LLMC 2012 limits, there is a policy option of denouncing the LLMC, but re-enacting many of its principles in national law outside of the convention. This would not necessarily be very radical. The LLMC 1976 and LLMC 1996 have not achieved the same sort of international acceptance as have the CLC and Fund Convention.[73] China, for example, has adopted limitation of liability principles in its national Maritime Code which are similar to the LLMC, although it is not a party. A denouncing State would be able to make modest changes to the LLMC scheme, while broadly keeping in conformity with it. One example would be to create a provision setting wholly stand-alone limits of liability for bunker pollution, while increasing the limits to the extent originally proposed by Australia. Indeed, it is arguable that this is what should have happened internationally. It is not simply that the LLMC 2012 limits of liability for bunker pollution might be too low to deal with incidents off sensitive costs, but that these limits may have to be shared with other claimants.

States considering denouncing the LLMC because of the risk of unmet bunker pollution claims should not naively think that if they enacted unlimited liability this would solve all of their problems. Under the Bunker Pollution Convention the insurers would not have a direct liability greater than the limit under the LLMC as amended.[74] A shipowner might have assets, but even if the ship does not sink the single shipowning company structure would effectively restrict what might be available.[75] Given that there is no international uniformity and a wide variety of limitation regimes already available, it seems unlikely that the Clubs or other insurers would restrict cover to a State which denounced the LLMC, but introduced its own principled limits. If there was a widespread series of denunciations, and in effect a move towards unlimited liability, the reaction of the Clubs might be to start imposing policy limits, eg based on the LLMC limits. International uniformity is a

---

[71] LEG 99/14, para 4.15–4.16, and Annex 2.

[72] Using the IMF rates on 25 June 2012, the limit would have been AU$17,201,050.

[73] As at 10 February 2012 the LLMC 1996 had 45 Contracting States: see LEG 99/10, 10 February 2012.

[74] See the Bunker Pollution Convention Arts 7(10), 7(1).

[75] Although charterers, managers and operators may also be liable under the Bunker Pollution Convention, they may not always have assets in the State.

worthwhile goal, but the failure properly to create separate bunker pollution limits may well undermine that goal. It may become politically difficult to justify a regime which provides limits for such claims if there is a disaster which also involved a collision with an innocent passenger ship. Governments may have difficulty in explaining that not only are there limits for pollution claims, but also for personal injury and death claims. Limitation of liability for passenger claims, and the Athens Convention 2002, is another story.

D. Hazardous and Noxious Substances

i. HNS Convention 1996

For over 30 years, there has been a major gap in the law concerning liability for damage (including pollution damage) caused by the carriage of hazardous and noxious substances (HNS), eg bulk or packaged chemicals, LPG or LNG. The world has been very fortunate in recent times in avoiding a major chemical disaster at sea or in port. Imagine if the containers on the *Pacific Adventurer* had contained a highly toxic pesticide in concentrated form; or if there was a major leakage of toxic fumes from a ship in Sydney Harbour; or if there was an explosion at a port of an LNG or LPG carrier. In addition to pollution there could also be loss of life and potentially enormous economic losses if large scale evacuations had to take place in major cities.

In many countries, in the event of an HNS type disaster, liability would have to be determined by the ordinary law of tort or delict (eg negligence and nuisance in the common law world). Some states, such as Australia, have national legislation which may provide some protection for government clean-up costs and private claims.[76] However, those claims would be subject to the general limits of liability under the LLMC, which, as already noted, may be relatively low and subject to sharing with other claimants. As with the case of oil, before the CLC, there was no internationally recognised scheme of compulsory insurance and direct action against insurers to prevent defendants hiding behind single ship companies where HNS liabilities may be involved.

To meet this gap in the law the IMO produced the *Convention on Liability and Compensation for Damage in Connection with the Carriage of Hazardous and Noxious Substances by Sea* (the HNS Convention) 1996, but it is not yet in force. It was modelled on the CLC 1992 and Fund Convention 1992. In a single convention[77] it aimed to create a similar strict liability regime[78] for hazardous and noxious substances *other* than oil or bunkers, with compulsory insurance for the shipowner, and a second tier fund contributed to by HNS importers.

---

[76] See TOMPA 1995, 2c(i), above.

[77] Not separate ones, as with the CLC and Fund Convention.

[78] The liability covers pollution damage but also extends to the risks of fire and explosion, including loss of life or personal injury as well as loss of or damage to property.

The HNS Convention 1996 would apply to bulk *and* packaged dangerous cargoes, but only those listed by reference to generic IMO categories. These include most harmful chemicals, but not all potentially noxious ones. In an incident such as that involving the containers of ammonium nitrate on the *Pacific Adventurer* it seems as if the cargo would have been covered,[79] probably as packaged cargo.[80] On 3 April 2010, the bulk carrier *Shen Neng 1*, carrying a cargo of 68,052t of coal, grounded on the Great Barrier Reef. She was eventually refloated, but if she had been totally lost the HNS Convention (if in force) would not have applied to any coal lost, as coal was excluded from the list of hazardous or noxious substances (along with iron ore, grain, bauxite, alumina and phosphate rock). As I understand the position, neither the Bunker Pollution Convention nor the HNS Convention would have provided compensation for reinstatement of the Great Barrier Reef caused by physical contact only, or for environmental impact assessments of damage caused by anti-fouling paint. Any liability for such losses would have to be sought in national law, but again subject to LLMC limits.[81]

It proved difficult after 1996 for States to be satisfied that the second tier HNS Fund (equivalent to that in the Fund Convention 1992) would actually be workable. This was partly because the chemical industry is much more diverse than the oil industry, thus creating potential difficulties in the compilation of records and the subsequent collection of financial contributions. In effect, there were fears that the second tier would not be financially viable. These practical concerns continued to delay entry into force of the HNS Convention 1996.

ii. HNS Convention 2010

In April 2010, the IMO agreed a Protocol to the HNS Convention 1996, aimed mainly at dealing with the practical problems about implementing the second

---

[79] There are potentially thousands of substances that could be covered in the HNS Convention, and inclusion is by reference to existing generic IMO lists. It was long recognised that this would present difficulties in determining if individual substances were or were not in the list and work on creating an indicative list was instigated by the IMO, with assistance from the secretariat of the IOPC Funds. An HNS database has been created with a searchable list (the HNS Finder, http://www.hnsconvention.org/Pages/FinderOverview.aspx): see IOPC/JUL11/5/1/1, 5 July 2011, para 3.16. The database seems reasonably consumer friendly and ammonium nitrate is clearly listed as an HNS substance.

[80] The cargo was shipped in bulk, although *within* standard freight containers (rather than strengthened, or special intermediate bulk, containers) – contrary to the IMDG (see ATSB Transport Safety Report, No 263 Final, 38–41). I assume that as it was shipped in containers, it would count as packaged HNS rather than bulk HNS (under the IMDG Code). In any event, this distinction does not affect *liability*, but rather whether the cargo is of a type that would be subject to contributions to the HNS Fund.

[81] Under the Great Barrier Reef Marine Park Act 1975 (Cth), s 38GA, civil penalties can be imposed up to a maximum corporate fine of 5,000 penalty units ($550,000), or if aggravated under s 38GA up to 50,000 penalty units ($5,500,000). Even the latter sum looks fairly small. It is assumed that these payments would be aggregated with civil claims for the purpose of limitation of liability (as Australia is a party to the LLMC), but the matter is not free from doubt. The issue of normal criminal fines is outside the scope of this chapter, but States are generally increasing the level of possible fines. Thus, in the Maritime Legislation Amendment Act 2011 (Cth), Australia has increased federal pollution fines to 20,000 penalty units, (Au$2.3 million).

tier fund. The 'HNS Convention 2010' will enter into force when two ratification criteria have been met: (a) at least 12 States, including four States each with not less than 2 million have ratified; and (b) the IMO has received information that those persons in such States who would be liable to contribute to the HNS Fund have received during the preceding calendar year a total quantity of at least 40 million tonnes of cargo (to contribute to the general HNS Fund).

Although the HNS Convention 2010 will supersede the HNS Convention 1996,[82] the essential structure of the latter has been retained, but the liability scheme has changed slightly in the first tier (ie equivalent to the CLC). In essence, if there is damage caused by bulk HNS (eg chemicals from a parcel tanker), compensation would be sought first from the registered shipowner from a minimum of 10 million sdr (about £9.88 million) for a ship of 2000 tons, up to a limit of 100 million sdr (about £98 million). Where damage is caused by packaged HNS (eg in containers), or by both bulk HNS and packaged HNS, the liability of the shipowner is a minimum of 11.5 million sdr (about £11.3 million) for a ship of 2000 tons, up to a maximum 115 million sdr (about £113 million). Once this first tier limit is reached, compensation would be paid from the second tier, the HNS Fund, up to a maximum of 250 million sdr (about £246 million). This is the total amount available, aggregated with the first tier. The HNS Fund limit has not increased since 1996,[83] although as already discussed, the LLMC 1996 limits (agreed at the same diplomatic conference), have since been increased by 51 per cent.

As long ago as 2002, the EU had adopted a decision[84] requiring all EU Member States to take the necessary steps to ratify the HNS Convention within a reasonable time; this progress was interrupted by the debates about the second tier's viability. Denmark became the first State to sign the HNS Protocol 2010 on 14 April 2011, and seven others also signed, subject to ratification or acceptance.[85] Despite the usual concerns about limitation of liability, it is my opinion that the amended HNS Convention should still be ratified by States such as the UK and Australia, thus adding to the suite of IMO liability conventions. Although States may face complaints from major importers about increased burdens, a Minister will be reluctant to stand in front of the cameras after a major chemical explosion in a port and say that his government has not quite got around to enacting an available convention. Maritime law only becomes sexy after the catastrophe. It might even be possible to consider interim national legislation designed to give effect to at least part of the HNS Convention scheme.[86]

---

[82] States have been advised by the IMO to ratify the Protocol rather than the 1996 Convention: see LEG 99/14, para 3.2.

[83] *cf* the Supplementary Fund figures in Table 1, and the recent moves by Australia to increase LLMC limits.

[84] 2002/971/EC.

[85] See also the 'Overview' of the HNS Convention 2010, a set of guidelines to help States give effect to it, at http://www.hnsconvention.org/Documents/HNS%20Overview.pdf.

[86] A State could not give full national effect to the convention as it stands, because the second tier fund requires international action. Interim legislation, imposing liabilities on the shipowner (mirroring the HNS first tier) might give some added protection to the State and individual claimants. For Australia, there is already some protection in legislation such as TOMPA, so this might hardly be a major step. The LLMC limits could still apply to such a national regime, though.

III. COMPENSATION FOR POLLUTION FROM OFFSHORE PLATFORMS

In the light of the experience with ships, it is appropriate to consider some possible solutions for liability in a *Deepwater Horizon*, or *Montara*, situation.

The *Deepwater Horizon* disaster involved the escape of hydrocarbons from the Macondo well in the Gulf of Mexico on 20 April 2010. There were explosions and fires on the *Deepwater Horizon* rig, resulting in loss of life and injury. In addition, there was widespread pollution involving the release of an estimated 4.9 billion barrels of oil over 87 days and compensation claims running into $billions, particularly concerning tourism and fishing.

The *Montara* incident on 21 August 2009, involved an uncontrolled blowout of oil and gas from the *Montara* Wellhead Platform, 250 km off the Australian coast. Oil and gas flowed into the Timor Sea for 10 weeks, possibly affecting 90,000 sq k. The amount leaked was up to 105,000 barrels (about 13,125 tonnes). There were unknown losses of gas and condensate. Gas leaks may involve more safety, than pollution, risks.[87]

A. New Multilateral Convention on Offshore Liabilities?

i. 1977–2001 proposals

In 1977, the Comité Maritime International (CMI) adopted a Draft Convention on Offshore Mobile Craft (the Rio draft).[88] It was mainly designed to clarify how far *existing* maritime rules applied to structures that might not be considered as ships, rather than to deal with pollution disasters.[89] The draft was submitted to the Legal Committee of IMCO (as IMO then was), but was never adopted.[90]

Contemporaneously with the CMI's Rio draft, a more significant stand-alone convention was adopted in Europe, the *Convention on Civil Liability for Oil Pollution Damage Resulting from Exploration and Exploitation of Seabed Mineral Resources* 1977 (CLEE 1977). This was largely modelled on the CLC 1969 and provided for liability of the 'operator' of an offshore 'installation', subject to limits for each installation and each incident of 30 million sdr (£29 million), rising to 40 million sdr (£39 million)[91] five years after the making of the Convention. To cover liability under the Convention, the operator was required to have 'insurance or other financial security to such amount, of such type and on such terms' as

---

[87] This seems to have been the case with the 25 March 2012 gas leak from the Elgin platform, 150 miles off the Scottish coast, where the leak was not stopped until 16 May, after the well was sealed with mud. There were risks to safety caused by the gas and a lighted flare (which was extinguished after six days).

[88] *CMI Documentation 1977* Vol I, 28; Vol III, p 124.

[89] Draft Art 8 would have applied the CLC to mobile offshore craft *carrying* oil, but not to blow outs. Any liability for these would remain with national law.

[90] This may have been in part a result of the opposition of the offshore industry, especially in the US, to international regulation.

[91] Conversion as at 1 June 2012.

the 'Controlling State'[92] shall specify, provided that this would not be less than 22 million sdr (£22 million) rising to 'not less than 35 million sdr' (£34 million) after five years. With a prescience for current concerns, the Controlling State was allowed to exempt the operator wholly or in part from this requirement where pollution damage was wholly caused by an act of sabotage or terrorism.

CLEE 1977 was specifically restricted to States bordering the North Sea, the Baltic or the North Atlantic. It never entered into force, perhaps in part because of the creation from 1974 of the voluntary OPOL agreement[93] – which itself was presumably designed to pre-empt the convention. There is also a suggestion that some thought that the CLEE limits were too high by reference to the LLMC 1976 limits then applicable to ships. On my calculations, the 40 million sdr limit would have been equivalent to that for a ship of some 400,000gt – larger than virtually all but a handful of ULCC tankers currently in operation. Even so, the comparison does not seem wholly inappropriate. Moreover, CLEE gave the Controlling State the right to opt for unlimited liability, provided that this was not discriminatory.

By 1990, the IMO was prompted by a number of interested States to ask the CMI to review the 1977 Rio Draft, to see if it needed updating or revising. A CMI International Sub-Committee met in 1992–1993, before presenting a revised draft convention at the 1994 CMI Sydney conference. The 'Sydney Draft Convention on Mobile Off-Shore Craft' continued to take the approach of looking at existing maritime conventions, eg relating to collision, arrest, salvage and limitation of liability, and then having these applied to offshore mobile 'craft' as defined.[94] A major criticism, particularly from the Canadian Maritime Law Association, was that the Sydney Draft was trying to apply existing conventions designed for ships to structures which were not ships.[95] At the 1994 conference the Canadians argued for a comprehensive convention designed specifically for all types of offshore operations, including those from fixed structures, and so the Conference resolved to set up a new working group.

Meanwhile, the Sydney Draft Convention was considered first at the IMO Legal Committee's 72nd Session in April 1995[96] where there was support for continuing work on offshore mobile craft. By the time of the IMO Legal Committee's 73rd Session in October 1995, there were already concerns about whether the work might exceed the technical competence of the IMO. The Sydney draft was, in effect, rejected, but there was some support (but with a low priority) for the CMI to continue its study on a more comprehensive draft treaty. Work was done for the

---

[92] ie the State with rights over the seabed where the installation is situated.

[93] See III.B.iv, below.

[94] Draft Article 1 provided:

In this Convention 'Craft' shall mean any marine structure of whatever nature not permanently fixed into the sea-bed which (a) is capable of moving or being moved whilst floating in or on water, whether or not attached to the sea bed during operations, and (b) is used or intended for use in the exploration, exploitation, processing, transport or storage of the mineral resources of the sea-bed or its subsoil or in ancillary activities.

[95] *CMI Yearbook 1994 Sydney II*, 168 *et seq.*

[96] See LEG 72/8, 27 January 1995.

CMI Antwerp conference in 1997,[97] but the proposed coverage was very diffuse. A discussion paper was presented to the 78th Session of the IMO Legal Committee in 1998, but it still focused very much on the application of traditional maritime law to mobile offshore units, and merely invited the Legal Committee to support any work to develop the convention to apply to fixed structures.[98]

The CMI was also up against a full IMO agenda and opposition from industry bodies, such as the International Association of Drilling Contractors (IADC), on the basis that no convention was 'necessary', or from the Oil Industry International Exploration and Production Forum (E&P Forum) that regional solutions might be better.[99] Although the matter was raised again by the CMI in subsequent IMO meetings,[100] by October 2001 the IMO Legal Committee had decided to delete the matter from its work programme, but noted that 'should the need arise' it could be reinstated – preferably by a proposal from a government.

In looking at the CMI's work as a whole, it seems fair to conclude that its contributions have been more useful academically, in identifying the problems, than in producing a workable draft convention that appealed to States. The concept of the Rio Draft was ahead of its time, but became outdated when it was realised that the main problem was not in trying to categorise offshore mobile craft. That still remains a live issue for some traditional maritime purposes, such as arrest, the application of the CLC, limitation of liability, or salvage. In some cases the answers have been developed within these particular areas of maritime law;[101] in others it is not a major issue.[102] The larger question is not really how far traditional maritime law needs to be adapted to fit new structures, but to consider afresh what sort of legal regime is necessary for them and to devise a separate instrument accordingly. It was always difficult to see how the Sydney Draft could easily have been adapted to such a purpose. For that reason the Canadian MLA did prepare a draft convention[103] which had a more focused approach than the Sydney Draft, and was discussed at the CMI's Vancouver conference 2004.[104] It was not taken up for use by the IMO. Even the Canadian draft was rather ambitious in its scope, eg for the establishment of an international register for offshore units.[105] It was always likely that it would

---

[97] See *CMI Yearbook 1996 Antwerp I*, 105 *et seq*, *CMI Yearbook 1997 Antwerp II*, 159 *et seq*, *CMI Yearbook 1998* 145 *et seq*.

[98] See IMO LEG 78/10, 13 August 1998.

[99] See IMO LEG 78/11, 2 November 1998.

[100] eg LEG 79/10, 12 February 1999 and LEG 79/11, 22 April 1999, 21.

[101] The Salvage Convention 1989 Art 3 clearly excluded mobile or fixed platforms when on location. The IOPC Fund has produced an identifiable position on FPSOs, see II.B.iv above.

[102] Arrest might be an example.

[103] 'Convention on offshore units, artificial islands and related structures used in the exploration for and exploitation of petroleum and seabed mineral resources' (May 2001 draft): see [2004] 1 *CMI Newsletter*, 1.

[104] *CMI Yearbook 2004*, 419.

[105] The draft did confront directly the difficult question of terminology. Discussions have tended to use a bewildering variety of descriptions for offshore craft, moving beyond the earliest usage of 'rigs', which could be mobile or fixed. The Canadian draft fixed on the UNCLOS Art. 60 concept of 'artificial islands' for fixed installations, and 'offshore units' for moveable structures (including those intended to be, but not yet, fixed to the seabed). Of course, the difficulty with producing such definitions is that they depend on having already determined the intended scope of the instrument as a whole.

take a disaster to prompt further action;[106] and then that a more narrowly focused instrument might be wanted to deal with that disaster, in particular concentrating on compensation for spills and blowouts.

ii. 2010–2012 Proposals

It was 2010 before a government, namely Indonesia, brought back to the IMO agenda the concept of a new international convention to create liabilities for spills from offshore wells.[107] Not surprisingly, this followed its experience of the *Montara* incident. It is notoriously difficult to add a new item to the IMO agenda, both for political and financial reasons.[108] Even with the possibility of utilising an existing model, such as CLEE 1977, the process to achieve an international convention could never be quick. On previous experience it can take a minimum of five years to agree a convention, but a more realistic estimate would be longer; and then up to 10 years for entry into force.

At the 97th Session of the Legal Committee in November 2010, most delegations expressed support, in principle, for the inclusion of an item in the Committee's work programme to consider liability and compensation issues for transboundary pollution damage resulting from offshore oil exploration and exploitation activities.[109] The Legal Committee also recommended to the IMO Council and Assembly that the IMO's Strategic Plan, Direction 7.2, needed to be revised to extend IMO's focus beyond shipping to 'offshore oil exploration and exploitation activities' and, more particularly, to cover not only pollution from ships, but also 'liability and compensation issues connected with transboundary pollution damage resulting from offshore oil exploration and exploitation activities.'[110]

By the 98th Session in April 2011, an informal consultative group consisting of representatives from 14 States, including Australia, had corresponded,[111] and a general legislative survey had been made.[112] It was agreed that Indonesia should continue to coordinate the informal intersessional consultative group. Indonesia hosted a conference in Bali in September 2011, and a wide variety of views were presented –from the need for a new multilateral convention,[113] to restricting any regime to national law.[114]

---

[106] As gloomily predicted by the Canadians, [2004] 1 *CMI Newsletter* 3.

[107] See IMO LEG 97/14/1, 10 September 2010.

[108] It may be significant that the Legal Committee had completed a number of major projects and some may see advantages in having a new target.

[109] Report of the Legal Committee on its 97th Session (LEG 97/15, 1 December 2010), para 14.10.

[110] Above, para 14.12.

[111] Including also industry bodies, such as the International Association of Drilling Contractors, and the International Association of Oil and Gas Producers: see LEG 98/13/1, 18 February 2011.

[112] See Leg 98/13, 18 February 2011.

[113] See S Rares, 'An international convention on offshore hydrocarbon leaks', [2011] *LMCLQ* 361.

[114] See R Shaw, 'Transboundary oil pollution damage arising from exploration and exploitation of offshore oil. Do we need an international compensation convention?' (2011) *CMI Newsletter No 3*, 18, 22.

In July 2011, the IMO Council requested the Legal Committee to re-examine, at its 99th Session, the proposed revision of Strategic Direction 7.2.[115] The decision was a result of a Brazilian challenge to the jurisdiction of the IMO. For the 99th Session of the Legal Committee in April 2012, Brazil reiterated its objections to consideration within IMO of a new multilateral convention.[116] These objections related first to the jurisdictional competency of IMO, but also to the substantive issue of whether such a convention was needed.

iii. Appropriateness of IMO to Consider Offshore Activities

The jurisdictional objections had been voiced when Indonesia made its 2010 proposal. Indeed, as already noted, concerns about the IMO extending its competence to offshore activities generally had been raised when the Sydney draft was being discussed in the mid-1990s.

The essential problem was that Article 1 of the IMO Convention 1948 on the 'purposes of the Organisation' refers repeatedly to 'shipping', eg the effects of 'shipping on the marine environment', or the 'prevention and control of marine pollution from ships'. This obviously raised doubts as to whether the IMO was allowed under its own IMO Convention 1948 to deal with matters other than ships. Further, UNCLOS only mentions the IMO in one small reference in the context of navigation, and in a number of places makes a distinction between ships and platforms.[117]

In a number of instances the IMO has considered offshore platforms, eg in the SUA Protocol 1988,[118] and in the removal of offshore installations,[119] but usually in the context of the safety of navigation.

The pragmatic approach is that the development of international law ought not to be hampered by technical objections where States recognise that there is a problem.[120] Even if there are doubts about the jurisdictional competency of IMO, there are precedents for joint projects with other UN bodies, including the ILO and UNCTAD. There is scope for the UN to approve joint drafting work where the subject matter crosses jurisdictional boundaries, as occurred with the International Convention on Arrest 1999, where IMO and UNCTAD were joint sponsors. Surely, work on any aspect of offshore activities (whether for safety or compensation) ought to involve the United Nations Environment Programme (UNEP), the International Seabed Authority (ISA), the United Nations Office of Legal Affairs/Division for Ocean Affairs and the Law of the Sea (UN/DOALOS) and the International Law

---

[115] The IMO Assembly in November 2011 merely noted the developments. See Leg 99/8, 16 February 2012, paras 3, 18–20, summarising the outcomes of the Council and Assembly meetings.

[116] LEG 99/13/1, 10 February 2012. See also the Report of the Legal Committee on the work of its 99th Session, LEG 99/14, 24 April 2012, 23–28.

[117] eg Arts 60, 80, 194, 208, 211.

[118] *Protocol for the Suppression of Unlawful Acts against the Safety of Fixed Platforms Located on the Continental Shelf 1988.*

[119] *Guidelines and Standards for the Removal of Offshore Installations and Structures on the Continental Shelf and in the EEZ 1989* (IMO resolution A.672(16)).

[120] See the arguments summarised in LEG 99/14, 25–28.

Commission.[121] Sometimes there can be time consuming skirmishes as to which UN body is the right one to take the lead.

It may well be that the IMO does not yet have special expertise in relation to the technical aspects of safety and regulation of platforms as opposed to ships, but there is no other UN organisation with comparable expertise. Moreover, IMO does have considerable experience now in developing liability and compensation regimes. From this conclusion, the Legal Committee reached a number of delicate compromises on the Indonesian proposal.[122]

First, the issue as to whether it was necessary to alter formally the Strategic Direction 7.2 was sidestepped. Although it was recognised that formal proposals might necessitate revisions, the Legal Committee decided to inform the IMO Council that it 'wished to analyse further the liability and compensation issues connected with transboundary pollution damage resulting from offshore oil exploration activities, with the aim of developing guidance to assist States interested in pursuing bilateral or regional arrangements, without revising SD 7.2'.[123] In effect, permission was being asked to keep discussing the issues without yet making any formal proposals. In the longer term there needs to be a more decisive decision as to where discussion of offshore activities is most properly located within the UN family.

Secondly, on the substantive issue 'The Committee recognized that bilateral and regional arrangements were the most appropriate way to address this matter; and that there was no compelling need to develop an international convention on this subject.'[124] The two parts of this decision are highly significant. The effect of the last part seems effectively to be major block to any future discussion of a multilateral convention on transboundary pollution damage, at least within IMO. The compromise is that IMO can keep discussing liability and compensation mechanisms, but only as a model to assist States who wish to create bilateral or regional schemes.

B. Liability Regimes: Possible Solutions

In the light of this highly important development, it is worthwhile to consider in outline the merits of the possible ways forward for liability regimes, in particular why there were objections to a multilateral approach based on the maritime model.

i. Advantages of a Convention-based Regime

There are many advantages of a multilateral convention-based regime to claimant States. First, there could be uniformity of rules for an industry that operates worldwide.

---

[121] In addition, it might be appropriate for there to be joint activity with the International Seabed Authority in so far as it has to perform functions (eg under UNCLOS Art 145) in relation to the protection of the marine environment in the Area, beyond national jurisdiction.
[122] LEG 99/14, 28.
[123] LEG 99/14, para 13.16.
[124] LEG 99/14, para 13.17.

Secondly, it would be more difficult for industry to resist international action than national legislation, especially where any regime is modelled on others already in use worldwide. Thirdly, risk could be spread internationally, rather than being targeted on one State. Fourthly, compulsory insurance provisions would more easily work where there was an inbuilt ability to seek reciprocal enforcement of judgments.

Although there now seems to be little prospect of a multilateral convention, it is still worthwhile to examine in outline the scope of any such convention in order to assess its value. The fundamentals of such a regime should be relatively easy to set out because of the experience that we have had with the maritime conventions. One would expect to see, as a minimum a strict liability regime with its boilerplate defences, coupled with compulsory insurance and direct action.[125]

ii. Difficulties with a New Multilateral Convention

The simple transposition of maritime liability principles might present real legal and commercial difficulties. There would be the inevitable debates about limitation of liability: should there be a limit and at what level? In the light of the US response to *Deepwater Horizon*, and BP's apparent agreement to have an open cheque book, would any State now agree to a regime with any limits of liability?[126] It may be that States with less international clout than the USA (and which are actively trying to attract and develop an offshore industry) will not be able to exert the same amount of influence. Moreover, any limitation debate will be intimately associated with the question of who will be the payer of claims and how will any payments be secured?

Compulsory insurance is the obvious method to ensure or guarantee payments, as with the CLC, but there are two main differences between the tanker regime and any offshore regime. First, while the International Group of P&I Clubs provides the majority of backing for the shipping industry, I am not aware of an equivalent insurance body for the offshore rig industry, both to represent the insurance interests in international negotiations for a convention, or to provide a settled and reliable long term guarantee for States.[127] Insurance markets can be very volatile and it may not be easy to ensure that there will be a lasting body of underwriters available to meet risks for the life of a convention, or that reinsurance could be obtained without limit.[128] It is highly unlikely that the Clubs would agree to extend their existing cover for rigs to include drilling liabilities, as these are simply not a mutual risk for the vast majority of their member owners.[129]

---

[125] See, eg S Rares, 'An international convention on offshore hydrocarbon leaks', [2011] *LMCLQ* 361.
[126] Even if the CLEE 1977 limits were adjusted to LLMC 1996 levels – on my calculations about £134 million (see 3 a(i), above).
[127] Insurance cover obviously exists already, but its extent is largely confidential, and many big players may simply self-insure.
[128] There were difficulties in the negotiation of the Athens Convention 2002 on carriage of passengers, when it was sought to find alternative insurance markets for claims, eg to base a convention on compulsory personal insurance for passengers, rather than on liability insurance for carriers (ie through the Clubs).
[129] There was a similar difficulty with passenger ship liabilities for those clubs with very few passenger ship members.

Secondly, a convention cannot easily discriminate between different categories of insurer in different States. The shipping conventions allow for certificates issued by insurers in *any* contracting State. This was a concern when the Bunker Pollution Convention was negotiated as, for the first time internationally, it effectively requires all types of seagoing ships to have insurance certificates. There was the prospect of smaller owners, in particular, relying on locally issued certificates that might not have been worth more than the paper they were written upon. There is a risk, therefore, that a State relying on a new offshore liability convention might find that a certificate has been issued in a small island State where it is not clear if there is effective insurance regulation.[130] To some extent, this risk can be reduced for platforms operating within a State's EEZ as the State is entitled to impose its own licensing requirements for drilling, independently of any offshore liability convention.[131] These licensing conditions should provide some protection against paper insurers. Moreover, as with the CLEE Convention 1977, it may be justifiable for the convention to leave approval of insurance to the State where the rig is situated. The disadvantage is the lack of uniformity, or an inhibition on the possibility of major insurance players emerging to cover a uniform risk.

A further distinction between tankers and platforms will be the availability of a second tier of compensation. The CLC/Fund regime and the HNS Convention are predicated on the notion of sharing risk between the vessel, on the one hand, and the oil and chemical industries on the other. Even assuming that there would be an insurer of the platform itself that was willing to accept third party liabilities, it seems unlikely that it could provide cover for the sort of liabilities predicted for *Deepwater Horizon*. The single tier CLEE Convention 1977 is therefore not entirely suitable for present day risks. The shipping experience is that it may be necessary to have some form of additional fund whose contributors go wider than those involved in the immediate incident. Could such a fund be created internationally, and how could it be financed? The obvious source is the oil and gas companies themselves, but how could a system work?

One source of a fund is to seek contributions from those companies involved in well operations, and to base contributions to any 'Offshore Operators' Fund' on the proportion of oil or gas extracted by such companies worldwide (or more accurately amongst those States party to such a convention). There are two difficulties. It would be necessary to create a new administrative structure which was able to deal with records and statistics from around the world. This is not necessarily straightforward, even in identifying the players, but it could be done. There is also the difficulty that US participation is highly unlikely, either because the US oil industry does not want to contribute to spills elsewhere in the world committed by other operators, or because the US itself would not accept any limits of liability. Could such a system work without US participation, or with only a small number of State parties?

---

[130] That this is not a fanciful risk is seen in the aftermath of the sanctions on Iran which have removed P&I cover (see eg Gard Circular 07–12, June 2012). There are suggestions that Iranian cargoes may obtain insurance from bodies set up in less developed states.

[131] See UNCLOS Arts 60, 80, 81.

The alternative to a wellhead fund is the IOPC/HNS model of a fund contributed to by oil and gas importers, still based on a post-spill levy. If the levy was calculated on the basis of oil or gas imports (rather than well-head flows) there might be said to be an overlap with the existing IOPC/HNS Funds. But this would not be a form of double taxation, unless a tanker collided with a rig.[132] The advantage of such a system would be that it could piggy-back on existing administrative arrangements, and that losses could be spread more evenly among users. Such a system could operate without the US, but would almost certainly need EU and Japanese involvement. There may be great hesitations in both of the latter to contribute, say, to a spill in African or Australian waters. Everyone can see that ships move around the world and that a ship carrying oil to Europe may cause risks in Africa. The connection between one State (or group of States) and a spill in a fixed facility in another part of the world may be more difficult to justify – especially when the State where the platform is located is extracting its own natural resources and imposing taxes accordingly.

Finally, there is the difficulty of deciding how far any regime would apply in waters outside the national jurisdiction of any State (eg the 200 mile EEZ, or the continental shelf), and the implications of this for UNCLOS, which declares seabed resources in the 'Area' to be the common heritage of mankind.[133]

In my view, there are likely to be significant difficulties in agreeing a multilateral two tier convention.

iii. Bilateral or Regional Conventions

The result of the IMO Legal Committee's decision in April 2012 is that there may be a greater focus on regional, rather than multilateral, conventions. To some extent, the financing problems described above might apply with even greater force to regional arrangements where there are likely to be small numbers of contracting States.

Studies within the IMO[134] have identified a number of existing regional conventions applicable to offshore activities.[135] The Nordic Environmental Protection Convention 1974[136] applies inter alia to 'the discharge from... installations of...gas or any other substance into...the sea...which entails... environmental nuisance.' It does not so much create new rights of compensation, but, under Article 3, provides that persons in one State can bring compensation issues before another State and that 'the question of compensation shall not be judged by rules which are less favourable to the injured party than the rules of compensation of the State in which the activities are being carried out.' The 1974 Convention does contain, however, a number of useful provisions dealing with procedural cooperation between the States.

---

[132] Not a fanciful situation where tankers load offshore.

[133] See UNCLOS Part XI, and Art 139 which places obligations on States in respect of damage.

[134] See also eg M. Kashubsky, 'Marine Pollution from the Offshore Oil and Gas Industry: Review of Major Conventions and Russian Law Part I', (2006) 151 *Maritime Studies* 1.

[135] In addition to OPOL, see III.B.iv below.

[136] Convention on the Protection of the Environment between Denmark, Finland, Norway and Sweden, 1974.

Similarly, the Barcelona Convention 1976 (and 1995 Protocol)[137] provides a general framework for cooperation between Mediterranean States to reduce pollution and, in Article 7 (as amended) obliges contracting States to 'take all appropriate measures to prevent, abate, combat and to the fullest possible extent eliminate pollution of the Mediterranean Sea Area resulting from exploration and exploitation of the continental shelf and the seabed and its subsoil.' Article 16 obliges the parties 'to cooperate in the formulation and adoption of appropriate rules and procedures for the determination of liability and compensation for damage resulting from pollution of the marine environment in the Mediterranean Sea Area.'

It is evident that these sort of regional conventions are drafted much more in the language of general public international law obligations, rather than the more precise private law influenced conventions such as the CLC.

It may be that it is easier, politically, to justify regional schemes, eg within Europe and the Gulf of Mexico. For States such as Australia, this is a significant disadvantage as it has relatively few neighbours with resources equivalent to its own. In any regional Australasian scheme, Australia may end up being the major contributor, eg to problems caused in Indonesia by *Montara* type spills. It would therefore be more attractive to create a much bigger Asian regional scheme including China, Japan and India. It is inevitable, however, that States will look to see where the offshore activity is taking place and assess the risks and advantages of a scheme on the basis of national interest, perhaps in a way that is more focused than where a multilateral instrument is being considered with many participants.

In my view, it may not be even harder to produce a two tier regional convention, although bodies such as the EU have greater legislative flexibility.[138] In the Australasia region, it is hard to see a State such as Australia being able to support politically a nationally levied (ie taxed) fund to support a neighbour. At the 100th session of the Legal Committee, in April 2013, Indonesia presented a set of principles for the recovery of compensation, but based on a single tier, compulsory insurance, model.

Although work on bilateral or regional models should be supported at the IMO, are there any shorter term solutions?

iv. Voluntary International or Regional Schemes

The comparative lack of legislative action in Europe may be due to the absence of a major rig or well pollution incident,[139] or the confidence in existing laws or arrangements. In 1974, an agreement called the 'Offshore Pollution Liability Agreement' (OPOL) was created;[140] the latest version is dated 1 October 2010.

---

[137] Convention for the Protection of the Mediterranean Sea against Pollution 1976 and Protocol of 1995 pertaining to offshore oil exploration and exploitation activities.

[138] See, eg T Markus, S Schlacke, N Maier, 'Legal Implementation of Integrated Ocean Policies: The EU's Marine Strategy Framework Directive' (2011) 26 *IJMCL* 59; S Boelart-Suominen, 'The European Community, The European Court of Justice and the Law of the Sea' (2008) 23 *IJMCL* 643

[139] The *Piper Alpha* disaster in 1988 involved loss of life, but there was no major pollution, see the *Cullen Inquiry* (1990).

[140] Although it came into force in 1975 (see http://www.opol.org.uk).

Its parties are 16 major operators of offshore facilities used in connection with exploration for or production of oil and gas. The preamble states its purpose as being for the parties

> to provide an orderly means for compensating and reimbursing any Person who sustains Pollution Damage and any Public Authority which incurs costs for taking Remedial Measures as a result of a Discharge of Oil from any Offshore Facility so used and located within the jurisdiction of a State denominated hereunder as a 'Designated State', provided that such Party is the Operator of the Offshore Facility and this Contract is applicable to that Offshore Facility.

As with the CLC, the liability is strict and there are similar defences (eg for war, or State faults). The parties agree to establish and maintain financial responsibility to fulfil their obligations, up to an overall maximum of US$250 million per incident. There is a maximum of US$125 million for remedial measures taken by any public authority and US$125 million for pollution damage (eg suffered by individuals or companies). As these sums are offered contractually, there can be no question of breaking the limits, and there is a comparatively short one year time bar (by comparison with the 3/6 year time bar under the CLC). From a State perspective there is some security in that the operators maintain a mutual guarantee, rather than having liability of a single operator with insurance backing, as under CLEE 1977.[141]

In the context of *Deepwater Horizon*, and even *Montara*, the OPOL sums are small, although they have been increased over the years.[142] But in the absence of any international convention, could such a voluntary system be of use to in, say, Australasia, or the wider Asia region? OPOL itself applies to named North Sea States (such as the UK, Denmark, Germany, France, Ireland, the Netherlands, and Norway) and 'any other State recognised as such under international law or custom which the Parties by appropriate amendment hereto under Clause X may so denominate.' OPOL is designed for the North Sea, and already excludes the Baltic and Mediterranean. It seems highly unlikely that the current companies would agree to an application to join from States elsewhere in the world, eg Australia. While discussions continue about possible international convention(s), it makes sense for a state such as Australia to precipitate a wider debate about why such a voluntary agreement should not be extended to other regions of the world, or at least replicated in other regions, eg Australasia. This would at least provide some measure of comfort to Indonesia.

Prior to the entry into force of the CLC 1969 and the Fund Convention 1971, the shipowners and the oil industry agreed voluntary schemes to provide equivalent (and in some cases extended) cover to State victims of pollution. These schemes were called TOVALOP[143] and CRISTAL,[144] and continued in existence in different

---

[141] Although applicants to become members of OPOL have to provide evidence of insurance 'acceptable to the [OPOL] Association' for $250 million per incident or $500 million pa.

[142] As at 1 January, 2010, the maximum limit was only US$120 million per incident.

[143] Tanker Owners Voluntary Agreement concerning Liability for Oil Pollution.

[144] Contract Regarding a Supplement to Tanker Liability for Oil Pollution.

forms until 1997 (when the CLC/Fund 1992 system was operational). Presumably the industries concerned in all the voluntary schemes have viewed them as in their best interests, eg to avoid more draconian national or international action. Nevertheless, they have been effective in providing some assurance to States and STOPIA and TOPIA continue to operate as voluntary agreements within the CLC/Fund system.

It is arguable that the only obstacle to an extended OPOL, or a series of regional OPOLs, is the willingness and ability of the industries to consider it. The mutuality of the 16 parties to OPOL would have to be replicated in a regional solution. The companies listed are those oil majors that one would expect to see, eg Amoco, BP etc, but for Australia there would presumably have to be other or different parties.[145]

v. Interim National Measures

It follows that, for the time being, any liability for well blowouts would have to remain with national law. The threat of huge liabilities under US law seems to have worked in producing compensation from BP after *Deepwater Horizon*. In the context of the *Montara* incident, a State such as Australia needs to assess what is the appropriate compensation environment which should apply in the interim before any international or regional action. This regime could be achieved by administrative action (through licensing), or by creating a new national liability regime.

The quickest and easiest way to achieve protection is through the imposition of very tight licensing terms, effectively contractual in nature. These might provide for strict liability with compulsory insurance, and some sort of bank or other cross-company guarantees. In an energy hungry market there may be players who are willing to accept stringent terms.

As happened with bunker claims, not subject to the CLC, many States could enact their own enhanced national legislation, using a CLC type model. This could be a single tier liability regime, possibly with some limits of liability[146] which could be insurable. The imposition of some sort of second tier national superfund for contingencies would inevitably be seen as a tax on the exploration industry. In Australia, for instance, that is likely to be highly controversial where the present government is under great political pressure for having introduced a new mineral resources tax. It is not clear if there would be the same level of support for a fund kept for possible future disasters, as opposed to using any 'tax' funds for other politically or socially desirable purposes.

Australia already has a 'National Plan to Combat Pollution of the Sea by Oil and Other Noxious and Hazardous Substances', and makes a levy raised on commercial shipping using Australian ports to finance it. There is a contingency fund for

---

[145] Including PTTEPAA (responsible for *Montara*), and other majors operating in the region such as Woodside.

[146] Although it appears that Norway and Germany have maintained unlimited liability, see *CMI Yearbook 1997 Antwerp II*, 172.

incidents where costs are incurred in responding to incidents when defendants cannot be identified, or clean-up costs cannot be recovered; this fund was accessed after the *Pacific Adventurer* incident. Could such a scheme be extended to cover levies on the offshore industry? Such levy systems work best when there are relatively small charges on a large number of operators; where there are large levies on a small number of operators there will be more resistance. Tactically, of course, the threat of such national action, backed by legislation, might be an incentive for the industry to produce a voluntary scheme.

IV. CONCLUSIONS: SCOPE OF MARITIME LAW

The discussions at the IMO about transboundary pollution have raised rather profound questions about the scope of maritime law. For most private practitioners of maritime law (at least in London), the subject is essentially one of private law, mainly of obligations arising in contract and tort, with a remedial structure based on normal rules of compensation, enforced internationally by the principles of private international law. In the last 30 years there have been increasing influences of international conventions (and enacting national statutes), but these have sometimes been viewed as merely 'intrusions' on maritime law principles established and litigated upon for generations.

For States, the focus of maritime law has primarily been of a public law regulatory nature, concerning safety, pollution prevention and, more recently, maritime security. The geographical scope has generally been limited to national waters (or national ships while overseas). The limits of action have been defined internationally very much by UNCLOS.

Of course, this private/public law distinction is oversimplified. Many maritime practitioners will have to advise clients on public law regulatory issues, including competition law, some of which have criminal law consequences. The advent of EU law has gradually produced a generation of UK lawyers whose views cannot be solely national. It is no longer so frightening to have to refer to an international legal instrument. Prior to the introduction of the LLMC 1976 in the UK, practitioners dealing with limitation of liability would have assumed that the law was created by, and found only in, the Merchant Shipping Acts; many might even have been unaware that the law was then based on the 1957 Limitation Convention. Modern methods of enactment have sensibly preferred, in general, to incorporate international private law conventions by means of a schedule,[147] Knowledge of public international law, especially UNCLOS, would not have been necessary to a traditional maritime practice, but has become central to States in negotiating about maritime activities.

---

[147] See, eg the Merchant Shipping Act 1995, Schs 5A, 6, 7 and 11; unfortunately the CLC and Fund Convention were rewritten into legal English. See generally N Gaskell, 'The Interpretation of Maritime Conventions at Common Law', in JP Gardner (ed), *United Kingdom Law in the 1990s* (British Institute of International and Comparative Law, 1990).

The work of the CMI was traditionally focused on the problems faced by maritime practitioners in private law, while the IMO was originally founded, as IMCO, with regulatory aims. The creation of the IMO Legal Committee after *Torrey Canyon* was a recognition of the need for private mechanisms (eg compensation) to be created in the hitherto public law field of maritime pollution. Over the last 30 years IMO has proceeded to produce a whole suite of maritime law conventions, dealing not only with pollution, but also passenger liability and wreck removal. The CMI's agenda has increasingly reflected the need to consider issues of public law (eg places of refuge, and crimes at sea), although it has lost its main role as a drafter of conventions.

The history of maritime law shows that it has always evolved to deal with new challenges thrown up by commercial development, including those offshore. The offshore industry developed with greater influences from land-based regimes and practices, eg on-shore drilling, than it did from maritime traditions. The offshore industry, influenced heavily by a US dislike of state interference, has been fiercely independent in creating its own cultures and practices, largely of self-regulation. Even the insurance arrangements have followed the artificial divide between 'maritime' and 'offshore', eg where different insurers are on risk when a platform is in transit to when it is in operation. Practitioners advising oil companies about the offshore developments have found that the boundaries between maritime law and offshore law are increasingly blurred; in some cases they are downright confusing.[148]

So far the offshore industry has managed to keep free of much international interference (and the UNCLOS Part XI concept of the common heritage of mankind has not yet really intruded significantly). It is sometimes harder to tell if the offshore industry would be more worried about the imposition of new legislation on offshore regulation than on offshore compensation.[149] Of course, it would prefer neither, but I suspect that it would more easily concede to a compensation regime which gave it legal and commercial certainty, than it would to an internationally controlled safety and environment regime that affected its day to day operations. Even in the US the need for better regulation has been recognised, but the transboundary debate at the IMO has illustrated that there is still a gaping hole in the international regulation of activities outside of existing coastal zones.

Still, it is hard to dispute that it is time to recognise that there is little place for artificial boundaries operating offshore which derive from historic commercial or legal distinctions.

---

[148] See generally M White, *Australia's Offshore Laws* (2009).
[149] See, eg LEG 99/14, para 13.10.

5

Shipping and the Marine Environment in the 21st Century

MICHAEL N TSIMPLIS

I. INTRODUCTION[1]

U NDER THE 1982 United Nations Convention Law on the Law of the Sea (UNCLOS),[2] states are obliged 'to protect and preserve the marine environment'.[3] The statement is very general and is not restricted to the marine environment within national jurisdiction but to the entire marine environment.[4]

---

[1] I would like to thank Prof Yvonne Baatz and Mr Richard Shaw for comments on the paper and Miss Adebowale Awofeso for assisting with the editing of the article.

[2] But arguably not under customary international law as it existed before the development of UNCLOS 1982.

[3] UNCLOS 1982 Art 192. This is a general statement that arguably binds not only the contracting states of UNCLOS 1982 but all states and one which is firmly accepted under customary international law. The term marine environment is not well defined. UNCLOS 1982 defines 'pollution of the marine environment' as,

> the introduction by man, directly or indirectly, of substances or energy into the marine environment, in-cluding estuaries, which results or is likely to result in such deleterious effects as harm to living resources and marine life, hazards to human health, hindrance to marine activities, including fishing and other legitimate uses of the sea, impairment of quality for use of sea water and reduction of amenities;

UNCLOS 1982 Art 1(1)(4). This is indeed a very wide definition which encompasses noise pollution (which affects mammals) and probably acidification of the oceans by human activities including burning of fossil fuels. But it does not tell us whether the marine environment and its protection refer, in addition to the ocean, to the interlinked and interconnected atmosphere and coastal zone. Probably it does not unless the atmospheric or land based pollution leads to the introduction of a pollutant substance or energy into the ocean causing deleterious effects. Thus, eg, CO_2 emissions which cause ocean acidification are probably covered by the definition. However increased CO_2 emissions which cause increases in atmospheric temperature that then lead to oceanic temperature increases are not clearly covered by the definition. It depends on whether the indirect introduction of substances or energy is to be read as encompassing all indirect consequences or is to be restricted to diffusion of the released pollutants or energy to the marine environ-ment. Thus, although it can be argued that the release of GHG by man in the atmosphere which leads to the introduction of energy into the oceans which may have, for specific species and regions deleterious effects, is marine pollution, the better view is that it is probably not covered by the UNCLOS 1982 definition.

[4] The International Court of Justice in the Legality of the Threat or Use of Nuclear Weapons, Advisory Opinion, ICJ Reports 1996, pp 241–42, para 29 stated:

> the environment is not an abstraction but represents the living space, the quality of life and the very health of human beings, including generations unborn. The existence of the general obligation of

Thus clearly the duty extends to activities of ships that operate in waters outside the jurisdiction of the flag state. Furthermore states are also under a duty to prevent, reduce and control pollution of the marine environment from every source by using the best practicable means and in accordance with their capabilities.[5] Thus states should develop shipping policies within this context for the twenty-first century. This appears easier said than done.

Shipping is one of the most dynamic and financially volatile global commercial sectors. It is the backbone of international trade. Due to its international character and the effects regulation may have on competitiveness, it is only when regulation is agreed internationally that improvements can be made. This is especially acute in relation to the environmental regulation of shipping.[6]

International agreements are a product of negotiation and ensure that some minimum standards are imposed on ships. However we will argue that existing international regulation is, even if it were to be assumed to provide the appropriate environmental standards, producing changes which are very slow and thus inefficient. It will be argued that in shipping too little is done too late, and potential deficiencies in the governance of shipping will be discussed.

We will assess the governance of the international maritime sector against the criteria of sustainable development and common but differentiated responsibility, both central in the development plans for the next century. This assessment is important because the sector's governance is based on an, arguably, outdated allocation of responsibility between states, coupled with the entrustment of powers for policing environmental standards in large areas of the oceans to small and unwilling states which prioritise the short-term financial benefits of shipping over any global or local social and environmental concerns. We will argue that the ability of the existing shipping governance to deliver on sustainable development can be questioned because the common but differentiated responsibility principle has been used so as to serve, not the needs of developing states, but the narrow financial interests of the shipping sector which flags its ships in developing states.

States to ensure that activities within their jurisdiction and control respect the environment of other States or of areas beyond national control is now part of the corpus of international law relating to the environment.
Furthermore in the Gabcikovo-Nagymaros Project, the ICJ Court had '… no difficulty in acknowledging that the concerns expressed by Hungary for its natural environment in the region … related to an "essential interest" of that State…' see p41 of the judgement. Thus it is arguable that there is a duty on states under customary international law not to harm the environment of other states or the environment at the high seas and that the concerns with respect to the marine environment expressed by state are legitimate and important. However, again, these decisions do not restrict the actions of states within their boundaries. With the marine environment the problem is that mixing of coastal waters with waters further from the coast dilutes the pollutants. To determine then that some activities of one state do not 'respect' the environment of other states would be very difficult. This leads to a continuing erosion of the baseline standards perpetuating the problem.

[5] (Art 194(1)). This may sound fair but there is no firm way of ensuring the capabilities of each state. It can be argued that this is a continuing obligation and that each state (and all states collectively) as they develop financially will increasingly have to deal with marine environmental pollution 'in accordance with its increase ability'. This necessarily points towards a revision of such arrangement imposed by all states.

[6] The importance of differences in working rights and conditions for seafarers is another very important area with similar difficulties.

We will further discuss the international environmental principles that are likely to shape shipping policy over the next decades. On the basis of the way these have been perceived within the shipping law negotiating forum, the IMO, the challenges for the shipping of the future will be examined and the capability of the established governance of shipping to meet these challenges will be analysed.

II. THE OCEANIC ENVIRONMENT AND SHIPPING

The discussion in this paper is based on a number of propositions. First we assume that the environment, and in particular the oceanic environment, has restrictions that arise from the physical limits of the oceans and the large but limited amounts of water contained. It follows that the addition of contaminants of pollutants at rates higher than such contaminants are removed by natural processes, from a location or from the ocean in total, will eventually lead to harmful alteration of the chemical consistency of parts end eventually the whole of the oceans. It also follows that any activity increasing the concentration of pollutants is taking the system towards saturation and that diffusive processes which take pollutants away from the source of pollution are not processes removing the pollutants but redistributing them within the oceans.

A second proposition is that the aquatic organisms, species and ecosystems also have specific limits of tolerance.[7] These are not uniform around the world[8] and also vary between species. The third proposition is that we presently do not know enough[9] and we will not be able to know for some time how high these limits are, or in other words, how tolerant the system is.[10]

---

[7] These can be demonstrated by the mortality rates of particular species in oil pollution incidents or through the establishment of alien species from ballast water. Both demonstrate extreme incidents of alteration of an ecosystem. The extent of oil pollution on the marine environment can be quantified on the basis of estimated loading. But to understand the impacts one has to look at the loading of specific chemical components, which include the polycyclic aromatic (multiple-ring) hydrocarbons, which must be taken into account as well as the sensitivity of the specific species present in a particular area to these chemical compounds (Oil in the Sea III: Inputs, Fates, and Effects Committee on Oil in the Sea: Inputs, Fates, and Effects, National Research Council, 2003). One can further argue that the impacts of an ecosystem will then depend on the sensitivity of specific components of the ecosystem to the compounds introduced, as well as to the general health (or tolerance) of the particular ecosystem, which would depend on the various pressures the ecosystem is under and which are not related to the particular pollution. However, contamination of waters by oil pollution has also been claimed to have long-term effects.

[8] This leads to the consequence that if contamination is source-generated rather than uniformly distributed, the risk for the various species would be higher. Thus coastal areas are at higher risks than open sea areas. The same argument could lead to the suggestion that shipping lanes should be uniformly distributed around the world to minimise the impacts of ship-generated pollution. The financial cost of adopting such a suggestion as general practice, as well as the inability to enforce it, makes it fanciful. It can also be argued that the additional time the ships would have to spend at sea and the additional number of ships could in effect lead to increase of pollutants.

[9] The Marine Strategy Directive, Directive 2008/56/EC of the European Parliament and of the Council of 17 June 2008 establishing a framework for community action in the field of marine environmental policy (Marine Strategy Framework Directive) sets this in the following terms:

The fourth proposition is that shipping activities contribute to the introduction of pollutants. Shipping, together with offshore drilling, fisheries, fish farming, pollution from land based activities and climate change are the major human activities that affect the marine environment. Shipping activities are presently not the major contributors of marine[11] atmospheric pollution over the oceans,[12] or to the global increase in greenhouse gas emissions.[13] It is, however, well established

Since programmes of measures executed under marine strategies will be effective only if they are devised on the basis of a sound knowledge of the state of the marine environment in a particular area and are tailored as closely as possible to the needs of the waters concerned in the case of each Member State and from the general perspective of the marine region or subregion concerned, provision should be made for the preparation at national level of an appropriate framework, including marine research and monitoring operations, for informed policymaking. At Community level, support for associated research should be continuously enshrined in research and development policies.

This is certainly a step in the right direction for the management of the European Seas. However it has to be appreciated that we lack basic knowledge concerning the pollution concentrations for many species and ecosystems, thus even if the directive is implemented the assumption about the lack of basic knowledge would still hold. What the Directive can establish though are base lines of what the status of the marine environment will be when it will be implemented.

[10] There is an important distinction between the development of scientific knowledge and the use of science in pollution litigation. The essential difference is that progress in science requires a theory which is developed, evaluated, disputed and improved continuously. It is the destiny of every scientific result that it will be doubted, improved, qualified, or rejected. Scientific development is based on observations conflicting with the dominant theory. From the legal point of view, the very existence of apparently conflicting scientific studies can be used to dispute the causation of damage arising from pollution. The latter technique has been used by the oil industry to dispute especially, the long-term effects of oil pollution on the marine environment. See also the way under the US system these legal objections are reduced or avoided in *Oil in the Sea III: Inputs, Fates, and Effects*, Committee on Oil in the Sea: Inputs, Fates, and Effects, National Research Council, 2003.

[11] Oil pollution from vessels for the period 1990–99 contributed 29% of the volume globally introduced, of which 8% was due to accidents and 21% due to operational discharges. In terms of anthropogenic oil pollution it is the biggest contributor. Land-based runoff accounts for about 11%, while extraction and transportation of oil with pipelines together with offshore facility incidents count for 7%. Natural seepage is the first overall contributor (47%) (National Research Council. *Oil in the Sea: input, fates and effects*, National Academy of Sciences, Washington, DC, 2003). It has also to be noted that the period 1990–99 used as reference for this study is a decade when the oil spilled had already been reduced to less than 20% in relation to what was spilled during the period 1975–80. It is not known how much larger operational oil discharge from shipping during the same period was. However it is not unreasonable to assume that the operational discharges were also correspondingly higher. Thus assuming natural seepage has remained unchanged – not necessarily a correct assumption as depletion of oil fields may have in fact reduced it too – this gives an estimate for the oil contribution from shipping in the 1970s of about 45% of the total contribution. Note that the earlier study by the same organisation in 1973 had significantly different estimates. The contribution from shipping was 35%, natural seepage was considered as 9.8% and land contributions were 54%. *Petroleum in the Marine Environment* (Washington, DC: National Academy of Sciences, 1975).

[12] Note that the shipping contribution to this type of pollution is not negligible. See, eg JJ Corbett, JJ Winebrake, EH Green, P Kasibhatla, V Eyring and A Lauer, *Mortality from Ship Emissions: A Global Assessment*, Environ, Sci Technol, 2007, 41 (24), pp 8512–18 who estimate that 60,000 cardiopulmonary and lung cancer deaths annually can be attributed to the air pollution caused from shipping. Note also that because ships emit pollutants in relatively cleaner areas their effects with respect to impacts on processes will be larger. See K Capaldo, Corbett JJ, P Kasibhatla, P Fischbeck and S.N Pandis, (1999) *Effects of ship emissions on sulphur cycling and radiative climate forcing over the ocean*, Nature, 400, 743–46 who estimate the indirect forcing effects caused by sulphates emitted from ships to be around 14% of the IPCC global anthropogenic sulphate estimate for 1990s.

[13] The shipping industry contributes around 3% of these emissions. However, future reductions of emissions in other sectors will lead to the increase in significance of CO2 emissions from ships, even if the actual amount of CO2 emitted were to remain unchanged.

that shipping activities have significant impacts on the marine environment and that overall they contribute to all of the aforementioned forms of pollution.[14]

The final proposition is that transport of goods by sea will increase in the future.[15] This assumption is based on the projected increase in the total human population and the increase of the number of wealthy people in the world.[16] The consequence will be that the contribution of shipping to marine, but also atmospheric pollution, will probably increase[17] even if cleaner ships and cleaner practices – when compared with present ships and practices – are to be employed.

---

[14] The spectacular character and the publicity that oil spills attract have the consequence that regulation and legislation with respect to such events are easier to develop due to public pressure. The cleanup cost for oil spills depends on the type of oil involved as well as the area where the oil spill occurs. The cost for cleanup of one tonne of cargo for The Prestige event was Euros 10.7 k (fuel oil) while the Exxon Valdez pollution incident was $70.5 k (crude oil) and the Erika was Euro 6.3 k (see MD Garza-Gil, A Prada-Blanco and MX Vazquez-Rodriguez,*Estimating the short-term economic damages from the Prestige oil spill in the Galician fisheries and tourism*, Ecological Economics 58 (2006) 842–49). Empirical analyses of oil spill costs based on data from the International Oil Pollution Compensation Fund suggest a relationship between the sum of the total socio-economic costs and clean-up costs in relation to clean-up costs of between 1.3 and 2.5 (see Kontovas et al (2010), An empirical analysis of IOPCF oil spill cost data, *Mar.Pollut. Bull,* 2010.05.2010). Note though that in that study very high values like the one for the Braer of a ration of 87.6 were eliminated as a wild point. Also the estimate of total socio-economic costs were necessarily, due to the source of data, based on the IOPCF definition of recoverable damage and did not include any assessment of ecosystem damage not payable under the IOPCF system. See also AKY Ng and S Song, 'The environmental impacts of pollutants generated by routine shipping operations on ports' (2010) 53*Ocean & Coastal Management* 301–311, who find the cost of environmental impact costs at Rotterdam port from MARPOL pollutants is between $1.5– 2 million per year, by assuming a cost of $100 per ton of seabird and $300 per ton of fish damaged. Thus the environmental effect of the port of Rotterdam is estimated to be about 1/80th of the clean up costs of *The Erika*. Note that these are of course only part of the impact; atmospheric pollution with effects on human health and the global environment, as well as slow degradation of the marine and coastal ecosystems are not accounted for. The port statistic of the American Association of Port Authorities – http://aapa.files.cms-plus.com/ PDFs/WORLD%20PORT%20RANKINGS%202009.pdf gives sizes of ports in relation to tonnage. Using them as guidance, the tonnage of Rotterdam is about 3% of the total tonnage of the top 125 ports. Assuming the tonnage is a good indicator of the emitted pollutants (this would imply the same level of enforcement of MARPOL at all these ports, a fact which is not true as only some of the MARPOL Annexes are compulsory), the effect of these top 125 ports is 33 times that of the port of Rotterdam. Thus this rough calculation suggests that the top 125 ports cause environmental damage equal to the Erika clean up costs every two years of their operation. Note that operational discharges are not restricted to ports. The above is a rough calculation and does not purport to be accurate. It is only used to compare order of magnitudes.

[15] Fig 1.1 of the Review of Maritime Transport, 2011, UNCTAD, demonstrates that world gross domestic product and world seaborne trade have both been increasing over the past 30 years. XX Li and J Wonham, 'Who is safe and who is at risk: a study of 20-year-record on accident total loss in different flags' 1999 26(2) *Maritime Pol MGMT* 137–144 state an average rate of increase for the period 1977–96 of 1.12%, with significant interannual variations.

[16] The Review of Maritime Transport, 2011, UNCTAD, reports that for the period 2006–10 more than half of the trade occurred in developing economies, which are also those with the fastest growing populations.

[17] If there is a rapid development of alternative energy resources that can drive ships and reduce the dependency of economies to fossil fuel, this assumption may be proven wrong. Oil cargoes correspond in volume to 30–40% of the cargoes carried between 2006–10 (Review of Maritime Transport, 2011, UNCTAD, Table 1.3, note the discrepancy with Table 1.4 which gives an estimate of 21–23%). Minimising the carriage of oil would reduce international trade significantly and reduce oil pollution at the same time. However this presently appears unlikely to happen within the next 3–4 decades.

Thus the problem – which has financial, social and environmental aspects – is how to develop the maritime transport sector so that the environmental degradation[18] caused, which is coupled with the limited capacity of the oceans, will not lead to catastrophic alterations to the marine environment and the services it provides.[19] For the time being we may call this process 'sustainable development of the maritime sector', as it is based on the three aspects that characterise sustainable development in general, namely financial, social and environmental issues. However it will become evident later that sustainable development is a particularly unclear term which cannot be constrained to one financial sector.

III. THE DEVELOPMENT OF A GLOBAL STRATEGY FOR THE MARINE ENVIRONMENT

Presently the world does not hold a realistic strategic vision about the marine environment[20] humanity would like to have.[21] Many states have not even considered how to develop a marine strategy. One of the exceptions is the EU where the Marine Strategy Framework Directive[22] sets the terms of the strategic goal as follows:

> The marine environment is a precious heritage that must be protected, preserved and, where practicable, restored with the ultimate aim of maintaining biodiversity and providing diverse and dynamic oceans and seas which are clean, healthy and productive.

---

[18] Within the Synthesis report on best practices and lessons learned on the objective and themes of the United Nations Conference on Sustainable Development UN A/CONF.216/PC/8, degradation of marine ecosystems is considered as one of the new and emerging challenges. It is highly arguable that this aspect of degradation is not new at all. However it is the realisation of the extent of the problems through international research synthesis reports, eg the Millennium Ecosystem Assessment, 2005, *Ecosystems and Human Well-being: Synthesis*, Island Press, Washington, DC, that justify the categorisation as new and emerging.

[19] Avoiding the problem by pointing out the contribution of other sectors to the degradation of the marine environment is beside the point. If the marine environment becomes too polluted to use and the species and ecosystems face catastrophic extinction, it does not matter which source tipped the balance. The approach that avoids action because of sectoral or even national interests is short-sighted in the long term and catastrophic for all states if the first proposition in this work is correct. Indeed the short-term benefits may have been taken by the sector or the particular states. However it is this exact point that needs to be addressed by international law: how will the strategic needs for humanity not be undermined by the short-term benefits of some states?

[20] The fragmentation of governance between fisheries, shipping, offshore activities, land-based pollution, climate change and biodiversity losses is evidence of the non-existence of a marine strategy.

[21] One of the problems is the appropriate baseline for the natural systems. Each generation starts from a different baseline usually documented on anecdotal evidence and not scientifically well-established reference parameters. See D Pauly, 'Anecdotes and the shifting baseline syndrome of fisheries' (1995) 10 (10) *TREE* 430 and JK Pinnegar and GH Engelhard, 'The 'shifting baseline' phenomenon: a global perspective' (2008) 18 *Rev Fish Biol Fisheries* 1–16. One major point is that the top of the trophic chain, the largest fish in the coastal region, have been subject to intense harvesting even before industrial fishing has started. A second point is that the timing of such effect as well as the initiation of industrial fishing started at different periods at the various parts of the world. Such a recent effect is evident around the islands and is likely to be the result of the development of amateur spear gunning over the last 20–30 years, though it is very difficult to prove. Notably, while for fisheries there is some understanding and some accounting of past fisheries in relation to water quality and composition of coastal waters there is not much information.

[22] Directive 2008/56/EC.

In that respect, this Directive should, inter alia, promote the integration of environmental considerations into all relevant policy areas and deliver the environmental pillar of the future maritime policy for the European Union.[23]

Nicely drafted and inspirational, but it is practically useless as most of the ideas conferred are very difficult to specify.[24] Some words, such as the 'diverse and dynamic oceans and seas', are meaningless while the requirement of them being clean, healthy and productive is a matter of standards which depend partly on the selected baseline that is not specified. The significance of the Marine Strategy Directive should not be underestimated. There is a clear objective of achieving or maintaining 'good environmental status' for the marine environment by year 2020 at the latest.[25] This is left to the Member States which are under an obligation to develop their own marine strategies and deal within broadly defined regions with the two major objectives: to protect and preserve the marine environment[26] and to reduce inputs and phase out pollution.[27]

On global scale the recent Rio+20 international Conference produced a rather long and repetitive text which includes a renewed commitment for the oceans and marine pollution and which indicates that the view of the participant states is that the issue of reducing marine pollution is a matter of implementation of existing legislation, including the IMO Convention,[28] rather than rethinking or readdressing the problem.[29]

It is true that without implementing in an appropriate manner existing policy instruments and laws, one cannot properly judge whether these are efficient or need improvements. However it is also true that the difficulties in the implementation

---

[23] S 3 of the Preamble.

[24] eg, we do not know whether and when the oceans or the ecosystems can be considered clean, healthy and productive.

[25] Art1(1).

[26] And where appropriate restore it, Art 1(2)(a).

[27] Art 1(2)(b). Scientific indicators will need to be defined and developed, and these have been developed on the basis of research funding provided by the EU. Thus the steps taken are the beginning of a long route towards minimising the impact of the EU on the marine environment. It is clear though, that the development of marine strategies, indicators and actions by each Member State will lead to differential standards or to differential implementation of the same standards. There is a risk that the whole exercise may end up being the development of a 'seal' of environmentally good statuses for the marine environment, without much impact on industrial and other activities.

[28] The only area where a commitment for a new instrument is given is for Marine Biodiversity beyond the areas of national jurisdiction (see A/CONF.216/L.1 Section 162).

[29] A/CONF.216/L.1 Section 163 of the head document titled: 'The Future We Want' includes the following:
We note with concern that the health of oceans and marine biodiversity are negatively affected by marine pollution, including marine debris, especially plastic, persistent organic pollutants, heavy metals and nitrogen-based compounds, from a number of marine and land-based sources, including shipping and land run-off. We commit to take action to reduce the incidence and impacts of such pollution on marine ecosystems, including through the effective implementation of relevant conventions adopted in the framework of the International Maritime Organization (IMO), and the follow-up of the relevant initiatives such as the Global Programme of Action for the Protection of the Marine Environment from Land-based Activities, as well as the adoption of coordinated strategies to this end. We further commit to take action to, by 2025, based on collected scientific data, achieve significant reductions in marine debris to prevent harm to the coastal and marine environment.

of these instruments are not occasional or circumstantial, but reflect inherent problems of the established governance which is in need of change.[30]

IV. SUSTAINABLE DEVELOPMENT AND SHIPPING LAW

One certain element of the future marine strategy, which has been used extensively for the past 35 years, is that it should contribute to the quest for sustainable development. Characterised some times as a contradiction in terms[31] and sometimes as an article of faith,[32] sustainable development is the principle under which economic, social and environmental issues are balanced in order to provide directions for the future.[33] The Brundtland report (1987) provides the most widely accepted – for policy determination – description of sustainable development: 'Sustainable development is development that meets the needs of the present without compromising the ability of future generations to meet their own needs.'[34]

The meaning of the word development[35] as well as the word sustainable,[36] and their interaction has been and continues[37] to be debated and analysed.[38] It is part of the common parlance that sustainable development should include free

[30] eg, as will be discussed later, flag state control for ships, or the lack of it, has long been recognised as an inherent problem for the implementation of shipping legislation. It was not until the development of an alternative implementation mechanism based on port state control that implementation improved.

[31] T O'Riordan, 'Future directions in environmental policy' (1985) 17 *Journal of Environment and Planning* 107–21.

[32] MK Tolba, *'The premises for building a sustainable society'*, Address to the world Commission on Environment and Development, October 1984 (Nairobi: UNEP 1984).

[33] Or, in a more cynical approach, to avoid the conflict between economic development and environmental degradation thus ensuring consensus behind a vague notion that can be interpreted in accordance with every state's interests.

[34] World Commission on Environment and Development, Our Common Future, (New York, Oxford University Press, 1987)

[35] Development is 'a process of directed change' (see Lele (1991)). It has been taken to mean increase in GDP, social welfare, general performance of economic or social indicators. With the emergence of geo-engineering options I would suggest that the general performance of the managed environment may need to be included. Of course without knowing where we want to go, the type of development needed is bound to remain unclear and contradictory.

[36] The term originates from the notion of renewable resources. Thus reaping the annual harvest and ensuring that you will have the ability to harvest at least the same next year is the requirement of a sustainable activity. However extrapolating this to the world economic production as a harvest that needs to be available or expanding every year is an erroneous interpretation of sustainability. There are two reasons for this. First sustainability must mean conservation of the environmental qualities, as otherwise the needs of future generations may not be able to meet their needs. Secondly the objectives set out of the WCED (1987) include: reviving growth and changing its quality; meeting essential needs for jobs, food, energy water and sanitation; ensure a sustainable level of population; reorienting technology and managing risk; merging environment and economics in decision making; reorienting international economics in decision making eradicating poverty. These objectives qualify sustainability only to those possible routes that can serve these objectives.

[37] It is important that the environmental problems have originally been seen as local and have attracted efforts for local solutions, subject to national governments or at worst to regional collaborations. Thus the development of global problems needing coordinated and consistent acts by all states have radically changed the basis of international negotiations.

[38] See SM Lele, 'Sustainable Development: A critical Review' (1991) 19 (6) *World Development* 607–21 for a thorough deconstruction of the terms.

trade[39] and the increase in global wealth.[40] Over the last 25 years the discussion has moved from 'What it means?' to 'How is it to be achieved?' and recently to 'How can it be measured?'[41] Sustainable development has been used to assess the development paths of states, regions as well as particular activities.[42]

The response to sustainable development largely depends on what one understands as its meaning. The mapping of notions of sustainable development can result in classifications in three categories.[43] The first works largely within retaining the *status quo,* but by improving the developmental path towards sustainability through undertaking technical measures or through increases socioeconomic well being and equality. The second category advocates reform of society by moving to eco-centred measures and in parallel improving socio-economic well being and equality concerns. The final category advocates social transformation along the lines of eco-centred measures with transformation of socioeconomic and equality values.[44] The established institutions including the OECD, the World Bank and the EU are within the first category, while the mainstream environmental NGOs are considered to be within the second group advocating reform.

Achieving sustainable development includes tackling global problems and their regional expressions. It is not a collection of sustainable financial sectors. Nor can it

[39] Environmental degradation in poorer countries is considered to be a consequence of poverty. The poor undertake the unsustainable use of resources because of the lack of other options. Thus economic development in these countries is considered to be the way in which environmental degradation will be reduced. However it is not necessarily true that global economic growth is a prerequisite for sustainable development. First the benefits of economic growth are unevenly distributed between states and benefit less the poorer of countries. Secondly, creating wealth beyond the point of depletion of the environmental resources does not lead to a sustainable future (see HE Daly, 'Toward some operational principles of sustainable development' (1990) 2 *Ecological Economics* 1–6). Furthermore, the assertion that protectionism is a major impediment to sustainable development (WCED, 1987, p 83) is debatable. Trade encourages the development of comparative advantages and specialisation. Both lead to increased depletion of local resources, selective degradation of biodiversity by selecting particular crops over others (RB Norgaard, 'Three dilemmas of environmental accounting' 1989 1 (4) *Ecological Economics* 303–14). Finally, trade and in particular shipping includes significant environmental impacts which are normally excluded from economic analyses (D McRobert, (1988) 11 (1) *Probe Post* 24–29).

[40] It should also be noted that the term wealth can be taken to mean solely economic wealth but can also be taken to mean social and economic wealth. What this would mean does depend to a large extent on the values of each society. Note that Morgan et al (2008) below, found in their analysis that despite the acceptance of sustainable development as a policy goal, increasing affluence has undermined ecological sustainability.

[41] See DD Morgan, M Wackernagel, JA Kitzes, SH Goldfinger and A Boutaud, 'Measuring sustainable development – Nation by Nation' (2008) *Ecological Economics* 470–74, who provide such a measurement finding that out of 93 countries included in their study, only one met the two criteria on which they assessed sustainability. Their study is restricted to 2003.

[42] See eg KJ Parikh (Ed) (1988) Sustainable development in agriculture (Dordrecht, Netherlands, Martinus Nijhoff) for a sectoral example, and see E Jordan, 'The governance of sustainable development: taking stock and looking forwards' (2008) 26 *Government and Policy* 17–33. For an example of a general activity (governance).

[43] B Hopwood, M Mellor and G O'Brien, (2005) 13 *Sustainable development* 38–52. Figure 1 in this paper is very helpful in understanding the range of political and economic views within the sustainable development notions and also for separating views which cannot be considered as relevant to sustainable development, either because they do not view environmental concerns as coupled with the developmental aspects (neo-liberal economists) or because they value the environment as a separate entity and determine the path of economic development subject to ecological values (eco-facists).

[44] Ecofeminists, ecosocialists, Indigenous movements are classified under this category.

be seen as the development of a sector which is more environmental friendly than before. Thus the development of shipping as a sustainable sector is not necessarily contributing to sustainable development. This can be easily demonstrated by the fact that the degradation of the marine environment, and particularly the coastal marine environment, is caused by various human activities – some based on the use of ships, some based on the sea bed and some based on land. Making each of the sectors sustainable, in the sense of zeroing their net impact on the environmental status quo,[45] could contribute to preserving the status of the marine environment. However achieving this objective would not mean achieving sustainable development unless the socioeconomic objectives are also achieved, a matter well beyond the capability of the shipping sector or the sectors contributing to ocean pollution alone.

Even if the net effect of the shipping sector is assumed to become environmentally balanced in terms of the everyday shipping operations, extreme events, catastrophic accidents and stresses from global factors like climate change mean that establishing neutrality in operational terms in a sector would not be sufficient unless the effects of these additional issues are factored in. The occurrences of these effects are to a large extent unpredictable, they vary with time, and their effects depend on the area of the world where these will occur. Thus the sustainable development for the shipping sector cannot, of itself, be an objective of a marine policy.

Nor can ecological and environmental neutrality be a sufficient target for shipping if global sustainable development is the objective. Surely then, improvement of environmental performance by reducing the impacts is no more than the expected development for any industrial sector and does not reflect by itself any tactical movement towards sustainability.

However, positioning sustainable development as a global or national target introduces a major problem because the development of sectoral regulation cannot readily be evaluated against the notion of sustainable development. Thus because the regulation of shipping cannot be evaluated against sustainable development on its own, any shipping regulation can be argued as contributing to sustainable development, as other sectors may compensate for its impacts where in fact, the realistic expectation for increases in pollution from land based activities may indeed make the sectoral success irrelevant in sustaining the status of the marine environment.

Thus it can be argued that minimisation of the environmental impacts of shipping below the point of neutrality should be the appropriate objective of a marine policy aiming at a sustainable marine environment. However this minimisation of impacts should be based on the cumulative effects human activities have on the ocean and should take into account the high uncertainty that exists in relation to the tipping points for species and ecosystems. There is also an additional issue of timing: if the tipping points are unknown and we believe we are moving towards them, it follows that we should change our behaviour sooner rather than later.

---

[45] By this we mean that the rate of introduction of pollutants in the marine environment is within the capability of the natural systems to remove them at local, regional and global scales and at all the relevant time scales.

Thus the extent a shipping policy contributes to sustainable development can probably be assessed on a) the net impacts the policy has on the marine environment; b) on the contribution this net impact of shipping has to the total anthropogenic net impact on the marine environment; c) on the contribution of the shipping activities to poverty eradication, the development of the poorest states; d) on the preservation of the marine environmental resources for the benefit of future generations; and e) on the time frame for the actions to improve the situation.

Within the Rio+20 Conference the commitment to sustainable development has been renewed.[46] A new term has been introduced that is expected to dominate the political and financial debate. This term, arguably as vague as sustainable development itself, is the development of 'green economy'.[47] With sustainable development not yet defined in a manner useful to be applied to the shipping, financial and environmental policies the introduction of the new term, whether considered as a particular path of sustainable development or a new term which redefines sustainable development, is likely to create further confusion and exasperation in relation to the objectives that need to be fulfilled by new shipping legislation.[48] However, if it is correct that green economy comes out of the 'growing recognition that achieving sustainability rests almost entirely on getting the economy right',[49] the environmental pillar of sustainable development becomes subsumed in the search, within a global economic crisis, of getting the economy right.[50]

Despite the interesting academic and political discussion, what is arguably missing and, it is submitted, is necessary as a first step, is a way through which legal instruments under discussion, as well as their alternative versions, are evaluated before being agreed within the context of sustainable development, green economy

---

[46] A/CONF.216/L.1 s 19. In s 20 an admission of slow or no progress in some aspects of sustainable development is admitted.

[47] The notion of green economy is apparently a product of the recent financial crises. One of the contributors of the reports on the green economy, M Khor says about green economy: 'It is an extremely complex concept and it is unlikely there can be a consensus on its meaning, use and usefulness and policy implications, in the short term.' See Transition to a Green Economy: Benefits, Challenges and Risks from a Sustainable Development Perspective, UNDESA DSD, UNEP, UNCTAD by: United Nations Department of Economic and Social Affairs (UNDESA), 2011, p 69.

[48] The Australian Delegation to Rio+20 submitted a proposal for the development of Blue Economy which one takes to mean a Green Economy for the oceans. By itself this separation of Economies is not productive because as explained, sustainable development is about peoples, societies and the global environment, rather than the development of separately sustainable financial sectors or areas of activities.

[49] See JA Ocambo, 'The Transition to a Green Economy: Benefits, Challenges and Risks from a Sustainable Development Perspective' UNDESA DSD, UNEP, UNCTAD by: United Nations Department of Economic and Social Affairs (UNDESA), 2011, p 4.

[50] There are two interesting aspects in this sense. The redefinition of sustainable development comes during a crisis, which is by far a crisis of the developed states. This is surprising as the Rio+20 Report suggests that the major difficulties in achieving sustainable development have been met by developing states (s 33). It must follow that developed states have made better progress towards sustainable development. From a long-term perspective one is tempted to argue that the present economic downturn is only a crisis when looked at from the point of view of a society expecting continuous economic growth as the norm. However this is clearly not necessary for sustainable development, thus it is unclear whether the development of the requirement of 'green economy' is a reiteration of the need for sustained economic growth, albeit within some limits concerned with environmental values, and social justice.

or any other benchmark developed at the highest political levels. If assessing sustainable development is a task for states rather than international organisations, then each maritime convention, as well as the alternative versions under discussion in the IMO, can be weighted by governments against the sustainable development requirements for each category of states. Whether the agreed legal instruments will contribute towards sustainable development depends on the governance of international shipping and the way they will be implemented.

V. THE GOVERNANCE OF INTERNATIONAL SHIPPING

Shipping activities are regulated through a delicate balance between flag state and coastal state interests, and with the International Maritime Organisation[51] as the major negotiating forum[52] for environmental matters concerning the shipping industry.[53]

The struggle between flag and coastal state interests[54] within the IMO is evident not only in the governance of the organisation[55] and the requirements for entry into force of the various IMO Conventions,[56] but in the substantive aspects of

---

[51] The Convention on the Inter-Governmental Maritime Consultative Organization Adopted by the United Nations Maritime Conference in Geneva on 6 March 1948 9 U.S.T. 621, 289 UNTS 48. Art 1 of the convention mandates the IMO to:

   provide machinery for co-operation among Governments in the field of governmental regulation and practices relating to technical matters of all kinds affecting shipping engaged in international trade; to encourage and facilitate the general adoption of the highest practicable standards in matters concerning the maritime safety, efficiency of navigation and prevention and control of marine pollution from ships; and to deal with administrative and legal matters related to the purposes set out in this Article.

[52] The IMO has been argued to have law-making powers under the tacit amendment procedure (see, eg RR Churchill and G Ulfstein, 'Autonomous Institutional Arrangements in Multilateral Environmental Agreements: A Little-Noticed Phenomenon in International Law' (2000) 94 (4) *The American Journal of International Law* pp 623–59). However, it is submitted that these should be seen as very restricted powers of amendment of technical or quantitative details granted to the IMO bodies by the contracting states of the relevant convention, and subject to an undergoing negotiating process and do not lead to the creation of legislative powers to any of the IMO bodies.

[53] For the way in which the IMO operates see RP Balkin, 'The Establishment and Work of the IMO Legal Committee' in MH Nordquist and JN Moore (eds), *Current Maritime Issues and the International Maritime Organisation* (Martinus Nijhiof Publishers), pp 291–308; N Gaskell, 'Decision Making and the Legal Committee of the International Maritime Organization', (2003) 18 (2)*The International Journal of Marine and Coastal Law* 155–214; Harrison, James, *Making the law of the Sea, Cambridge Studies in International and Comparative Law* (Cambridge University Press, 2011), in particular Ch 6, pp 154–99.

[54] It is an oversimplification to distinguish between the interests of flag states against those of coastal states, as many states have both interests. It is arguably better to look at the way states compete for a share in international shipping by facilitating the needs of part of the shipping market which survive by opting for minimum regulation.

[55] See the Constitution of the Maritime Safety Committee of the Inter-Governmental Maritime Consultative Organization, Advisory Opinion of 8 June 1960: ICJ Reports 1960, p 150. For commentary see KR Simmonds, 'The Constitution of the Maritime Safety Committee of IMCO' (1963) 12 (1) *The International and Comparative Law Quarterly* 56–87 and for potentially recurring problems see Ademuni-Odeke, 'From the "Constitution of the Maritime Safety Committee" to the "Constitution of the Council": Will the IMCO Experience Repeat Itself at the IMO Nearly Fifty Years On? The Juridical Politics of an International Organization' (2007) 43 *Texas International Law Journal* 55–113.

[56] Most of the IMO conventions require for entry into force a minimum number of contracting states, which must, in addition, cover a proportion of global tonnage. In one of the latest IMO Conventions-

conventions agreed.[57] The dominance of the shipping industry can also be shown in the role of the various non-governmental organisations, of which those representing the shipping sector have been shown to be more influential in affecting the views of the decision-making state delegations than those representing environmental interests.[58]

The negotiations at the IMO are conducted on the basis of the jurisdiction rights flag states have on ships. Some of these rights are well established, some are more open to debate. It is well established that flag states are free to prescribe laws and regulations for ships registered with them and entitled to fly their flag. They have enforcement rights on their ships in all of their jurisdictional zones and in the high seas. UNCLOS restricts the freedom of flag states by imposing on them in relation to ship source pollution,[59] the IMO standards as compulsory minima, and also imposing obligations for their enforcement. Flag states[60] are under strict obligations to enforce the adopted rules for ship source pollution wherever the ship is and irrespective of where the violation takes place.[61] This obligation involves taking measures to restrict the vessel from sailing, providing immediate investigation for particular breaches, instituting proceedings and ensuring sufficiently high fines are imposed to discourage parties from breaching the law.[62]

The need for cooperation between coastal states and flag states arises from the division of jurisdiction over the oceans, which for the environmental aspects of shipping concerns the territorial sea,[63] the Exclusive Economic Zone,[64]

The Hong Kong International Convention for the Safe and Environmentally Sound Recycling of Ships, 2009 adopted at a diplomatic conference held in Hong Kong, China, from 11 to 15 May 2009 – the requirements include, in addition to 15 states covering 40% of the global tonnage, that 'to the combined maximum annual ship recycling volume of those States must, during the preceding 10 years, constitute not less than 3 per cent of their combined merchant shipping tonnage'.

[57] There is no doubt that the support for entry arrangements are there to support the actual implementation of each convention which otherwise may come into force but be inefficient. However, the ability of flag states themselves to bring IMO Conventions into force in essence indicates the very significant powers these have in deciding what laws and regulations will come into force. In essence, flag states could themselves have implemented such measures on their ships without the support of the coastal states. The negotiation process at the IMO arguably plays two roles: first it eliminates competition elements form the essential parts of shipping regulation between flag states. Secondly, the standards negotiated are probably stricter than most flag states themselves would implement. In exchange, flag states obtain a restriction of coastal state powers of legislation and enforcement in the sense that compliance with the IMO requirements is, in most cases, and certainly in Construction, Design, Equipment and Manning (CDEM) regulations, considered as sufficient to satisfy coastal state requirements and therefore restricts enforcement by the coastal state to the implementation of such agreed measures.

[58] See eg, G Peet, 'The Role of (Environmental) Non-Governmental Organisation of the Marine Environment Protection Committee (MEPC) of the International Maritime Organization (IMO), and at the London Dumping Convention (LDC)' (1994) 22 *Ocean & Coastal Management* 3–18.

[59] Art 211(3).

[60] The flag state has the right to requisition its ships wherever they are. See *The Broadmaybe* [1916] P 64; *The Arantzazu Mendi* [1939] P 37; *Lorentzen v Lydden* [1942] 2 KB 202.

[61] Art 217.

[62] Art 217.

[63] See UNCLOS Art 2. Coastal state is sovereign although foreign ships are entitled to the right of innocent passage. States may establish a territorial sea which extends up to 12 miles from the baselines

the high seas[65] as well as special areas like straits used in international navigation,[66] and archipelagic waters.[67] The freedom of navigation at the high seas where enforcement jurisdiction is solely for the flag state has been an important area of conflict which in environmental terms is likely to become more important. In essence the question is whether, on realising that the marine and in general the global atmospheric environment has limited capacity, coastal states can only avoid degradation of the marine environment by becoming able to enforce regulatory arrangements applicable to all ships sailing the oceans. Clearly an attempt by more than one state to develop such exclusive rights would lead to trade conflicts at the very least. The IMO-based instruments provide appropriate standards that are enforced and inspected

(Art 3). Within the territorial sea the coastal state has wide jurisdiction in prescribing and enforcing navigational and environmental rules but this jurisdiction is co-existent with the right of innocent passage which is granted to all ships of all states. The term passage may include two ways of travelling (Art 18). First it covers passing through the territorial sea without going to a port, internal waters or other facility of the coastal states. The second situation concern ships going to or coming from a port or other facility of the coastal state. For vessels on innocent passage destined for or coming from ports or facilities of the coastal state jurisdiction Art 25(2) provides for the prevalence and enforcement of the laws applicable of the coastal state. The passage must be continuous and expeditious (Art 18). The passage must also be innocent which is defined as not been 'prejudicial to the peace, good order or security of the Coastal State' (Art 19(1)). The same art contains an exhaustive list of activities which may make the passage non-innocent including 'wilful and serious pollution contrary to this convention' Art 19(2)(h).

[64] States are entitled to claim an EEZ up to 200 miles from their baselines (Art 57). The designation of EEZs only means extension of the coastal state's jurisdiction on specific issues and does not affect the rights of other states in all other aspects. Thus the EEZ can be viewed as a zone where the High Seas regime governs most activities but the coastal state has jurisdiction with respect to exploitation and exploration of resources and the protection of the marine environment. In the EEZ all states enjoy amongst other freedoms the freedom of navigation in the same way as in the high seas (Art 58(1)). However exercising such freedoms they shall have 'due regard to the rights and duties of the coastal State and shall comply with the laws and regulations adopted by the coastal State...'.Art 58(3). Coastal states are entitled under Art 211(5) to adopt laws and regulations for the control of pollution from vessels. However only laws and regulations giving effect to 'generally accepted international rules and standards established through the competent international organisation or general diplomatic conference' are permissible (Art 211(5)). The competent international organisation is generally accepted to mean the IMO. The enforcement rights of the coastal state in the EEZ with respect to ship source pollution are limited. Specifically if a vessel is at the EEZ or the territorial sea of a coastal state and there are clear grounds for believing that, while in the EEZ, it has violated any applicable international standards the coastal state may ask the vessel to provide information. Such information includes the ship's identity, port of registry, last and next port of call and other relevant information relevant to establishing the existence of the violation (Art 220(3)). Where there are clear grounds that substantial discharge causing or threatening significant pollution has taken place the coastal state can physically inspect the vessel if the required information is not provided or where it is evident that it is not true. Furthermore if where there is clear objective evidence that a ship has committed a violation of international standards that has resulted in a discharge which caused major damage or threat of major damage to the coastal state the coastal state can institute proceedings and detain the vessel is needed.
[65] There is limited jurisdiction by the coastal state on the high seas under both customary international law and UNCLOS. The basic regime is exclusive flag state jurisdiction (Art 94). Coastal states have no enforcement rights against foreign flagged ships, except a right to visit in the particular circumstances (Art 110) of suspected piracy, unauthorised broadcasting and slave trade or where the ship has no nationality.
[66] UNCLOS Part III.
[67] UNCLOS Part IV.

when a ship visits a port.[68] However it remains arguable that this arrangement may not be sufficient for the future. First, ships which pollute, wherever they do so *de facto,* exploit the common oceanic resource and therefore affect the interests of all coastal states and bring the marine system closer to saturation. Secondly, the principle of freedom of navigation has been based on the interests of trading states and other states in general.[69] Therefore it is arguably sanctioned as a principle of international law only to the extent that it still serves the purpose for its existence.

It has been pointed out that the notions of freedom of the high seas, including navigation as well as fishing, have been developed at times where there was no understanding of the limited capacity of the seas to accept pollution or provide resources.[70] The assumption of Grotius has been that 'they could not forbid navigation, whereby the sea loseth nothing'.[71] It is easy to demonstrate that the sea has lost species, ecosystems and had its physical characteristics altered partly due to shipping and marine pollution from shipping. Thus the underlying argument for the freedom of navigation is in the process of being removed, and sooner or later will have to lead to an alteration in the views the states collectively have with respect to marine pollution and end exclusive flag state rights. There are various ways in which such a change can be achieved. With marine pollution gradually becoming more important, introducing an exception in respect of enforcement jurisdiction in the high seas for marine pollution or suspected marine pollution would not, in the view of the author, be considered unreasonable, as its effects are equally important for the long term economic and environmental development of the oceans as the existing exceptions to piracy, slave trading and unauthorised broadcasting.[72] An alternative way for regulation would be the development of an international intergovernmental body responsible for the sustainable use of the oceans, which would prescribe the minimum environmental standards for ships

---

[68] UNCLOS Art 218 provides:

When a vessel is voluntarily within a port or at an off-shore terminal of a State, that State may undertake investigations and, where the evidence so warrants, institute proceedings in respect of any discharge from that vessel outside the internal waters, territorial sea or exclusive economic zone of that State in violation of applicable international rules and standards established through the competent international organization or general diplomatic conference.

Under customary international law the coastal state has sovereign rights over its ports and internal waters. It is on the basis of this sovereignty that it regulates access to its ports. See the ICJ decision on Military and Paramilitary Activities in and against Nicaragua (*Nicaragua v United States of America*) Judgement on the Merits, Para 213.

[69] See D Vidas, 'Responsibility for the Seas' in D Vidas (ed), *Law, Technology and Science for Oceans in Globalisation* (Leiden/Boston: Martinus Nijhoff Publishers/Brill, 2010) 1–40. The 1609 work of Grotius, Mare Liberum, was in essence a commissioned document to justify the capture and sale of a Portuguese ship by two Dutch ships. In that sense it was an assessment of the powers of the coastal state in a remote part of the ocean rather than a statement of ideological principle of freedom.

[70] See D Vidas, Responsibility for the Seas, who states:

...scientific findings and facts. Findings that clearly demonstrate why the key factual basis on which the ideology of Mare Liberum was founded can no longer retain it validity. And, just as in the time of Grotius, it is not about validity as such: it is about ultimate purpose.

[71] *Mare Liberum*, Ch 5 p 37.

[72] UNCLOS Art 111.

and which could rely on enforcement on contracting states' powers. A third way could be the carving up of the oceans so that coastal states overtake responsibility for the applicable environmental standards. This last solution is probably the least attractive, as coastal states have patently failed to protect their coastal marine environment and it is doubtful that they would perform better when extensive environmental areas are subjected to their jurisdiction.

Enforcement of stringent conditions for entry to ports in respect of environmental standards and conduct of ships during the exercise of the freedom of navigation is a fourth option which actually does not require a dramatic or revolutionary approach. It is strongly arguable that the right of coastal states to impose conditions for entry to foreign ships is very wide under customary international law. This right has in practice been restricted through the adoption of international treaties.[73] States also generally avoid exercising jurisdiction on matters internal to the ship, if these do not affect the interests of the State.[74] Clearly, on the basis of the basic assumption that the capacity of the oceans to assimilate pollution is limited, pollution incidents cannot be considered as internal to the ship.

There are already several examples where States do exercise such jurisdiction against foreign ships for the enforcement of international treaties, even where the flag State is not a signatory to the treaty.[75] This suggests that there is a right to exercise jurisdiction on ships voluntarily entering the ports of a State.[76]

---

[73] Thus there is an obligation not to discriminate under UNCLOS (see Arts 24(1)(b), 25(3), 119(3), and 227) and under International Trade law (see Art XX General Agreement on Tariffs and Trade 1994; 1867 UNTS 190; GATT 1994). See also the discussion in EJ Molenaar, 'Port State Jurisdiction: Toward Comprehensive, Mandatory and Global Coverage' (2007) 38 (1–2) *Ocean Development and International Law* 225–57(33).

[74] There is a dictum by a Judge of the International Court of Justice which suggests that State are required to 'exercise moderation and restraint as to the extent of jurisdiction assumed by its courts in cases having a foreign element, and to avoid encroachment on a jurisdiction more properly appertaining to, or more appropriately exercisable by another State'. (*Barcelona Traction Case* (1970) ICJ Rep 3, 105 (Judge Fitzmaurice)). The reference to jurisdiction in this statement is about jurisdiction on the merits, with respect to a default by a foreign company that should have been dealt with by the courts of the State where the company was established. The statement has limited value as it was in a separate judgement and the court did not discuss or decide such issues. If correct, it could probably be taken to mean in the shipping context, that an issue can be regulated by another State, the port State would be better off restricting its actions. For shipping matters, the jurisdiction of the flag State or issues concerning the ship's conduct in the ports or internal waters of another State are examples which would probably be covered by this suggested principle. However, the practice of port State control suggests that in the field of environmental protection (whether this is pollution or fisheries), the safety of navigation, employment or seamen, human rights, and health considerations indicate that exercise of the inherent powers of the coastal State are generally welcomed and considered as safeguards against deficient flag State controls to fishing.

[75] In fisheries, the rights of States to impose conditions for port entry with respect to fisheries under the 1982 UNCLOS are enhanced by the UN Fish Stock Agreement which in Art 23(1) states:
A port State has the right and the duty to take measures, in accordance with international law, to promote the effectiveness of subregional, regional and global conservation and management measures. When taking such measures a port State shall not discriminate in form or in fact against the vessels of any State.
The European Court of Justice in Case C-286/90, (*Anklagemyndigheden (Public Prosecutor) and Peter Michael Poulsen, Diva Navigation Corp.*) permitted the confiscation of 22 tons of salmon caught outside the waters of Member States on the basis of EC Regulation (EEC) No 3094/86. According to the judgement, the regulation became enforceable because of the presence of the ship in a Danish port. This was considered to be consistent with international law. CDEM standards are primarily determined

However States prefer to act under international arrangements rather than rely on such inherent powers unilaterally, probably because of the loss of competitiveness and the commercial disadvantages to the ports of the State imposing such conditions, where other nearby States are not imposing such restrictions.[77] The conclusion that the port State has powers to set conditions for entry and to enforce them does not necessarily mean that such conditions can be arbitrary and without a jurisdictional basis. Thus it may be necessary to differentiate between conditions for entry referring to the ship's conduct when these operate in internal territorial or archipelagic water, and conditions referring to the EEZ of the coastal State or the high seas.[78]

through IMO instruments. However there is residual prescriptive jurisdiction and States have exercised it. Following the Prestige incident, the Spanish government excluded all single hull tankers from Spanish ports: 24343 Royal Decree-Law 9/2002 of 13th December and the EC in response to Spanish and French pressure accelerated the phasing out of single hull tankers for the carriage of heavy oils by unilaterally developing legislation. This also led to accelerated phasing out by the IMO. Note that the EC phasing out was in force a year and a half (1/10/2003) before the IMO Resolution MEPC.111 (50) (5/4/2005). S 4115 of OPA 90 US 1990 Oil Pollution Act also had the effect of excluding double hull tankers larger than 5,000 grt before any IMO agreement was reached. The 1996 Stockholm agreement provides another example of where a group of States exercised their jurisdictional right to impose conditions for entry in relation to CDEM. Council Directive 2005/33/EC (July 2005) imposes maximum limits of sulphur content on passenger vessels operating between EU ports and when they are within EU ports, irrespective of flag. Molenaar (2007) reports a ruling of the Environmental Court of Appeal in Sweden which decides, amongst other issues, that nothing in the 1982 UNCLOS or MARPOL 73/78 prevents a port from establishing stricter – than MARPOL – non-discriminatory measures in relation to nitrogen oxide emissions.

Not all courts agree on the scope of this inherent jurisdiction: In *Sellers v Maritime Safety Inspector*, Mr Sellers, the master of a foreign pleasure craft was fined for leaving New Zealand without the radio tranceiver required by local law and without an emergency location beacon on board. The CA reversed the conviction. In their view New Zealand:

...has no general power to unilaterally impose its own requirements on foreign ships relating to their construction, their safety and other equipment and their crewing if the requirements are to have effect on the high seas. Any requirements cannot go beyond those generally accepted, especially in the maritime conventions and regulations; we were referred to no generally accepted requirements relating to the equipment particularly in issue in this case so far as pleasure craft were concerned. In addition, any such port State powers relate only to those foreign ships which are in a hazardous state.

MARPOL and SOLAS contain the 'no more favourable' treatment of ships of non-contracting States, which in essence obliges foreign ships of non-contracting States to follow the rules of the port State or face the same consequences as if they were non-compliant ships of a contracting State. The Maritime Labour Convention 2006 also contains the 'no more favourable' treatment provision under Art 5(7). Art 15 of 2001 Underwater Cultural Heritage Convention provides that 'States Parties shall take measures to prohibit the use of their territory, including their maritime ports .... in support of any activity directed at underwater cultural heritage which is not in conformity with this Convention.' The overall development of international law arguably demonstrates that such enforcement jurisdiction exists, and that IMO-based conventions utilise them through the 'no more favourable treatment' requirement, as it is unarguable that the insertion of the 'no more favourable treatment' in the IMO conventions create extended enforcement rights against non-contracting states. The difference between the *Poulsen* case and the *Sellers* case above is arguably indicative of how the various national courts chose to exercise the existing jurisdiction.

[76] What each State has to provide to all foreign personalities, companies, and arguably ships, is the protection of the national law (see Barcelona Traction Case (1970) ICJ Rep 3, Judgment para 33).

[77] EJ Molenaar, in 'Port-State Jurisdiction: Towards Mandatory and Comprehensive Use', suggests a more restrictive position by accounting five grounds under which such jurisdiction could be justified and by distinguishing between the right to restrict access from that of exercising jurisdiction. He also suggests that the type of enforcement action is also relevant.

[78] For an analysis of the jurisdictional bases that are exercised, see the Report of the Task Force on Extraterritorial Jurisdiction (International Bar Association, sa). This position is preserved to a large extent under UNCLOS. Note also that under Art 25(2) 'the coastal State also has the right to take the necessary

Thus the governance of international shipping has been dominated by three factors. First, the need for states to attract shipowning companies to their registers in order to achieve financial income from these activities. Secondly, the need for coastal state to develop trade and related activities by encouraging ships to use their facilities. Thirdly, to protect their coasts and population from the risks of shipping accidents and pollution. Shipping companies have used the competition between states to negotiate international environmental requirements and standards, without losing any freedom in relation to their ability to establish business anywhere in the world, but with some restrictions in relation to the applicable environmental and construction standards, especially those agreed through the IMO.

VI. OBSTACLES TO THE PRODUCTION SHIPPING LEGISLATION FOR SUSTAINABLE DEVELOPMENT

The IMO as a negotiating forum has been very successful in terms of the number[79] of new conventions agreed.[80] More importantly there is evidence that the adopted legislation has achieved significant improvements[81] in terms of the safety of carriage of polluting substances.[82] However there are significant implementation problems with several IMO instruments. [83] Some of these problems arise due to the reluctance[84] or inability of flag states to enforce the measures agreed, and some related to delays by coastal states in providing reception facilities for pollutants or providing appropriately trained personnel.

steps to prevent any breach of the conditions to which admission of those ships to internal waters or such a call is subject', with respect to ships proceeding under innocent passage to a port or facility.

[79] The number of Conventions and Protocols agreed at the IMO in the 1970s was 22, 8 were agreed in the 1980s, 13 in the 1990s, 13 in the period 2000–10, overall 56 binding legal instruments, is by all measures a remarkable evidence of consensus building and regulatory work.

[80] It has to be recognised that the IMO governance of shipping is not solely dependent on binding arrangements. A significant part of the negotiation process results in guidelines which are then left to the various states to implement.

[81] This may be interpreted as a justification of the processes and techniques used in the IMO. However they can also be argued simply as an indication that regulation works. In such a case the issue is whether the legal instruments negotiated at the IMO achieved the optimal improvements or not – an almost impossible question to answer in such general terms.

[82] Thus the number of oil spills as well as the total volume of oil from accidental spills from ships has been reduced for the period 1970–99. By contrast the oil spill incidents and the amounts of spillage from offshore facilities and pipeline incidents have been increasing. The top 10% of the oil spills account for 63% of the oil spilled over the period 1970–99. (P Burgherr, 'In-depth analysis of accidental oil spills from tankers in the context of global spill trends from all sources' (2007) 140 *Journal of Hazardous Materials* 245–56.)

[83] S Knapp and PH Franses, ('Does ratification matter and do major conventions improve safety and decrease pollution in shipping?' (2009) 33 *Marine Policy* 826–46) provide statistical analyses on the effects the various conventions have on shipping accidents and on marine pollution. The effect of regulation in terms of accidents cannot be statistically demonstrated and in fact, the negative effects of legislation were higher than the positive but with, in most cases (55.1%), no effect. They attribute this ineffectiveness to implementation problems. However the statistics for oil spills are very clear.

[84] P Burgherr (2007) fn 13, suggests that the reduction in oil pollution was higher in the EU and other OECD states, lesser in Flags of Convenience and there was in fact an increase in pollution incidents

There is little doubt that the work at the IMO and its subsequent implementation has led to reduction of the impact most ships have on the marine environment. There is also evidence that the collective impact of such improvements in relation to some environmental impacts have led to reduction of pollution from ships.[85] However it is impossible to find evidence that the development of the shipping sector as a whole has a neutral environmental effect, in other words it can be considered as sustainable on a strict sectoral approach, or that it contributes to sustainable development in the broader sense.[86]

It can be argued that the legal work at the IMO reflects sustainable financial development for the sector, if this is defined as maximisation of financial activity for the shipping sector, while negotiating environmental standards to their minimum possible. In other words, it can be argued that the IMO legal work is only performed to avoid reaction from other sectors or parts of the society. Before providing particular examples of proposed legal instruments developed at the IMO that support the previous assertions, we discuss the reasons why the IMO operates in the present way.

The primarily industrial character of the IMO can partly be attributed to its historical development.[87] Although established in 1948, it was only in 1984 when the IMO formally acquired a mandate[88] that included the impact of shipping on the marine environment.[89] During this period of time, significant changes in the perception of the interaction between financial activities and environmental concerns have taken place. The Declaration of the United Nations Conference on the Human Environment[90] was a significant milestone linking environmental concerns with financial activity. Its dominant perception, as evident in the preamble,

and oil spill volumes from ships flying the flags of other non-OECD states. However it appears that significant variations between the various flag of convenience states are to be expected as the oldest of them improve their regulatory records, thus pushing old and bad ships as well as unscrupulous owners to newly formed registers (see T Alderson and N Winchester, 'Globalisation and de-regulation in the maritime industry' (2002) 26 *Marine Policy* 35–43 who perceive the difference between the new and old FOC registers in 'this explicit resentment of the possibility of regulation' p 42).

[85] eg oil pollution from accidents.
[86] Shipping is claimed to presently be the least polluting way and most economic way of carrying goods around the world. However this is not, by itself, a contribution to sustainability.
[87] The IMCO was originally established following a Resolution (28 March 1947) of the UN Maritime Conference convened by the Economic and Social Council of the United Nations. The Resolution refers to the possibility of including the removal or prevention of unfair restrictive practices by shipping concerns and to issues on safety of life at sea, but not to the marine environment. Not surprisingly then the Convention on the Intergovernmental Maritime Consultative Organization (IMCO), Geneva, (6 March 1948) does not mention the marine environment either under Art I(a).
[88] Resolution A.400 (X) of 17 November 1977 replaced the original Art I(a) with the following text:
To provide machinery for co-operation among Governments in the field of governmental regulation and practices relating to technical matters of all kinds affecting shipping engaged in international trade; to encourage and facilitate the general adoption of the highest practicable standards in matters concerning maritime safety, efficiency of navigation and prevention and control of marine pollution from ships; and to deal with administrative and legal matters related to the purposes set out in this Art;.
The amendments came into force on 10 November 1984.
[89] The International Convention for the Prevention of Pollution of the Sea by Oil, 1954 was agreed earlier.
[90] Stockholm, 16 June 1972.

is one where economic development and environmental quality are linked. The source of the dilemma between economic development and environmental preservation is considered there to be different between developed and developing countries. For developing countries under-development is seen to be the source of most environmental problems, while for the developed countries it is the way industrialisation has progressed that poses the conflict.[91] Thus since the very early days in the negotiations for the development of commonly accepted environmental principles, a distinction has been drawn between developing and developed states. This distinction is only partly true in shipping. It is for example self-evident that states that trade in large quantities of goods face higher risks of shipping incidents. It is also true that for developing states, an oil pollution incident from a shipping accident, even if extensive, is unlikely to overshadow environmental problems relating to water provision or the general population health. This differentiation in the source of the environmental problems admittedly requires differentiation in the response to the problem. And where an international response is orchestrated, it would logically follow, first, that an agreement can only be achieved if the different stages of financial development are taken into account, and secondly that the response agreed tackles the source of the problems which differs between states. Thus in general, the common but differentiated responsibility of states in relation to environmental problems can, in a very general sense, be argued as a logical consequence of the distinction in their particular needs and problems at a particular point in time.[92] Thus the common but differentiated responsibility is strongly established as part of the primary objective of the sustainable development.

Common but differentiated responsibility does not appear consistent with the major legal shipping instruments, as these have been established through negotiations at the IMO. One, for example, could argue that common but differentiated responsibility means that developing states (or their ships) should be permitted to operate at lower environmental standards, if their performance is linked to the provision of wealth to the developing state, thus reducing poverty and enabling the particular state to deal with it more pressing internal environmental

---

[91] In the preamble it is stated: 'In the developing countries most of the environmental problems are caused by under-development' while 'in the industrialized countries, environmental problems are generally related to industrialization and technological development'.

[92] It can also be argued on the basis of the aggregate character of pollution which historically has been caused by developed states. This argument has been used especially in relation to pollutants which have long life spans in the environment. See, eg, Montreal and UNFCCC. This argument is however, in the view of this author, wrong on several grounds. If correct, it would imply that the citizens of a state have responsibility for the actions (or at least the environment related actions) of the previous generation(s). But state practice points against such a principle. On purely moral grounds, the actions of a state must be judged in accordance with the principles prevailing at the time the actions were taken, and not on the basis of retrospective actions. The ancient governance system of Athens was a democracy in relation to the equivalent systems at the time, but could never be considered as democratic nowadays, as the financial production was based on slavery. Finally on the personal level, it can be argued by each human being that their rights cannot be prejudiced in relation to the rights of people of the same generation because of the actions of their predecessors. Furthermore, the allocation of rights to the use of natural resources (or the right to exploit them) cannot be considered as granted to states that cover a period of time. No state has the right to appropriate any part of the common resources and every state is under a duty not to harm neighbouring states on the basis of activities taking place in their territory.

problems.[93] Is it then appropriate that ships of developing states involved in international trade operate with reduced environmental standards? Several objections can be raised against such a suggestion. First, the limited capacity for the oceans restricts any approach which will increase the concentration of pollutants over the amount the oceanic systems can remove.[94] A second objection is that the development of wealth by international trade is not necessarily restricted to the importing or the exporting state, but also to the state involved in the transfer of goods, the states and institutions that provide the financing and even to the states that dominate the dispute resolution process. Thus it cannot be said that making the operation of ships of a developing state cheaper would promote the economic development of any particular developing state or indeed the flag state. On the contrary, it can be argued that as the capital for shipping comes primarily from developed states, the most significant benefits will be received by developed states.

Of course, the reason the IMO-based instruments demonstrate a non-discriminatory approach between flag states is not concerned with any of the previous two arguments, but is based on the belief that non-discriminatory trade policies are an essential element of the global market.[95] The non-discrimination between flag states has thus been an established norm in shipping laws.[96] The relationship between the flag state and the shipowner is an issue that has been hotly contested during the past three decades and is likely to continue been contested as one of the sources of inefficient shipping legislation. In my view this is an issue which disorientates the discussion on sustainability. This view is supported by a number of observations.

[93] This is implicitly recognised under all IMO conventions which normally exclude from their ambit ships constraint within national waters, thus permitting different standards to be imposed nationally on such ships. The application of IMO conventions are uniform in relation to ships employed in international shipping.

[94] eg, this could be achieved if the pollution from ships of developed states was reduced so as to compensate for the excess pollution of developing states' ships. Note that the limited capacity of the oceans to hold pollutants can be also used as an argument against the exception of ships employed within national limits.

[95] This can be seen expressed in general terms in Art I of the General Agreement on Tariffs and Trade which came into force on 1 January 1948. Its present extent and continuing support can be seen in the eighth of the United Nations Millennium Goals which states: 'Develop further an open, rule-based, predictable, non-discriminatory trading and financial system' (target 8a), and in the proposal of the World Trade Organisation for the 2012 United Nations Conference on Sustainable Development where at in publication 'Harnessing trade for sustainable development and a green economy' a proposed affirmation to a commitment of the states to 'promote an open and equitable rules-based multilateral trading system that is non-discriminatory' is suggested (at p 2). Within this context shipping is considered within the category of 'Services' which include 'transport, finance, telecoms and law'.

[96] The non-discriminatory policy principles have led to the inclusion of an obligation for 'no more favourable treatment' in international shipping legislation. As a result ships flying the flag of non-contracting states to a specific shipping convention become subject to enforcement measures for environmental protection arrangements agreed under international conventions as if the flag state has agreed to these because otherwise their treatment would have been 'more favourable' than that of the ships of contracting states. Thus the choice of contracting states to impose measures on their ships is changes to an obligation to impose the same measures to all ships. While there is no doubt to the author that such jurisdiction exists, if such restrictions are considered conditions for entry, the effect is to impose on foreign ships measures not agreed by the flag state whose jurisdiction is claimed at the same time to be predominant.

VII. WHO IS NEGOTIATING AT THE IMO? THE GENUINE LINK ISSUE

Ships have been trading before the development of the nation-state and the associated symbol of flag. In the past the flag of the ship entitled the ship to protection by the flag state[97] and for some periods of time was used as a barrier to foreign traders.[98] The present arrangements under international law are based, on one hand on the powers a state has to determine who can fly the flag on a ship and, on the other hand on the freedom of the shipowner to move his capital and thus chose the state in which the ship can be registered at.[99] Thus states can select the ships that can fly their flag,[100] but at the same time by raising the operational standards may be losing out[101] on taxation and other related revenue.[102] In the

[97] Flags and symbols of origin have been used since antiquity. However the link between the flag and the state and the link with ship registration is much more recent and came about the early 17th century. See JHK Mansell, 'An analysis of flag state responsibility from an historical perspective: delegation or derogation' (2007), PhD Thesis, University of Wollongong, New Zealand, http://ro.uow.edu.au/theses/742.

[98] JHK Mansell, *ibid* at p 33 traces laws to that effect back to 1381.

[99] JHK Mansell, *ibid* points out at p 28 that the term flag state also describes entities which are not states under international law and still operate registers. Dependent territories, The Red Ensign Group, and Taiwan are some examples.

[100] *The Muscat Dhows* Case (France and Great Britain), Award of the Tribunal, 8 August 1905, Scott, Hague Court Reports 95 (1916); *The Virginius*, 2 Moore, Digest of International Law, 895 (1906) and the *Schooner Exchange v Mcfaddon* 11 US (7 Cranch) 116 (1812). See also *The I'm Alone* (1933), 29 AJIL 326 (1935) and *Furness, Withy & Co. v RederiaktiegolabetBanco* [1917] 2 KB 873.

[101] The general assumption that multinational companies move to countries with lower environmental standards has been significantly challenged on the basis of statistical evidence (see GS Eskerland and AE Harrison, 'Moving to greener pastures? Multinationals and the pollution haven hypothesis' (2003) 70 *Journal of Development Economics* 1–23. Understanding the behaviour of land based companies is complex and depends on several factors. Thus, labour costs, intangible assets like managerial abilities technology, business relations as well as whether the cost of environmental abatement decreases with increasing volume of production all play a role in determining whether relocation is appropriate or not. Thus while pollution abatement costs were found to be significantly correlated when compared with foreign investment, the corresponding increase was very small (about 0.5% for a doubling of the abatement costs). In addition, it became smaller and insignificant when additional parameters were added to the statistical model. Despite the challenge on the conventional wisdom about the behaviour of multinational companies, shipping companies must have a different behaviour. First they are not subject to the various restrictions described above. Shipping companies can register at a particular state and conduct their business from another state – thus the intangible assets issue is not coupled with the flag. The labour issue is coupled with that of the flag as several flag states require a minimum number of seafarers to be nationals of the flag states. This necessarily leads to the selection of flags that do not impose such restrictions. The cost of relocation is very small thus the financial, administrative and environmental issues are those that determine the choice of flag for the shipowner. In this context it is surprising that the flag state obligations are not equally restricted, eg the protection of its ships is an obligation for the flag state. This is only common sense as the flag state collects the taxation from the ship. Thus the navies of the open registers should provide protection for ships against eg pirates. Why other states with powerful navies but not a large commercial fleet get involved with protecting foreign flagged ships at areas at risk, thus imposing costs on their tax payers, is not very clear. One explanation could be that the fear of the economic consequences of disruption of trade leads them to prioritise the security of maritime routes as the lesser evil.

[102] This is a major difference between investing in a land based company and in a shipping company. In the first case not only does the company have to comply with the operational requirements of that state, but the decision to move to another state, if the laws of the original state become unfavourable, will also involve significant costs. Such changes are by contrast quick and cheap in the shipping sector. In essence a shipowner can keep his capital moving between states by changing his flag, thus continuously

end,[103] in an open financial market where the capital cannot be constrained within national boundaries, it is self-evident that shipowners will seek to minimise their costs by re-flagging to the most advantageous register.[104]

To the extent that the shipowners' practice did not directly affect the interests of other states, it remained at state level unopposed, and formed a principle of customary international law.[105] UNCLOS has confirmed that the nationality of the ship is that of the flag state, and that the flag state determines the conditions for permitting vessels to fly its flag.[106] The expectation then is that the flag state will exercise its effective control over its ships in all necessary respects, including their environmental conduct. In practice, the willingness and the capability of some states to deliver efficient control over their ships is lacking behind that of other states. In some cases the state's right to determine the conditions for registration of ships has been enforced by tax benefits and lax legislation regarding crewing, safety and pollution standards.[107] Thus the two issues, a claimed disinterest for safety for flags of convenience[108] and competition between flag states, have been

minimising his operational obligations. States can only compete by making the economic environment more favourable to the shipowner – an aspect which can be seen as a recipe for a race to the bottom. International agreements, to an extent, serve the purpose of establishing the 'bottom', the minimum standards. However the way shipping companies have been operating by choosing the optimum financial environment is clearly in line with the concept of globalisation. This is nicely demonstrated by JR Barton, 'Flags of Convenience: Geoeconomics and regulatory Minimisation' (1999) 90(2) *Tijdschrift von Economische en Sociale Geographie* 142–55.

[103] Whether other states are bound to recognise the granting of nationality to a ship started being contested in *The Nottebohm Case* (*Liechtenstein v Guatemala*) International Court of Justice April 6, 1955, ICJ 4, where the ICJ held that the granting of Liechtenstein nationality to a German national living in Guatemala did not oblige Guatemala to recognise the nationality where there was no real prior connection with Liechtenstein. If the ICJ's position is considered equally applicable to ships then the international arrangements for ship registration is undermined. However, most ships operating in international trade do not have permanent and close links with any territory. Their owners or managers or crew members may have, but the ships as such are unlikely to be within the territory of the flag state for long, whether the flag state is a flag of convenience or an open register. Thus the application of the test to ships is probably inappropriate. Of course the major question is whether the right to question the nationality of the ship and disregard it exists. State practice suggests that even if it were to exist it is one that is not normally exercised.

[104] JR Barton, attributes the following characteristics to a flag of convenience: It allows foreign nationals to own or control ships under its flag; provides easy registration and deregistration procedures; minimal or no taxation for profits; fees for registration and tonnage are minimal; foreign crews can be used; legislation for controlling shipping companies is minimal or non-existent; the ships cannot be requisitioned. (JR Barton, 'Flags of Convenience; Geoeconomics and regulatory Minimisation' (1999) 90(2) *Tijdschrift von Economische en Sociale Geographie* 142–55

[105] See MS McDougal, WT Burke and IA Vlacic, 'The maintenance of public order at Sea and the Nationality of Ships' (1960) *Yale Law School, Faculty Scholarship Series* Paper 2610.

[106] 1982 UNCLOS Art 91.

[107] See eg RM M'Gonigle and MW Zacher, *Pollution, Politics and International Law* (University of California Press, 1979) where the performance of tankers registered at flags of convenience is discussed. Also note that the growth of the global fleet is not uniformly distributed across the countries but has favoured open registries and recently, new maritime nations (KX Li and J Wonham, 'Who is safe and who is at risk: a study of 20-year-record on accident total loss in different flags' (1999) 26, *Maritime Policy & Management* 137–44). The issue is of course more complicated. The history of open registers goes back to probably the early 1920s.

[108] This appears to be difficult to prove conclusively and depends on the statistics used, the period concerned and the underlying assumption which reflect in the grouping of the various states. The

confused and argued together. The financial issues arising from the re-flagging of ships to open registers have led to the development of the requirement of a genuine link, which has found its way to UNCLOS and requires that 'there must exist a genuine link between the State and the ship.'[109] The rationale for the 'genuine link' requirement can be supported on the basis of judicial statements,[110]

> A merchant fleet is not an artificial creation. It is a reality which corresponds to certain indispensable requirements of a national economy. As an aspect of the economic activity of a country, it governs the amount of the normal movement of its international trade. It cannot be used for other purposes, save only when a great development of commercial activity leads a country – as in the case of nations which are ultra-developed economically – to use its fleet industrially for the provision of services. The flag-that supreme emblem of sovereignty which international law authorizes ships to fly-must represent a country's degree of economic independence, not the interests of third parties or companies. This is a consequence of the very structure of world economy, of which merchant shipping, is one of the principal supports.

From the standpoint of investment of national capital the above statement was probably arguable at the time it was made. However since then, the world has moved towards globalisation of economy. Capital cannot be claimed to be linked

argument has been made that some open registers have better records than many traditional maritime countries and could not find differences on the averages rates of loss (eg the studies of KX Li and J Wonham, 'Who is safe and who is at risk: a study of 20-year-record on accident total loss in different flags' (1999) 26, *Maritime Policy & Management* 137–144). However T Alderton and N Winchester, 'Flag states and safety: 1997–1999' (20020 29 (2) *Maritime Policy & Management* 151–62) find that both older and newer open registers have more than twice the casualty rates of national registers. At the same time it is true that in all published classifications there are open registers that perform much better than some flag states. In a more comprehensive and statistically more complete study, S Knapp and PH Franses, 'Econometric analysis on the effect of port state control inspections on the probability of casualty. Can targeting of substandard ships for inspections be improved?' (2007) 31 *Marine Policy* 550–63 find that the open registers do worse in respect of very serious accidents but perform equally well to other flags in respect of serious and less serious accidents. The important point is that the division of states as open registers and national registers is to this extent misleading. However, it is probably still a good reflection of the grouping for negotiations at the IMO with the open registers, old and new resisting new regulation against national registers.

[109] *Ibid.* The issue was first raised in relation to seafarers' rights by the International transport Worker's Federation (see McDougal et al, 1960, above). Note that the wording of Art 5 of the 1958 Convention of the High Seas stated: '*There must exist a genuine link between the State and the ship; in particular, the State must effectively exercise its jurisdiction and control in administrative, technical and social matters over ships flying its flag*'. Thus the genuine link requirement was expressed in terms which turned on the phrase 'must effectively exercise' and could be seen as a dual test (see McDougal et al 1960, above). These requirements have in UNCLOS been separated and appear as a requirement for a genuine link (Art 91) and as obligations of the flag state (Art 94). Thus, under UNCLOS the genuine link requirement is not connected, in my view, to the way the flag state exercises it control. However the difference is marginal. Even under Art 5 of the 1958 Convention it would have been extremely difficult to argue that the lack of effective jurisdiction deprives the ship of the genuine link, simply because no flag state can seriously claim a continuous exercise of jurisdiction and control on ships, and then the matter turns on how often, in what way and against what standards jurisdiction and control are destined to be judged against.

[110] ICJ, Advisory opinion, 8 June, 1960, Constitution of the Maritime Safety Committee of the Inter-Governmental Maritime Consultative Organization, Dissenting Opinion of Lucio M Moreno Quintana, p 4. Note that because the majority's decision accepts the use of registered tonnage to determine the largest shipping nations, the issue of genuine link, which then appeared in Art 5 of the 1958 Geneva Convention, was raised but considered irrelevant to the issue in question.

with one particular state, whether in shipping or elsewhere. Furthermore with many shipping companies entering the international stock markets, trying to identify a national link to a particular shipping company cannot go much further than identifying the country where the company is registered or the place where decisions are made from, thus obscuring the requirement for a link with the owner to a link with the manager or operator of the company.

The 'genuine link' requirement was heavily criticised well before it was included in UNCLOS. McDougal et al (1960) have distinguished two major groups of principles in international law of the sea. In essence the first group concerns the overriding principle of the widest possible access to the shared used of the oceans. The second subsidiary group of principles concerns the most economically efficient ways of ensuring the implementation of the first group. These would include issues about international competition between flag states, worker's rights etc. Within this framework McDougal et al (1960) consider the attempt to establish a genuine link as aiming in resolving difficulties in the second set of issues which, however, will have the effect of altering the well balanced and long established first group of principles. The argument was that the market can sort itself out and that an interference with the market by introducing the genuine link requirement will be economically damaging. Thus they stated that 'Any unnecessary interference with the traditional freedoms of access and shared competence can be expected only to reduce the total amount of values created for sharing among all participants in the exploitation of the oceans.'[111]

In essence the claim is that if every state is entitled to assess the genuine link requirement and thus dispute the entitlement of the flag state to exercise jurisdiction, then such vessels will be considered arbitrarily stateless, the right to innocent passage may be denied for such ships and would lead to discrimination in international trade. The critical analysis of McDougal et al is exemplary and detailed. However, since it was written, environmental concerns and values have increased significantly. The danger of bringing the environment to pollution concentrations that may cause significant alterations and the vulnerability of ecosystems to multiple stresses were not predominant parameters in their analysis. Pollution control was in fact referred to in their work but only very briefly and only as part of the type of measures ensuring the most economic implementation of the primary right of share in the use and exploitation of the oceans. Arguably if pollution and environmental degradation from ships affects the central right of the McDougal et al analysis, that is, the possibility of having shared resources, in the oceans, then arguably the conclusion of their analysis must be different. Thus, although the Mc Dougal et al analysis is preferable to the view of the Judge Moreno Quintana above, neither of them is, it is submitted, an appropriate reflection of the present situation. [112]

---

[111] McDougal et al, *supra* at page 36.

[112] Of course it must be recognised that environmental regulations also affect the second set of principles of McDougal et al's classification and are partly concerned about optimisation of financial benefits, as well as competitiveness issues as they affect the cost of transport.

Notably UNCLOS does not specify when a link is to be considered genuine, nor does it expressly determine who has the authority and the task to determine the existence of a genuine link.[113] However, to my knowledge, there has not been any case where a state enforced rights on the basis of the absence of a genuine link between a ship and the claimed flag state. Thus it can be argued that either the genuine link requirement is in practice considered demonstrated by the fact of registration, or that the requirement altogether as a matter of state practice is of no further relevance to environmental concerns of international law.[114] In my view the requirement of a genuine link is not a useful or appropriate target for the development of a marine policy for sustainable development.[115]

VIII. ENVIRONMENTAL PROTECTION AND SUSTAINABLE DEVELOPMENT IN RECENT IMO INSTRUMENTS

In order to characterise the legal work undertaken at the IMO, two important aspects of its recent work are considered as examples and compared with legal developments dealing with broader issues and are not restricted to a specific sector.

A. Scrapping of Ships[116]

Ship-breaking, an integral part of the shipping industry, is a profitable activity concentrated in developing states[117] which raise issues of health and safety of the

---

[113] The UN Convention on Registration of Ships, Geneva, 7 Feb 1986 does deal with the way the genuine link should be established. However, it requires 40 signatures covering 25% of the world's gross tonnage. It only has 14.

[114] See also the discussion by PS Dempsey and LL Helling, 'Oil Pollution by Ocean Vessels – An Environmental Tragedy: The Legal Regime of Flags of Convenience, Multilateral Conventions, and Coastal States' (1981) 10 *Denver Journal of International Law & Policy* 37.

[115] Only if the term 'genuine' is taken to mean something not fraudulent might it have a meaning. Thus if a ship has fraudulent documents suggesting it is registered at the flag state, then it may be considered stateless, as a fraudulent link claimed on documentation cannot be considered as having any validity. However if fraud is used in obtaining genuine documents from the flag state, then it is arguable that the nationality of the state must be recognised and the flag state should deal with the issue of fraud under its laws. Of course on notional grounds, having a genuine link established between all flag states and their ships on the grounds advocated by Judge Moreno Quintana would have made the delineation of state interests much easier to deal with. However this is not a problem specifically restricted to shipping. All sectors involved with international transactions have the same issues and these arise primarily through international trade arrangements, not by the special rule for flag state jurisdiction over ships.

[116] See also D Wall and MN Tsimplis, 'Selling ships for scrap' (2003) 1 *LMCLQ* 254-264; MN Tsimplis, 'The Hong Kong Convention on the Recycling of Ships' (2010) *LMCLQ* 305.

[117] The ship-breaking industry is presently located in developing states. India, Bangladesh, Pakistan, China and Turkey are some of the most important ship-breaking countries. The existence of ship-breaking operations is essential for the livelihoods of thousands of families from the most deprived parts of these countries. See eg the report by Prasanna Srinivasan 'The Basel Convention of 1989 – A developing country's perspective' available from: http://www.libertyindia.org/pdfs/basel_convention_srinivasan.pdf.

workers,[118] environmental protection[119] as well as financial issues.[120]

The export of hazardous wastes is regulated by the 1989 Basel Convention on the Control of the Transboundary Movements of Hazardous Wastes and Their Disposal, (Basel Convention).[121] The Basel Convention applies to all international carriage of hazardous wastes whether by land, air or sea, but not to national carriage. The 1989 Basel Convention applies to hazardous wastes[122] which are subject to transboundary movement,[123] (hereinafter 'transport'). Such wastes are hazardous if they fall within the rather involved Convention definition,[124] or if they are deemed hazardous under the domestic legislation of a party to the Convention that is involved in the transport of the waste.

Parties to the Basel Convention are under a general obligation to minimise the generation of hazardous wastes[125] and to ensure that there are adequate disposal facilities within the generating State.[126]

States Party to the Basel Convention can only transport hazardous wastes to other States party to the Convention, whilst transport from and to non-party States is precluded.[127]

---

[118] Environmental NGOs have suggested that 16% of all shipyard workers employed in ship-breaking in India suffer from asbestosis. Many of the yards employ children as workers. The International Labour Organisation (ILO) has been involved in the process of the development of the new Convention and will continue its collaboration in developing detailed guidelines for the adoption of safe procedures in the dismantling of ships. See the news release: 'ILO welcomes new regulations on ship breaking as crisis boosts the industry available from': http://www.ilo.org/global/about-the-ilo/press-and-media-centre/insight/WCMS_106542/lang--en/index.htm.

[119] The scrapping procedure may releases substances to the atmosphere, to the ground and to marine environment. The applicability of the various regulatory and liability regimes normally applicable to ships could be an issue for ships and structures destined for recycling. Thus issues related to the management of the ballast water can be important (see the MEPC 44/16 submission by Friends of the Earth International in 1999), however it is unclear whether the 2004 International Convention for the Control and Management of Ships' Ballast Water and Sediments (not yet in force) will be applicable in all cases where the ship is destined for recycling.

[120] Recycling is presently profitable for shipowners and this is an incentive to ensure that their ship reaches the recycling destination. However, if recycling stops being profitable the ship may be abandoned in a port or scuttled. See IMO LC 27/14, where the issue is described as an important problem for developing states without the appropriate resources to deal with it. The Legal Committee considers it as a matter for the port state to resolve with the flag state and the shipowner where abandonment takes place. Arguably this is not a realistic prospect in many situations. However the issue of abandonment is not dealt with under the SRC.

[121] The Convention has 175 parties and entered into force in 5 May 1992. The UK ratified the Basel Convention in February 1994. In the UK any export of hazardous wastes to a non-OECD country is completely banned, by virtue of the EU adoption of the 1995 amendment to the Basel Convention: The Ban Amendment to the Basel Convention on the Control of Transboundary Movements of Hazardous Wastes and their Disposal, Geneva, 22 September 1995. The Ban Amendment must be ratified by three-fourths of the Parties who accepted it in order to enter into force. At the moment 69 States have ratified the Protocol.

[122] Art 2.1 of the Basel Convention defines '*wastes*' as '*substances or objects which are disposed of or are intended to be disposed of or are required to be disposed of by the provisions of national law*'.

[123] Art 2.3 of the Basel Convention defines '*transboundary movement*' as,
any movement of hazardous wastes or other wastes from an area under the national jurisdiction of one State to or through an area under the national jurisdiction of another State or to or through an area not under the national jurisdiction of any State, provided at least two States are involved in the movement.

[124] Under Art 1.1(a) of the Basel Convention hazardous wastes are those listed in Annex I of the Convention, unless they are devoid of the characteristics that are contained in Annex III.

[125] *Ibid,* Art 4.2(a), '*taking into account social, technological and economic aspects*'.

[126] *Ibid,* Art 4.2(b).

[127] Basel Convention 1989, Art 4.5.

The majority of ships that are at the end of their lives contain hazardous chemical constituents within their structural make-up, if not in their cargo residues.[128] Thus the procedure applicable for all hazardous wastes and the restrictions in exports are also applicable to ships destined for recycling.[129] The Basel Convention prohibits the exportation of hazardous wastes if a State of export believes that the wastes will not be managed in an environmentally sound manner.[130] Shipbreaking operations in non-OECD countries, such as India, Pakistan and Bangladesh, do not always constitute environmentally sound management as defined in the Convention.[131] Consequently, transboundary movement of ships destined for shipbreaking may be prohibited under the Basel Convention and the 1995 Basel Convention Ban Amendment which completely prohibits exports of hazardous wastes for final disposal and recycling from OECD countries to non-OECD countries.

The Conference of the Parties to the Basel Convention has passed the problem to the IMO. The Hong Kong International Convention for the Safe and Environmentally Sound Recycling of Ships, 2009 (SRC),[132] a legal instrument agreed at the IMO, attempts to provide a solution to several of the problems raised. It does so, not by only adopting general principles of law but by devising a system of control and standards through the ship construction and the ship recycling industry.

The SRC accepts that recycling is the best option for decommissioned ships. However the way the SRC arranges for the recycling of ships including hazardous materials onboard ships is only partly consistent with the Basel Convention.

First the SRC applies only to ships larger than 500 grt which are registered to a contracting state.[133] Secondly, ships operating only within waters under the sovereignty and jurisdiction of the flag State are excluded from the application of the SRC. Thirdly, military ships and any governmental ship of a contracting state employed in non-commercial service[134] are also excluded from the SRC. The recycling of ships is regulated under the SRC through the International Inventory of Hazardous Materials Certificate ('IHM'), a key certificate for the operation of

---

[128] A ship can certainly be classed as an '*object*' under Art 2(1) of the Basel Convention, and the further definition of '*disposal*' encompasses those operations which lead to recovery/recycling. Bearing in mind that scrapping of vessels is generally undertaken to recover material, eg scrap steel for steel mills and also fuel oils and machinery components, ships destined for shipbreaking will typically contain several of the materials listed in Annex I as hazardous wastes. In addition to this there are a host of other specific wastes contained in ships destined for shipbreaking, which are listed in Annex VIII of the Basel Convention. Under the above arguments ships are considered as falling under the Basel Convention's scope. However, the literal reading of the Convention indicates that ships were not considered when the Convention was agreed and they fall uneasily within the scope of the Basel Convention (MN Tsimplis, 'Liability and Compensation in international transport of hazardous wastes by sea: The 1999 Protocol to the Basel Convention' (2001) 16 (2) *International Journal of Coastal and Marine Law* 295–347).

[129] State-owned ships and war ships are not excluded from the scope of the 1989 Basel Convention.

[130] *Ibid*, Art 4(2)(e). Environmentally sound management is defined as meaning: 'taking all practicable steps to ensure that hazardous wastes or other wastes are managed in a manner which will protect human health and the environment against the adverse effects which may result from such wastes.' *ibid*, Art 2(8). There is a reciprocal obligation upon the State of import as well. Art 4(2)(g).

[131] See, eg, the various articles published by Greenpeace: http://www.greenpeace.org/international/en/publications/.

[132] SR/CONF/45, 19 May 2009. The SRC was agreed on 15 May 2009.

[133] Or operating under the contracting state's authority Art 3(1).

[134] Art 3(2).

the SRC. Existing ships are under an obligation to comply with the requirement to have onboard an inventory of hazardous materials at the latest five years after the entry of the SRC into force[135] or before recycling, if this less than five years from the entry into force of the SRC.[136] However the International Certificate (IHM) for an existing ship, defined as being a ship other than a new ship,[137] is to be produced before recycling as the initial and final survey are to be conducted at the same time.[138] Ships registered in non-contracting states cannot be issued with IHM certificates.[139] The SRC requires that with respect to ships flying the flag of states that are not contracting states to the Convention, the contracting states should ensure that '… no more favourable treatment is given to such ships.'[140] How this will be achieved is not clear and guidelines will be developed.[141]

The SRC avoids the solution adopted by the 1989 Basel Convention, where it is up to the exporting state to decide whether environmentally sound recycling can be achieved at the state of import. Instead it requires the development of recycling facilities in contracting states which can ensure appropriate environmental standards. The SRC is also incompatible with the 1995 Basel Amendment (Ban), through which no hazardous wastes are to be exported in developing countries. The SRC preserves the status quo by improving the conditions under which recycling takes place. Under the SRC, recycling is permitted only at authorised,[142] ship recycling facilities[143] which, in addition, are authorised to perform all the necessary recycling actions the ship recycling plan provides for.[144]

Whether the SRC will succeed in ensuring the environmentally sound recycling of most ships in existence is questionable. Significant ambit is given to each recycling state to establish its own requirements for recycling, and what effects these will have in practice is unknown. Furthermore there is no control of flag-changing to non-contracting states thus avoiding the legal requirements of the SRC.

It can be argued that arranging for an improvement of the present recycling conditions can only be beneficial. It can further be argued that shipping has developed a realistic and practical approach to the problem posed by the recycling of hazardous materials of ships, and that this will be achieved without compromising the financial benefits for the developing states from the recycling

---

[135] The five-year period applies only if it is not practicable to have the IHM inventory onboard earlier.
[136] Reg 5.2
[137] Reg 10.3
[138] Reg 11
[139] Reg 12.4
[140] Art 3(4).
[141] See MEPC 59/3/4.
[142] The final survey provides for compliance with the IHM, that the Ship Recycling Plan appropriately reflects the IHM information as well as the requirement for safe-for-entry and safe-for-hot work requirements, and that the Ship Recycling facilities hold valid authorisation under the SRC (Reg 10.4).
[143] A Ship Recycling facility is, under Art 2.11, a defined area, site, yard or facility, used for the recycling of ships. Thus, any area where activities of ship recycling take place intentionally is subject to this definition, provided that it is somehow defined as such, probably under the requirements of national law.
[144] Reg 8(1.2).

work. Furthermore it can be argued that by keeping the cost of recycling low, the financial incentives will ensure that shipowners recycle their ships. The gradual removal of very hazardous materials from the construction or repair of ships will further improve the conditions for recycling, albeit in 20–30 years' time. Is this arrangement a contribution to sustainable development? Surely it does not go as far as reforming the ship recycling practice? Nor does it follow the 1989 Basel Convention basis whereby developed states take responsibility for the reduction of hazardous wastes and their exportation. They simply appear as adjustments to the present situation that they could safely be classified as techno-centred. They can be seen as opening the door of gradual improvements, as a number of guidelines are likely to determine the efficiency of the SCR. On the other hand, they can also be seen as closing the door of fundamental reform and make the application of the 1995 Basel Convention Ban unarguable, to the extent that the SCR covers a particular type of ship. Since states have agreed to the SCR, the effort will be on bringing it into force and implementing it. Whether the effects will be those necessary for sustainable development will not be assessed for a very long time. The present financial needs of some leading developing states have clearly overshadowed the environmental and socio-economic concerns. The only party that comes up clearly better are shipowners, who can claim compliance with recycling principles and retain the profit of recycling in developing states. Note also that the exclusions of small ships and ships constrained within national waters is an expression by the common but differentiated responsibility arrangement, as well as the discretion granted to recycling states in relation to establishing what each of them considers an appropriate system.

B. Greenhouse Gas Emissions from Ships[145]

The response of the shipping sector through the IMO to the control and reduction of greenhouse gas emissions appears to be developing in similar lines.

The general obligation imposed on all states to stabilise GHG at levels not dangerous for humans and the environment[146] is to be fulfilled within the context of common but differentiated responsibility. The Kyoto Protocol excludes GHG from ships from its operation, and imposes an obligation on contracting states of Annex I to 'pursue limitation or reduction of emissions of greenhouse gases … working through … the International Maritime Organization…'. The reference to the IMO as the forum of regulation or reduction of GHG does not by itself exclude the application of the common but differentiated responsibility arrangement under the UNFCCC, but it creates a paradox. Flag states, most of which are developing states, can and have argued that the obligation imposed under the Kyoto Protocol implies that the GHG emission reduction in the shipping sector should be undertaken by

---

[145] An interesting collection of papers can be found in Asariotis R and Benamara H, (2012), Maritime transport and the Climate Change Challenge, Routledge.p 327.

[146] UNFCCC Art 2.

developed states, as it has already been arranged for GHG reductions in general under the Kyoto Protocol. Taking into account that most of the capital invested in shipping does not arise from open register developing states, the position adopted reflects a major leakage to any efforts in reducing GHG emissions from shipping.

In response to calls for reduction of GHG from shipping, 20 years after the 1992 UNFCCC, the IMO has adopted the Energy Efficiency Design Index (EEDI) for new ships[147] and the Ship Energy Efficiency Management Plan (SEEMP) for all ships. However the EEDI will concern the gradual development of an engineering index (in itself debated) which will in the future, depending on further negotiations, lead to improvements of energy efficiency from ships and possibly reduction of emissions. [148] The second part of the system is voluntary and will not have implementation options, unless coastal states chose to enforce it unilaterally. In essence the IMO system, 20 years after the 1992 UNFCCC, will deal with GHG emissions for the next generation of ships which will become fully efficient in 20–25 years and which will, apparently lead to actual increase of emissions from ships by more than 40 per cent. In the meantime, the focus of the organisation will naturally be on the technical implementation of the EEDI while GHG emission from shipping will grow.

Thus the systemic or systematic delays and redefinition of the problems within the IMO can be argued as grounds for avoiding efficient environmental implementation.[149]

IX. THE FUTURE OF SHIPPING LEGISLATION

When governance from the world outside shipping is compared with the IMO-agreed shipping instruments, the contribution of the shipping legislation to

---

[147] For an outline of the EEDI see Chrysostomou A and Vagslid E S, Climate Change: a challenge for IMO too, Chapter 6 in Asariotis R and Benamara H, *Maritime transport and the Climate Change Challenge*, (Abingdon: Earthscan, 2012) 75–111. According to this report (and the IMO GHG study of 2009), ships have emitted 870 million tonnes of CO_2. The projections for all SRES scenarios except the A1FI are bound by emissions of around 1,500 million tonnes of CO_2 annually by 2030 (figure 6.9 of Chrysostomou and Vagslid, 2012) The EEDI is projected under the same paper to reduce the emissions by up to 240 million tonnes of CO_2 annually by 2030. This means, if my understanding is correct, that the emissions from shipping will in 2030 be around 1,260 million tonnes of CO_2 annually; that is, an increase of emissions from shipping by 44% on the 2009 IMO study estimate. Taking into account that the normal way of estimating reduction/increase of emissions globally is by reference to 1990, one can argue that by 2030 the emissions from ships would be even higher. Chrysostomou and Vagslid (2012) consider the introduction of mandatory measures in MEPC 62 to introduce the measures through MARPOL ANNEX VI as a 'historic agreement'. While it is fully understandable that people fighting for some improvement in a completely unregulated situation are jubilant for this development, the question is posed once more on whether these measures can be argued or heralded as leading to greenhouse gas emission reductions and to sustainable development. The author, on the basis of the numbers stated above considers them simply inadequate.

[148] The EEDI will apply to new ships only thus in essence gradually improving the emissions from the sector as older ships are taken out of use. This exception of old ships coupled with exemptions granted to developing states until 2019 will reduce the effects of the EEDI.

[149] The author is very much aware of the difficulties in the development of a post-Kyoto protocol and the operation of the European Emission Trading System (ETS). Within this context one can even argue that the IMO action is a success. This does not change the fact that it is inadequate and possibly ineffective.

sustainable development becomes questionable. The two examples described above indicate that the ability of the IMO as a forum to agree on generally accepted practical arrangements which improve on the existing situation come at the price of delays and concessions to the shipping industry. It can be argued that the IMO legislation is about the future of shipping and not about the immediate improvement in the environmental performance of the shipping sector. The exclusion of existing ships and the clear choice to apply new environmental standards to new ships, often with a horizon of 5 to 10 years, results in a slow reduction of the environmental impact of individual ships. The well-known problems faced in the implementation of the IMO conventions coupled with the increase in the number of ships that follow the expansion of international trade is likely to result in a total increase of the impact the shipping sector has on the marine environment in the heavier shipping routes. Thus the success of the IMO shipping laws in being agreed and in providing a global framework for the sector does not appear sufficient to ensure even a shipping sector with neutral contribution to the environment. Furthermore there is presently no method by which to assess the impact of shipping legislation towards sustainable development.

Thus the shipping of the future must (a) be part of a path for the sustainable development of each state; and (b) consider the (unknown) limits of tolerance of the various aspects of the marine environment.

How these will be taken into account and implemented by developing rules which will correspond to regional needs for development is difficult to detail.

However there are various ways with which the international community can try to resolve these issues. One is to include shipping in the sustainability consideration of each state. This would mean that the impact of shipping to the marine environment of the coastal state would be a matter for each state. Thus heavily impacted areas would need to be more regulated than others. The limited capacity of each region would then need to be taken into account in order to develop the appropriate shipping regulation. This line of thinking implies that diversification of the rules for shipping based on the areas of trading and the vulnerability of the marine environment at each location will need to be developed. Thus the future may require moving away from the globally uniform rules for all ships and develop additional to the IMO minimum standards regionally appropriate regulations. Preservation of the present status with gradual increase in the strictness of the environmental regulations is an alternative path. To decide which is the appropriate way to follow a comparison between the impacts regional strict environmental regulation has against less strict global regulation is required.[150] For example, by identifying the major trade routes and assuming new strict regional laws by the trading states an alternative path to the shipping of the future can be developed and compared with the present uniform application of shipping laws. In such a scenario the global minimum standards for the operation of ships as agreed in the IMO conventions will be used as the basis of the high seas while the strict regional

---

[150] Assessing the speed of implementation of each type of regulation would also be crucial in view of the delays presently encountered with IMO-based legislation.

standards will push the most profitable part of the shipping sector towards higher environmental standards.

Arguably, providing enforcement rights at the high seas for marine pollution to all states would also be an important step to consider. This can only be done with the development of a comprehensive global system of environmental conventions appropriate for the various areas of the high seas. At the beginning compliance with existing IMO Conventions can be required. Thus marine pollution of the high seas (damage to the commons), will be considered as grave an offence as piracy, slave trafficking and unauthorised broadcasting, a possibility worth considering as an alternative to haphazard port state enforcement.

However, it has to be recognised that even if enforcement rights at the high seas are granted to coastal states[151] for marine pollution purposes and even if shipping regulations reflect regional needs and vulnerability at each area, there will be no guarantee that the shipping of the future will contribute to sustainable development, unless an integrated assessment of all marine activities and impacts are combined with the corresponding land-based activities.

Maybe those who claim that sustainable development is misguided and more rhetoric than active are right. And it is certainly true that the most likely outcome is that some states will not follow sustainable paths of development. But even then, it makes sense to respect the limits of the capacity of the marine environment to sustain pollutants. The present inability to accurately assess the limits of the capacity of the marine environment to the various sources of pollution is certainly frustrating, but our knowledge improves and respecting this principle will dictate the development of shipping policy and laws.

Practical criteria quantifying the impact of shipping and the suggested changes of shipping legislation on the marine environment, and the way these affect the financial, social and environmental aspects of sustainable development will need to be developed and incorporated, in assessing the proposals put forward for shipping laws at the IMO or other national and international *fora*. Sustainability impact assessment will need to be defined and scored. Such procedures will require a different type of governance with a more important role given to quantifying environmental risks and sustainability requirements and taking into account long term financial consequences.[152]

Changes in the ownership of the commercial fleet and re-flagging may also be an important challenge for the future. The differential development between rich and poor countries is only partially reflected in the world of shipping. The registration

---

[151] This would require a modification of UNCLOS Art 110. However it is arguable that jurisdiction for enforcement of pollution and emission laws from ships would make more sense and be more appropriate, than the existing provisions under Art 109 on unauthorised broadcasting, an activity uncomfortably sitting together with piracy, slave trading, as well as a ship without a flag or refusing to show its flag under Art 110.

[152] There is a lively discussion on how this can be achieved. One concept developed is that of reflexive governance (see for various aspects of it: J-P Voß, D Bauknecht, R Kemp (eds), *Reflexive Governance for Sustainable Development* (Edward Elgar Publishing Inc, 2006). For the difficulties involved in linking scientific uncertainty with policy see also Stohr C and I Chabay, 'Science and Participation in Governance of the Baltic Sea fisheries' (2010) 20 *Environmental Policy and Governance* 330–63.

of ships has long been used as a legitimate commercial tool in attracting tonnage in exchange for granting financial advantages to shipowners, sometimes in forms of tax relief and labour law, and sometimes in terms of reduced requirements for compliance with safety and environmental regulations. This has been debated primarily on state jurisdiction and flag state rights, which, it is submitted, have been proven as inconclusive and unproductive for any progress to be made. However there is no reason why competitive advantages cannot co-exist with international legitimacy in terms of environmental protection and sustainable development. This will be assisted by an assessment of the sustainable development of each state coupled with the duty not to reach the capacity of the marine environment to accommodate pollutants.

Part 2

Developments in the Law Concerning Carriage of Goods and International Trade

6

Reflections on the Rotterdam Rules

REGINA ASARIOTIS*

IN 1982, when the Institute of Maritime Law (IML) was established at Southampton University, the Hamburg Rules[1] were four years old. Having been adopted in 1978, the Hamburg Rules did not, however, enter into force until 1992. Twenty years later, in 2012, they continue to co-exist at the international level with the 1968 Hague-Visby Rules,[2] in force in most of the main shipping nations, but also with the 1924 Hague Rules,[3] the first internationally agreed cargo-liability regime – adopted almost a century ago – and still in force in the United States.

The Hamburg Rules are in force and, therefore, cannot be described as a failure altogether. However, they have so far failed to achieve the main objective of any international Convention in the field of commercial law, which is to create genuine uniformity of law at the international level. Instead of replacing their predecessors, the Hague Rules and Hague-Visby Rules, the Hamburg Rules represent another – third – set of international rules in the field. The unsatisfactory 'stalemate' created by the co-existence of three different 'competing' international liability regimes, has given rise to an increasing proliferation of diverging national laws. As a result, the legal framework governing carrier liability has become increasingly complex. Today, twenty years after the entry into force of the Hamburg Rules, this remains the status quo, to the delight of maritime lawyers and to the chagrin and cost of commercial parties engaged in international trade.

But what is to be made of the Rotterdam Rules, the *United Nations Convention on Contracts for the Carriage of Goods Wholly or Partly by Sea*?[4] In 2012, the year

---

* The views expressed in this article are those of the author and do not necessarily reflect those of the UNCTAD Secretariat.

[1] United Nations Conventions on Contracts for the Carriage of Goods by Sea, 1978.

[2] International Convention for the Unification of Certain Rules of Law Relating to Bills of Lading, 1924 (Hague Rules), as amended by the Visby and SDR Protocols 1968 and 1979.

[3] International Convention for the Unification of Certain Rules of Law Relating to Bills of Lading, 1924.

[4] The Convention was adopted by the United Nations General Assembly on 11 December 2008. The full text of the Convention is available on the UNCITRAL website at www.uncitral.org. Please note that there has been a correction regarding 'certain errors in articles 1 (6) (a) and 19 (1) (b) of the authentic text', effective 25 January 2013. The relevant text relates to the obligations and liabilities of a performing party. Also available on the UNCITRAL website (under 'Working Group Documents') are all working documents pertaining to the negotiations (Working Group III).

the IML celebrates its 30th anniversary, the Rotterdam Rules are four years old. Having been adopted in 2008, following many years of deliberation under the auspices of UNCITRAL, high hopes were pinned on the success of the Rotterdam Rules, intended as a modern successor to the Hague Rules, Hague-Visby Rules and Hamburg Rules. However, the Rotterdam Rules have as yet been ratified by only two States.[5] As a further 18 ratifications are required for their entry into force, it is at present anyone's guess if and when the Rotterdam Rules will enter into force.[6]

The important question, however, is not so much whether the Rotterdam Rules are likely to enter into force soon, but rather whether entry into force of the Rotterdam Rules would make things better. That is to say, whether the Rotterdam Rules would be able to deliver in two key respects, namely: (a) establish a modern international liability regime that successfully addresses the needs of commercial parties; and (b) offer the prospect of genuine international uniformity of law in the field. The first requires that the Rotterdam Rules address substantive issues in a manner better suited to the conditions of modern commercial practice than the three international liability regimes currently in force; the second requires not only that the Rotterdam Rules succeed in attracting widespread international adoption but also that they establish a set of rules which are easy to interpret and apply across jurisdictional borders, thus providing legal certainty and reducing the need for costly litigation.

Forming a view on these issues requires a degree of understanding which is not easy to obtain. In fact, the number, length and complexity of provisions in the Rotterdam Rules are such that even a knowledgeable observer will find it difficult to form a clear opinion about the content and implications of the Rotterdam Rules, without spending a considerable amount of time. With ardent proponents of the Rotterdam Rules insisting that the Rules offer the *panacea*, much of what has been published on the subject highlights only the perceived virtues of the Rules, without any hint of a critical assessment. This includes not only brief summary pieces, but also some of the academic commentary.

The author has, over time, carefully analysed key features of the Rotterdam Rules in some detail and published a number of academic papers on the subject.[7] While

---

[5] Spain was the first State to ratify the Convention on 19 January 2011, followed by Togo, on 17 July 2012. Relevant information about the status of ratification is available on the UNCITRAL website (www.uncitral.org).

[6] It should be noted that Contracting States are required to denounce the Hague Rules, Hague-Visby Rules or Hamburg Rules upon ratification. Following entry into force, such denunciation is technically a condition for accession (Art. 89). As a result, States will not be able to adhere to any other maritime liability regime with respect to their trade with States that have chosen not to become party to the Rotterdam Rules.

[7] See R Asariotis, 'Allocation of Liability and Burden of Proof in the Draft Instrument on Transport Law' (2002) *LMCLQ* 382; R Asariotis, 'Main Obligations and Liabilities of the Shipper' (2004) *Transportrecht* 284; R Asariotis, 'The End of the Bill of Lading as we Know it?' *DC-PRO*, 11 April 2008 (http://focus.dcprofessional.com/ExpertView.asp); R Asariotis, 'What Future for the Bill of Lading as a Document of Title?' (2008) *JIML* 75; R Asariotis, 'Burden of Proof and Allocation of Liability for Loss Due to a Combination of Causes Under the Rotterdam Rules' (2008) *JIML* 537; R Asariotis, 'Loss Due to a Combination of Causes: Burden of Proof and Commercial Risk Allocation', in D Rhidian Thomas (ed.), *A New Convention for the Carriage of Goods by Sea – The Rotterdam Rules* (Lawtext, 2009) 138; R Asariotis, 'UNCITRAL Draft Convention on Contracts for the Carriage of Goods Wholly or Partly by

these may be consulted by the interested reader for more detailed consideration and for further references,[8] this contribution presents the outcome of the analysis in context, so as to provide a birds-eye view and to enable the reader to better assess some of the implications that entry into force of the Rotterdam Rules may have. The analysis is not comprehensive, but focuses on some important elements of the Rules. Issues considered have been selected with the two key 'benchmarking criteria' noted above in mind, ie (a) how the Rotterdam Rules compare to their predecessors in terms of addressing substantive issues and (b) whether the Rotterdam Rules promote greater legal certainty at the international level.

I. WHAT TYPES OF ISSUES ARE ADDRESSED IN THE ROTTERDAM RULES?

The Convention is primarily intended to be a modern successor to existing international conventions in the field of carriage of goods by sea, ie the Hague-Rules 1924, the Hague-Visby Rules (HVR) 1968/1979 and the Hamburg Rules 1978. Therefore, the Rotterdam Rules provide in large part for a substantive liability regime, albeit with significant changes to existing regimes in terms of structure, wording and substance. Some key issues arising in this context will be considered further, below. A few points are, however, already worth noting. In particular: (a) the commercial *quid pro quo* inherent in the Convention, on balance, appears to favour the interests of the carrier rather than shipper – this is in contrast to the position under any of the existing international conventions in the field; (b) although the Rotterdam Rules are in principle mandatory, significant freedom of contract exists in relation to so-called 'volume contracts'– a new type of contract, based somewhat on the US concept of a 'service contract'; and (c) the Rotterdam Rules liability regime – which is exclusively maritime in nature – may also apply to contracts for multimodal transport that include an international sea-leg.[9]

In addition to the types of issues covered in the Hague-Visby and Hamburg Rules, several chapters of the new Convention are devoted to matters which, for the first time, would be subject to international uniform law, such as delivery of the

---

Sea: Mandatory Rules and Freedom of Contract', in A Antapassis, L Athanassiou and E Rosaeg (eds), *Competition and Regulation in Shipping and Shipping Related Industries* (Martinus Nijhoff, 2009), 349; R Asariotis, 'The Rotterdam Rules: A Brief Overview of Some of their Key Features' [2009] *European Journal of Commercial Contract Law* 111.

[8] The relevant publications provide fuller analysis and discussion of individual aspects of the Rotterdam Rules (and of earlier draft versions of the Convention), as well as further references, in particular to other academic writing. A bibliography relating to the Rotterdam Rules is also available on the UNCITRAL website at www.uncitral.org/pdf/english/bibliography/Rotterdam_Rules.pdf.

[9] The substantive scope of application and the provisions regulating the application of the Convention to multimodal transport remained controversial, even at the UNCITRAL Commission meeting at which the final text was agreed, with some States proposing to make the multimodal application of the new international regime optional, or proposing to provide for continued applicability of existing national law. Others expressed concern about the suitability of the substantive liability regime in the context of international multimodal transportation. See A/63/17 at paras 23, 93–98 and 270–78.

goods,[10] transfer of rights[11] and right of control.[12] Relevant provisions are entirely new and untested and, for this reason alone, will be subject to extensive litigation if and when the Convention enters into force. The Rotterdam Rules also provide for electronic communication and the issue of electronic substitutes for traditional paper documents, largely by recognising contractual agreements in this respect and by according electronic records similar status to paper-based documents.[13] This is in principle a good thing, although the relevant framework does not really help to make the much-needed electronic equivalent of the traditional bill of lading a reality. In essence, if and when such a commercially viable electronic equivalent emerges, the Rotterdam Rules would provide a framework to allow for its use.

Two separate chapters provide complex rules on jurisdiction and arbitration.[14] These chapters are optional, and will only be binding on Contracting States that have declared their intention to be bound. Absent such declaration, national rules would apply, including in respect of the question of whether contractual choice of a forum (jurisdiction or arbitration) is permissible and under which circumstances. As a result, unless all of the Contracting States choose to adhere to the relevant chapters on jurisdiction and arbitration, there is a significant potential for parallel legal proceedings in different Contracting States and, ultimately, conflicting judgments.

The above very cursory overview of what is regulated in the Rotterdam Rules shows that they are very ambitious in their scope of coverage. Many of the provisions are new, lengthy and highly complex, with extensive cross-references as well as imprecise or ambiguous wording – which would remain to be tested in the courts. This, unfortunately, makes national differences in their interpretation and application likely and may give rise to significant litigation. With 96 Articles, the Rotterdam Rules are also significantly longer than the Hamburg Rules, which consist of 34 Articles, or the Hague-Visby Rules, which are set out in no more than 16 Articles and, nevertheless, after many years of judicial interpretation, continue to attract new case law.

II. TO WHICH CONTRACTS WOULD THE CONVENTION APPLY? – CONTRACTS FOR THE INTERNATIONAL CARRIAGE OF GOODS WHOLLY OR PARTLY BY SEA

The Rotterdam Rules apply to international contracts of carriage,[15] provided the contract involves an international sea leg and the contractual place of receipt,

---

[10] C 9.

[11] C 11.

[12] C 10.

[13] See in particular c 3, dealing with electronic transport records.

[14] C 14 and 15. For a considered analysis, see YM Baatz, in YM Baatz, C Debattista, F Lorenzon, A Serdy, H Staniland, M Tsimplis, *The Rotterdam Rules: A Practical Annotation* (London, Informa, 2009) 211 *et seq.*

[15] Note that charterparties are expressly excluded, as are 'other contracts for the use of a ship or for any space thereon' and contracts of carriage in non-liner transportation, except where 'there is no charterparty or other contract for the use of a ship or of any space thereon and a transport document or an electronic transport record is issued' (Art 6). While the Convention does not apply as between original parties to any of these contracts, it does apply 'as between the carrier and the consignee, controlling part or holder that is not an original party ...', see Art 7.

loading, discharge or delivery is located in a Contracting State (Article 5). Contract of carriage is defined, in Article 1(1), as

> a contract in which the carrier, against the payment of freight, undertakes to carry goods from one place to another. The contract shall provide for carriage of goods by sea and may provide for carriage by other modes of transport in addition to sea carriage.

Thus, as is also apparent from the rather cumbersome full title of the Convention, the Rotterdam Rules apply not only to contracts of carriage by sea from or to a Contracting State, but also to contracts involving other modes, as long as the contract 'provides' for carriage of goods by sea.

What exactly this means will depend on the interpretation by national courts, which may vary. One commentator's summary of some of the questions that may arise highlights the potential for different outcomes, depending on national courts' approach to interpretation:

> Does the Convention apply if the contract required the goods to be carried by sea but there was in fact no sea carriage as the goods were carried by some other mode in breach of contract? Here the Convention would seem to apply. Does the Convention apply if the contract required the goods to be carried by air but they were in fact carried by sea in breach of contract? Here the Convention would seem not to apply. Does the Convention apply if the contract is not 'mode specific', or contains a liberty or contractual option to carry by sea and the goods are in fact carried in whole or in part by sea? Might it be said that, in this example, the contract does 'provide for carriage by sea' in that it sanctions carriage by sea? If so, why does the Convention not apply where the carrier has a contractual liberty to carry by sea but in fact the goods are not so carried? A logical answer in both cases might be that it is irrelevant whether or not the actual carriage was by sea and that an option to carry by sea is not sufficient to satisfy the requirement that 'the contract shall provide for carriage by sea'. I suspect however that courts may be reluctant to construe the phrase so narrowly. It would not be surprising if it were held that, where the contract contained an option to carry by sea and that option was exercised so that part of the carriage was actually by sea, the contract is to be read as though the contract provided for that part of the carriage to be by sea.[16]

Irrespective of the lack of precision in the definition of contract of carriage, what is clear, however, is that there is no requirement that the carriage 'by other modes' must be ancillary to the sea carriage or must be shorter than the sea carriage. Thus any multimodal contract involving an international sea leg may be covered by the Rotterdam Rules, irrespective of which mode of transport is dominant.

III. WHICH RULES APPLY IN RELATION TO MULTIMODAL TRANSPORT INVOLVING A SEA LEG?

The issue of potential overlap or conflict with existing international conventions applicable to road, rail, air and inland waterway carriage has, to some extent, been

---

[16] A Diamond, 'The Rotterdam Rules' [2009] *LMCLQ*, 445 (451–52).

addressed in a separate provision – Article 82. The provision gives precedence to international conventions on road, rail, air and inland waterway carriage currently in force (and any future amendments thereto 'on carrier liability for loss of or damage to the goods'), 'to the extent that such convention according to its provisions', applies beyond pure unimodal transportation by road, rail, air and inland waterway, respectively.[17]

However, otherwise, substantive rules pertaining to other modes of transport come into play only (a) in relation to losses *arising solely before or after sea-carriage*, and (b) even then only in the form of *mandatory* provisions on '*the carrier's liability, limitation of liability, or time for suit*' contained in any international convention that would have applied mandatorily to the stage of carriage where the loss occurs, *had a separate unimodal transport contract been made* (Article 26).

These specific mandatory provisions – and only these – would, in a cargo claim, or in a claim by the carrier against the shipper (eg in connection with dangerous goods), have to be applied in context with the substantive remaining body of provisions in the Rotterdam Rules. For instance, if a loss arose during the road leg of a multimodal transport which, hypothetically, would have been subject to the CMR (Convention on the Contract for the International Carriage of Goods by Road 1956, as amended), then 'carrier liability, limitation of liability and time for suit' would be determined by the CMR. In every other respect, however, the lengthy and complex provisions of the Rotterdam Rules (eg shipper liability, delivery, jurisdiction, documentation, rights of suit etc.) would remain relevant.

In all other cases, that is to say where no international unimodal convention would have been applicable (had a separate unimodal contract been made), or where a loss could not be localised, the provisions of the Rotterdam Rules, ie of a substantively maritime liability regime, would apply to determine the parties' rights and the incidence and extent of any liability.

In this context it should be noted that apart from the provisions in Articles 1, 82 and 26, none of the remaining 93 Articles in the Rotterdam Rules makes reference to carriage by modes other than sea-carriage; all of the substantive liability provisions are based exclusively on maritime law concepts and principles, without particular regard to the application of the Rotterdam Rules in a multimodal transport context. For instance, while an express seaworthiness obligation is set out in a provision entitled 'specific obligations applicable to the voyage by sea',[18] no equivalent obligation is envisaged in respect of road or rail carriage. Thus it would seem that a carrier may be under no obligation to ensure the 'roadworthiness' of any vehicle that may be used as part of a multimodal contract.[19] Existing national laws on

---

[17] However, it has been argued that despite the intention, inherent in Art 82, of avoiding conflict with existing unimodal transport conventions, the potential for such conflict remains, in particular in respect of the CMR. See Diamond, n 16 above, at 454–55 for a considered discussion.

[18] Art 14.

[19] Courts may of course imply such a duty but, as a matter of interpretation, application of Art 14 by analogy may be difficult to justify, given that the legislator has given its attention to the matter. The title of Art 14 makes it clear that the provision sets out 'Specific obligations applicable to the voyage by

multimodal transportation will play no role in relation to contracts falling within the scope of the new Convention. Moreover, contractual solutions would only be permissible within the narrow parameters of the Convention itself, ie effectively only in the context of a 'volume contract'.[20]

IV. OBLIGATIONS AND LIABILITY OF THE CARRIER

A. The Basic Framework

Under the Rotterdam Rules, the carrier (as well as any 'maritime performing party',[21] such as potentially a terminal operator) is under a number of obligations, breach of which gives rise to liability. The liability of the carrier under the Rotterdam Rules is subject to financial limitation (Article 59),[22] with limitation amounts higher than in the Hague-Visby Rules or Hamburg Rules, but lower than in international conventions on carriage of goods by land or air. Limitation of liability for loss caused by delay is regulated separately (Article 60),[23] but liability for delay only arises in cases where a time for delivery has been agreed in the contract (Article 21). In contrast to the Hague-Visby and Hamburg Rules, the relevant liability limits apply to 'breaches of [the carrier's] obligations under this Convention', ie are not restricted to 'loss or damage to or in connection with the goods' (*cf* Art. IV, r. 5(a) HVR) or 'loss resulting from loss of or damage to goods' (*cf* Art. 6(1)(a) Hamburg Rules). The carrier may lose the right to financial limitation of liability in case of recklessness or intent (Article 61), but remains entitled to limitation in cases of deviation amounting to a 'breach of obligation' under 'the applicable law'.[24] All claims are subject to a two-year time bar (Article 62), which may be extended by declaration.

---

sea'. A chapter entitled 'Additional provisions relating to particular stages of carriage' has been included in the Convention, but contains only three provisions. In addition to Art 26, ('Carriage preceding or subsequent to sea carriage'), this includes Art 24 ('Deviation') and Art 25 ('Deck cargo on ships').

[20] Volume contracts are discussed further below. See also Arts 79 and 80.

[21] Art 19 specifies the circumstances under which a 'maritime performing party' is subject to the obligations and liabilities of a carrier. The concept is defined in Art 1(6) [performing party] and 1(7) [maritime performing party]. Accordingly, a 'maritime performing party' is a performing party to the extent that it performs or undertakes to perform any of the carrier's obligations, at the carrier's request or under its supervision, during the period between arrival of the goods at the port of loading of a ship and their departure from the port of discharge of a ship. An inland carrier is a maritime performing party only if it performs or undertakes to perform its services exclusively within a port area. See also n 4, above

[22] 875 SDR per package or other shipping unit or 3 SDR per kilogram of gross weight, whichever amount is the higher.

[23] 2.5 times the freight.

[24] Unreasonable deviation is not a breach of obligation under the Convention. Art 24 does, however, stipulate that if deviation amounts to a 'breach of obligation' under the 'applicable law', the carrier and performing carrier remain entitled to rely on 'any defence or limitation' under the Rotterdam Rules. Under English common law, the question of whether a deviation amounts to a breach of contract is well established and would probably be easy to answer. If the applicable law is that of a civil law jurisdiction, the position may be less clear, in particular if and when national legislation based on the Hague-Visby Rules will have been replaced by the Rotterdam Rules.

Deck carriage, which is regulated in some detail in a separate provision, Article 25, deserves special mention. Carriage of goods on deck is covered by the Rotterdam Rules and is in general permissible, including in cases where such carriage is 'in accordance with the contract of carriage, or the customs, usages or practices of the trade in question'.[25] However, the carrier is not liable for 'special risks involved in … carriage on deck', except in relation to containers[26] carried on specially fitted decks (Article 25(2)). Thus, a simple contractual 'liberty to carry on deck' clause would suffice to trigger a statutory exclusion of liability for any loss related to deck carriage, other than in the context of container carriage.[27]

In cases where neither law, nor contract, customs, usages or practices of the trade permit carriage on deck, 'the carrier is liable for loss of or damage to the goods or delay in their delivery that is exclusively caused by their carriage on deck and is not entitled to rely on the defences provided for in Article 17' (Article 25(3)).[28] If goods are carried on deck in breach of an express agreement to the contrary, the carrier loses its right to limitation of liability 'to the extent that such loss, damage or delay resulted from their deck carriage' (Article 25(5)).[29]

The carrier's main obligations include the duty to carry the cargo and deliver the goods to the consignee (Article 11) and a duty of care, during the carrier's period of responsibility, ie from receipt to delivery of the goods (Articles 13(1) and 12). The carrier is also bound to exercise due diligence to make and keep the vessel seaworthy (Article 14) – this includes (a) physical seaworthiness of the vessel, as well as (b) manning, supply and equipment, and (c) cargoworthiness of the vessel.[30] In contrast to the Hague-Visby Rules, the seaworthiness obligation is a continuous one, applying throughout the voyage, and there is no general reversal of the burden of proof regarding the exercise of due diligence (*cf* Article IV, r.1 HVR).[31]

---

[25] See Art 25(1)(c). Under Art 25(1)(a) and (b), goods may also be carried on deck if 'such carriage is required by law' or 'they are carried in or on containers or vehicles that are fit for deck carriage and the decks are specially fitted to carry such containers or vehicles'.

[26] Note, however, the wide definition of 'container' in Art 1(26), which refers to 'any type of container, transportable tank or flat, swap-body, or any similar unit load used to consolidate goods, and any equipment ancillary to such load'.

[27] A contractual liberty to carry on deck will be sufficient to bind third parties that have acquired a negotiable transport document in good faith, see Art 25(4).

[28] Regarding 'the defences provided for in Article 17', see below, text following n 32 and n 38.

[29] *cf Daewoo Heavy Industries Ltd v Klipriver Shipping Ltd (The Kapitan Petko Voivoda)* [2003] EWCA Civ 451, where the Court of Appeal held that a carrier remains entitled to the limitation of liability in accordance with the Hague Rules. For a critical comment on the decision, see R Asariotis, 'Kapitan Petko Voivoda Judgment Raises Weighty Questions' (2003) *Lloyd's List* 2 July 2003.

[30] Note the text of Art 14(c):

Make and keep the holds and all other parts of the ship in which the goods are carried, and any containers supplied by the carrier in or upon which the goods are carried, fit and safe for their reception, carriage and preservation.

[31] Art 14 sets out the carrier's seaworthiness obligation but does not refer to the burden of proof regarding the exercise of due diligence. Art 17(5) contains detailed rules on the burden of proof in cases of unseaworthiness and, under Art 17(5)(b)(ii) the burden of proof regarding the exercise of due diligence is on the carrier. However, it is important to note that the application of the provision is restricted to cargo claims (see the title of c 5: 'Liability of the carrier for loss, damage or delay', as well as the wording used in Art 17(1), 'The carrier is liable for loss of or damage to the goods, as well as delay in their delivery') and, in contrast to Art IV, r 1 HVR, does not cover liability of a shipper, which is regulated separately, in c 7. See further text to n 68, below.

Instead, the central provision dealing with the (fault-based) liability of the carrier for loss, damage or delay in the context of a cargo claim, Article 17, which sets out a list of exceptions to liability, also contains detailed and complex rules on burden of proof. Important issues arising in relation to the burden of proof will be considered further, below.[32]

The list of exempting 'events or circumstances' set out in Article 17(3) (a)–(o) corresponds to some extent to the list of exceptions set out in Article IV rule 2 of the Hague-Visby Rules, but differs in a number of respects, including some which reflect substantive differences in liability under the Rotterdam Rules as compared with the Hague-Visby Rules. While it is not possible to consider these differences fully here, the following should particularly be noted:

- The exemption for 'negligence in the navigation or management of the ship' – a special feature of the Hague Rules and Hague-Visby Rules (*cf* Article IV rule 2(a) HVR) that is without parallel in any other transport convention – has, as was to be expected, been omitted. The fire exemption (*cf* Article IV rule 2(b) HVR) has been modified and no longer protects the carrier in cases where the claimant is able to establish negligence;[33] however, it would appear that the carrier would be free from liability if the cause of the fire was unclear.[34] It should be noted that the exemption only applies to 'fire on board the ship', but not to fire on any other vehicle that may be used as part of a multimodal transport.
- The carrier is exempt from liability for loss, damage or delay due to 'act or omission' of not only the 'shipper' (or owner of the goods, as well as their agents and servants, *cf* Article IV rule 2 (i) HVR), but also of 'the documentary shipper, the controlling party, or any other person for whose acts the shipper or documentary shipper is liable'.[35]

---

[32] See below section B, text to n 37–47.

[33] See Art 17(3) (f). Note that the relevant burden of proof regarding negligence on the part of the carrier's servants, agents or subcontractors is on the claimant (see Art 17(4)).

[34] The carrier may also become liable 'for all or part of the loss' in cases where the loss was 'caused by or contributed to by' unseaworthiness of the vessel and the carrier was unable to prove that 'it complied with its obligation to exercise due diligence pursuant to Art. 14' (see Art 17(5)). Thus, similar to the position under the Hague-Visby Rules, the carrier would be liable in cases where the underlying cause of the fire was the unseaworthiness of the vessel and the carrier was unable to establish the exercise of due diligence in the relevant respects, *cf* only *Papera Traders Co Ltd v Hyundai Merchant Marine Co. Ltd and The Keihin Co Ltd (The Eurasian Dream)* [2002] EWHC 118 (Comm) in particular at para 123 *et seq*. However, in cases where a loss was due both to fire and unseaworthiness, a carrier may be better off under the Rotterdam Rules: this is due to the fact that under Art 17, a carrier may be exempt from part of its liability without having to prove the proportion of loss not due to its breach/fault; see further n 43, below, and accompanying text.

[35] See Art 17(3) (h). Explicit reference is made to 'act or omission of the shipper, the documentary shipper, the controlling party, or any other person for whose acts the shipper or the documentary shipper is liable pursuant to article 33 or 34'. A 'documentary shipper' is defined in Art 1(9) as 'a person, other than the [contracting] shipper, that accepts to be named as "shipper" in the transport document or electronic transport record'. Art 33 deals with 'Assumption of shipper's rights and obligations by the documentary shipper' and makes it clear that the documentary shipper is subject to the same liabilities as the shipper; Art 34 covers 'Liability of the shipper for other persons' and makes it clear that the shipper is liable for 'acts or omissions of any person ... to which it has entrusted the performance of any of its obligations', except for the carrier or a performing party acting on behalf of the carrier. The wording of Art 17(3) (h) appears to imply that the documentary shipper may also be liable for the acts or omissions of third parties it – or the shipper – engages.

- Some exempting events/circumstances are new, without express parallel in the Hague-Visby Rules. They include 'loading, handling, stowing or unloading of the goods' performed pursuant to a FIOS type agreement (except if carried out by/on behalf of the carrier), which is now expressly permitted under Article 13(2),[36] as well as 'reasonable measures to avoid or attempt to avoid damage to the environment' (Article 17(3)(i) and (n)).

- Moreover, the list of exempting events/circumstances includes 'acts of the carrier in pursuance of the powers conferred by articles 15 and 16' (Article 17(3)(o)). Article 15 deals with potentially dangerous cargo and gives the carrier broad rights, 'notwithstanding' its obligations regarding delivery of the goods and care of cargo (Articles 11 and 13), to dispose of goods which 'are, or reasonably appear likely to become ... an actual danger to persons, property or the environment' during the carrier's period of responsibility. Article 16 gives the carrier a broad right to 'sacrifice goods at sea when the sacrifice is reasonably made for the common safety or for the purpose of preserving from peril human life or other property involved in the common adventure'. Importantly, this right to sacrifice arises 'notwithstanding Articles 11, 13 and 14', ie also arises in cases where the carrier was in breach of its obligations to take care of the cargo and to exercise due diligence in respect of the vessel's seaworthiness. Thus, depending on what courts make of the provision(s), cargo interests may have to shoulder a loss due to underlying negligence by the carrier.

A preliminary observation that may be made at this point is that, by virtue of the fact that the content and wording of the list of exempting events/circumstances – and, more generally, Article 17 – differs from the equivalent provisions in the Hague-Visby Rules, there may be potentially significant differences in the application of the provisions and, ultimately, in the practical outcome of cargo claims. Existing case law on Article IV rule 2 HVR will not be directly applicable and potentially extensive litigation may be required to gain a clear understanding of the new rules.

Moreover, attention should be drawn to the fact that the application of the relevant rules on carrier obligations/liability in the context of a multimodal transport contract is particularly unclear. For instance, as already noted above, while there is an express seaworthiness obligation, no equivalent obligation exists in respect of vehicles other than ships, which may be used in the performance of a multimodal transport contract. Whether courts would imply certain obligations in a multimodal context would remain to be seen.

Also worth noting are a number of points which are of particular relevance in the context of contracts conducted on the carrier's standard terms, ie contracts of adhesion. First, the carrier's period of responsibility (receipt to delivery) may be

---

[36] See also *Jindal Iron and Steel Co Ltd v Islamic Solidarity Shipping Co Jordan Inc (The Jordan II)* [2004] UKHL 49, where the House of Lords considered similar clauses to be compatible with the Hague-Visby Rules. The fact that the question came to be decided by the House of Lords indicates that the legal position under the Hague-Visby Rules required judicial clarification. The House of Lords appears to have been reluctant to 'rock the boat' at a time when international negotiations on the Rotterdam Rules were underway (see the speech of Lord Steyn, at para 31), but may have underestimated the impact that its decision in the matter had on the outcome of the negotiations.

contractually defined (ie restricted) to cover only the period from initial loading to final unloading under the contract (Article 12(3)). Secondly, the carrier's responsibility for certain functions, such as loading, handling, stowing and unloading may be contractually transferred to the shipper, documentary shipper or consignee (Article 13(2)). Thirdly, the carrier's liability for special cargo and for live animals may be contractually limited or excluded (Article 81). Therefore, a carrier may only be liable from loading to discharge and for only some of the carrier's functions set out in the Convention.

B. Burden of Proof in Respect of Cargo Claims

Of particular practical relevance in relation to the liability of the carrier under the Rotterdam Rules are the applicable rules on burden of proof, in particular in cases where several causes have contributed to cause a loss. As has been explained in considerable detail elsewhere,[37] the rules on burden of proof within the scheme of the Convention appear to differ significantly from those in the established maritime liability conventions, to the detriment of the shipper, thus resulting in an important shift in commercial risk allocation.

With respect to cargo claims, rules on burden of proof are set out in great detail in Article 17.[38] The provision is lengthy and complex and does not lend itself to being summarised. However, in overview, Article 17 provides as follows:

- According to Article 17(1) 'The carrier is liable for loss of or damage to the goods as well as delay in their delivery, if the claimant proves' that the loss/damage/delay (hereafter loss) 'or the event or circumstance that caused or contributed to it took place during the carrier's period of responsibility ...';
- Article 17(2) provides that 'the carrier is relieved of all or part of its liability ... if it proves that the cause or one of the causes of the loss ... is not attributable to its fault or to the fault of any person referred to in article 18';[39]
- Article 17(3) provides that 'the carrier is also relieved of all or part of its liability if ... it proves that one or more of the [listed events or circumstances] caused or contributed to the loss ...';
- Article 17(4) qualifies the position by providing that, notwithstanding Article 17(3), the carrier is liable for 'all or part of the loss, damage, or delay' in cases where

---

[37] For detailed analysis, see Asariotis, 'Burden of proof' (2008) and Asariotis, 'Loss Due' (2009). See also Asariotis, 'Allocation of liability' (2002) and Asariotis, 'Main obligations' (2004) relating to earlier draft versions of the Rotterdam Rules (n 7).

[38] Note the title of the chapter 'Liability of the carrier for loss, damage or delay' which makes it clear that the relevant rules do not apply to liability of a shipper under c 7. See also n 31, above.

[39] Art 18 states that the carrier is liable for the breach of its obligations under the Convention caused by the acts or omissions of any performing party (defined in Art 1(6)), the master or crew of the ship, employees of the carrier or a performing party or 'any other person that performs or undertakes to perform any of the carrier's obligations under the contract of carriage, to the extent that the person acts, either directly or indirectly, at the carrier's request or under the carrier's supervision or control'.

the claimant proves that the fault of the carrier or of a person referred to in article 18 caused or contributed to the event or circumstance on which the carrier relies; or ... proves that an event or circumstance not listed ... contributed to the loss ... and the carrier cannot prove that this ... is not attributable to its fault or to the fault of any person referred to in article 18;

- Article 17(5) also qualifies the position by providing that, notwithstanding Article 17(3), the carrier is liable for 'all or part of the loss, damage, or delay' in cases where 'the claimant proves that the loss was or was probably caused by or contributed to by' unseaworthiness and the carrier cannot disprove causality or cannot prove compliance 'with its obligation to exercise due diligence pursuant to article 14';
- Article 17(6) provides for proportionate liability of the carrier 'when the carrier is relieved of part of its liability pursuant to this article'. Thus, Article 17(2)–17(5) respectively needs to be considered in context with Article 17(6).

Throughout Article 17, reference is made to the fact that a carrier may be relieved of 'all or part of its liability' depending on what 'caused or contributed to' the loss/damage/delay, but no further guidance is provided to make it clear under which circumstances the carrier would be relieved of all, as opposed to only part, of its liability.[40] In cases where the carrier is considered to be 'relieved of part of its liability', proportional allocation of liability is envisaged, notably without any reference to the relevant burden of proof.[41]

Careful analysis of the operation of the provisions of Article 17 in context[42] suggests that in cases where fault of the carrier combines with another cause to produce a loss, a carrier would be relieved of part of its liability without having to prove the proportion of loss not due to its own breach. This would be in marked difference to the Hague-Visby Rules, or indeed the Hamburg Rules, where the carrier could only escape liability to the extent that it could prove that a distinguishable proportion of the loss was due to an excepted peril.[43] This difference could have

---

[40] For different possible approaches to interpretation, see in more detail Asariotis, 'Loss Due' (2009), at 150 (n 7).

[41] Art 17(6): 'When the carrier is relieved of part of its liability pursuant to this article, the carrier is liable only for that part of the loss, damage, or delay that is attributable to the event or circumstance for which it is liable pursuant to this article'.

[42] See Asariotis, 'Loss Due' (2009), at 145–58 (n 7).

[43] See Art 5(7) Hamburg Rules. For jurisprudence to similar effect regarding the Hague and Hague-Visby Rules, see, in England, *Gosse Millerd Ltd v Canadian Government Merchant Marine Ltd* (1928) 32 Ll L Rep 91 (98), [1929] AC 223 (241) (HL), cited with approval in *Silver v Ocean SS Co* [1930] 1 KB 416 (430, per Scrutton LJ); *Smith Hogg & Co v Black Sea & Baltic General Insurance Co Ltd* [1940] AC 997, (1940) 67 Ll L Rep 253 (HL); *Government of Ceylon v Chandris* [1965] 3 All ER 48, [1965] 2 Lloyd's Rep 204 (216); *The Torenia* [1983] 2 Lloyd's Rep 210 (218); *The Mekhanik Evgrafov and Ivan Derbenev* [1987] 2 Lloyd's Rep 634 (636); *Northern Shipping Co v Deutsche Seerederei GmbH and Others, The Kapitan Sakharov* [2000] 2 Lloyd's Rep 255 (see particularly the statement by Auld, LJ, at 269–70). See also *The Popi M* [1985] 1 WLR 948, [1985] 2 All ER 712, [1985] 2 Lloyd's Rep 1 (HL), where Lord Brandon of Oakbrook cited with approval an *obiter dictum* by Scrutton LJ in *La Compania Naviera Martiartu v The Corporation of the Royal Exchange Assurance* (1922) 13 Ll L Rep 298 (304), [1923] 1 KB 650 (657). The position is similar in other jurisdictions, see *Schnell & Co v SS Vallescura*, 293 US 296 (1934), (1934) AMC 1573 and more recently *The OOCL Inspiration* [1998] AMC 1327 (US CA 2nd Circuit); *The Pacific Clipper* [1992] LMLN 329 (Can S Ct British Columbia); *Great China Metal Industries Co Ltd v Malaysian International Shipping Corp Berhad (The Bunge Seroja)* [1998] HCA 65; [1999] 1 Lloyd's Rep 512 (HC (AUS)).

considerable implications for the practical outcome of cargo claims, where much may depend on the available evidence. In cases where evidence on the relevant proportion of loss due to different identified causes was not available, as for instance is often the case where unseaworthiness has contributed to a loss, a carrier's liability under the Rotterdam Rules would seem to be significantly reduced, compared with established liability regimes: in most cases, the carrier would be liable for less than the full loss claimed, subject always to monetary limitation.

It has been suggested that this critical change to the established position regarding the burden of proof and allocation of liability of loss due to a combination of causes may be justified in view of the elimination of the 'nautical fault' defence.[44] The same rationale appears to have prompted a similar approach to proportional allocation of liability that had been adopted as part of proposals for a new Carriage of Goods by Sea Act[45] in the United States, in the late 1990s.[46] Judging from the number of decided cases, however, the practical relevance of the 'nautical fault' defence appears to be limited; its elimination would, therefore, seem to be less important in practice than the changes to the rules on allocation of liability, which potentially affect a large number of cargo claims, in particular those where unseaworthiness of the vessel has been identified as a contributory cause. As was said by Lord Wright in *Smith Hogg & Co Ltd v Black Sea & Baltic General Insurance Co Ltd*,[47] a charterparty dispute before the House of Lords:

> In truth, unseaworthiness, which may assume according to the circumstances an almost infinite variety, can never be the sole cause of the loss. At least I have not thought of a case where it can be the sole cause. It must, I think, always be only one of several co-operating causes.

[44] See for instance UNCITRAL working document A/CN.9/WG.III/WP.34, a submission by the United States, at para 15. References in the document to paragraphs of a 'commentary' relate to UNCITRAL document A/CN.9/WG.III/WP.21.

[45] See s 9(e) Senate Staff Working Draft for a Carriage of Goods by Sea Act 1999, 24 September 1999, available on the US Maritime Law Association's website at www.mlaus.org (Committee on Carriage of Goods). The provision is not drafted in identical terms, but reflects a similar approach. For a comment on an earlier (and in this respect identical) Senate Staff Working Draft, see R Asariotis and MN Tsimplis, 'The Proposed US Carriage of Goods by Sea Act' [1999] *LMCLQ* 126. (Republished in [1999] *LMCLQ 25th Anniversary Issue*, 11).

[46] By way of background, see MLAUS Document No 724, 3 May 1996 (at www.mlaus.org), which reproduces the *Final Report of the Ad Hoc Liabilities Study Group*, together with some related documents, and an early draft of what later became the Senate draft US COGSA 1999. The relevant 'COGSA Proposal Summary' lists changes to the burden of proof and proportional allocation of liability for loss due to a combination of causes as one of seven changes to the existing US COGSA 1936. See also M Sturley, 'Proposed Amendments to the Carriage of Goods by Sea Act', (1996) *Houston J.Int.L* 609, [Vol 18:609 1996] at p 631, where it is explained, with reference to a joint-fault scenario (loss resulting from some combination of heavy weather and negligent navigation):

> [W]ith the total elimination of the navigational fault exception, the rule in Schnell v Vallescura would require the carrier either to prove absence of negligence or to prove the extent to which the loss is attributable to each cause. Carrier interests suspect that in many courts this burden would be impossible to carry, and that they would lose the benefit of all of the exceptions found in subsection 4(2) of the [1936] Act whenever navigational fault was a plausible argument.

Against this background, two suitably worded provisos were introduced, one of which 'to overrule Schnell v Vallescura and adopt the modern comparative fault approach applied by the Supreme Court to collision cases ...'

[47] [1940] AC 997, (1940) 67 Ll L Rep 253 (259).

V. OBLIGATIONS AND LIABILITY OF THE SHIPPER

A. The Basic Framework

The shipper's obligations and liability under the Rotterdam Rules – set out in a separate chapter 7 – are more extensive than in the Hague-Visby Rules and are, for the first time, mandatory.[48]

Detailed obligations are set out in Article 27, regarding the preparation and delivery of the goods for carriage. Thus, the shipper 'shall deliver the goods in such condition that they will withstand the intended carriage, including their loading, handling, stowage, lashing and securing, and unloading, and that they will not cause harm to persons or property'.[49] Where the shipper is responsible for 'loading, stowing, handling, or unloading of the goods' under a FIOS type agreement in accordance with Article 13(2), he must 'properly and carefully' perform any relevant obligation. Finally, 'when a container is packed or a vehicle is loaded by the shipper, the shipper shall properly and carefully stow, lash and secure the contents in or on the container or vehicle, and in such a way that they will not cause harm to persons or property'.

Article 28 sets out a duty of both the shipper and the carrier to respond to requests from each other to provide 'information and instructions required for the proper handling and carriage of the goods'.

Article 29 sets out wide-ranging information and documentation requirements with which the shipper must comply. Thus, the shipper shall provide, in a timely manner, information, instructions and documents relating to the goods that are not otherwise reasonably available to the carrier and that are reasonably necessary for (a) the proper handling and carriage of the goods, including precautions to be taken; and (b) compliance by the carrier with law, regulations or other requirements of public authorities in connection with the intended carriage. The obligations in Article 29 may become particularly relevant in the context of maritime and supply-chain security requirements.[50] Potentially extensive loss could arise, for instance, as a result of a delay of the vessel (and possibly third-party liability of the carrier), arising from the shipper's failure to provide documentation or information that is required for maritime security-related purposes.

---

[48] See n 81, below.

[49] It is interesting to note that the shipper is expressly under an obligation to ensure that the goods will 'withstand the intended carriage'. Clearly, if the cargo, when delivered for carriage was not in a state so as to withstand the intended carriage the carrier would, in any event, incur no liability in a cargo claim. The specific purpose of including an express obligation to this effect in chapter 7 is, therefore, not entirely clear.

[50] For information on some of these, see UNCTAD, *Container Security: Major initiatives and related international developments* (UNCTAD/SDTE/TLB/2004/1), available at www.unctad.org/ttl/legal and R Asariotis, 'Implementation of the ISPS Code: an overview of recent developments', (2005) *JIML* 266–87. For an interesting charterparty case in which liability arose in connection with security regulations, see *Hyundai Merchant Marine Co Limited v Furnace Withy (Australia) Pty (The Doric Pride)* [2006] EWCA Civ 599.

In respect of the obligations under Articles 27–29, the shipper's liability is, in principle, fault-based. This is not expressly stated in the relevant provisions, but follows from the wording of Article 30(2), which provides that:

> ... the shipper is relieved of all or part of its liability if the cause or one of the causes of the loss or damage is not attributable to its fault or to the fault of any person referred to in Article 34.[51]

The introductory words to that same provision also make it clear that in respect of another set of obligations, set out in Articles 31 and 32, the possibility for the shipper to be relieved of all or part of its liability is not envisaged, ie that the relevant liability of a shipper shall be strict.[52]

Under Article 31(1), the shipper is obliged to provide timely and accurate information required for the compilation of the contract particulars and the issuance of the transport document (or electronic record). This includes information relating to the goods, but also the name of the shipper, consignee (if any) and the name of the order party (if any); according to Article 31(2), the shipper is deemed to have guaranteed the accuracy of the relevant information at the time of receipt by the carrier and is under an express statutory duty to indemnify the carrier against loss or damage arising from inaccurate particulars.[53] Once again, it should be noted that some of the information to be provided by the shipper may be required for security-related purposes; inaccurate information,[54] even if tendered in good faith by the shipper, could potentially give rise to significant delay of the vessel, ie result in a significant loss for which the shipper would be liable strictly – and without the benefit of monetary limitation of liability.

Article 32 sets out special rules on dangerous goods,[55] more particularly 'goods which by their nature or character are, or reasonably appear likely to become, a

---

[51] This is complemented by a further special rule (Art 30(3)) on proportional allocation of liability, which applies in cases 'when the shipper is relieved of part of its liability pursuant to this article...', ie in cases which may arise from the application of Art 30(2).

[52] See Art 30(2), which commences by stating: 'Except in respect of loss or damage caused by a breach by the shipper of its obligations pursuant to articles 31, paragraph 2, and 32 ...'.

[53] See Art 31:
(1) The shipper shall provide to the carrier, in a timely manner, accurate information required for the compilation of the contract particulars and the issuance of the transport documents ..., including the particulars as referred to in article 36, paragraph 1 [ie description of the goods, leading marks, number or packages/pieces or quantity and weight of the goods, the latter "if furnished by the shipper"]; the name of the party to be identified as the shipper in the contract particulars; the name of the consignee, if any; and the name of the [order party] if any.
(2) The shipper is deemed to have guaranteed the accuracy at the time of receipt by the carrier of the information that is provided according to paragraph 1 ... The shipper shall indemnify the carrier against loss or damage resulting from the inaccuracy of such information.

[54] Please note that failure to provide the information 'in a timely manner' (as required in Art 31(1)) may also give rise to liability but, in view of the wording of Art 30(2), liability would in these cases probably not be strict.

[55] Art 32 provides:
When goods by their nature and character are, or reasonably appear likely to become, a danger to persons, property or the environment: (a) the shipper shall inform the carrier of the dangerous nature or character of the goods in a timely manner before they are delivered to the carrier or a performing party. If the shipper fails to do so and the carrier or performing party does not otherwise

danger to persons, property or the environment'. The shipper is under obligation to 'inform the carrier of the dangerous nature or character of the goods before they are delivered to the carrier or a performing party' and is liable to the carrier for loss or damage resulting from failure to do so, unless carrier or performing carrier 'otherwise have knowledge' of the dangerous nature/character of the goods. The shipper is also under obligation to mark or label dangerous goods in accordance with any relevant requirements imposed by law, regulations or public authorities that are applicable during any stage of the intended carriage. 'If the shipper fails to do so, it is liable to the carrier for loss or damage resulting from such failure'.

It should be noted that according to Article 34, the shipper is liable for 'the breach of its obligations ... caused by the acts or omissions of any person, including employees, agents and subcontractors, to which it has entrusted performance of any of its obligations' (other than the carrier or performing carrier).

Also important to note is that parties other than the contractual shipper may become liable for breach of the obligations set out in chapter 7. Thus, a final consignee who, as 'holder',[56] makes a claim under the contract may become liable for breach of any of the shipper's obligations.[57] Moreover, under Article 33, a so-called 'documentary shipper', ie a party who is not the contracting shipper but who 'accepts to be named as "shipper" in the transport document' (Article 1(9)), such as an FOB seller, is expressly 'subject to the obligations and liabilities imposed on the shipper', in addition to the shipper itself.[58]

---

have knowledge of their dangerous nature, the shipper is liable to the carrier for loss or damage resulting from such failure to inform; and (b) the shipper shall mark or label dangerous goods in accordance with any law, regulations or other requirements of public authorities that apply during any stage of the intended carriage of the goods. If the shipper fails to do so, it is liable to the carrier for loss or damage resulting from such failure.

[56] Holder is defined, in Art 1(10)(a) as:
A person that is in possession of a negotiable transport document and (i) if the document is an order document, is identified in it as the shipper or the consignee, or is the person to which the document is duly endorsed; or (ii) if the document is a blank endorsed order document or bearer document, is the bearer thereof; ...
Part (b) of the provision deals with electronic transport records.

[57] See Art 58(2) which states that a 'holder' who 'exercises any rights under the contract of carriage' also 'assumes any liabilities imposed on it under the contract of carriage to the extent that such liabilities are incorporated in or ascertainable from the negotiable transport document'. It has been argued, with reference to the wording of Art 79(2)(b) (which, *inter alia*, prohibits contractual increase of 'the liability of the shipper, consignee, controlling party, holder or documentary shipper for breach of any of its obligations under this Convention') that the statutory obligations set out in chapter 7 may be personal to the shipper and cannot be contractually transferred to a third-party consignee (ie 'holder'), see S Baughen, 'Obligations of the Shipper to the Carrier' (2008) *JIML* 555 at 564 and the discussion by R Williams, 'Transport Documentation under the New Convention' (2008) *JIML* 566 at 583. If this view is correct, it would seem that Art 58(2) serves no useful purpose. Moreover, if all obligations in c 7 are personal to the shipper (and 'documentary shipper'), it would follow that a final consignee would in no case become liable for loss arising from the shipment of dangerous cargo. This would be an unusual result and not easy to justify.

[58] The provision expressly refers to the obligations and liabilities imposed pursuant to chapter 7 as well as those pursuant to Art 55. That provision deals with additional information, instructions or documents to be provided, upon request of the carrier or a performing party, by the controlling party; if the controlling party cannot be located or is unable to provide the information, the shipper or, if the shipper cannot be located, the documentary shipper 'shall provide such information, instructions, or documents'. See also n 35, above.

This '*all for one and one for all*' approach means not only that the carrier has several legs to stand on. It also means that parties engaged in international sales on shipment terms may have to re-assess their risk exposure: an FOB seller would be well advised to avoid being identified as shipper in a bill of lading; a final consignee who has bought CIF should note that it may risk becoming liable to the carrier for a loss arising from matters that are entirely within the sphere of control of the original shipper.[59]

While claims against the shipper are also subject to a two-year time bar, a shipper, unlike a carrier, does not benefit from any monetary limitation of liability. This absence of a financial cap on the shipper's liability is not negotiable: contractual limitation of the shipper's mandatory liability is expressly inadmissible.[60]

Thus, under the Rotterdam Rules, mandatory standards of liability are imposed on two commercial parties who contract with one another. While one party benefits from a financial cap on its potential liability, enabling it to factor in the commercial risk associated with the venture, the other party does not. Carrier and shipper are, therefore, on not quite an 'equal footing' as regards their commercial risk-exposure – and the insurability of all relevant risks.

But would any of this matter in practice? After all, under the Hague-Visby and Hamburg Rules, too, the liability of the shipper is not subject to monetary limitation and only a large shipper with significant bargaining power would be in a position to take advantage of the possibility to contractually negotiate any exclusion or limitation of its liability *vis-à-vis* a carrier.

Arguably it would, in particular as a result of the burden of proof in relation to the incidence and allocation of liability under Chapter 7.

B. Burden of Proof Issues Arising in the Context of Claims by the Carrier for Breach of the Shipper's Obligations[61]

While detailed rules on burden of proof apply in relation to the carrier's liability for cargo, the relevant rules in Chapter 7 are much less explicit. A basic rule, set out in Article 30(1), states that 'the shipper is liable for loss or damage sustained by the carrier if the carrier proves that such loss or damage was caused by a breach of the shipper's obligations under this Convention'. Nothing further, however, is said on the burden of proof. As a result, in relation to claims against the shipper (or another party liable for breach of the shipper's obligations), courts would have to fall back

---

[59] This includes the shipper's strict obligation regarding the accuracy of contract particulars under Art 31(2), see n 53, above. Note that an equivalent obligation under Art III, r 5 HVR is expressly personal to the shipper and would not affect a third party consignee. As regards fault-based liability of the shipper, it might be argued that the consignee and documentary shipper cannot be held liable for loss due to fault on the part of the shipper. However, given that the matter is not expressly addressed and in the light of Art 33 and Art 58(2) (see nn 35 and 57), this argument is difficult to sustain.

[60] Art 79(2) (b).

[61] For detailed analysis, see Asariotis, 'Loss Due', (2009) 161–67 (n 7). Note that the rules on burden of proof under Art 17 are not applicable to liability of a shipper under c 7; see further Asariotis, 'Loss Due', (2009) at 165 (n 7).

on the general principle: 'he who alleges must prove', ie whoever wishes to rely on a certain proposition must provide the relevant evidence.[62] Applying this general rule to shipper liability, the position may be summarised as follows:

While liability of the shipper for breach of obligation under Articles 27 to 29 is, in principle, fault-based, it appears that the carrier benefits from a reversal of the burden of proof regarding the fault of the shipper. This follows from the wording of Article 30(2), which envisages that

> … the shipper is relieved of all or part of its liability if the cause or one of the causes of the loss or damage is not attributable to its fault or to the fault of any person referred to in article 34.

As the provision is worded in the form of an exception to liability, on the basis of general principles, the burden of proving the absence of fault would be on the shipper, rather than the carrier.[63]

The shipper would thus appear to be liable unless it could disprove fault (its own and fault on the part of anyone it engages). This will, in many cases, be a heavy burden to discharge. In cases where the shipper could establish that part of a loss was due to a cause not attributable to its fault, (ie could establish another contributory cause, such as a *force majeure* type event or breach of obligation by the carrier), the shipper would be entitled to partial relief from liability.

How would the relevant proportional liability of the shipper be assessed in these cases? According to Article 30(3):

> When the shipper is relieved of part of its liability pursuant to this article, the shipper is liable only for that part of the loss or damage that is attributable to its fault or to the fault of any person referred to in article 34.

It would seem that in the absence of clear evidence on the respective proportion of loss due to the different causes the relevant extent of the shipper's liability would be a matter for assessment by the court.

In respect of the shipper's strict obligations, ie where loss arises from a breach of obligation regarding the shipment of dangerous cargo (Article 32), or from a failure to provide accurate information required for the compilation of the contract particulars and the issuance of the transport documents (Article 31(2)), the Rotterdam Rules envisage liability of the shipper upon simple proof of breach of obligation and causality. Partial relief from liability is *expressly* not envisaged.[64]

---

[62] See *Aktieselskabet de Danske Sukkerfabrikker v Bajamar Compania Naviera SA (The Torenia)* [1983] 2 Lloyd's Rep 210, 215, per Hobhouse, J: 'The legal burden of proof arises from the principle: He who alleges must prove. The incidence of the legal burden of proof can therefore be tested by answering the question: What does each party need to allege?' See also C Ezeoke 'Allocating onus of proof in sea cargo claims: the contest of conflicting principles' [2001] *LMCLQ* 261, with further references. The party bearing the burden of proof 'bears the risk of non persuasion on any given proposition'. That party therefore has to bring relevant evidence or will lose the argument and have to accept defeat on a particular issue.

[63] If this analysis is correct, or, more to the point, if this view is taken by courts in future case law under the Convention, the provision effectively serves to reverse the burden of proof in respect of shipper's fault: in the absence of evidence, the shipper would be presumed to be at fault.

[64] As noted above (nn 51–52), the possibility of partial exemption from liability is envisaged within the parameters of Art 30(2) and (3). The introductory words of Art 30(2) make it clear, however, that

This could have important practical implications for the outcome of claims by the carrier against the shipper (or, as appropriate, the 'documentary shipper' or 'holder'[65]), in particular in cases where unseaworthiness of the vessel may have contributed to a loss of the carrier arising from the carriage of dangerous cargo.

Under existing liability regimes, the shipper is strictly liable for losses due to the carriage of dangerous cargo (shipped without the carrier's knowing consent), but benefits from a reversal of the burden of proof in respect of the carrier's seaworthiness obligation: the carrier must disprove negligence; moreover, once a breach of the carrier's seaworthiness obligation has been identified as a contributory cause, the carrier bears a heavy evidential burden regarding the proportion of loss not due to its own breach.[66] If the carrier is unable to discharge this burden – ie in the absence of relevant evidence – the carrier must shoulder the entire loss.[67]

This is not the case under the Rotterdam Rules. The shipper does not benefit from a reversal of burden of proof in respect of the carrier's seaworthiness obligation;[68] a rule envisaging partial relief from liability and proportional allocation of liability is *expressly* not applicable in cases where loss arises from the shipment of dangerous cargo (Articles 32, 30(2) and (3)). Thus, whereas under the Hague-Visby Rules and Hamburg Rules, in cases where unseaworthiness can be identified as a contributory cause a shipper would, in many instances, be free from liability, under the Rotterdam Rules a shipper may, in many instances, become liable in full for any of the potentially considerable losses sustained by the carrier (eg loss of a vessel,

---

the possibility of partial exemption from liability is not envisaged in respect of the shipper's strict obligations, ie where loss is due (at least partly) to inaccurate contract particulars or, much more importantly, dangerous goods. Proportional allocation of liability under Art 30(3) is contingent on partial relief from liability under Art 30(2), ie is also not envisaged in these cases.

[65] See text to n 56 and n 57, above.

[66] See Art 5(7) of the Hamburg Rules. For very clear judicial guidance and a full discussion of relevant case law in relation to Art IV r 6 HVR, see in particular the decision of the Court of Appeal in *Northern Shipping Co v Deutsche Seereederei GmbH and Others, The Kapitan Sakharov* [2000] 2 Lloyd's Rep 255. The Court of Appeal made it clear that the principle was the same as that applicable to a breach of Art III r 1, where the shipowner pleaded an excepted peril under Art IV r 2, namely that it was for the shipowner to establish that the whole or a specific part of the damage or loss was caused by the excepted peril (see particularly at 269–70). See also the Court of Appeal decision in *The Fiona* [1994] 2 Lloyd's Rep 506, (particularly at 519 and 521), confirming the decision at first instance [1993] 1 Lloyd's Rep 257 (286). Importantly, the Court of Appeal in *The Kapitan Sakharov* did not agree with the claimant shipowner's argument that it should be indemnified under Art IV r 6 HVR for the whole loss, *as no such loss would have occurred but for the shipment of undeclared dangerous cargo.* The Court of Appeal expressly rejected the shipowner's submission that *The Fiona* should be distinguished, as in contrast to that case, the original shipment of the dangerous goods in *The Kapitan Sakharov* was the *initial* or indirect cause of the whole loss. See [2000] 2 Lloyd's Rep 255 (269–70) per Auld, LJ.

[67] *Ibid.* See also the judgment of Clarke J in *Compania Sud Americana de Vapores SA v Sinochem Tianjin Import and Export Corp (The Aconcagua)* [2009] EWHC 1880 (Comm) (affd by the Court of Appeal at [2010] EWCA Civ 1403), at para 333: 'It is well established that a carrier … is not entitled to an indemnity under Article IV, Rule 6 [HVR] if its loss results from two causes (a) the shipment of dangerous goods not knowingly consented to; and (b) the carrier's overriding obligation of seaworthiness under Article III, Rule 1 [HVR]: *The Fiona* [1994] 2 Lloyd's Rep 506; *The Kapitan Sakharov* [2000] 2 Lloyd's Rep 255. It is not necessary to determine whether the carrier's breach was the dominant or merely an effective cause.'

[68] See n 31 and text to n 38, above.

third-party liability).[69] It is in the context of cases involving both dangerous cargo and unseaworthiness that the absence of a financial cap on the shipper's liability is likely to be of particular practical relevance. Other scenarios are, however also worth considering. For instance, cases where dangerous goods as well as negligent navigation may have contributed to a loss; or cases where a security-related delay of a vessel, due to inaccurate particulars, may have been compounded by unseaworthiness.

In any event, much would depend on what courts may make of the complex provisions in context. There is certainly considerable scope for litigation.

VI. DELIVERY OF THE GOODS

A separate chapter dealing with delivery of the goods (chapter 9),[70] provides for a new obligation on the part of the consignee to accept delivery of the goods from the carrier (Article 43)[71] and includes detailed rules on delivery of the goods under different types of transport documents/electronic records. Leaving aside the position under electronic records, for the purposes of the chapter, reference needs to be made to the definitions, in Article 1, of the terms 'transport document', 'negotiable transport document', 'non-negotiable transport document', 'holder', 'consignee', 'shipper', 'documentary shipper' and 'controlling party' as well as to

---

[69] For a full analysis, see Asariotis, 'Loss Due' (2009), at 164–67 (n 7). In brief: the substantive rules in Art 30(2) and (3) expressly do not apply in cases where loss is due (at least partly) to inaccurate contract particulars or, much more importantly, arises in connection with the shipment of dangerous goods (see nn 51–52 and accompanying text, above). Thus, no special rule is included in the Convention to deal with the question of burden of proof and allocation of liability in cases where the carrier's loss may be due both to breach of the shipper's dangerous goods obligations and another cause, such as unseaworthiness of the vessel. Depending on the view taken by courts in the interpretation and the application of Arts 30 and 32, it would seem that, where unseaworthiness and dangerous goods had combined to produce a loss of the carrier, the shipper may either: (a) always be held liable in full or, more likely, (b) be held liable in full unless it could establish unseaworthiness *and* lack of due diligence of the carrier as a contributory cause. The relevant burden of proof regarding lack of due diligence/negligence would appear to be on the shipper, rather than the carrier, as the seaworthiness obligation is given no outstanding importance within the scheme of the Convention and, in marked contrast to Art IV r 1 of the Hague-Visby Rules, no 'freestanding' rule provides that in cases of unseaworthiness the burden of proof regarding negligence shall be reversed (ie that the carrier must prove the exercise of due diligence or be liable for breach of its seaworthiness obligation). Even if a shipper could successfully discharge this very onerous burden of proof, the question still remains as to how liability should be allocated between the parties. In the absence of evidence on the respective proportion of loss due to the different causes, courts may opt for a 50:50 apportionment or apply another formula. In any event, what seems clear is that there is no basis in the Rotterdam Rules to suggest that courts may continue to take the established judicial approach as developed over many years in relation to Art IV r 6 of the Hague-Visby Rules.

[70] For comment on relevant aspects of the draft Rotterdam Rules, see Asariotis, 'Main Obligations' (2004); Asariotis, 'The End of the Bill of Lading' (2008) and Asariotis, 'What Future for the Bill' (2008) (n 7).

[71] The provision, entitled 'Obligation to accept delivery' states that 'the consignee that demands delivery under the contract of carriage', shall accept delivery at the time or within the time period and at the location agreed in the contract or failing such agreement at the time and location at which 'having regard to the terms of the contract, the customs, usages or practices of the trade and the circumstances of the carriage, delivery could reasonably be expected'. The term 'consignee' is defined as 'a person entitled to delivery of the goods under a contract of carriage or a transport document' (Art 1(11)).

Article 51 (the provision that identifies the controlling party depending on which type of document has been issued) and to Article 57 (the provision that – for negotiable transport documents only – states how rights may be transferred).[72] The relevant terms and their definitions offer much scope for litigation, not just because in each case the relevant wording is new and untested, but also because of imprecise or ambiguous drafting.[73] Here and there it appears that – possibly inadvertently – there have been changes to the traditional understanding of established terms.[74]

Importantly, the chapter also includes complex new rules to effectively shift the risk of delayed bills of lading from carrier to consignee.[75] Under certain circumstances, the carrier may deliver the goods without surrender of a negotiable transport document provided the document 'expressly states that the goods may be delivered without surrender of the transport document'.[76] Thus, in cases where the final consignee/endorsee of goods shipped under a negotiable transport document (ie a bill of lading),[77] typically a CIF buyer in a chain of contracts, (a) is notified of the arrival of the goods at destination but is late in requesting delivery of the goods from the carrier – for whatever reason – or (b) fails to identify itself properly,[78] or (c) cannot be located, the carrier may deliver the goods without the need for surrender of the bill of lading, according to alternative delivery instructions from the original shipper – or documentary shipper.[79]

Therefore, a final consignee/endorsee, having paid its seller, under a CIF contract, against tender of a negotiable transport document, may – in some circumstances –

---

[72] See further R Thomas, 'A comparative Analysis of the Transfer of Contractual Rights Under the English Carriage of Goods by Sea Act 1992 and the Rotterdam Rules' (2011) *JIML* 437. The Rotterdam Rules do not address the transfer of rights under a non-negotiable transport document. Thus some aspects of these documents are regulated, including the right of control, whereas the transfer of rights depends on national law. Much litigation may be expected in this respect, given that national statutes will often cover the right of control as well and relevant provisions would have to be reconciled.

[73] For more detailed consideration of the provisions set out in c 9, see C Debattista in: YM Baatz et al (ed), *The Rotterdam Rules: A Practical Annotation*, at 123 *et seq*.

[74] Note, for instance, a new separate requirement, under Arts 47(1)(a)(i) and 1(10)(a)(i), for the holder of an order bill of lading to 'properly identify itself', in order to obtain delivery from the carrier. Under English law, surrender of the bill of lading by the lawful endorsee would be sufficient. See also C Debattista, previous n, at para [47–48]. For the definition of 'holder', see n 56, above.

[75] See in particular Art 47(2) which deals with negotiable transport documents/records and 46(2) which deals with a 'non-negotiable transport document that requires surrender'.

[76] Art 47(2). The need for such a statement to be included in the document was only introduced as a last minute amendment to the Convention, before its adoption. For a comment on the previous version of the relevant provision, see Asariotis, 'The End of the Bill of Lading' and Asariotis (2008), 'What Future for the Bill' (n 7).

[77] The Rotterdam Rules do not expressly refer to bills of lading or to documents of title. However, they distinguish between two types of 'transport document', namely the 'negotiable transport document' and the 'non-negotiable transport document', each of these terms being defined separately (see Art 1(14), 1(15) and 1(16)). The definition of 'negotiable transport document' is apt to cover an order or bearer bill of lading, provided the bill of lading is not marked 'non-negotiable' or 'not negotiable'.

[78] As noted in n 74, above, the holder of an order bill of lading, in addition to surrendering the document, needs to 'properly identify' itself, to obtain delivery of the goods.

[79] Note that under Art 46(2) the position is similar in respect of a 'non-negotiable transport document that requires surrender', ie a straight bill of lading of the kind considered in *JI MacWilliam Company Inc v Mediterranean Shipping Company SA (The Rafaela S)* [2005] UKHL 11.

be left empty-handed and unable to sue the carrier for misdelivery.[80] The provision, apparently intended to provide a solution to the practical problem of negotiable bills of lading being delayed in a chain of international transactions involving different buyers and banks, may seriously undermine the document of title function of the negotiable bill of lading, which is key to its use in international trade.

In addition, however, there are practical questions that arise, including the following: assuming that a carrier asks an original shipper for delivery instructions, what is the shipper, who may have no contact whatsoever with the final consignee, to do? The shipper, being a CIF seller or an FOB buyer in the first of a chain of string sales, would have normally already been paid by its own buyer against tender of documents and no longer have any legitimate interest in the goods. Therefore, although expressly 'authorized' by the Rotterdam Rules, the shipper should refuse to provide delivery instructions, or risk later becoming exposed to a claim for conversion by the lawful consignee. If, however, the shipper (or documentary shipper) were to refuse to provide delivery instructions, the rules on 'goods remaining undelivered' set out in Article 48 would become relevant.

Under Article 48, where goods remain 'undelivered', under any type of transport document or electronic record (negotiable or non-negotiable) the carrier may, after giving reasonable notice, dispose of the goods in a number of ways, at the risk and expense of 'the person entitled to the goods'. This includes storing, unpacking or even destroying the goods, or selling them on, in which case the carrier would keep the proceeds in trust, but would be able to deduct 'any costs … and any other amounts that are due to the carrier in connection with the carriage of those goods'. The carrier would only be liable for loss of or damage to the goods if the claimant could prove that the carrier had failed to take reasonable steps to preserve the goods and 'knew or ought to have known that the loss or damage to the goods would result from its failure to take such steps'. Cargo interests should clearly take note of these new provisions but, in any event, once again, considerable litigation would be required, before it is clear how the provisions are to be interpreted in commercial practice.

VII. VOLUME CONTRACTS

Although, in general, mandatory minimum standards of liability[81] apply to contracts covered by the Rotterdam Rules,[82] this is subject to an important exception. So-

---

[80] Under Art 47(2)(e), weak protection is afforded to 'a holder that becomes a holder after such delivery [of the goods] and that did not have and could not reasonably have had knowledge of such delivery at the time it became a holder'. Relevant knowledge is presumed if 'the contract particulars state the expected time of arrival of the goods, or indicate how to obtain information as to whether the goods have been delivered'.

[81] Art 79 envisages that, unless otherwise provided, a contract term is void to the extent that it 'directly or indirectly excludes or limits' the obligations and liability of the carrier, maritime performing party, shipper, consignee, controlling party, holder or documentary shipper. In respect of the obligations or liability of the carrier or maritime performing party contractual increase of obligation/liability is, however, permitted.

[82] See n 15, above and accompanying text.

called 'volume contracts' which, for the first time, are regulated in an international convention, are subject to special rules providing for extensive freedom of contract. This represents an important novel feature, distinguishing the new Rotterdam Rules from existing conventions in the field and, therefore, is of particular interest.[83]

A volume contract is very broadly defined in Article 1(2) as:

> a contract of carriage that provides for the carriage of a specified quantity of goods in a series of shipments during an agreed period of time. The specification of the quantity may include a minimum, a maximum or a certain range.

Parties to a volume contract may derogate from the provisions of the Convention (Article 80), subject to certain conditions and subject to some statutory limits to the right to derogate.

These statutory limits to the right to derogate include, on the *carrier* side: (a) the loss of the right to financial limitation of liability in case of recklessness or intention (Article 61); and (b) the obligation, under Article 14(a) and (b), to make and keep the ship seaworthy and to properly crew, equip and supply the ship. Not mentioned in this context is the third aspect of the carrier's seaworthiness obligation, ie the obligation to make and keep the vessel cargoworthy (*cf* Article 14(c));[84] therefore, contractual derogation in this respect would, quite surprisingly, be permitted. Thus, under a volume contract, a vessel may not necessarily have to be cargoworthy.

As concerns obligations and liabilities of the *shipper*, no derogations are permitted regarding (a) the duty to provide documentation, instructions and information under Article 29, and (b) the obligations and (strict) liability arising in the context of dangerous goods, under Article 32. From a shipper's perspective, it is important to note that its liability arising from breach of Articles 29 and 32 – which may be extensive, such as in the case of damage, loss or delay of a vessel – may not be contractually excluded, limited or modified. This means that a shipper would always be exposed to potentially extensive (and 'unlimited') liability under the Rotterdam Rules for losses arising from the carriage of dangerous cargo or breach of the obligation to provide certain documentation, information and instructions.

Volume contracts are exempt from the mandatory scope of application of the liability regime, based on the proposition that these types of contract are concluded between parties with potentially equal bargaining power.[85] However, the definition of a volume contract is extremely wide and no minimum quantity of cargo is prescribed. It would therefore seem that almost any type of contract in the liner-trade might be devised as a volume contract, subject to almost complete freedom of contract.[86] Given that liner carriage is dominated by a small number

---

[83] For more detailed analysis and comment by the author, see Asariotis, 'UNCITRAL Draft Convention' (2009). For further references see also Asariotis, 'The Rotterdam Rules' (2009) (n 7).

[84] See n 30, above.

[85] See only the Report of the UNCITRAL Working Group on the work of its final session in January 2008, A/CN.9/645, at para 36.

[86] Experience with US 'service contracts', under which in some trades reportedly more than 80% of cargo is carried and on which volume contracts under the Rotterdam Rules are, to an extent, modelled (see also nn 90–93 and accompanying text, below), suggests that these types of contracts may be used

of global liner-carriage operators,[87] the question arises as to whether the statutory safeguards included in the Rotterdam Rules are effective to protect small parties against the use of volume contracts as contractual devices to circumvent the mandatory liability regime.

As between carrier and shipper, derogations from the Convention set out in a volume contract are binding, even if the contract has not been individually negotiated.[88] Although the shipper must be given the opportunity to contract on terms of the Convention without derogation, in practice, a shipper may find itself under commercial pressure to agree to a volume contract, such as where a much higher freight rate would apply unless consent was given. Similarly, while third parties are only bound by volume contracts if they 'express[ly] consent' to be bound,[89] it is not clear whether this will ensure the effective protection of small third-party consignees who, in practice, may find that their only commercially viable choice is to give their consent. Thus, depending on the approach taken by courts in the application of the relevant provisions, it would remain to be seen whether the statutory safeguards are adequate to ensure that notional agreement of a volume contract may not be used as a contractual device to circumvent otherwise applicable mandatory liability rules, to the detriment of a small shipper or consignee.

It is important to note that the concept of the volume contract is to an extent modelled on that of the US 'service contract',[90] defined in the Shipping Act of 1984[91] in broadly similar, albeit more restrictive terms.[92] However, while service contracts

---

not only as between large shippers and carriers, but also for the carriage of very small quantities, such as 10 or 20 TEUs or even 1 TEU. See *The Impact of the Ocean Shipping Reform Act of 1998*, a study published by the FMC in 2001 (www.fmc.gov/assets/1/Page/OSRA_Study.pdf), at 18–19, 84–85. Of the 1,000 service contracts sampled for the purposes of the study, 60% were for 100 TEUs or less, with cargo quantities ranging from as low as 1 TEU. Less than 10% of contracts sampled contained any provisions on contractual terms such as carrier liability.

[87] See UNCTAD, Review of Maritime Transport 2012, Table 2.6, according to which the top 20 service operators of container ships control around 70% of global TEU capacity.

[88] Art 80(2). Derogations are binding provided the volume contract 'contains a prominent statement that it derogates from [the] Convention' and 'prominently specifies the sections of the volume contract containing the derogations'. Derogations may not be 'incorporated by reference from another document nor … included in a contract of adhesion that is not subject to negotiation'. The shipper must be 'given an opportunity and notice of the opportunity to conclude a contract … without any derogation'.

[89] Art 80(5). Derogations in a volume contract are binding for 'any person other than the shipper' provided that

(a) Such person received information that prominently states that the volume contract derogates from [the] Convention and gave its express consent to be bound by such derogations and; (b) Such consent is not solely set forth in a carrier's public schedule of prices and services, transport document or electronic transport record.

[90] The concept of what was to become a 'volume contract' was first introduced, as part of the negotiations, in the form of a proposal for an 'Ocean Liner Service Agreement' (UNCITRAL document A/CN.9/WG.III/WP.34) a type of agreement 'modelled on the "service contract" created by the US Shipping Law of 1984'; see MF Sturley, T Fujita, G van der Ziel, *The Rotterdam Rules* (London, Sweet & Maxwell, 2010) at 13.044. Further details about the relevant drafting history are provided at 13.040-48.

[91] The Shipping Act of 1984, 46 USC app § 1701 et seq, was amended by the Ocean Shipping Reform Act of 1998 ('OSRA 1998'), Pub L 105–258, 112 Stat 1902 (1998) effective 1 May 1999.

[92] See the definition in s 3(19) of the Shipping Act of 1984 (as amended by OSRA 1998):

Service contract means a written contract, other than a bill of lading or receipt, between one or more shippers and an individual ocean common carrier or an agreement between or among ocean

are heavily regulated and their use is subject to oversight by the Federal Maritime Commission (FMC),[93] volume contracts at a global level would not be subject to any meaningful controls.

The provisions on volume contracts may – if and when the Convention enters into force – have important repercussions, both for commercial contracting practice and, more generally, for the prospects of international legal uniformity in the field of carriage of goods. If, in future practice, the use of volume contracts with contractual modification of the provisions of the Convention were to become the norm, the potential benefits associated with an internationally uniform liability regime would, in the longer run, fail to materialise altogether.

VIII. SUMMARY

The Rotterdam Rules introduce a number of important changes to the position under existing international maritime liability regimes. Views on the commercial *quid pro quo* inherent in the Rotterdam Rules will vary, depending on whose interests are seen as more important: those of the carrier or those of the shipper/consignee. However in terms of substance, the Rotterdam Rules appear overall to be more favourable to carriers than any of the existing international conventions in the field.

While the Hague Rules, Hague-Visby Rules and Hamburg Rules are primarily geared towards protecting smaller shippers and consignees against a carrier's unfair standard contract terms, the Rotterdam Rules appear to be designed for use by commercial parties who are potentially equal negotiating partners. As a result, there is an important shift in the established commercial risk allocation between carriers and shippers/consignees. The obligations and liabilities of the shipper, which are more extensive and detailed than under existing maritime liability regimes, are for the first time mandatory, and the shipper, in contrast to the carrier, is not entitled to monetary limitation of liability. This approach appears somewhat inequitable, but also difficult to justify. Traditionally, the rationale for mandatory regulation of commercial contracts for carriage of goods by sea has been one of public policy: inequality of bargaining power in the context of contracts of adhesion giving rise to the need for protection against unfair contract terms.[94] It is this rationale which

common carriers in which the shipper makes a commitment to provide a certain minimum quantity or portion of its cargo or freight revenue over a fixed time period, and the individual ocean common carrier or the agreement commits to a certain rate or rate schedule and a defined service level, such as, assured space, transit time, port rotation, or similar service features. The contract may also specify provisions in the event of nonperformance on the part of any party.

[93] For further information, see www.fmc.gov/resources/how_to_file_service_contracts.aspx. There are obvious differences regarding the definition and specific regulation of service contracts under US legislation and of volume contracts under the Rotterdam Rules. In particular, it should be noted that in the United States, the ocean transport industry is subject to oversight by the Federal Maritime Commission, with primary statutory guidance provided in the Shipping Act of 1984.

[94] This in particular, given the use of the bill of lading in international trade on shipment terms and the position of a third party consignee. As will be recalled, the cargo-claimant may be the final buyer

explains why the established maritime liability regimes provide for mandatory minimum standards only in respect of *carrier* liability.

The Rotterdam Rules impose mandatory liability on the shipper without, however, any apparent rationale, other than that the modern shipper is much more the carrier's equal and no longer in need of protection. If this be the case, then why have mandatory standards of liability at all, why not leave commercial parties to agree as they wish? This in particular, as a special contractual vehicle for use by contracting parties with potentially equal bargaining power has been established in the form of the 'volume contract', to allow for significant freedom of contract. If the *mandatory* application of the Rotterdam Rules liability regime is, in any event, effectively restricted to what may be called contracts of adhesion, it is difficult to see the justification for adopting an approach less protective of shippers and third-party consignees than existing maritime liability regimes.

Moreover, the rules on burden of proof seem to be more advantageous to carriers than those in the Hague-Visby Rules or Hamburg Rules, with potentially important consequences for the outcome of legal disputes between carrier and cargo interests.[95] The issue is of particular relevance where unseaworthiness of the vessel has contributed to a loss. This is not only because unseaworthiness, in English law often referred to as an 'overriding obligation' of the carrier,[96] typically becomes an operative cause of a loss in combination with some other factor[97] and, in these cases, the relevant proportion of loss due to the different causes may be particularly difficult to prove. Unseaworthiness is also often one of the causes of a potentially major *loss of the carrier*, namely in cases where unseaworthiness, in combination with the shipment of dangerous goods, leads to damage or loss of the vessel or results in extensive third-party liability of the carrier. In particular in this context, the question of who bears the relevant burden of proof and of how, in the absence of evidence, liability should be allocated is of major commercial significance.

Under existing international conventions, provided the cargo claimant can establish a loss, the carrier is presumed to be liable.[98] Where different causes have

---

in a string of CIF contracts. With risk of loss or damage of the goods in transit on the buyer, the final consignee will have to pay its seller even if no goods arrive and will instead have to pursue a cargo-claim against the carrier.

[95] While the text of relevant provisions has undergone some change during the negotiations, a potential shift in commercial risk-allocation arising from regulation of burden of proof under the draft Convention was apparent as early as in 2002. See Asariotis, 'Allocation of liability' (2002) and Asariotis, 'Main Obligations' (2004) (n 7).

[96] In respect of the overriding nature of the seaworthiness obligation under the Hague Rules, see particularly the dictum of Lord Somervell of Harrow in the Privy Council decision in *Maxine Footwear Co Ltd v Canadian Government Merchant Marine* [1959] AC 589 (602–03). See also *Mediterranean Freight Services Ltd v BP Oil International Ltd (The Fiona)* [1994] 2 Lloyd's Rep 506, per Hirst LJ at 519.

[97] See text to n 47, above.

[98] The Hamburg Rules contain a clear and categorical presumption of fault, neatly summarised in the Common Understanding, set out in its Annex II:

It is the common understanding that the liability of the carrier is based on the principle of presumed fault or neglect. This means that, as a rule, the burden of proof rests on the carrier but, with respect to certain cases, the provisions of the Convention modify this rule.

contributed to a loss, the carrier can only escape liability to the extent that it can establish a quantifiable proportion of the loss not due to its breach. Any evidentiary problems are those of the carrier and, in the absence of evidence on how much of a loss may be attributed to a cause for which the carrier is not responsible, the carrier would be liable for the entire loss. This is expressly the position under Article 5(7) of the Hamburg Rules;[99] in respect of the Hague and Hague-Visby Rules, the same follows from jurisprudence at a high level – at least under current US and English law.[100]

In contrast, the Rotterdam Rules envisage proportional allocation of liability but say nothing on who shall bear the burden of proof with regard to the respective *proportions* of loss due to different contributory causes. Thus, in the absence of relevant evidence, the carrier would be liable for only part of the loss claimed. This represents a clear departure from the established approach, resulting in a shift in commercial risk-allocation between carrier and cargo.[101] While proportional allocation of liability under the Rotterdam Rules is seen by some as justified in view of the elimination of the 'nautical fault' defence[102] it is submitted that the 'art of tuning the burden of proof'[103] has arguably been taken one step too far:

This common understanding is also reflected in Art 5(1) of the Hamburg Rules, which sets out the basis of liability. The Hague-Visby Rules are less explicit on the matter and, of course, also contain two exceptions to liability which are available in cases of fault. However, the basic premise is the same: the carrier is liable unless it can establish the loss is covered by an exception to liability. See further Asariotis, 'Allocation of liability' (2002), Asariotis, 'Burden of proof' (2008) and Asariotis, 'Loss Due' (2009) (n 7).

[99] The provision states with exemplary clarity:
Where fault or neglect on the part of the carrier, his servants or agents combines with another cause to produce loss, damage or delay in delivery the carrier is liable only to the extent that the loss, damage or delay in delivery is attributable to such fault or neglect, provided that the carrier proves the amount of the loss, damage or delay in delivery not attributable thereto.

[100] See nn 43, 57 and 58, above.

[101] This is readily acknowledged by some of the Rotterdam Rules' most ardent proponents, in particular in the United States. See, eg MF Sturley, 'The Carrier's Liability under the Rotterdam Rules: the "Well-balanced Compromise" of Article 17', in *Scritti in onore di Francesco Berlingieri, Il Diritto Marittimo* (2010) Vol I, at 977 (994): 'The Hamburg Rules and many national legal systems [see, eg Schnell v Vallescura] impose an insuperable burden on carriers to prove the allocation for responsibility among the various causes when cargo is lost, damaged, or delayed as a result of multiple causes. The Convention's imposition of new responsibility made it necessary to revise that approach. Art 17(6) accordingly announces a new rule for allocating responsibility in multiple causation cases'. See also MF Sturley, 'Modernizing and Reforming US Maritime Law: The Impact of the Rotterdam Rules in the United States' (2009) 44 *Texas International Law Journal* 427 at 448: 'Although the Hamburg Rules adopted the Vallescura Rule, the Rotterdam Rules implicitly reject this approach'. To the same effect, see also C Hooper, 'The Rotterdam Rules: Simpler than they Appear' (2009) 40 *The Arbitrator* 5, available at www.smany.org/sma/pdf/Vol40_No3_Apr2009.pdf. For the assumption that 'the so-called "Vallescura principle" is provided by the new Convention as well', see, for instance, A von Ziegler, in von Ziegler, Schelin and Zunarelli (eds), *The Rotterdam Rules 2008* (Kluwer, 2010) at para 5.2.6.

[102] See nn 44 and 46, above and accompanying text.

[103] The expression was coined by A Diamond, writing in 1978, as part of his comments on the absence of special provisions dealing with nautical fault in the Hamburg Rules. Describing the quandary draftsmen of international conventions may find themselves in, he states:
There may be an unanswerable case in a particular situation for excluding liability for negligence but they are precluded from excluding it. Again they may wish to give an exclusion for negligence as a trade off for a concession on some other point. So they try to do indirectly what they dare not

relevant adjustments to the burden of proof could have much wider repercussions for the outcome of claims, in particular in cases where loss is due at least in part to unseaworthiness of a vessel.

In relation to *claims by the carrier* against the shipper for loss arising in connection with the shipment of dangerous goods (eg loss of or damage to the vessel), the rules on burden of proof matter even more and appear particularly onerous for the shipper, especially in cases where unseaworthiness has been a contributory factor.[104] In the absence of evidence on how much of the loss was due to the different cooperating causes, a shipper would, under existing international regimes, not be liable at all, whereas under the Rotterdam Rules, a shipper could, depending on what courts make of the provisions, often become liable in full.

The complex provisions which, under certain circumstances, permit the carrier to deliver the goods without surrender of a negotiable transport document and to dispose of 'undelivered' goods in a number of ways, are both new and problematic. While the relevant provisions appear to be designed to address the practical problem of bills of lading arriving late at the port of discharge and not being available when the vessel is ready, they may seriously undermine the document of title function of the negotiable bill of lading, which is key to its use in international trade A negotiable bill of lading provides its holder with independent documentary security, as the carrier may only hand over the goods against surrender of the document. If goods are delivered without surrender of the bill of lading, a carrier may become liable for misdelivery to the lawful holder of the bill. Under the Rotterdam Rules, the carrier would be permitted, in certain circumstances, to deliver the goods to a party other than the lawful holder of the negotiable bill of lading, provided the transport document contains a statement giving the carrier this option.

This statutory solution resembles, in its aims, a controversial practice emerging among some liner carriers in the early 2000s, who by way of including suitable clauses in their standard transport documents, sought to make surrender of the negotiable bill of lading optional rather than required.[105] While it is by no means clear whether courts would give effect to relevant bill of lading clauses under the Hague-Visby Rules, it is clear that courts would have to give effect to the statutory solution envisaged in the Rotterdam Rules, if and when the Convention enters into force. More likely than not, following entry into force of the Rotterdam Rules, many liner carriers would be inclined to include a standard term in their bills of lading to allow (in certain circumstances) for delivery of the goods without surrender of the document.

---

do directly: rather than exclude liability for negligence, they attempt by means of 'tuning' to deter the claimant from pursuing his claim. Such attempts I would regard as inadmissible and doomed to failure.
See A Diamond, 'The Legal Analysis of the Hamburg Rules, Part I', in *The Hamburg Rules– A one day Seminar Organized by Lloyd's of London Press, 28 September 1978 CMI* (London 1978), at p 12.

[104] See above, text to n 64 *et seq*.
[105] An example for such a clause can be found in the 2003 edition of the *Maersk Sealand Bill of Lading for Ocean Transport or Multimodal Transport* which, however, was later withdrawn.

The net-upshot is that under the Rotterdam Rules a lawful bill of lading holder, such as a CIF buyer, having paid its seller against tender of the documents, may be left empty-handed and without rights of recourse against the carrier.[106] Unpaid sellers or banks too, could be affected in similar ways. Thus sellers, buyers and banks engaged in international trade and in need of independent documentary security would be well advised to carefully take note and (try to) ensure that any 'negotiable transport document' they accept does not permit delivery of the goods without surrender of the document.[107]

More generally, shippers and consignees using any type of transport document or electronic record (negotiable or non-negotiable) should be aware that their new statutory obligation to accept delivery has teeth: if goods remain 'undelivered', the carrier may be entitled to dispose of the goods in a variety of ways, at the risk and expense of the person entitled to the goods. How the complex new provisions in chapter 9 will be applied in practice remains to be seen, but much litigation may be expected.

The regulation of volume contracts in the Rotterdam Rules, also new and untested, may lead to a state of affairs in which freedom of contract becomes the norm and in which strength of bargaining power matters more than it has, since the advent of the Hague Rules in 1924. This is of particular concern from the perspective of small shippers and consignees who, as a result of commercial pressure, may effectively have to agree, in exchange for an acceptable freight rate, to contractual terms set unilaterally by one of a small number of large global liner-carrying companies. Larger shippers too, should be aware that their potentially extensive liability under the Rotterdam Rules for loss arising (at least in part) from the carriage of dangerous goods would be non-negotiable, even in the context of a volume contract. More generally, extensive use of volume contracts in future commercial contracting practice – with teams of lawyers negotiating additions, deletions and amendments to provisions of the Rotterdam Rules – could effectively mean less, rather than more, legal certainty at the international level. Most likely, courts in different jurisdictions would take different views on the construction and interpretation of such volume contracts and any 'modified version' of the Rotterdam Rules.

In relation to regulation of liability arising from multimodal transport involving an international sea leg, the Rotterdam Rules adopt an approach which is potentially problematic and unlikely to create the much-needed international uniformity. While the present international framework is complex,[108] entry into force of the Rotterdam Rules would, it is submitted, make it even more so.

---

[106] The position is similar in the case of a straight bill of lading containing an *express* provision requiring its surrender, such as the *MSC bill of lading*, available at www.mscgva.ch/bl_terms/bl_standard_terms.html. Para (2) of Art 46 allows the carrier, under certain circumstances (ie where the document is not available when the goods arrive and the carrier cannot find the consignee), to request delivery instructions from the shipper or documentary shipper. The carrier would be discharged of its delivery obligation despite a clear indication on the document that its surrender is required. Any independent documentary security that a shipper or consignee may associate with this document (*cf The Rafaela S* [2005] UKHL 11) would be seriously undermined.

[107] As regards straight bills of lading, see previous n 106.

[108] For a detailed overview of the complexity of the current international liability framework, see UNCTAD, *Multimodal Transport: the Feasibility of an International Legal Instrument*, UNCTAD/SDTE/TLB/2003, in particular Table 1. The report is available at www.unctad.org/ttl/legal.

As only multimodal contracts that 'provide for' international carriage of goods by sea would be governed by the Rotterdam Rules, the question of whether an individual contract envisaging/permitting multimodal transport falls within the definition of 'contract of carriage' is important. However, given the lack of precision in the definition of the term, courts in different states may adopt different views on the matter, leading to varying outcomes; commercial parties will have to foot the bill and contend themselves with lack of certainty. Moreover, even if a multimodal contract falls within the definition of a contract of carriage, the question as to the applicable substantive rules remains a difficult one to answer.

The Rotterdam Rules preserve the application of international conventions on road, rail, air and inland waterway carriage *to the extent that they apply, according to their own provisions, beyond pure unimodal transportation*. Once again, this will require judicial interpretation of the potentially relevant unimodal conventions, arguably with differing outcomes depending on the jurisdiction. In cases where no existing unimodal convention takes precedence, and the Rotterdam Rules are applicable, substantive liability rules would vary, depending on: (a) whether a loss could be attributed to a particular non-maritime leg of the multimodal transport; and (b) whether existing international conventions governing carriage of goods by land or air would have applied, had a separate contract been made for that particular leg of the transport:

- In cases where a loss could not be localised, as will often be the case in containerised transport, the substantively maritime liability regime set out in the Rotterdam Rules would apply – in all its complexity.
- The position would be the same in cases where a loss arose during land transport, but none of the existing unimodal international conventions would have been applicable (had a separate contract been made for that particular leg of the transport). Judges would be required to ensure that the substantively maritime Rotterdam Rules apply in a meaningful and uniform manner to such claims.
- Finally, in cases where a loss could in fact be attributed to a mode of transport other than sea-carriage *and* one of the existing unimodal transport conventions would have applied (had a separate unimodal contract been made), courts in different jurisdictions would have to apply a complex mixture of substantive rules in context: *mandatory provisions on 'carrier liability, limitation of liability or time for suit'* contained in the relevant unimodal land or air convention, *together with the remainder of the Rotterdam Rules*. Clearly, this in particular is a challenging task likely to result in nationally differing approaches and, ultimately, judgments.

More generally however, and most importantly, the complexity and considerable scope for interpretation inherent in the Convention means that extensive litigation is likely to be required to gain a clear understanding of the new rules, with courts in different jurisdictions adopting potentially differing approaches to interpretation and application of the provisions.[109] This outlook may be somewhat

---

[109] The likelihood of nationally varying outcomes of disputes, conflicting legal proceedings and, ultimately, conflicting judgments at international level is further compounded by the fact that as noted

good news for maritime lawyers, but not for commercial parties in international trade. It is particularly unfortunate in respect of a new international convention, a main purpose of which is to enhance legal certainty at the international level.

IX. CONCLUDING REMARKS

As was noted at the outset, at this juncture, the question is really whether the Rotterdam Rules offer a substantive set of rules that is better suited to the needs of modern commercial practice than existing regimes, and whether their entry into force would enhance legal certainty at the international level.

The text of the Rotterdam Rules is there for anyone to study and reflect upon. Much has been and will be written about the Convention. This author's analysis of some of the key features of the Rotterdam Rules suggests that they are problematic, in particular from the perspective of a shipper, but also for reasons which are not related to conflicting commercial interests.[110] Above all the Rotterdam Rules are, unfortunately, exceedingly complicated. This, it is submitted, is their 'Achilles heel'. Whatever else one may make of the substantive content of the Rules, it appears beyond argument that the entry into force of the Rotterdam Rules would give rise to extensive – and costly – litigation. This prospect should be of some concern to potentially affected commercial parties.

Whether the Rotterdam Rules have a future can, at this stage, only be a matter of conjecture. As will be recalled, the Hamburg Rules entered into force but failed to attract the support of any of the main shipping nations. There have been a number of reasons for this 'rejection', including an increase in the carrier's liability as compared with the Hague-Visby Rules, and the omission of the notorious 'nautical fault' defence. However, arguably one of the main reasons why the Hamburg Rules have never really taken off was that they were not seen to offer sufficient benefits to make up for the fact that they were different from the Hague-Visby Rules – in terms of style and structure – and, as a result, would require extensive judicial clarification. Whether a similar cost-benefit analysis in respect of the Rotterdam Rules produces a different result remains to be seen. The Rotterdam Rules may well fare better than the Hamburg Rules – if a sufficient number of shipping nations are persuaded that ratification is in their best interest. But they could also fare worse – and become a mere footnote in the history of Transport Law.

---

above, chapters in the Convention setting out rules on jurisdiction and arbitration are optional for Contracting States and, as a result, contractual jurisdiction and arbitration clauses may be valid under the same conditions in only some, but not all, Contracting States.

[110] A number of relevant issues had already been highlighted as potentially problematic in 2002, when a first consolidated Draft Instrument on Transport Law became available as document A/CN.9/ WG.III/WP.21. See UNCTAD, *Commentary on Draft Instrument on Transport Law*, UNCTAD/SDTE/ TLB/4 (2002). See also UNCTAD/SDTE/TLB/2004/2. Both documents are available at www.unctad. org/ttl/legal.

7

Multimodal Transport Evolving: Freedom and Regulation Three Decades after the 1980 MTO Convention

FILIPPO LORENZON

MORE THAN THREE decades after the adoption of the 1980 MTO Convention, the world of international trade is not yet able to rely on a proper international liability regime for multimodal carriage. This is notwithstanding considerable investments of time and resources by international[1] and regional organisations, a significant regional attempt to create a more or less uniform multimodal liability framework,[2] the development of multimodal provisions in unimodal transport conventions[3] and – lastly – the interesting development of the Rotterdam Rules.[4]

International trade law is usually responsive to the needs of its industry and steadily follows technological developments, economic and political change and market practices.[5] At a relatively early stage of the container revolution, standard form contracts[6] and associated trade practices were quickly developed by the industry to try and solve the most common difficulties faced by multimodal transport operators. Unsurprisingly the international regulator also attempted to follow.[7] Equally unsurprisingly, the regulator failed and the issue of multimodal carriage was left to piecemeal provisions in unimodal conventions. The Rotterdam

---

[1] In particular from the United Nation Conference for Trade and Developments (UNCTAD) and the United Nation Conference for International Trade Law (UNCITRAL).

[2] On the institutional side a particular effort towards uniform liability has been made by the European Commission.

[3] As Art 18.4 of the 1999 Montreal Convention; Art 2(1) of the CMR; Art 1.4 of the COTIF-CIM 1999; and partly Art 2.2 of the CMNI in respect of sea and inland waterways transportation.

[4] The 2009 UN Convention on the Carriage of Goods Wholly or Partly by Sea.

[5] On the private and non-regulatory side, the effort to tackle the issue of the liability of multimodal transport operators has been very intense: FIATA, ICC and BIMCO are only the most prominent private international bodies who have worked towards an industry led practical solution.

[6] Eg the FIATA Multimodal Transport Bill of Lading, the UNCTAD/ICC Rules for Multimodal Transport Documents (ICC Publication 481) and COMBIDOC first, followed by COMBICONBILL, COMBICONWAYBILL, MULTIDOC 95 and MILTIWAYBILL 95 from BIMCO.

[7] With the 1980 United Nations Convention on International Multimodal Transport of Goods.

Rules have now made a last attempt with the so-called 'maritime plus'[8] approach where unimodal thinking is extended to multimodal transport.

The proliferation of attempted 'solutions' to a relatively simple 'problem' however, has generated a serious legal difficulty: a number of legally binding regimes at risk of conflicting with each other and make a true multimodal regime hardly possible to devise. *This* technological change, a natural evolution of the surge of international trade in manufactured goods, and the ever-increasing geographical split between producers and consumers, seem to have been incapable of developing a legal regime fit to deal satisfactorily with the issues it generates.

The very special circumstances surrounding this paper and the very purpose of this book provide the perfect opportunity to try and understand whether the *quasi*-perfect mechanism of evolution has failed multimodal transport law or – to the contrary – has worked brilliantly and contributed substantially to take containerisation to its current success. This will be done by looking at the aim of evolution in international trade practice and applying it to the current state of play of the multimodal carriage liability. The discussion will revolve around the concept of evolution and its suggested applicability to international trade practice; the multimodal liability conundrum and its current contractual solutions will be the starting point of this analysis, which will then shift towards international and regional attempts at unification in order to evaluate the reason behind their failures in evolutionary terms. It will be concluded that the possibility of a uniform liability regime is certainly possible and technically more desirable than all current approaches; but the market evolves its own way and will maintain its freely self-determined course as long as it proves competitive and eventually successful.

I. THE CONCEPT OF 'EVOLUTION'

The necessary starting point for any discussion on evolution must be Charles Darwin and his much discussed theory. A legal article is certainly not the most obvious place to discuss such a theory but it would be extraordinary if a rule which has inspired so much debate and research was to be considered *a priori* unsuitable for legal reasoning.

A good, recent and apt formulation of this theory may be found in Prof Ruse's book on Darwinism, where the author states:

> Not all organisms that are born survive and (more importantly) reproduce. Those that are successful in the struggle will tend to do so, because they have features not possessed by the unsuccessful. Thus there will be a constant selecting or winnowing, with only the successful passing on features to future generations. Supposing a continual supply of new variations and that these variations are in fact heritable, given sufficient time, one will get full-blown coverage: what Darwin called 'descent with modification' and we call 'evolution'.[9]

---

[8] B Marten, 'Multimodal Transport Reform and the European Union: A Treaty Change Approach' (2012) 36 *Tulane Maritime Law Journal* 741, at 754.

[9] M Ruse, *Dawinsim Defended: A Guide to the Evolution Controversies* (1982, Addison-Wesley, Canada), at p 26.

If we accept this as a good definition of evolution of the species, can we adopt it in the context of international trade? It is here suggested that when it comes to international commerce, where the law constantly changes to follow new industry needs or overcome problems or situation created by practice, major accidents and new risks, the concept of evolution is extremely apposite. Evolving means first and foremost striving for success, resolving, improving, making more efficient and reliable: the very essence of commerce.

Multimodal containerised transport is extremely successful worldwide, its lack of a uniform legal regime notwithstanding. This must mean one of two things: (a) the industry has evolved to live with the shortcoming of the international legal environment for containerised cargo; or (b) such legal environment is perfectly suitable for multimodal carriage. Both alternatives would explain the current state of play. None of them would require the intervention of a *deus ex machina* to fix what is clearly not broke.

Some evidence to support the first alternative can be found in a 2003 UNCTAD report[10] according to which a large percentage of operators expressed serious concern about the inefficiency of the current legal regime. However, in a similar market consultation conducted on behalf of DG TREN at the Institute of Maritime Law in Southampton in 2006[11] the industry appeared not keen on undergoing any radical change. This was partly attributed to the fact that UNCITRAL was then drafting the Rotterdam Rules, partly because the proposal came from a regional source as the EU rather than from a truly global player but – most interestingly – because there was no perceived need to undertake the cost and uncertainty of legal change.

Strong evidence in support of the second alternative is to be found in the massive development of containerised transport and its current volumes and routes, the massive surge of container terminals worldwide and the political strive towards intermodal integration, dry ports and multimodal distribution centres. How could this happen if the international legal regime surrounding multimodal transport was so inefficient and unpredictable? And really, is it?

II. THE MULTIMODAL TRANSPORT PROBLEM

Every contract for the carriage of goods implies a relationship of bailor, bailee and bailment, according to which the carrier must deliver the goods at destination in the same condition as they have been received by it at the place of loading. The carrier is strictly liable for failure to do so; unless due to act of God,[12] enemies of the sovereign of the carrier,[13] inherent vice[14] and jettison, save

---

[10] UNCTAD, Multimodal Transport: The Feasibility of an International Legal Regime, UNCTAD/SDTE/TLB/2003/1.

[11] F Lorenzon, M Clarke, J Ramberg, R Herber, *Integrated Services in the Intermodal Chain*, available at http://folk.uio.no/erikro/WWW/cog/Intermodal%20liability%20and%20documentation.pdf.

[12] *Nugent v Smith* (1876) 1 CPD 423.

[13] *Russell v Niemann* (1864) 17 CB NS 163.

[14] *The Barcore* [1896] P 294 and *Hudson v Baxendale* (1857) 2 H&N 575 for its insufficient packing version.

for its negligence.[15] Common carriers can however avail themselves of their contractual freedom to reduce or exclude their exposure to the principles of bailment and the liabilities connected thereto.

Although read strictly *contra proferentem*,[16] such clauses have produced appalling results in practice, as it happened in the English case *The Kapitan Sakharov*.[17] It is in particular for the protection of third party cargo interests from the unfair results of smart exclusion clauses that compulsory international legislation restricting freedom of contract started to develop at the end of the nineteenth century.

Before considering whether the current lack of a multimodal regime at international level is a problem requiring a legislative solution, it should be established whether there is an actual need for a compulsory legal regime for multimodal transport.[18] The first question which must be asked therefore is whether the current contractual framework for multimodal transport produces unfair results.

Current commercial practice appears to use multimodal transport documents in both negotiable and non-negotiable form. Negotiable multimodal bills in use include BIMCO's 'MULTIDOC 95', 'COMBICONBILL' and the FIATA Multimodal Transport Bill of Lading. Some multimodal carriers and NVOCC have adopted their own in-house standard form (eg P&O Nedlloyd's Bill of Lading for Combined Transport or Port to Port shipment). Among non-negotiable transport documents specifically devised for multimodal transport, two are worth mentioning for their widespread use in commercial transactions: BIMCO's MULTIWAYBILL and COMBICON-WAYBILL. Some carriers have also drafted their own in-house seawaybill (eg P&O Nedlloyd's Non-Negotiable Waybill for Combined Transport shipment or Port to Port Shipment).[19]

All these documents provide for a more or less complete contractual liability regime with clear rules on the basis of liability,[20] available defences in different stages of the voyage,[21] limitation[22] and time bar.[23] It is certainly true to say that each and every bill of lading devises its regime somewhat differently, on the basis of the concept of what is known as the limited network liability system, with the benefit of avoiding as much as possible, interference with mandatory regimes applicable to unimodal segments of the adventure. In practice, this means that the outcome of every single claim depends on the wording of the contract and the specific circumstances of the case. But is this not the case for any unimodal bill or waybill subject to compulsory international legislation?

---

[15] *Aktieselskabet de Danske Sukkerfabrikker v Bajamar Compania Naviera SA (The Torenia)* [1983] 2 Lloyd's Rep. 210; the 'exception to the exception' argument.

[16] *Glynn v Margetson* [1893] AC 351.

[17] [2000] 2 Lloyd's Rep 255.

[18] For some interesting thoughts on the concept of multimodalism, see R Thomas, 'Multimodalism and Through Transport – Language, Concepts and Categories' (2012) 36 *Tulane Maritime Law Journal* 37.

[19] F Lorenzon, M Clarke, J Ramberg, R Herber, *Integrated Services in the Intermodal Chain*, available at http://folk.uio.no/erikro/WWW/cog/Intermodal%20liability%20and%20documentation.pdf, at 30.

[20] Eg MULTIDOC 95, cl. 10; FIATA Bill, cl. 6.

[21] Eg MULTIDOC 95, cl. 11; FIATA Bill, cl. 6.6.

[22] Eg MULTIDOC 95, cl. 12; FIATA Bill, cl. 8.

[23] Eg MULTIDOC 95, cl. 4; FIATA Bill, cl. 17.

Moreover, it is also true to say that this practice does not appear to have created particularly hash or unfair results on cargo interests. The market for multimodal carriage is certainly not as concentrated as it is for single mode transport operators and competition among different players, coupled with the favourable conditions of the last decades and the current shipping crisis, have not offered fertile soil for the development of dubious exclusion clauses.

The dissatisfaction expressed by the industry in the abovementioned studies[24] may well be understandable in the context of small and medium enterprises trying to access the market, but the remarks made are rather general and appear not to indicate any particular practice, clause or legal device affecting the efficiency of the system. It seems also very clearly connected with the fact that the lack of a mandatory legal regime makes it difficult to predict *a priori* the amount of compensation to which cargo interest and their insurers may be able to recover from the carrier in any given transport. However, this does not seem to be attributable to the lack of an international multimodal convention, but rather the presence of a number of unimodal conventions of mandatory nature. In practice, different regimes will be applicable to each leg of the voyage and this leads to multiple problems especially where there is overlap, conflict and discrepancy between the applicable regimes as to the same issue. The way the international community has tackled this conundrum is to develop what may be referred to as 'multimodal thinking for unimodal transport' approach; ie a philosophical endemic distortion of the unimodal regimes which seeks to tackle specific multimodal problems on a piecemeal basis.[25] A good example of this approach is how ro-ro carriage is dealt with in the CMR and CIM/COTIF. Article 2(1) of the CMR states:

> Where the *vehicle containing the goods* is carried over *part* of the journey by sea, rail, inland waterways or air [...] this Convention shall nevertheless apply to the whole of the carriage. Provided that to the extent it is proved that any loss, damage or delay in delivery of the goods which occurs during the carriage by the other means of transport was not *caused* by act or omission of the carrier by road, but *by some event which could only have occurred in the course of and by reason of the carriage by that other means of transport*, the liability of the carrier by road shall be determined [according to the relevant unimodal convention]. If, however, there are no such prescribed conditions, the liability of the carrier by road shall be determined by this Convention. (*emphasis* added)

A similar provision is to be found in Article 1(4) of the COTIF/CIM 1999:

> When international carriage being the subject of a single contract of carriage includes carriage by sea or transfrontier carriage by inland waterway *as a supplement to carriage by*

---

[24] UNCTAD, Multimodal Transport: the feasibility of an international legal regime, UNCTAD/SDTE/TLB/2003/1; and F Lorenzon, M Clarke, J Ramberg, R Herber, *Integrated Services in the Intermodal Chain*, available at http://folk.uio.no/erikro/WWW/cog/Intermodal%20liability%20and%20documentation. pdf. For some further reflections on the need for industry support, see B Marten, 'Multimodal transport reform and the European Union: a minimalist approach' (2012) 2 *European Transport Law* 129, at 138–41.

[25] See R Herber, 'The European Legal Experience with Multimodalism' (1989) 64 *Tulane Law Review* 611; B Marten, 'Multimodal transport reform and the European Union: a minimalist approach' (2012) 2 *European Transport Law* 129; and V Ulfbeck, 'Multimodal transports in the United States and Europe – Global or regional liability rules?' (2009) 34 *Tulane Maritime Law Journal* 41.

rail, these Uniform Rules shall apply if the carriage by sea or inland waterway is performed on [specific] services. (*emphasis* added)

These provisions are all complex variations of ad-hoc solutions to specific problems but are certainly *not* multimodal in nature. Even clearer is the multimodal provision in the 1999 Montreal Convention. Article 18(4) of the MC99 provides that:

> The period of the carriage by air *does not extend to any carriage by land, by sea or by inland waterway* performed outside an airport. If, however, such carriage takes place in the performance of a contract for carriage by air, for the purpose of loading, delivery or transhipment, any damage is *presumed*, subject to proof to the contrary, to have been the result of an event which took place during the carriage by air. If a carrier, *without the consent of the consignor, substitutes* carriage by another mode of transport for the whole or part of a carriage intended by the agreement between the parties to be carriage by air, such carriage by another mode of transport is deemed to be within the period of carriage by air. (*emphasis* added)

Again it is clear that the MC99 is not a multimodal convention, but includes a test based on the performance of the contract; a test of a contractual nature. The Montreal approach can certainly not be defined as an 'air plus' solution, as the extra-modal application only comes into the picture when the extra-modal carriage is made in performance of a contract for the carriage of goods by air; or as an unauthorised alternative performance. Although wider in effect and more forward thinking than the CMR and CIM/COTIF provisions, this is again clearly multimodal thinking for unimodal transport.

These solutions – as well as they may have worked in practice addressing the specific issues concerned – are and will remain unsuitable for tackling multimodal transport liabilities in full. As a matter of policy, unimodal regimes are negotiated with the parties concerned with, and to tackle the specific needs of, specific unimodal carriage: there are no 'perils of the sea' for those driving a lorry, or any need to excuse a rail carrier for failure to deliver due to its 'attempting to save life or property at sea'. Similarly, a limitation per 'package or unit' would make no commercial sense in carriage by air.

It is submitted that the only way to tackle multimodal transport issues is to approach it with true multimodal thinking. However, in evolutionary terms, this has so far proven unsuccessful.

III. MULTIMODAL TRANSPORT REGIMES EVOLVING: EARLY ATTEMPTS AT UNIFORMITY

The legislative history of multimodal transport legislation began as early as the 1930s,[26] and evidences a long-standing political desire to create a uniform regime

---

[26] As evident in the Preparation of a Preliminary Draft of a Convention on International Intermodal Transport. See UNCTAD Document TD/B/AC.15/2, 1973, at p 3. On a full history of the development of multimodal transport legislation see J Ramberg, *The Law of Transport Operators in International Trade* (Stockholm, 2005).

for this type of transportation.[27] The International Institute for the Unification of Private Law (UNIDROIT) led the way in terms of pushing for a multimodal transport regime, and finally published a draft regime in 1965. And then in 1969, the Comité Maritime International (CMI) adopted the Draft Convention on Combined Transport, also known as the Tokyo Rules, albeit with some differences to the UNIDROIT draft. The Rome Draft followed, the efforts of the United Nations Economic Commission for Europe (UNECE), combining the two drafts. The Rome Draft further developed into the TCM (Transport Combine de Merchandise) Draft, a failure. In the words of a later commentator:

> Efforts to preserve the existing unimodal conventions resulted in an intermodal convention too weak to achieve the objective of uniformity and efficiency in intermodal transportation [...]. Furthermore, given continued applicability of various unimodal conventions limits and the addition of yet another document to the already mandatory existing ones, it was clear that the TCM Draft Convention would not, in actuality, result in any simplification.[28]

The next attempt was made by UNCTAD who began working on a multimodal transport convention in the early 1970s. The United Nations attempt culminated in the adoption of the United Nations Convention on International Multimodal Transport of Goods in 1980.[29] The convention developed some of the solutions underpinning the previous attempts and tried to address the problems raised by multimodal transportation in a comprehensive and relatively practical manner, including the delicate issues of documentation[30] and the liability of the multimodal transport operator[31] and the consignor.[32] The convention provides for the possibility of issuing one document – the so-called MT Document[33] – to cover the entire transportation period and for the Multimodal Transport Operator to undertake the liability of the whole period in which it is 'in charge' of the goods, ie, from the time it takes the goods in charge until the time of delivery.[34] After 33 years the MT Convention has attracted only 6 signatories and 11 parties, nowhere near the 30 needed for the Convention to enter into force.[35] As an early commentator remarked during a Conference held in Southampton in 1980:

---

[27] This was inspired by the need to '(i) simplify the transport document so that one document would serve several stages of the carriage where more than one means of transport was used; (ii) ensure that the shipper/consignee could pursue their claim against one party responsible rather than against several carriers involved.' M Faghfouri, 'International Regulation of Liability for Multimodal Transport – In Search of Uniformity' (2006) Vol 5, No 1, *WMU Journal of Maritime Affairs*, 95–114, at p 96.

[28] K Nasseri, 'The Multimodal Convention' (1988) 19(2) *Journal of International Maritime Law*, at pp 230–35.

[29] The United Nations Convention on International Multimodal Transport of Goods, done at Geneva on 24 May 1980 (hereafter *The MT Convention*), on which see R De Wit, *Multimodal Transport: Carrier Liability and Documentation* (London, 1995).

[30] *MT Convention*, Arts 5–13.

[31] *MT Convention*, Arts 14–21.

[32] *MT Convention*, Arts 22–23.

[33] *MT Convention*, Art 5.

[34] *MT Convention*, Art 14. See also M Faghfouri, 'International Regulation of Liability for Multimodal Transport – In Search of Uniformity' (2006) Vol 5, No 1, *WMU Journal of Maritime Affairs*, 95–114, at pp 97 and 98.

[35] See Art 36.

[...] the Multimodal Transport Convention has... been regarded as somewhat peculiar and has been approached with considerable uneasiness. Several reasons may explain this. The multimodal transport contract and the multimodal transport operator are new concepts. They are, however, contractual concepts akin to those applied in other parts of the law of carriage. Thus, the M.T.O. is the one contracting to carry goods multimodally, viz. by several modes of transport. Differences still exist. The familiar, existing conventions all apply only to contracts for particular types of carriage (unimodal carriage). Also, much of the thinking in the field of transportation is based on status, and again, by tradition, we are operating within a unimodal framework.[...] The new multimodal concepts is based on a different approach because it corresponds to a new system for the transportation of goods, based mainly on containerisation and other forms of unitisation of goods [...]. The implications of the new system of transportation for the existing commercial and legal traditions provide a key to understanding why the Convention has sometimes been thought to raise problems. However, it is clearly not the Convention itself, but the development of new transportation techniques and their implications which are the essential difference [...]. Uncertainty as to the future role of multimodal transport and the consequences for present transportation patterns has contributed to the uneasiness in many quarters.[36]

Others have attributed the failure of the MT Convention to the fact that 'the shippers were uncertain as to the benefits the Convention might offer them, while the maritime industry offered resistance and resorted to adverse lobbying, neither of which heightened the chances of the Convention.'[37]

After the MT Convention, more attempts were made at uniformity with different approaches. The UNCTAD/ICC Rules for Multimodal Transport Documents 1992 have tried the way of adopting a uniform contractual framework, which has proved very popular. [38] The UNCTAD/ICC Rules represent the most successful attempt to achieve uniformity so far, and this – it is submitted – is a remark worthy of careful reflection. The most important feature of these rules would appear not to be the unoriginal limited network limitation system or the promise of the MTO to undertake liability from the place of receipt to that of delivery, nor the availability of some defences specifically confined to maritime and inland waterways transport. Their success seems to be based on their contractual and hence relatively flexible nature. In evolutionary terms, the widespread acceptance of the UCITRAL/ICC Rules proved a remarkable step forward.

The lack of success in finding a worldwide standard solution does not mean that regional agreements could not and have not been reached, and South America has

---

[36] E Selvig, 'The Background to the Convention', in *Multimodal Transport – the 1980 U.N. Convention*, Papers of a One Day Seminar, Southampton University Faculty of Law, 12 September 1980, at p A1–A2.

[37] M Hoeks, *Multimodal Transport Law: The Law Applicable to the Multimodal Contract for the Carriage of Goods* (2010: Kluwer Law International), p 22.

[38] M Hoeks argues that 'As long as there is no international regime regulating multimodal transport the transport sector will make use of these kinds of contracts [such as the UNCTAD/ICC Rules for multimodal transport documents] to negate as much of the uncertainty concerning the applicable legal regime as possible. That this system seems to be working to a large extent can be deduced from the fact that there are some experts who suggest that there is no need for a new regulatory system, since the existing private law arrangements are satisfactory. Logic tells us however, that a new system would be more effective since contractual rules such as the UNCTAD/ICC Rules do not set aside any mandatory arrangements and thus the uncertainty regarding the legal regime that applies is not lifted entirely. What is more, contractual provisions such as paramount clauses choosing a certain regime as the law applicable to the contract may even enhance the confusion'. *ibid*, at p 24,

led the way in this direction. The Andean Community, current member states of which are Bolivia,[39] Colombia, Ecuador and Peru, has in fact developed its own regional liability system.[40] The Andean Community regional agreement is applicable to contracts of international multimodal transport, provided that the place of taking charge or delivery of the goods by the multimodal transport operator, as defined in the multimodal transport contract, is located in any of the member states.

Another South American regime may be found in the Partial Agreement for the Facilitation of Multimodal Transport of Goods, signed in April 1995 among the member states of Mercosur:[41] Argentina, Brazil, Paraguay, Uruguay and Venezuela.[42] Other examples include the Latin American Integration Association (ALADI) Agreement on International Multimodal Transport 1996; the Association of South-East Asian Nations (ASEAN) Draft Framework Agreement on Multimodal Transport (final draft, as of 19–20 March 2001).[43] And more recently, there was the April 2008 Draft Convention on International Multimodal Transport of Goods in The Arab Mashreq,[44] which was set to be open for signature by members of the United Nations Economic and Social Commission for Western Asia (UNESCWA) [45] in 2008/2009, but had to be postponed for further industry consultation.[46] The project is now in the hands of the Arab League.

At national level, multimodal regimes also exist[47] such as in Germany,[48] India,[49] China,[50] Argentina,[51] Brazil,[52] Mexico[53] and Netherlands.[54] But these are not the focus of this research.

---

[39] Bolivia recently became an accessing member of Mercosur in December 2012, and there is doubt as to their continued membership of the Andean Community. http://www.aljazeera.com/indepth/features/2012/12/20121231123114400572.html (last accessed on 9 May 2013)

[40] Decision 331 of 4 March 1993, as modified by Decision 393 of 9 July 1996: 'International Multimodal Transport'.

[41] Partial Agreement for the Facilitation of Multimodal Transport of Goods, 27 April 1995.

[42] Venezuela recently obtained full membership of Mercosur in July 2012, having left the Andean Community in 2006 to join Mercosur.

[43] See UNCTAD, Implementation of Multimodal Transport Rules – Comparative Table, UNCTAD/SDTE/TLB/2/Add. 1, 9 October 2001, p 6–9, for a comparison of these regional regimes as to Scope of application, Documentation, Period of responsibility, Basis of liability and limitation, Delay in delivery, time bar, jurisdiction, etc. Accessible at http://unctad.org/en/Docs/posdtetlbd2a1.en.pdf (last accessed on 9 May 2013).

[44] Accessible at http://css.escwa.org.lb/SessionDOCS/25-L-9.pdf (last accessed on 9 May 2013).

[45] Current members being Egypt, Bahrain, Iraq, Jordan, Kuwait, Lebanon, Oman, Palestine, Qatar, Saudi Arabia, Sudan, Syria, Yemen, UAE, Tunisia, Libya and Morocco.

[46] See also, J-M Moriniere, 'A Multimodal Transport Convention for the Middle East?' July, 2008, accessible at http://www.forwarderlaw.com/library/view.php?article_id=506 (last accessed on 9 May 2013).

[47] Again, see UNCTAD, Implementation of Multimodal Transport Rules – Comparative Table, UNCTAD/SDTE/TLB/2/Add. 1, 9 October 2001, p 10–17 for a comparison. Accessible at http://unctad.org/en/Docs/posdtetlbd2a1.en.pdf (last accessed on 9 May 2013).

[48] Transport Law Reform Act 1998.

[49] Multimodal Transportation of Goods Act, 1993 (No. 28 of 1993).

[50] 3 different sets of provisions – Maritime Code, 1993, Ch IV, Sec. 8: Special Provisions Regarding Multimodal Transport Contract; Regulation Governing International Multimodal Transport of Goods by Containers, 1997; and Contract Law, 1999, Ch 17, Sec. 4: Contracts for Multimodal Transportation.

[51] Law No. 24.921: Multimodal Transport of Goods, Official Bulletin 12 January 1998.

[52] Law No. 9.61 of 19 February 1998 on Multimodal Transport of Goods.

[53] Regulation on International Multimodal Transport, 6 July 1989.

[54] Civil Code, book 8, title 2, section 2.

IV. THE EU ATTEMPT: A MISSED OPPORTUNITY?

The surge in volume of containerised transport within, from and to Europe and the continuous attempts of the Union to optimise intermodal exchange, minimise the use of the carbon inefficient road transport and push the development of rail, inland waterways and EU cabotage solutions were eventually bound to come to the issue of multimodal liability. In order to justify a European regional approach to the issue of multimodal liability, the EU looked at the current legal system and found it inadequate to support intra-European free trade and an active hindrance to trade integration. According to the Commission of the European Communities, the utmost inadequacies of transport law as a whole may be summarised as follows:[55]

> The consequence of current arrangements is therefore a patchwork of regimes which fails to capitalize on modern IT-based communications systems and practices, which impedes the introduction and use of a single multimodal waybill/transport document, and which does not reflect fully the increased use of containerized transportation operating across different modes, making mode-specific liability arrangements inappropriate. In cases of loss or damage to goods, this creates uncertainty as to the time of loss/damage, uncertainty as to mode and identity of the carrier; and uncertainty as to the applicable legal regime for liability and its effects.[56]

A 2009 European Commission study also details the insufficiencies of transport law as follows:

> The present legal framework determining a carrier's liability consists of a confused jigsaw of international conventions designed to regulate unimodal carriage, diverse national laws and standard term contracts. [...] As every intermodal transaction is made up of unimodal stages, there are a number of mandatory international liability regimes which are potentially applicable, depending on their scope of application and the stage of transport where a damage or loss occurs. Accordingly, two different regimes may apply to the same claim or the regime which applies can only be identified when it is clear during which stage of the transport a loss/damage occurred. Where the stage of transport during which a loss or damage occurred cannot be identified, where loss or damage occur gradually, or in the course of (value-added) services ancillary to transportation (eg warehousing), a carrier's liability will often depend on national laws and/or contractual agreement. As a result, both the applicable liability rules and the degree and extent of a

---

[55] *Issues Relating to the Physical Movement of Consignments (Transport and Transit) & Payment, Insurance and other Financial Questions Affecting Cross-border Trade in Goods*, G/C/W/133, 3 December 1998, at. 3, accessible through http://www.wto.org/english/tratop_e/tradfa_e/tradfa_overview1999_e. htm

[56] A similar comment had been made a few years earlier by R De Wit, stating that 'the increased use of containers has illustrated very clearly the greatest shortcoming of transport law: the vast differences between the rules governing the different transport modes. Different grounds of liability, different limitations of liability, different documents with a different legal value, different time bars, these are all historically grown traits of the various legal regimes. Where it may perhaps be said that this particularism did not constitute such a formidable problem when unimodal transport was still predominant, its drawbacks become glaringly obvious when attempts are made to combine different transport modes, and, inevitably, their different legal regimes, into a single transport operation governed by a single contract.' R De Wit, *Multimodal Transport: Carrier Liability and Documentation* (London: LLP, 1995) at p 7.

carrier's liability vary greatly from case to case and are unpredictable. Liability for delay in delivery is not always covered by the same rules as liability for loss of or damage to the goods.[57]

Against this background, the Directorate-General for Energy and Transport of the European Commission (DG TREN) of the EU commissioned two studies[58] to the Institute of Maritime Law to evaluate the feasibility of a uniform liability regime for Europe and attempt an easy and clear draft for a non-mandatory European alternative of the regulation of multimodal transport. The draft was prepared by Prof Clarke, Herber, Lorenzon & Ramberg, and submitted on 21 September 2005. The aim was a set of uniform intermodal liability rules which 'concentrate the transit risk on one party and which provide for strict and full liability of the contracting carrier (the intermodal operator) for all types of losses (damage, loss, delay) irrespective of the modal stage where a loss occurs and of the causes of such a loss'[59] and to form the 'basis for further discussion with all industries concerned to find a satisfactory solution to the problems identified in the current practice of multimodal transport',[60] the end result being for the Commission to approve a multimodal transport regulation based on their proposals.

The ISIC project proposed that the Transport Integrator (the multimodal carrier) would be 'strictly liable for loss of or damage to the goods occurring between the time he takes over the goods and the time of delivery, as well as for any delay in delivery (Article 8.1), unless and to the extent the Transport Integrator proves that it was caused by circumstances beyond his control (Article 8.4).'[61]

The system is designed around the creation of the Transport Integrator, essentially a forwarder who assumes direct responsibility for carrying the goods on a multimodal basis and responsible – irrespective of whether the damage is localised or not – for loss, damage and delay. According to its Article 2:

> The provisions of this Regime shall mandatorily apply to all contracts of transport between places in two different States, if
> (a) the place for the taking in charge of the goods by the Transport Integrator as provided for in the contract of transport is located in a State member of the European Economic Community, or
> (b) the place for delivery of the goods by the Transport Integrator as provided for in the contract of transport is located in a State member of the European Economic Community,
> unless the parties to the contract have agreed that it shall not be governed by the Regime.[62]

---

[57] *International Transportation and Carrier Liability,* June 1999, section 1.

[58] R Asariotis, HJ Bull, MA Clarke, R Herber, A Kiantou-Pampouki, D Moran-Bovio, J Ramberg, R de Wit, S Zunarelli, *Intermodal Transportation and Carrier's Liability,* EC Contract n. EI-B97-B27040-SIN6954-SUB (1999).

[59] TREN/G3/25/2004, at p 7.

[60] Clarke, Herber, Lorenzon & Ramberg, *Integrated Services in the Intermodal Chain (ISIC) – Draft Final Report Task B,* September 2005, available at http://folk.uio.no/erikro/WWW/cog/Intermodal%20liability%20and%20documentation.pdf, at p 2.

[61] Clarke, Herber, Lorenzon & Ramberg, *Integrated Services in the Intermodal Chain (ISIC) – Draft Final Report Task B,* September 2005, at p 7.

[62] *Ibid,* Art 2.

In turn, 'contract of transport' is defined in Article 1(a) to mean:

> [...] a contract whereby a Transport Integrator undertakes to perform or procure the transport of goods from a place in one country to a place in another country, whether or not through a third country, involving at least two different modes of transport, and to deliver the goods to the consignee.[63]

The idea behind this opt-out EU solution is that the Transport Integrator will have access to mutual liability insurance to cover its exposure towards shippers and consignees under its contract and – in turn – will be entitled to recourse actions against its unimodal contractors under the relevant liability regime. Admittedly, the system adds a further layer between the consumers of the transport services and the actual carriers involved in the transportation. However, its truly multimodal approach would seem a simple and efficient way to tackle the complexities of the network liability system and partly avoid issues of conflicts of conventions.[64]

As the Authors of the accompanying report put it:

> The strict liability established by the Regime [...] is expected to facilitate claims settlements, especially when compared with liability for presumed fault which often encourages fruitless efforts to rebut the presumption. As a quid pro quo for the strict liability and the monetary limit of 17 Special Drawing Rights, the Regime makes the monetary limit of 17 Special Drawing Rights for all practical purposes unbreakable. If nonetheless Transport Integrators find that the Regime works to their disadvantage, they have the opportunity of opting out of the Regime (Article 2).[65]

And this last point on the possibility of the Freight Integrator to opt out of the regime altogether should not be underestimated in evolutionary terms, given the success contractual solutions have encountered in this area of transport.

Notwithstanding the efforts of the European Commission and the investment made in the research leading to, and the consultations following, the ISIC Project,[66] the decision made by the UNCITRAL to make the Rotterdam Rules a 'maritime plus' convention and hence – in substance – an international multimodal regime, has led to the decision to halt progress on the European project until the global solution was put to the test.[67]

---

[63] *Ibid*, Art 1(a).

[64] *Ibid*, at 12 and ff.

[65] *Ibid*, at 11.

[66] The European Commission issued a Communication on Freight Transport Logistics in Europe (COM(2006)336) supported by the Transport Council in December 2006. The European Parliament gave a positive opinion in September 2007 (P6_TA(2007)0375). Finally. the European Economic and Social Committee broadly welcomed the approach adopted by the Commission (TEN/262) although the attention appeared to shift on a fall back multimodal liability clause (COM(2007) 96 final, at 3).

[67] Notwithstanding some relatively recent debate, no further action has been taken at EU level. See European Commission, *Commission Staff Working Document: accompanying the White Paper – Roadmap to a single European Transport Area – Towards a Competitive and Resource Efficient transport system*, SEC(2011)391 final.

V. UNIMODAL THINKING FOR MULTIMODAL TRANSPORT: THE ROTTERDAM RULES

The latest international attempt at creating a uniform regime on multimodal transport was made with the adoption in 2008 of the United Nations Convention on the Contracts of International Carriage of Goods Wholly or Partly by Sea (the Rotterdam Rules).[68]

Although drafted to replace the Hague, Hague-Visby and Hamburg Rules and hence conceived at first as a unimodal regime, the Rotterdam Rules are clearly designed as a multimodal convention. Their Article 1.1, in fact reads:

> 'Contract of carriage' means a contract in which a carrier, against the payment of freight, undertakes to carry goods from one place to another. The contract shall provide for carriage by sea and may provide for carriage by other modes of transport in addition to the sea carriage.

This approach has become known as the 'maritime plus' approach and makes the convention applicable to the carriage by sea and – where the contract of carriage provides for a further leg through a different mode of transport – also to that extra leg, irrespective of the means chosen. The Rotterdam Rules attempt to resolve issues of conflict of conventions via *ad hoc* provisions aimed at creating a limited network liability system.[69]

In essence, Article 26 applies the network liability system typical of multimodal transport legislation to the effect of applying the unimodal regime applicable to a specific mode of transport in all circumstances in which the event which has caused loss of or damage to the goods, or an event or circumstance causing a delay in their delivery has been localised, provided such event is the exclusive cause of the loss, damage or delay.[70] Where the damage is not localised the Convention applies.

The Rotterdam Rules are not in force and have attracted just a handful of ratifications so far.[71] Certainly their progress has been slowed down by the financial crisis and the dramatic way in which it has affected the world of shipping. The truth however is that the limited network approach adopted by the Rules is nothing new or original. In evolutionary terms moreover it has two major shortcomings: firstly, it only applies to multimodal carriage with a sea leg. If the container is carried by truck, road, waterways and delivered again by truck, the Rules are not triggered

---

[68] For a more detailed discussion of the Rotterdam Rules, see Y Baatz, C Debattista, F Lorenzon, A Serdy, H Staniland, M Tsimplis, *The Rotterdam Rules: A Practical Annotation* (London, 2009), (hereinafter *The Rotterdam Rules: A Practical Annotation*); R Thomas (ed), *The Carriage of Goods by Sea under The Rotterdam Rules* (London, Lloyd's List, 2010)

[69] See Articles 26 and 82. On the matter of conflict of conventions under the Rotterdam Rules see among others C Hancock QC, 'Multimodal transport and the new UN Convention on the Carriage of Goods' (2008)14 *Journal of International Maritime Law* 484; *The Rotterdam Rules: A Practical Annotation*, at [26–01] and [82–01] and ff. See also E Rosaeg, *Conflicts of conventions in the Rotterdam Rules* (2009)15 *Journal of International Maritime Law* 238.

[70] *The Rotterdam Rules: A Practical Annotation*, at [26–01].

[71] Article 94 of the Convention provides that the Convention will enter into force after 20 member states have ratified the Convention. The Convention might have 24 signatories, but so far only 2 states have ratified it: Spain and Togo.

and the contract fails to be subject to the regime. It is submitted that this would significantly disturb the current way multimodal transport operators run their everyday business – as compliance with the convention may be truly burdensome – without the benefit of a uniform liability system at all.

Secondly, the Rotterdam Rules are drafted firmly with sea carriage in mind; evidence of this may certainly be found in the list of excepted perils contained in Article 17, among which 'perils of the seas',[72] 'piracy',[73] 'fire on the ship'[74] are really only relevant to sea transit. In essence, the Rotterdam Rules are designed to apply to some and not all multimodal carriage, but conceived mainly following the maritime approach: they are underpinned by unimodal thinking but applied to (some types of) multimodal transport.

If we return to the historical development of unimodal transport conventions and the need to limit freedom of contract to avoid punishing exclusion and limitation clauses in multimodal carriage, the key policy question to be asked is whether it is still true today that cargo interests are in need of protective legislation. If not, the *raison d'etre* of the limitation to freedom is simply not there. Does multimodal carriage need the *deus ex machina* of supranational legislation? Are opt-in regimes, model laws or contractual solutions not enough? None of this has been considered by the Drafting Group.[75]

The Rotterdam Rules are an 'evolution' of the Hague-Visby and Hamburg systems[76] and – as such – are a pure breed maritime regime in relation to the liability system, documents and delivery, shippers' duties and liabilities, identity of carriers and performing parties, etc. The problem with the liability regime for multimodal transport – the existence of which is questionable – has been identified as the *'inefficiency and uncertainties inherent to the network liability system'*.[77] If this is the problem, by definition the Rotterdam Rules are not the solution as they adopt the very same network system for localised accidents at the cost of 'infecting' – so to speak –other modes of transport and their liability regimes for non-localised or continuous damages, with the added disadvantage of providing for a much lower level of compensation.[78]

---

[72] Art 17(3)(b).

[73] Art 17(3)(c).

[74] Art 17(3)(f).

[75] MF Sturley, T Fujita & G Van Der Ziel, *The Rotterdam Rules: The U.N. Convention On Contracts For The International Carriage Of Goods Wholly Or Partly By Sea* (London: Sweet & Maxwell 2010) at [4-005].

[76] *Ibid.*

[77] UNCTAD (SDTE/TLB/2003/1) and the EU Commission (TREN/G3/25/2004).

[78] M Hoeks, *Multimodal Transport Law: The law applicable to the multimodal contract for the carriage of goods* (2010: Kluwer Law International), p 478: 'All in all, it can be said that from a legal point of view the Rotterdam Rules are a far cry from being perfect. Their multimodal rules are complex, leave gaps and despite valiant attempts the Convention fails to prevent all envisioned conflicts with the existing uniform carriage law. However, one might ask whether perfection is ever attainable in international law, as it is inevitably the result of political compromise. One thing is certain, if the Rotterdam Rules do enter into force, the best we can do is hope that it is accepted globally instead of sporadically. Only then will the new regime add to the much sought-after uniformity of carriage law. If accepted globally, it will even cause the European transport conventions to generate more uniformity, as courts all around the

While it is probably right to say that 'this approach was, in truth, correct – at least in the short term',[79] it falls short from being a true multimodal solution.

VI. MULTIMODAL THINKING FOR MULTIMODAL TRANSPORT?

The only way to achieve a truly multimodal regime must be that of taking a firm multimodal approach, look at the container itself as a single mode of transport and design a special regime applicable to containerised carriage.[80] A number of conventions are already in place to regulate containers[81] and it would be enough to go one step further to regulate the liability of the container carrier. It may well be argued that whether a container is put on wheels, rails, barges or ships, goods are carried not only in the box, but *by* the box.[82] Just because it does not move unaided should not necessarily mean it is not a means of transport/carriage.

However, what should be the main consideration before new approaches are explored is whether a compulsorily applicable multimodal regime is really needed. If it is, who needs protection? Who should negotiate? Who should compromise? The ISIC project shows clearly that a uniform liability regime is possible and may be adopted, but is it really necessary?

On this point, the European Association for Forwarding, Transport, Logistic and Customs Services (CLECAT),[83] whilst commenting on the ISIC Project, raised some serious doubt:

> Is there an identified need for such a regime? Our answer is simply no, for two reasons. First, although we acknowledge that there is no simple and unique rule to calculate liability in intermodal transport, clear rules and division of responsibility exist. The market offers solutions (eg FIATA Multimodal Bill of Lading, which has been in use for a couple of decades) that are tailored and suited to the most sophisticated shippers' demands. Second, we do not think that an EU-regime would enhance the use of intermodal transport, perhaps quite the opposite. Indeed, our experience tells us that the choice of the transport mode by the freight service provider AND his customer is rarely, if ever, made on the basis of the legal framework that governs it. The key factors are and will certainly remain the cost and quality of service. These ideas were expressed in clear terms by 100% of the

globe are then forced to apply the provisions on carrier liability, limitation of liability and time for suit of these treaties through Article 26 RR. Whether the new Convention will be this successful in terms of acceptance is more likely to be subject to political considerations than to its legal accomplishments however. On the whole, the new regime cannot be considered completely recommendable from a purely theoretical juridical point of view.'

[79] C Hancock QC, *Multimodal transport and the New UN Convention on the Carriage of Goods* (2008)14 *Journal of International Maritime Law* 484, at 495.

[80] This is sometimes referred as the *'sui generis* approach', see, eg B Marten, *Multimodal Transport Reform and the European Union: a Minimalist Approach* (2012) 2 *European Transport Law* 129, at 143–44.

[81] Eg such as the United Nations/IMO Customs Convention on Containers, 1972.

[82] But according to De Wit in R De Wit, *Multimodal Transport: Carrier Liability and Documentation* (London: LLP, 1995) at p 4, *'Multimodal transport is a legal concept [whilst] container transport is a technical concept.'*

[83] Also the Comité de Liaison Européen des Commissionaires et Auxiliaires de Transport du Marché Commun.

stakeholders invited to participate as advisors in the project and to speak at the hearings where the Commission asked them to express their views.

Secondly, beyond the lack of need for a new regime, CLECAT sees possible negative effects in the proposed system. Indeed, it would first add complications because of the mere fact that it would be 'just another liability regime', lacking the necessary universality in order to make it functional worldwide. Transport is characterised by globalisation and we take the view that any framework liability regime should thus stem from international initiatives. In addition, the proposed system would surely lead to a substantial increase in costs, and in particular insurance costs. When one looks at the current differences of liability ceilings in the different transport modes (between 2 and 17 SDR's), the choice of the upper ceiling seems overambitious. No insurer would absorb extra liability at zero cost and this additional cost would simply be brought onto the end user's account. Since the cost is one of the key elements in the choice of a transport mode, this could lead to an increased use of the CMR and road transport, which is considered by many users as more simple and effective, to the detriment of intermodal (or comodal) solutions offered by MTI's.

In view of the above, CLECAT would like to inform all those concerned that its certainly cannot encourage this additional attempt to table draft uniform intermodal liability rules, as contained in the ISIC study. Instead, CLECAT generally advocates 'voluntary enhanced awareness programmes' to improve knowledge of existing liability regimes, as well as a more extensive use of one of the best practices in this regard, the FIATA Multimodal Bill of Lading. Resources can be profitably devoted to enhancing the level of awareness of operators and users by making appropriate vocational training trails available. CLECAT, in conjunction with FIATA (our sector's mouthpiece at UN level), has participated actively in the important work which is being carried out by UNCITRAL and likely to produce a comprehensive international proposal in the near future. For this reason, with all best intentions, alternative proposals would not reach any other result but detracting from the resources already devoted to this complex agenda. [84]

And much of the industry consultation following the ISIC Project led to very similar results. And if the industry does not need a uniform liability regime, the very basic policy considerations raised should lead to the conclusion that the evolution is not leading in that direction.

This may also be proven by some new political pressure imposed by the EU onto its Member State towards the ratification of the Rotterdam Rules. In a recent document, the European Parliament stated:

> Calls on Member States speedily to sign, ratify and implement the UN Convention on Contracts for the International Carriage of Goods Wholly or Partly by Sea, known as the 'Rotterdam Rules', establishing the new maritime liability system.[85]

Interestingly the Rules are referred to as 'a maritime liability system' as opposed to a multimodal one.

---

[84] CLECAT Position Paper in the Joint ECMT/UNECE Working Party/Group on Intermodal Transport and Logistics, *Reconciliation and Harmonization of Civil Liability Regimes in Intermodal Transport*, Informal document No. 6 (2006), 7 September 2006.
[85] EU Parliament Resolution, 2009/2095/INI.

CONCLUSION

This paper started from one factual observation: containerisation as technological change, successful evolution of way in which international trade in manufactured goods has developed over the last decades has been incapable of triggering the development of a uniform legal regime. What is certainly less clear is why this is the case.

May it be possible that the *quasi*-perfect mechanism of evolution has failed multimodal transport law? If it is true that the theories of evolutionism can be applied to international trade and freedom as its natural environment, why no multimodal convention has been successful so far?

Paraphrasing Prof Ruse's definition,[86] it could be said that: 'Not all legal solutions that are born survive and (more importantly) reproduce. Those that are successful in the struggle will tend to do so, because they have features not possessed by the unsuccessful.' A uniform liability regime is certainly possible and probably technically more desirable than the current fragmented system which sees well tested contractual devices filling the gaps left among multimodal provisions in unimodal compulsorily applicable legal regimes. The 1980 MT Convention has been certainly the most ambitious among the attempts to solve the multimodal conundrum but, as history shows, has been unsuccessful. And so far the same can be said of the regime proposed by the ISIC Project at EU level.

What appear to have thrived are multimodal afterthoughts in single mode regimes where extra-modal scenarios are tackled with minimum possible interference with other conventions; and more recently – with the Rotterdam Rules – the unimodal plus solution. But more than any other solution, what seems to have conquered the highest degree of success is freedom of contract and its ever-converging expressions to be found in current multimodal documentation.

These solutions prove without a doubt that unimodal thinking is unsuitable for tackling multimodal transport, as different modes of carriage present different practical problems requiring different policy considerations, involving different social parties and different market forces. And multimodal carriage is a different mode of transport with its own problems, complexities and market.

The aim of evolution is ultimately survival and the rules of nature are such that only the strongest survive. In the current financial climate, this has proven true even for international trade players, including multimodal carriers, forwarders and NVOCCs. If only the strongest survives in a competitive context, then multimodal transport is very strong indeed and it has proven to be here to stay. And so has its legal regime, as confusing or complex as it may be.

Perhaps the future will see multimodal transport operators opt in to the uniform liability regime proposed by the draftsmen of the ISIC project as an extra service to their customers, similar to a non-compulsory ISO standard. Or maybe they will commence lobbying for a new global and truly multimodal regime to support

---

[86] M Ruse, *Darwinsim Defended: A Guide to the Evolution Controversies* (Canada, Addison-Wesley, 1982), at p 26.

all the way through to ratification. Whatever the future has in store, the current multimodal liability regime based on freedom of contract and the promotion of international best practices is certainly well-evolved to cope with the industry's needs and will further develop to allow more growth and success. Leaving it free to keep developing seems the best way to ensure it will keep thriving.

8

Incorporation of Charterparty Clauses into Bills of Lading: Peculiar to Maritime Law?[1]

MELIS ÖZDEL

MARITIME LAW HAS, over the years, played a central role in the evolution of modern contract law. Anyone taking even a quick glance at the last century's judicial decisions can hardly fail to see this. The celebrated House of Lords judgment in *The Hongkong Fir*[2] represents only one example out of many illustrating the appreciable impact of maritime cases on the development of contract law. It would, however, be naive to think that the influence goes only in one direction and that maritime law itself gains little or nothing from the classical doctrines of contract law. These two areas of law must be perceived as closely interlinked, feeding upon each other. Nonetheless, on some occasions, maritime lawyers take the view that their cases lie outside the boundaries of the traditional rules of contract law.[3] This paper asks whether the incorporation of charterparty clauses into bills of lading ought justifiably to be ring-fenced away from the rules of notice in general contract law.

Incorporation clauses have been, and remain, commonplace in bills of lading. The frequent use of these clauses is mainly due to the shipowners' desire to ensure that they could turn to and face bill of lading holders on the same terms as their respective charterparties. If successful, incorporation enables shipowners to rely on their rights and obligations under the charterparty against bill of lading holders, who have the ultimate interest in the cargo and who will thus claim delivery at the discharge port.[4]

---

[1] This section is dedicated to Charles Debattista of Stone Chambers, *formerly* Professor of Commercial Law at the University of Southampton, Law School, for his significant contribution to English Maritime Law. I am grateful for his invaluable comments and suggestions on earlier drafts of this section. All errors and omissions remain my own.

[2] [1962] 2 QB 26 (HL).

[3] *Photo Production v Securicor* [1980] AC 827, [1980] 1 Lloyd's Rep 545 (HL), Lord Wilberforce at 550.

[4] However, it must be noted that it may prove difficult to enforce such contractual rights, in particular the right to lien the cargo for the sums due under the charterparty, against the bill of lading holder in a foreign jurisdiction. See, for instance, *The Sinoe* [1972] 1 Lloyd's Rep 201.

From the perspective of bill of lading holders, the main cause for concern arising from the incorporation clauses is evident: copies of the charterparties seldom travel with bills of lading, and the holders hardly ever have the chance and the right[5] to see the relevant charterparty terms. Against this backdrop, it is not surprising that effectiveness of the incorporation clauses in bills of lading has, for more than a century, been hotly disputed in courts and tribunals. Also not surprisingly, the charterparty terms sought to be carried across to bills of lading have been at great variance; ranging, inter alia, from provisions on demurrage, cesser and freight, through to forum selection clauses.

From the perspective of a non-maritime contract lawyer, it is difficult to see why the legal effect of the incorporation clauses in bills of lading could not be determined through the application of the contractual doctrine of notice – a classical rule of contract law on incorporation of terms which have not been individually negotiated by the parties.[6] On the surface, there seems to be nothing to prevent adoption of such a basic contract law thinking for resolution of this issue. The contractual doctrine of notice has already been extended from cases involving parties who have unequal bargaining powers,[7] to commercial transactions entered into between parties standing on an equal footing.[8] Furthermore, the doctrine provides a simple and flexible test, the application of which can make sense in different contractual and factual circumstances. Why would this accepted, general and flexible doctrine not do the job for maritime lawyers as it does for contract lawyers?

I. THE CONTRACTUAL DOCTRINE OF NOTICE

The contractual doctrine of notice dictates that without the proferens giving 'reasonably sufficient'[9] notice of their terms to the other party, the terms will not be incorporated.[10] As is clear from the ticket cases in which this doctrine is rooted, the

---

[5] *Finska Cellulosaforeningen v Westfield Paper Co Ltd* [1940] 2 All ER 473, where it was held that the seller was not obliged to tender a copy of the charterparty referred to in the bill of lading to the buyer. However, see the views of Donaldson J in *SIAT di dal Ferro v Tradax Overseas SA* [1978] 2 Lloyd's Rep 470 at 492, which suggest that the buyer will be entitled to sight of the relevant charterparty where the incorporated charterparty terms affect the rights of the buyer. See further C Debattista, *Bills of Lading in Export Trade*, 3rd edn (Haywards Heath: Tottel Publishing, 2008) para 8.34; M Bridge, *Benjamin's Sale of Goods*, 8th edn, (London: Sweet & Maxwell, 2010) para 19-041.

[6] This doctrine would appear to derive from the well-known ticket cases, see *Parker v South Eastern Railway Co* (1877) 2 CPD 416 (CA); *Thornton v Shoe Lane Parking Ltd* [1971] 2 QB 163; *Thompson v London Midland and Scottish Rly Co* [1930] 1 KB 41.

[7] *Parker v South Eastern Railway Co* (1876–77) LR 2 CPD 416; *Thornton v Shoe Lane Parking Ltd* [1971] 2 QB 163; *Thompson v London Midland and Scottish Rly Co* [1930] 1 KB 41.

[8] *Interfoto v Stiletto Visual Programmes* [1989] QB 433; *Poseidon Freight Forwarding Co Ltd v Davies Turner Southern Ltd* [1996] 2 Lloyd's Rep 388; *Circle Freight International Ltd v Medeast Gulf Exports Ltd* [1988] 2 Lloyd's Rep 427.

[9] *Parker v South Eastern Railway Co* (1876–77) LR 2 CPD 416, Mellish LJ at 424.

[10] *Hood v Anchor Line Ltd* [1918] AC 837, Lord Viscount Haldare at 844. This rule will not apply where there is a 'constant' course of dealing with the parties. A set of terms will be deemed to be incorporated by such a course of dealing, see *McCutcheon v David MacBrayne Ltd* [1964] 1 WLR 125, Lord Reid at 128; *British Crane Hire Corporation Ltd v Ipswich Plant Hire Ltd* [1975] QB 303, Lord Denning at 310; *Henry Kendall v Lillico* [1969] 2 AC 31.

notice itself need not spell out the terms:[11] a mere reference to the terms would thus be sufficient for incorporation, if the party has reasonably and sufficiently been put on notice at the time of contract conclusion[12] and can readily get access to the terms.[13] It is also well established that where, by virtue of its effect and nature,[14] a term is found to be onerous or unusual, the test for its incorporation becomes more stringent: such terms can be incorporated only if they have been 'fairly' and specifically brought to the attention of the other party.[15] This inquiry is most simply formulated under the so-called 'red hand' rule;[16] whereby, in words stated by Lord Denning in J *Spurling v Bradshaw*, 'the more unreasonable a clause is, the greater the notice which must be given of it'. Thus, as his Lordship put it, some provisions would need to be 'printed in red ink on the face of the document with a red hand pointing' to them.[17]

With respect to the question of how much is required for sufficient notice, which is a matter of fact,[18] further guidance can be drawn from the much-cited *Interfoto* case.[19] There, Bingham LJ (as he then was) suggested that sufficiency of notice must be assessed through both contractual and factual analyses.[20] At the contractual level, the courts examine 'the nature of the transaction in question and the character of the parties to it'[21]; and at the factual level, they go on to decide whether in light of the circumstances it is fair to make the party bound by the relevant term.[22] As is clear from the observations above, the doctrine of notice gives rise to a form of good faith in the context of contract formation,[23] and it offers a fact-driven analysis to provide 'piecemeal solutions' for the cases of incorporation.[24] Is this basic and flexible rule applicable to the incorporation of charterparty clauses into bills of lading?

---

[11] *Thompson v London Midland and Scottish Rly Co* [1930] 1 KB 41.

[12] *Olley v Marlborough Court Ltd* [1949] KB 532. Where the notice is provided after the contract conclusion, the terms can be incorporated by a 'constant' course of dealing with the parties, see n 9 above.

[13] See n 10 above.

[14] *Ocean Chemical Transport Inc v Exnor Craggs Limited* [2000] 1 All ER (Comm) 519,[1999] WL 1142725, Evans LJ at para 47; *Parker v South Eastern Railway Co* (1876–77) LR 2 CPD 416, Mellish LJ at 424.

[15] *Thornton v Shoe Lane Parking Ltd* [1971] 2 QB 163, Megaw LJ at 172–73; *Hood v Anchor Line Ltd* [1918] AC 837, Lord Dunedin at 846–47; *Parker v South Eastern Railway Co* (1876–77) LR 2 CPD 416, Mellish LJ at 424; *Interfoto v Stiletto Visual Programmes* [1989] QB 433.

[16] E McDonald, *Exemption Clauses and Unfair Terms,* 2nd edn (Tottel Publishing, 2006) pp 16, 19.

[17] [1956] 1 WLR 461, 466

[18] *Hood v Anchor Line Ltd* [1918] AC 837, Lord Haldane at 844. See also E McDonald, *Exemption Clauses and Unfair Terms*, 2nd edn, (Tottel Publishing, 2006) pp 16, 19.

[19] [1989] QB 433

[20] *Interfoto*, Bingham LJ at 439.

[21] *Interfoto*, Bingham LJ at 439, 445.

[22] *Ibid*.

[23] *Interfoto*, Bingham LJ at 445.

[24] *Ibid*. See also, *Hood v Anchor Line Ltd* [1918] AC 837, Lord Viscount Haldare at 844; *Parker v South Eastern Railway Co* (1876–77) LR 2 CPD 416, Mellish LJ at 421–22.

II. INCORPORATION OF CHARTERPARTY CLAUSES INTO BILLS OF LADING

As maritime lawyers know, the incorporation of charterparty clauses into bills of lading is resolved strictly pursuant to a set of peculiar and sophisticated rules which have grown out of a large body of English maritime case law. The rules are popularly known as the rules of incorporation, and they set out four main hurdles that must be overcome to achieve incorporation. These hurdles are namely[25] the rules of formality for incorporation, and the issues of description, manipulation and consistency.

A. The Rules of Formality

In the decision making process, the rules of formality come first.[26] For a charterparty to qualify for incorporation, it must be reduced to writing by the time the bill of lading is issued.[27] Charterparties made by or evidenced under fax or telex exchanges are considered as written, so long as these exchanges either clearly stipulate the terms of the charterparty or refer to a written charterparty.[28] These requirements apply also to any alterations to the charterparty.[29] Hence, only those written alterations made when or before the bill of lading is issued can be incorporated.[30] There are also formalities for the bill of lading to incorporate. The bill of lading must contain an express incorporation clause which demonstrates an intention to incorporate.[31] In this respect, incorporation can succeed despite the fact that the charterparty is not clearly identified, particularly since a pre-printed incorporation clause itself with no charterparty details is accepted to manifest an intention to incorporate.[32]

Where the incorporation clause does not contain any charterparty details and where there is more than one charterparty, which charterparty is deemed to be referred to in the bill of lading? The solution for this is the general presumption that the head charterparty is intended to be incorporated.[33] This presumption is not followed in cases where the head charterparty is a time charterparty. In

---

[25] See C Debattista, *Bills of Lading in Export Trade*, 3rd edn (Haywards Heath, Tottel Publishing, 2008) paras 8.14–8.19.

[26] Undoubtedly, the preliminary stage is to determine what law governs the incorporation of charterparty clauses into bills of lading. This issue is decided pursuant to the legal system which would govern the bill of lading, if the charterparty were deemed to be incorporated, see *The Heidberg* [1994] 2 Lloyd's Rep 287; *The Wadi Sudr* [2009] 1 Lloyd's Rep 666, reversed on other grounds by the Court of Appeal in [2010] 1 Lloyd's Rep 193. On this issue, see further M Ozdel, 'Presumptions on the law governing the incorporation clauses: should the putative applicable law lead the way?' (2011) 4 *Journal of Business Law* 357.

[27] *The Heidberg* [1994] 2 Lloyd's Rep 287, 304; *The Petr Schmidt* [1995] 1 Lloyd's Rep 202.

[28] *The Epsilon Rosa* [2003] 2 Lloyd's Rep 509, 515.

[29] *Fidelitas Shipping Co v V/O Exportchleb* [1963] 2 Lloyd's Rep 113.

[30] *Ibid.*

[31] *The San Nicholas* [1976] 1 Lloyd's Rep 8.

[32] *The Garbis* [1982] 2 Lloyd's Rep 283, 287; *The Ikariada* [1999] 2 Lloyd's Rep 365, 372; *The San Nicholas* [1976] 1 Lloyd's Rep 8, 12; *The SLS Everest* [1981] 2 Lloyd's Rep 389, 391–92.

[33] *The San Nicholas* [1976] 1 Lloyd's Rep 8.

such cases, the presumption shifts to the sub-charterparty, provided that it is a voyage charterparty.[34] Where there is no hierarchy between charterparties (ie in the case of slot charterparties), the bill of lading is matched with the charterparty which was entered into for the carriage of the goods covered by the bill of lading.[35] These presumptions may not be followed, when this makes more sense commercially.[36]

B. The Description Test

When the charterparty from which terms are incorporated is identified either expressly by the parties or ex post by the courts, it becomes necessary to proceed to the description issue. At this stage, which particular charterparty provisions are aptly described and thus carried across to the bill of lading, is decided on the true construction of the words of incorporation in the bill of lading.[37] General words of incorporation which refer to at least all the terms, conditions and exceptions of the charterparty are prima facie sufficient to incorporate charterparty clauses which are germane to the shipment, carriage and discharge of cargo.[38] Charterparty clauses which are not germane, such as jurisdiction and arbitration clauses, can only be brought into the bill of lading through a specific reference in the incorporation clause.[39]

C. The Manipulation Test

Having identified which particular charterparty clauses are aptly described through the words of incorporation, the next step is to decide whether the clauses can be applied, mutatis mutandis, to the parties to the bill of lading. Where a charterparty clause has a restrictive wording, the courts may engage in 'verbal manipulation' of the wording in order for the clause to make sense and be applicable in the context of the bill of lading.[40] Therefore, the courts may read those charterparty clauses referring to the charterer, shipowner and charterparty as though they refer to the bill of lading holder, carrier and to the bill of lading, respectively.[41] Where a charterparty clause, for instance, places liability on the charterer, the courts may

---

[34] See *The SLS Everest* [1981] 2 Lloyd's Rep 389. The position is not clear where the sub-charterparty is also a time charterparty; see *The Vinson*, 25 April 2005, 677 LMLN 1.

[35] *The Wadi Sudr* [2009] 1 Lloyd's Rep 666, para 110, quoting G Treitel and FMB Reynolds, *Carver on Bills of Lading*, 2nd edn (London, Sweet and Maxwell, 2005) para 3-026, reversed on other grounds by the Court of Appeal in [2010] 1 Lloyd's Rep 193.

[36] *The Vinson*, 25 April 2005, 677 LMLN 1; *The Heidberg* [1994] 2 Lloyd's Rep 287.

[37] *The Varenna* [1984] QB 599.

[38] *TW Thomas v Portsea Steamship Co Ltd (The Portsmouth)* [1912] AC 1.

[39] *The Delos* [2001] 1 Lloyd's Rep 703; *Siboti K/S v BP France SA* [2003] 2 Lloyd's Rep 364; *The Nerano* [1996] 1 Lloyd's Rep 1; *The Rena K* [1978] 1 Lloyd's Rep 545. On the contrary, see *The Merak* [1965] P 223, which can hardly be reconciled with the other decisions so far as the description issue is concerned.

[40] *The Merak* [1965] P 223, Russell LJ, at 259–60.

[41] *The Annefield* [1971] P 168, Lord Denning MR, at 184.

extend application of the clause to the bill of lading holder.[42] The courts do not, however, engage in verbal manipulation of a demurrage clause which imposes the liability to pay demurrage exclusively upon the charterer,[43] unless the demurrage clause is specifically referred to in the words of incorporation.[44]

D. The Consistency Test

The last remaining hurdle is the rule of consistency: whether manipulated or not, the imported charterparty clauses will be ruled out if they are 'repugnant'[45] to the nature of the bill of lading[46] or are inconsistent with the express terms therein.[47] Charterparty clauses which are inapplicable, 'surplus', 'insensible' or 'inconsistent' are jettisoned from the bill of lading at this final stage.[48]

III. WHY NO DOCTRINE OF NOTICE?

In light of these discussions, the rules of incorporation and the contractual doctrine of notice do not appear to stand on the same footing. This view is strengthened by the fact that the contractual doctrine of notice has almost never formed part of the reasoning of those maritime decisions establishing the rules of incorporation. Despite this seeming separation between the contractual doctrine of notice and the rules of incorporation, the question is: would the contractual doctrine of notice, in essence, the 'red hand' rule, bring about the same result in the incorporation of charterparty clauses into bills of lading? If the result of applying both tests is the same, this would mean that the rules of incorporation are simply a maritime expression of the contractual doctrine of notice. For purposes of deciding whether the rules of incorporation can be treated as such, our analysis will be based on two key questions which will be answered by reference to case law. First, would the charterparty clauses which can get through the rules of incorporation also be able to fulfil the tests under the contractual doctrine of notice? Secondly, could charterparty terms fail to make it through the maritime tests where the bill of lading holder had actual notice of the terms? If the answer to the first question is No and the answer to the second question is Yes, then it will be fair to say that these two sets of rules do not just appear dissimilar, but also operate differently.

---

[42] *The Constanza M* [1981] 2 Lloyd's Rep 147, 154, where the court acknowledged the difficulty in manipulating the words 'charterer is to pay freight', while also stating that manipulation of that wording was possible.

[43] *The Miramar* [1984] AC 676, which was followed in *The Spiros C* [2000] 2 Lloyd's Rep 319. For manipulation of arbitration clauses, see *The Nerano* [1994] 2 Lloyd's Rep 50; *The Rena K* [1978] 1 Lloyd's Rep 545.

[44] See *The Rena K* [1978] 1 Lloyd's Rep 545; *Adamastos Shipping Co Ltd v Anglo-Saxon Petroleum Co* [1959] AC 133, [1958] 2 WLR 688.

[45] *Diederichsen v Farquharson Brothers* [1898] 1 QB 150, 158.

[46] *Gullischen v Stewart Brothers* (1883–84) LR 13 QBD 317.

[47] *Gardner v Trechmann* [1884–85] LR 15 QBD 154; *Hamilton & Co v Mackie Sons* (1889) 5 TLR 677.

[48] *The Varenna* [1984] QB 599, 616.

IV. WOULD THE CHARTERPARTY CLAUSES WHICH CAN GET THROUGH THE RULES OF INCORPORATION ALSO BE ABLE TO FULFIL THE TESTS UNDER THE CONTRACTUAL DOCTRINE OF NOTICE?

For present purposes, we will initially compare the contractual doctrine of notice with the maritime tests through examination of the requirements for the time and form of notice. Thereafter, we will analyse the whether the 'red hand' rule would bring about different results, if it were applied to the incorporation of charterparty terms into bills of lading.

A. The Time and Form of Notice

Case law suggests that charterparty terms, on many occasions, would not be incorporated into bills of lading, if the contractual doctrine of notice were applied. As will be recalled, the contractual doctrine of notice permits incorporation only if the party has 'reasonably and sufficiently' been put on notice of the referred terms at the time the contract was concluded[49] and can readily get access to the terms.[50] Astonishingly for contract lawyers, the rules of incorporation do not require the referred charterparties to be readily accessible to bill of lading holders. Furthermore, it will be remembered that incorporation can succeed even if the bill of lading does not even expressly identify which particular charterparty is being referred to.[51] Given this difference in approach between the contractual doctrine of notice and the rules of incorporation, it is clear that terms from charterparties which are not made available to bill of lading holders for inspection would not be incorporated, if the contractual doctrine of notice was applied.

From a general contract law perspective, the difficulties with incorporation in the maritime sphere are substantial: a bill of lading holder cannot reasonably be treated as having been put on notice, where the referred charterparty is neither identified in the bill of lading nor made accessible to the holder. However, from the point of view of maritime lawyers, contractual doctrine of notice sets the bar too high for incorporation of charterparties into bills of lading. It would perhaps come as a surprise to non-maritime contract lawyers that bill of lading holders, whether they be shippers or receivers, do not in most cases have access to the relevant charterparty terms. A shipper to whom a bill of lading incorporating charterparty terms may not himself be a charterer, in which case he will not have sight of the charterparty from which terms are incorporated. Moreover, a bill of lading holder who has bought the goods has no implied right under the sale contract to sight of the charterparty.[52]

The absence of an implied obligation on a seller to tender a copy of an incorporated charterparty raises what must, for general contract lawyers, be another maritime

---

[49] See n 8 and 11.
[50] See n 12.
[51] See n 31.
[52] See n 4.

mystery. Non-maritime contract lawyers might be forgiven for asking why the rules of incorporation require that a charterparty be reduced to writing by the time the bill of lading is issued. In the absence of an implied obligation on the part of carriers and sellers to tender copies of the charterparties, why have a requirement that they should be in writing? Again, the justification for this has its roots exclusively in maritime law. To accept that oral charterparties can be incorporated into bills of lading would run counter to the well-settled rules established in *Leduc v Ward:*[53] oral arrangements made between the shipper and carrier cannot vary the terms of the bill of lading, and the bill of lading is conclusive evidence of contract of carriage between the carrier and transferee of the bill of lading. Obviously, incorporation of oral charterparties would also create a great deal of difficulty in ascertaining the terms of carriage.

B. The 'Red Hand Rule'

There is another stumbling block which could stand in the way of incorporation of charterparty terms into bills of lading, if the contractual doctrine of notice were applied: the 'red hand rule', whereby onerous or unusual terms can only be incorporated if they have been 'fairly' brought to the attention of the other party. Would maritime cases be decided differently, if the red hand rule were applied to the incorporation of charterparty terms into bills of lading?

At first glance, it seems that the question above cannot be answered decisively, inasmuch as sufficiency of notice under the red hand rule is determined through both contractual and factual analyses. To put it another way, the question of whether a term is incorporated is not just a matter of contract construction under the red hand rule. Hence, if the red hand rule was applied to the incorporation of charterparties into bills of lading, it would be necessary to construe the words of incorporation in light of the circumstances of the individual bill of lading holder. The upshot of this is evident: the legal effect of incorporation clauses would vary depending on the actual position of every subsequent bill of lading holder.

Indeed, the argument that application of the red hand test would probably bring about different results can be supported through analysis of the decision in *The Garbis.*[54] There, Goff J decided that a charterparty clause which the arbitrators found unusual was nonetheless incorporated into the bill of lading through general words of incorporation. The major underpinning for this ruling was that despite being unusual, the clause was germane to the shipment, carriage and discharge of goods. Another decisive factor was the all-embracing incorporation clause, which contained a reference to 'all the terms whatsoever' of the charterparty. With regard to the impact of such an approach on the bill of lading holders, Goff J said:[55]

---

[53] (1888) LR 20 QBD 475. On this issue, see further C Debattista, 'The Bill of Lading as the Contract of Carriage—A Reassessment of *Leduc v Ward*' (1982) 45 *Modern Law Review* 652.

[54] [1982] 2 Lloyd's Rep 283.

[55] *Ibid* at 289.

If a receiver of goods accepts a bill of lading in this form without ascertaining the terms of the charter-party, he must accept that his contract with the shipowner for the carriage of the goods, contained in or evidenced by the bill of lading, is subject to the charter-party terms relevant to the loading, carriage and discharge of the goods, even though they may be unusual terms and may limit the shipowners' liability.

Even though the speech of Goff J in *The Garbis* is clearly addressed to bill of lading holders, the dispute in *The Garbis* was actually between a shipowner and a charterer. In narrow terms, the case was concerned with the responsibility for the detention of the vessel arising from the master's refusal to sign the bill of lading as presented by the charterer. Nevertheless, the decision gives some support to the argument that general words of incorporation are apt to describe and incorporate onerous and unusual charterparty clauses. If the red hand test, instead of the rules of incorporation, were in place in *The Garbis*, would the case be decided differently? Since the red hand rule requires that the offending clause is fairly brought to the attention of the other party, the unusual charterparty clause in *The Garbis* would probably not be incorporated through general words of incorporation. Therefore, regardless of any expansive language in the incorporation clause, the unusual charterparty clause would only safely be incorporated through specific reference to it in the incorporation clause.

For present purposes, the House of Lords judgment in *The Jordan II* also deserves attention.[56] There, the bill of lading holder was left with no remedy against the shipowner for damage to cargo which occurred during loading operations carried out by the charterer pursuant to the FIOST clause.[57] In the charterparty context, the FIOST clause had the effect of relieving the charterer of expenses and liability for, inter alia, loading operations. When this clause was carried across to the bill of lading and was held to be applicable in this context, the shipowner was discharged of liability also towards the bill of lading holder. If the red hand rule was applicable to the question of whether the FIOST clause was incorporated, would this bring about a different result? It is again not possible to answer this question with certainty, given the unpredictability arising from the application of the contractual doctrine of notice. Nevertheless, if the red hand rule was applicable to the case, it would appear that the House of Lords in *The Jordan II* would at least be slow to hold that the FIOST clause, the application of which brought about onerous results for the bill of lading holder, was incorporated into the bill of lading through general words of incorporation.

To sum up, the cases discussed so far support the argument that charterparty terms which can be carried across to the bill of lading through application of the rules of incorporation would not be incorporated if the doctrine of notice were operative. As has been examined, the two main reasons for this are: first, the

---

[56] [2004] UKHL 49, [2005] 1 WLR 1363.

[57] FIOST stands for 'free in and out, stowed and trimmed'. These clauses purport to relieve shipowners at least of the costs arising from loading, discharge, stowage and trimming, and it depends on the language of the clause as to whether shipowners can also transfer the responsibility for these operations to the respective charterers. See *The Jordan II* [2002] EWHC 1268 (Comm) paras 16–18.

difference in approach between the rules of incorporation and the contractual doctrine of notice as to time and form of notice; and secondly, the red hand rule under the contractual doctrine of notice. Does this all mean that the contractual doctrine of notice has no influence on the rules of incorporation?

C. The Influence of the Red Hand Rule

While the red hand test has never been directly applied to the incorporation of charterparties into bills of lading, one seminal maritime decision, *The Miramar*[58] suggests that the red hand test subliminally influences the rules of incorporation: the manipulation test. In *The Miramar*, the issue was whether the charterparty demurrage clause in an Exxonvoy 1969 form was incorporated into the bill of lading and whether it was binding upon the bill of lading holder. While holding that the incorporation clause was apt to describe and carry the demurrage clause across to the bill of lading, Lord Diplock did not allow manipulation of the words 'charterer is to pay demurrage' in the incorporated demurrage clause. Had the words been manipulated, this would have resulted in the imposition of demurrage charges personally upon the bill of lading holders. When hinging on the restrictive language as a justification for the ruling, he added[59]:

> My Lords, I venture to assert that no business man who had not taken leave of his senses would intentionally enter into a contract which exposed him to a potential liability of this kind; and this, in itself, I find to be an overwhelming reason for not indulging in verbal manipulation of the actual contractual words used in the charter-party so as to give to them this effect when they are treated as incorporated in the bill of lading.

It is striking that the reasoning of Lord Diplock is similar to the underlying objective of the red hand rule, which is to prevent the imposition of onerous liabilities arising from the application of terms that are not individually negotiated. Viewed in this light, the ruling in *The Miramar* suggests two key points. Firstly, the red hand rule has some influence on the manipulation test, although it does not save bill of lading holders from onerous or unusual charterparty clauses which are couched in broad language to encompass the holders. Secondly, the decision also illustrates that application of the doctrine of notice in a maritime context may in some cases bring about the same results. Having discussed the probable effects of the contractual doctrine of notice in a maritime context, it is now timely to move on to the second question central to our discussion.

---

[58] [1984] 2 Lloyd's Rep 129.
[59] *Ibid* at 132.

V. COULD CHARTERPARTY TERMS FAIL TO MAKE IT THROUGH THE MARITIME TESTS WHERE THE BILL OF LADING HOLDER HAD ACTUAL NOTICE OF THE TERMS?

The crucial point here is this: imagine that a bill of lading holder was given sight of a charterparty from which terms have been incorporated into the bill of lading – assume, therefore, full notice – would that fact in and of itself ensure effective incorporation of those terms into the bill of lading? In a great number of maritime cases, the courts have stressed that neither the inability of the bill of lading holders to have sight of the relevant charterparty, nor their actual knowledge of the charterparty, is relevant to the question of incorporation.[60] The upshot of this is that the rules of incorporation do not permit incorporation of a charterparty into the bill of lading merely because the holder has been provided with a copy of the relevant charterparty. The rules of incorporation therefore bring about different results from those which can be reached under the contractual doctrine of notice. These will be illustrated through further examination of the description and consistency tests.

A. Description Test

In light of the observations above, a charterparty clause which would be incorporated under the contractual doctrine of notice will not be incorporated under the rules of incorporation, where the words of incorporation do not aptly describe the relevant charterparty clause. With these considerations in mind, the court in *Serraino & Sons v Campbell and others* ruled against incorporation of a charterparty exclusion clause which purported to relieve the carrier of liability for the cargo loss or damage occasioned by, inter alia, the negligence of the master.[61] The clause could not be imported into the bill of lading, for the incorporation clause in question – which made a reference only to all the conditions of the charterparty – was inapt to incorporate the exclusion clause. Such charterparty clauses could only sufficiently be described through a specific reference to 'exceptions',[62] unless the word 'term'[63] or a word with the broadest possible meaning such as 'whatsoever' were inserted

---

[60] *Wegener v Smith* (1854) 15 CB 285, 287; *Fry v Chartered Mercantile Bank of India, London, and China* (1865–66) LR 1 CP 689; *Russell v Niemann* (1864) 144 ER 66, 70; *Serraino & Sons v Campbell and others* [1891] 1 QB 283, Lord Esher MR at 290; *Gray v Carr and another* (1870–71) LR 6 QB 522, 532–33. Interestingly, the court in *Gray v Carr* referred to the fact that a copy of the charterparty was provided to the bill of lading holder in question. However, it appears that the judgment did not rest on this fact.

[61] [1891] 1 QB 283. See also, *Manchester Trust v Furness* [1895] 2 QB 539. There, it was held that where the bill of lading contains a reference to a charterparty, the bill of lading holder cannot be taken to have notice of all the terms in the charterparty. This decision is the authority for the proposition that the doctrine of constructive notice does not extend to commercial transactions.

[62] Given that the charterparty clauses of this type are known as negligence clauses, a specific reference to 'negligence clause' in the words of incorporation will also suffice for purposes of incorporation, *The Northumbria* [1906] P 292. See also, G Treitel and FMB Reynolds, *Carver on Bills of Lading*, 2nd edn (London, Sweet and Maxwell, 2005) para 3-018.

[63] *Fort Shipping v Pederson* [1924] 19 Ll L Rep 26.

into the incorporation clause.[64] Consequently, applying the description test in a strict sense, the court in *Serraino v Campbell* gave no weight to the fact that the bill of lading holders had actual notice of the charterparty terms due to their being the charterer.[65]

Similarly, the rule that general words of incorporation can incorporate only those charterparty provisions which are germane to the shipment, carriage and discharge of goods has also strictly and consistently been applied in maritime cases. Following the decision in *Thomas v Portsea*[66] where this rule was established, the courts in *The Varenna*[67] and *Siboti K/S v BP France SA*[68] decided against incorporation of charterparty forum selection clauses through general words of incorporation. In so holding, the courts did not inquire as to whether the bill of lading holders were provided with copies of the relevant charterparties. Nor did they ask whether it would be fair to hold these parties bound by the forum selection clause. They adhered to the description test without considering the factual circumstances of the individual bill of lading holders. This approach received further judicial support by HH Judge Diamond QC in *The Heidberg*.[69] There, he stated that the test is not whether the charterparty terms have been fairly and reasonably brought to the notice of the bill of lading holder.[70]

Despite this consistent line of maritime cases, an obviously confusing twist in the application of the description test was seen in the curious case of *The Merak*.[71] There, the charterparty arbitration clause was held to be incorporated through the words of incorporation which read 'all terms, conditions, clauses and exceptions as per charterparty'. In support of this finding, the court relied on the comprehensiveness of the word 'clause' in the incorporation clause, alongside the charterparty arbitration clause which required arbitration of disputes arising out of 'any bills of lading issued hereunder'. It is, at any rate, clear that these two patterns of reasoning cannot be reconciled with the settled rules of incorporation: pursuant to the decision in *Siboti K/S v BP France SA*, the word 'clause' must be treated as inapt to describe a charterparty arbitration clause, particularly since the all-encompassing word 'whatsoever' was held insufficient to incorporate a jurisdiction clause.[72] Also, in light of the ruling in *The Varenna*, the description tests need to be carried out solely through the words of incorporation in bills of lading, for the bill of lading is accepted as the primary document to be considered for incorporation.[73]

For present purposes, it must be noted that the incorporation clause in *The Merak* case mistakenly referred to 'clause 32' of the relevant charterparty instead of 'clause 30', which was the correct arbitration clause. Observing the principle of

[64] *The Garbis* [1982] 2 Lloyd's Rep 283.
[65] [1891] 1 QB 283, 297.
[66] [1912] AC 1.
[67] [1984] QB 599.
[68] [2003] 2 Lloyd's Rep 364.
[69] [1994] 2 Lloyd's Rep 287.
[70] *Ibid*, at 313.
[71] [1965] P 223.
[72] [2003] 2 Lloyd's Rep 364.
[73] [1984] QB 599.

general contract law that a contract cannot be rectified to the detriment of a third party, the court stood against rectification of the mistaken reference. Since the bill of lading was not in the hands of the shipper, the reference was considered as merely superfluous and was discarded. Notably, the bill of lading holder was also the charterer and party to the charterparty which was sought to be incorporated. When holding in favour of incorporation and treating the mistake *nihil ad rem*, the knowledge of the holders, which they happened to have because they were also the charterers, was given no weight by the majority. Instead, they relied on the two main underpinnings which are, with respect, contrary to the settled principles of incorporation. In support of these findings, unlike the majority, Davies J said[74]:

> Whatever might have been the position if this bill were in the hands of a stranger to the charterparty of April 21, these plaintiffs were parties to it and therefore must be taken to have had knowledge of all its terms. They knew therefore that clause 30 was nihil ad rem. They knew that by clause 32 arbitration was provided for not only for disputes arising out of the charterparty but also for those arising out of any bill of lading issued thereunder ... In the light of all these circumstances, it is impossible to hold that clause 32 was not incorporated into the bill of lading.

Considering the long line of authorities with regard to incorporation in bill of lading cases, it is prudent not to place too strong a reliance on this statement of Davies J. Throughout the discussions, we have seen that the words of incorporation and certainly not the actual knowledge of the bill of lading holder are decisive when choosing which particular charterparty provisions can be carried across to the bill of lading. Perhaps for these reasons, the court in *The Federal Bulker*[75] treated the facts of *The Merak* as unique and unusual, suggesting that this ruling would be of limited application. Nonetheless, the decision in *The Merak* illustrates that application of the rules of incorporation and the contractual doctrine of notice may, in only very exceptional circumstances, bring about the same result.

B. Consistency Test

In addition to the discussions above, a charterparty clause which would cross the bar of contractual doctrine of notice does not satisfy the rules of incorporation where that clause is 'repugnant, inconsistent or insensible'[76] in the context of the bill of lading. In *Gullischen v Stewart Brothers*,[77] the court did not allow the consignee to rely on the incorporated charterparty cesser clause, when the same party was also the charterer and shipper of the goods. While accepting that this clause releases the charterer of liabilities, the court nevertheless held this party responsible for the charges under the bills of lading, given that he was also the cargo receiver. Releasing the holder of liabilities by reason of the cesser clause would have created

---

[74] [1965] P 223, 255–56.
[75] [1989] 1 Lloyd's Rep 103.
[76] *The Varenna* [1984] QB 599, 616.
[77] (1883–84) LR 13 QBD 317.

an unbusinesslike result which the shipowner could not reasonably be deemed to have intended, and the clause was thus treated as not 'sensible' in a bill of lading context.

C. Influence of the Doctrine of Notice?

It follows from the above that the courts in maritime cases approach the question of incorporation within the realms of contract construction, observing the utmost necessity of ensuring that the bill of lading provides invariable terms of carriage to every indorsee. This well-settled approach taken in maritime cases leads to the conclusion that charterparties which would qualify for incorporation under the contractual doctrine of notice may not be incorporated through application of the rules of incorporation. As has been stated, the main barriers against incorporation are the description and consistency tests.

On closer inspection of two maritime tests, could it be said that they are ring-fenced away from the contractual doctrine of notice? Inasmuch as the description and consistency tests do not require assessment of fairness in light of the actual position of the individual bill of lading holder, this question must be answered in the affirmative. Nonetheless, one may also see that the rationale behind the description and consistency tests is similar to that behind the contractual doctrine of notice: the maritime tests would appear to be based on the assumption that the holders do not have actual knowledge of the terms of the charterparty referred to. Proceeding on that assumption, the description test requires the words of incorporation in the bill of lading to alert the holders when their carriers seek to incorporate a charterparty clause which is not germane to the shipment, carriage and discharge of goods. Along the same lines, the consistency test prevents the incorporated charterparty terms from varying the express bill of lading terms.

CONCLUSION

Central to this paper was the question of whether the rules of incorporation are simply a maritime expression of the contractual doctrine of notice. To put it simply, we asked whether the question of incorporation both in maritime and non-maritime contexts is, in essence, determined by one method, albeit expressed in different language. In reaching a conclusion, we first looked at the probable effects of the application of the contractual doctrine of notice on the incorporation of charterparty clauses into bills of lading, and we later examined whether the terms which are incorporated through the application of the contractual doctrine of notice can also satisfy the rules of incorporation. Our analysis, which was based on these two key questions, yields the conclusion that the contractual doctrine of notice is distinct from the rules of incorporation in terms of their operation and the results they create, although the decision in *The Miramar* demonstrates a subliminal influence of the red hand rule on the manipulation test. English courts have long treated the incorporation of charterparty clauses into bills of lading as an issue peculiar to maritime law. Some might argue that application of the contractual doctrine of notice, which is chiefly based on fairness, would come at the expense of certainty and predictability under bills of lading. Hence, the rules of incorporation have much to commend them, for they provide specific solutions to maritime issues.

9

Certificate Final Clauses in International Trade: Some Recent Developments

ALEXANDER SANDIFORTH

INTRODUCTION

IN INTERNATIONAL TRADE the fact that the goods have to travel long distances, under the supervision of a carrier, means that there can be uncertainty for the parties on both sides of the sale contract. How will the seller get paid? Is there any guarantee that the buyer will receive the goods? What if the goods are damaged when they arrive at the place of destination or are of a lesser quantity than the buyer was expecting?

In this area of English law, freedom of contract generally prevails.[1] Therefore the answers to the above questions will often be found in the sale contract itself which, generally speaking in cases where the goods are traded in bulk and carried on board a ship, is likely to have been concluded on fob,[2] cif,[3] or c&f[4] terms.

For the purpose of this chapter, the two most important features of such contracts are that the 'legal' risk of physical loss or damage to the goods passes from the seller to the buyer on (or as from) shipment[5] and that the seller is not giving an undertaking as to the arrival of the goods at the discharge port.[6]

---

[1] Section 55(1) of the Sale of Goods Act 1979 which applies to contracts for the sale of all types of goods. See also sections 3, 6, 26, 27 and Schedule 2 of the Unfair Contract Terms Act 1977.

[2] Free on board.

[3] Cost, insurance and freight.

[4] Cost and freight.

[5] *Comptoir d'Achat et de Vente du Boerenbond Belge S/A v Luis de Ridder Limitada (The Julia)* [1949] AC 293, (1948–49) 82 Ll L Rep 270 in respect of cif and c&f contracts. Under an fob contract the goods must, given the seller's obligation to deliver free on board, be appropriated to the contract by shipment at the latest. Thus risk cannot pass 'as from' shipment – see *Esteve Trading Corp v Agropec International (The Golden Rio)* [1990] 2 Lloyd's Rep 273 at p 276 col 2 and *Scottish & Newcastle International Ltd v Othon Ghalanos Ltd* [2008] UKHL 11, [2008] 1 Lloyd's Rep 462 at [35(ii)].

[6] *cf* the concept of a cif 'delivered' contract, where the seller does give an undertaking as to the date of arrival of the goods at the discharge port. Such contracts have become increasingly prevalent, particularly in the oil trade. Under such a contract, in the event that the goods fail to arrive and the buyer has, and exercises, his option to terminate the contract, risk (and title) in the goods re-vest in the

Thus, if the seller, under eg a cif contract, can demonstrate that he has 'shipped'[7] conforming goods, then what happens to the goods after this point in time is not the seller's concern. The risk of loss of and/or damage to the goods has passed to the buyer,[8] whose recourse (if any) is to bring a claim against the carrier or insurer.[9]

Today, the virtually invariable practice favoured by sellers to allow them to demonstrate compliance with the contract of sale *vis-à-vis* the shipment of bulk goods of the contractual quality and thus provide certainty on this extremely important issue, is to insert into the sale contract a 'certificate final clause'.[10]

GENERAL PRINCIPLES OF CERTIFICATE FINAL CLAUSES

A certificate final clause may cover a number of things. First, the clause will provide for the sampling/inspection/testing and subsequent certification[11] to be carried out by an independent surveyor/inspector and the method by which the surveyor/inspector is to be appointed. Second, the clause may provide for a specific sampling/inspection/testing method[12] or 'customary' method[13] to be used. Third, it will provide for the results to be 'final and binding for both parties', sometimes 'save fraud or manifest error'.[14] The clause may also, and often does, deal with the quantity of goods loaded.

The intention behind such a clause is clear. It is designed to prevent the buyer from adducing evidence that the goods were not as described by the certificate at the moment when risk in the goods passed from seller to buyer ie loading/shipment. Although not an exemption clause, a certificate final clause will be subject to strict

---

seller. However clear words are needed to create such an obligation on the seller – see *Vitol SA v Esso Australia Ltd (The Wise)* [1989] 2 Lloyd's Rep 451 and *Erg Petroli SpA v Vitol SA (The Ballenita and The BP Energy)* [1992] 2 Lloyd's Rep 455.

  [7] This being 'provisional delivery' – see *Schmoll Fils & Co Inc v Scriven Bros & Co* (1924) 19 Ll L Rep 118 per Roche J at p 119 col 1.

  [8] *cf* the discussion about 'prospective' and 'continuing' warranties by Rix LJ *in KG Bominflot Bunkergesellschaft Für Mineralöle mbH & Co v Petroplus marketing AG (The Mercini Lady)* [2010] EWCA Civ 1145, [2011] 1 Lloyd's Rep 442 at [18], discussed later in this chapter.

  [9] Under a c&f or fob contract, a prudent buyer should have effected his own insurance. Alternatively the contract may require him to do so – see eg clause 13 of the Federation of Oils, Seeds and Fats Associations Limited ('FOSFA') contract number 53. The seller may also have sellers' interest insurance to cover the eventuality that the goods are lost/damaged but the buyer fails to pay.

  [10] It is possible, albeit increasingly difficult in some trades, for the buyer to purchase goods on terms which do not include a certificate final clause. However, the buyer can often expect to pay a premium as a result.

  [11] Such certification will generally speak only to the quality of the goods – see the comments of Lloyd J in *NV Buge v Compagnie Noga d'Importation et d'Exportation SA (The Bow Cedar)* [1980] 2 Lloyd's Rep 601 at p 603 col 2.

  [12] For example, sampling as per the sampling rules number 124 of the Grain and Feed Trade Association ('GAFTA') and subsequent testing as per GAFTA Register of Analysis Methods number 130.

  [13] See for example the clause in *Veba Oil Supply and Trading GmbH v Petrotrade Inc (The Robin)* [2001] EWCA Civ 1832, [2002] 1 Lloyd's Rep 295.

  [14] The phrase 'manifest error' refers to 'oversights and blunders so obvious and obviously capable of affecting the determination as to admit of no difference of opinion' per Tuckey LJ in *The Robin* above n 13 at [33].

interpretation[15] and should therefore be clearly and carefully drafted. Care must also be taken to ensure that any other terms of the sale contract are not inconsistent with the certificate final regime, a point which recently came before the commercial court in *R G Grain Trade LLP v Feed Factors International Ltd*,[16] one of two decisions examined below.

Although the intention behind a certificate final clause may be clear, the effect is not always as straightforward. For example, a certificate which speaks to quality yet does not speak to description[17] will not be binding in respect of the latter[18]. However, where the description of the goods includes a statement about quality and the contract provides for a certificate which is final as to quality, then the certificate will be final as to that part of the description of the contract goods.[19]

Also far from straightforward is the effect which such a clause has on the basic statutory implied term found in section 14(2) of the Sale of Goods Act 1979 ('the 1979 Act') that the goods supplied must be of 'satisfactory quality'.

A clause satisfying the requirements set out above contains no express reference that the parties intend to exclude the operation of section 14(2) of the 1979 Act. However, if the alleged 'defect' is something covered by the certificate,[20] then the effect of the clause would appear to preclude the buyer from raising an argument that the goods are not of satisfactory quality on the basis of this defect.

However, if the 'defect' is something that falls outside the scope of the certificate, then it is submitted that this can give rise to a breach of the section 14(2) implied term,[21] notwithstanding the fact that the clause may purport to make the certificate 'final as to quality and condition at time and place of loading'. For this reason a well drafted sale contract should contain an appropriate clause dealing with the section 14(2) implied term.[22] The relationship between such certificates and implied terms was recently considered by the Court of Appeal in *The Mercini Lady*.[23]

---

[15] See the comments of Diplock LJ in *W N Lindsay & Co Ltd v European Grain & Shipping Agency Ltd* [1963] 1 Lloyd's Rep 437 at p 445 col 1.

[16] *RG Grain Trade LLP v Feed Factors International Ltd* [2011] EWHC 1889 (Comm), [2011] 2 Lloyd's Rep 432.

[17] The types of contract under consideration are invariably contracts for the sale of unascertained goods and will thus all be sales by description – see *Wallis Son & Wells v Pratt & Haynes* [1911] AC 394 and section 13(1) of the Sale of Goods Act 1979.

[18] *The Bow Cedar* above n 11 per Lloyd J at p 603 col 2. See also *Peter Cremer GmbH v General Carriers SA (The Dona Mari)* [1973] 2 Lloyd's Rep 366 at p 375 col 2 (distinction between quality and condition of goods) and section 14(2B) of the Sale of Goods Act 1979.

[19] *Alfred C Toepfer v Continental Grain Co (The Penquer)* [1974] 1 Lloyd's Rep 11 per Lord Denning MR at p 13 col 2, referred to with approval by Lord Diplock in *Berger & Co Inc v Gill & Duffus SA* [1984] AC 382 at p 393 para H – p 394 para A, [1984] 1 Lloyd's Rep 227 at p 232 col 2 – p 233 col 1.

[20] An example of this would be where the alleged 'defect' is that the goods have a lower protein content than the contract provides for. However, the process employed in the certification procedure encompasses analysis of the goods' protein content.

[21] See the comments of Rix LJ in *The Mercini Lady* above n 8 at [41].

[22] Such clauses are briefly considered later in this chapter.

[23] Above n 8.

THE RELATIONSHIP BETWEEN CERTIFICATES AND IMPLIED TERMS: *THE MERCINI LADY*

A cargo of gasoil was shipped on board the *Mercini Lady* pursuant to an fob contract which contained *inter alia* the following terms:

12. QUANTITY/QUALITY
Quantity and quality, basis shoretank to be determined by a mutually agreed independent inspector at the loading installation, in the manner customary at such instillation. Such determination shall be final and binding for both parties except in case of fraud or manifest error...

15. RISK AND TITLE FOB Antwerp
Each delivery shall be completed and title shall vest absolutely in buyer when the product passes the vessel's permanent hose connection at the port of loading at which time buyer assumes all risks pertaining thereto.

18. OTHER CONDITIONS
There are no guarantees, warranties or misrepresentations, express or implied, [of] merchantability, fitness or suitability of the oil for any particular purpose or otherwise which extend beyond the description of the oil set forth in this agreement.

The shore tank analysis[24] indicated that the gasoil met the specification stipulated in the contract. However, the buyer contended that notwithstanding an admission that the gasoil was of the contractual specification as it was loaded on board the *Mercini Lady*,[25] when it arrived at destination it did not conform to the contractual specifications and the seller was therefore in breach.

As a result, the buyer sought trial on a number of preliminary issues.[26] These included whether or not the seller was in breach of the implied term of satisfactory quality pursuant to section 14(2) of the 1979 Act and/or a similar term implied at common law, both of which the buyer said meant that the seller was under an obligation to deliver gasoil which would remain of satisfactory quality for a reasonable time *after* delivery on board the *Mercini Lady*. The seller contended that such was inconsistent with the notion that risk of loss/damage to the gasoil passed incrementally as it was loaded on board the *Mercini Lady* and that clause 18 of the sale contract excluded the possibility of the implication of a term either by section 14(2) of the 1979 Act or at common law.

Mr Justice Field[27] determined these preliminary issues in favour of the buyer. His judgment appeared to suggest that there was a 'continuing' warranty[28] implied

---

[24] This meant that the certificate certified the 'quantity and quality' of the gasoil *before* shipment. Therefore the point at which the gasoil was certified and the point at which risk and title passed to the buyer (as per clause 15 of the contract of sale) were different. See also n 5 above.

[25] Hence the reason the buyer could not rely on the decision in *Mash & Murrell Ltd v Joseph I Emanuel Ltd* [1961] 1 Lloyd's Rep 46 (reversed on appeal ([1961] 2 Lloyd's Rep 326) but not on this point).

[26] This meant that there were no findings of fact which led to the argument becoming 'unsatisfactorily speculative' per Rix LJ at [65]. Notwithstanding this it is submitted that for the reasons given in this chapter, the judgment is highly instructive, demonstrating that a certificate may not in fact be as final as the parties to the sale contract may think. The subsequent findings of fact are reported at [2012] EWHC 3009 (Comm), [2013] 1 Lloyd's Rep 360.

[27] [2009] EWHC 1088 (Comm), [2009] 2 Lloyd's Rep 679.

[28] See section 11(3) of the 1979 Act.

by statute[29] and at common law that the goods must continue to conform with the contract for a reasonable time *after* shipment[30] and that clause 18 of the sale contract did not prevent the implication of either term.

The impact of Field J's decision was to effectively render the certificate obtained at loading worthless, despite the fact that it was expressed to be 'final and binding'. Whilst the judgment cast no doubt that the certificate was indeed final and binding as to the quality/quantity of the oil,[31] it was expressed to be so only at the point just prior to loading.[32] The certificate said nothing as to the quality/quantity of the oil *after* this point, ie after shipment, and given the implied terms as to the quality of the gasoil *after* shipment, all the buyer would need to do to succeed in his claim[33] would be to adduce evidence that the gasoil was not of the contractual quality at the discharge port.

The practical effect of Field J's judgment was that the seller was still 'on risk' in respect of the goods complying with the implied terms as detailed above, notwithstanding clause 15 of the sale contract. This in turn meant that the certificate provided the seller with no finality as a matter of practicality and therefore no certainty, notwithstanding the clear intention that it provide otherwise and preclude the buyer from making the arguments it had.

In the Court of Appeal, the parties were in agreement[34] that if clause 18 of the sale contract did not exclude the statutory implied term that the goods would remain in conformity with the contractual specification for a reasonable time *after* delivery on board the *Mercini Lady*, then such a term could only operate at a fixed point in time,[35] namely the point of delivery, ie the time at which the gasoil was loaded on board the *Mercini Lady*. This once again gave the certificate teeth *vis-à-vis* the statutory implied term, since the buyer would have to prove that the gasoil was defective in the sense alleged at this point in time, which he could not do due to the fact that the certificate said that the gasoil was of the correct specification at this time.[36]

In respect of the implied common law term, which was also said to operate at a fixed point in time, ie at the point of delivery,[37] the Court of Appeal unanimously held that there was no basis on which to imply such a term. In the words of Lord Justice Rix, the contract made it clear that:[38]

---

[29] As per section 14(2) of the 1979 Act.

[30] Derived from the decision in *Mash & Murrell Ltd v Joseph I Emanuel Ltd* above n 25.

[31] Although the wrong test at loading had in fact been used, the buyer's case was argued on the basis that the certificate was still final and binding and 'that the gasoil was within specification at loading'– see the comments of Rix LJ at [25] and n 24 above.

[32] ie the shore tanks.

[33] Assuming that the voyage was uneventful, ie the deterioration was not a result of the carrier's actions.

[34] Above n 8 at [21].

[35] Hence the terminology 'prospective' warranty – above n 8.

[36] Above n 31.

[37] However, the term sought to be implied meant that if the gasoil arrived outside its specification, the seller would have been in breach of the sale contract rather than the buyer having evidence to merely allege that the seller was in breach at the point of delivery, ie loading – see [23]–[24].

[38] At [40]. Note however the qualifications to this statement *vis-à-vis* 'risk' and at [16] *vis-à-vis* 'durability'.

the specification [of the gasoil] ha[d] to be met at the time of delivery,[39] that the intention [was] that the gasoil should be inspected by an independent inspector prior to loading 'basis shoretank'…and that the inspector's determination should be conclusive.

Finally, as to whether clause 18 of the sale contract excluded the implication of the statutory implied term, Rix LJ held that Field J had decided this point correctly and that the clause did not operate to exclude the implication of 'conditions' since it referred only to 'guarantees, warranties or misrepresentations'.[40] However, whilst the law is 'very strict'[41] and Rix LJ had 'sympathy'[42] for the seller's case on the point, like Field J he was ultimately bound on the point.[43]

Thus, the *Mercini Lady* reiterates that *caveat emptor* still rules in this area of English law, that the parties will be held to their contractual bargain and that attempts to effectively reallocate some of the risk in shipment contracts[44] via a re-characterisation of a seller's duties are unlikely to succeed.

The judgment also highlights the possibility that a 'final' certificate may not in fact be final as to *all* matters of quality, notwithstanding the fact that there was no dispute between the parties about the certificate itself[45] and a seller would be unwise to consider a certificate final clause in a sale contract as providing it with an absolute defence to any claim about issues of quality *per se*, unless the clause is carefully drafted (and many are not).

Furthermore, the judgment also serves as a warning that if the parties wish to exclude the implication of terms as to quality in their contracts, then they must be precise when drafting their contracts. Whilst the current position in English law[46] is undoubtedly out of step with the commercial reality, until the Supreme Court gets to grapple with this point, it is not going to change.

Notwithstanding the above, the effect and usefulness of the statutory implied terms will of course depend on the facts of the case. Undeniably, a 'final' certificate will often mean that a buyer will be faced with an insurmountable hurdle and thus provide the contracting parties with certainty.

However, it is submitted that this may not always be so. What if the alleged defect falls outside any specified testing method? Although Rix LJ considered this point hypothetically,[47] it is submitted that it must surely be correct that a certificate can only be evidence of the results of the process which has been undertaken to produce it. Put another way, it is submitted that a certificate expressed to be final and binding as to 'quality' cannot in fact be final and binding as to every conceivable issue of quality *per se* unless the clause is appropriately drafted.

---

[39] ie the point of loading in accordance with clause 15 of the sale contract.

[40] *Wallis Son & Wells v Pratt & Haynes* [1911] AC 394 at p 398.

[41] M Bridge (ed), *Benjamin's Sale of Goods*, 8th edn (London, Thomson Reuters (Legal) Ltd, 2010) para 13-025 p 681.

[42] At [62].

[43] *cf* the conclusion reached by Cooke J in *Air Transworld Ltd v Bombardier Inc* [2012] EWHC 243 (Comm), [2012] 1 Lloyd's Rep 349 at [31].

[44] ie contracts concluded on fob, cif, or c&f terms.

[45] Above n 31.

[46] Above n 43.

[47] At [41] and [42]. See also the comments of Hamblen J, [2012] EWHC 3009 (Comm), [2013] 1 Lloyd's Rep 360 at [46] and [49].

In the absence of such drafting, it is further submitted that the contract itself may support the above conclusion. Imagine the situation where a seller must, in order to obtain payment, provide the buyer with certificates on a number of parameters, all of which relate to the quality of the goods but only one/some of which are expressed to be final and binding. It surely cannot be correct that a seller can hide behind the final and binding certificate(s) unless the alleged defect can be said to be dealt with by the certificate(s) in question.

These issues are of course matters of construction of the contract of sale. This may in fact go even further and indicate that notwithstanding the presence of a certificate final clause, the parties did not intend to provide for a certificate final regime at all. Such an argument was successfully advanced by the buyer in *RG Grain Trade LLP v Feed Factors International Ltd.*[48]

INCONSISTENCY WITH A CERTIFICATE FINAL REGIME: THE *RG GRAIN* DECISION

In *RG Grain*, one of the issues in dispute was whether or not the sale contract created a certificate final regime. The sale contract contained *inter alia* the following terms:

> Quality and condition to be final at time and place of loading as per certificate of first class superintendent approved by GAFTA at seller's choice and expense.
> The buyers have the right to appoint their own GAFTA approved supervisor at their expense. In this case the sampling to be done conjointly, as per GAFTA terms and conditions.
> 2nd analysis, if any, as per Salamon and Seaber, London…
> Seller to provide the following documents:
> …
> Quality Certificate
> Contract: Gafta 119

Gafta 119 contained *inter alia*, the following terms:

> 5. QUALITY
> Official…certificate of inspection, at time of loading into the ocean carrying vessel, shall be final as to quality.
> 16. SAMPLING AND ANALYSIS AND CERTIFICATE OF ANALYSIS – the terms and conditions of GAFTA Sampling Rules No 124 are deemed incorporated into this contract

GAFTA's sampling rules contained *inter alia*, the following terms:

> 4. QUALITY CERTIFICATION AT TIME OF LOADING
> Where the contract provides that a certificate of inspection of a superintendent…at time of loading shall be final as to quality, then the superintendent…shall be solely responsible for drawing samples and Rules…5[49] do not apply.

---

[48] Above n 16.
[49] This provision allowed for the buyer to accept the seller's analysis or obtain a second analysis from Salamon & Seaber, failing which the seller's analysis would be final and binding.

At loading the buyer exercised his option to appoint a supervisor and joint sampling was carried out and certificates were issued by the superintendent appointed by the seller, which indicated that the goods were in accordance with the specifications in the sale contract.

However, the buyer's own analysis indicated that the cargo was off specification in some aspects and they sent samples to Salamon & Seaber accordingly, the analysis of which indicated that the cargo was off specification *vis-à-vis* protein and fibre content. This led to the buyer rejecting the goods and the documents.

Mr Justice Hamblen, upholding the decision of the GAFTA Appeal Board, held that as a matter of construction of the sale contract, the certificates issued by the seller's superintendent were not final and binding in circumstances where the buyer had elected to appoint his own supervisor.

Although the clause did not expressly state that the second analysis was the buyer's right, this was clearly what was contemplated. The clause appeared immediately after a provision giving the buyer the right to appoint a supervisor and in GAFTA 124, the right to call for a '2nd analysis', was generally a right given to the party that had not arranged the first analysis. Furthermore, to hold otherwise would deprive the clause of all meaningful effect since if the seller's analysis was final and binding, the second analysis would have no realistic application.[50]

CONCLUSION

The importance of certainty in commercial transactions was recognised by Lord Mansfield as long ago as 1774[51] and international trade is obviously no different in this regard.

When it comes to disputes about the quality of goods sold, a certificate final regime is designed to provide certainty on both sides of the contract. As Lord Denning MR stated in *Alfred C Toepfer* v *Continental Grain Co*:[52]

> it must be remembered that numerous persons act on the faith of the certificate, such as the buyers, sub-buyers, bankers lending money and so forth.

Although this undeniably still holds true, since 1983 when *Toepfer* was approved by the House of Lords in *Berger & Co Inc v Gill & Duffus SA*,[53] it has almost three decades later become virtually impossible in some trades to buy on anything other than certificate final terms when contracting on fob, cif or c&f terms. Whilst goods of course continue to be traded on the strength of the documents, the effectiveness of the certificate final regime has been called into question by trading houses and trade associations alike due to the tension it necessarily creates between the desire for certainty on the one hand and the ability of a seller[54] to effectively exclude its

---

[50] [17]–[19].
[51] *Vallejo v Wheeler* (1774) 1 Cowp 143 at p 153.
[52] Above n 19 at p 13 col 2.
[53] Above n 19.
[54] In practice, it is very often the seller that is in control of sampling/testing at the port of loading.

liability for claims relating to issues of quality on the other with appropriately drafted wording in the contract of sale. It remains to be seen whether international trade will continue along the certificate final route.

However one thing is certain. If a seller wishes to sell on certificate final terms to protect himself against such claims, both decisions examined in this chapter demonstrate that care must be taken to ensure that the rest of the sale contract is consistent with that intention and that the clause is appropriately drafted to provide the finality sought. If not, then the certainty the certificate is designed to provide may in fact prove to be wholly illusionary.

Part 3

Development in Marine Insurance, Jurisdiction and Enforcement

10

Thirty Years of Inherent Vice – From Soya v White *to* The Cendor MOPU *and Beyond*

JOHANNA HJALMARSSON AND JENNIFER LAVELLE[1]

INTRODUCTION

IN NOVEMBER 1982, the House of Lords gave judgment in *Soya GmbH Mainz Kommanditgesellschaft v White*.[2] Lord Diplock gave what has for thirty years remained the seminal definition of the concept of inherent vice. That concept had until then quite surprisingly remained undefined through the centuries,[3] although not for lack of cargoes subject to inherent vice. On the contrary, until refrigeration quite changed the rules of the game, a significant proportion of all cargoes were subject to the exclusion from cover for loss caused by inherent vice, now enshrined in the law of England and Wales by the Marine Insurance Act 1906, section 55(2)(c).[4] In the twentieth century, containerisation and refrigeration were game changers to the business of cargo transport, with the result that many previously sensitive and perishable cargoes were suddenly

---

[1] The authors are indebted to Professor Rob Merkin for his comments on a draft of this chapter. Any errors are attributable solely to the authors.

[2] [1983] 1 Lloyd's Rep 122, Lords Diplock, Keith, Scarman, Roskill and Templeman.

[3] For some of the earlier cases discussing the concept of inherent vice, see *Dyson v Rowcroft* (1802) 3 B&T 474; *Boyd v Dubois* (1811) 3 Camp 133; *Koebel v Saunders* (1864) 17 CBNS 71; *Blower v Great Western Railway Co* (1872) LR 7 CP 655; *British & Foreign Marine Insurance Co v Gaunt* [1921] 2 AC 41; *Traders and General Insurance Association v Bankers & General Insurance Co* (1921) 9 Ll L Rep 223; *Maignen & Co v National Benefit Assurance Co* (1922) 10 Ll L Rep 30; *Wilson, Holgate & Co Ltd v Lancashire and Cheshire Insurance Corp Ltd* (1922) 13 Ll L Rep 486; *ED Sassoon & Co Ltd v Yorkshire Insurance Co* (1923) 16 Ll L Rep 129; *Bird's Cigarette Manufacturing Co Ltd v Rouse* (1924) 19 Ll L Rep 301; *CT Bowring & Co Ltd v Amsterdam London Insurance Co Ltd* (1930) 36 Ll L Rep 309; *Whiting v New Zealand Insurance Co Ltd* (1932) 44 Ll L Rep 179; *Gee and Garnham Ltd v Whittall* [1955] 2 Lloyd's Rep 562; *FW Berk & Co Ltd v Style* [1955] 2 Lloyd's Rep 382; *Overseas Commodities Ltd v Style* [1958] 1 Lloyd's Rep 546; and *Albacora SRL v Westcott & Laurance Line Ltd* (1966) 2 Lloyd's Rep 53.

[4] Hudson and Madge describe the exclusion as one 'of considerable antiquity', which is recognised by the maritime law of all countries, at p 20 of NG Hudson and T Madge, *Marine Insurance Clauses*, 4th edn (London, LLP, 2005).

susceptible to transportation for several weeks without noticeable deterioration and it was even possible to let produce ripen in transit. The goalposts in the transportation of sensitive cargoes had obviously shifted, but it was not clear how. It was against this background that the question of the meaning of 'inherent vice' first arose in modern times in the case of *Soya v White*, giving rise to several subsequent cases that opened issues which have now been brought to a conclusion by the judgment of the Supreme Court in *The Cendor MOPU*.[5]

It is appropriate first to set out some of the legislative and contractual background to the issue. Convenient as it might seem, it would be wrong to start this discussion by offering a definition of the concept of inherent vice, for reasons that will become quite obvious. The colourful expression 'inherent vice' is found in section 55(2)(c) of the 1906 Act, which reads:

> Unless the policy otherwise provides, the insurer is not liable for ordinary wear and tear, ordinary leakage and breakage, inherent vice or nature of the subject-matter insured, or for any loss proximately caused by rats or vermin, or for any injury to machinery not proximately caused by maritime perils.

Inherent vice also makes an appearance in the standard cargo insurance clauses most in use. The Institute Cargo Clauses (A), (B) and (C) in both their 1982 and 2009 incarnations contain an exclusion of loss caused by inherent vice in clause 4.4, which reads as follows.

> 4. In no case shall this insurance cover
>
> ...
>
> 4.4 Loss damage or expense caused by inherent vice or nature of the subject matter insured.

Having commented on the exclusion thirty years ago in 1982, the House of Lords, now succeeded by the Supreme Court, had a renewed opportunity to return to the exclusion and to finally settle its scope in 2011, in the case of *The Cendor MOPU*.[6] Next, the factual background to these two key cases should be set out.

I. FACTUAL BACKGROUND

In *Soya v White*,[7] the courts had been asked to draw a line of principle or law – not of evidence or fact – between events that are inevitable and those that are fortuitous; a task made more difficult by events that are covered, although

---

[5] *Global Process Systems Inc v Syarikat Takaful Malaysia Berhad (The Cendor MOPU)* [2011] UKSC 5; [2011] 1 Lloyd's Rep 560. The judgments of the lower courts are reported at [2009] EWCA Civ 1398, [2010] 1 Lloyd's Rep 243 (Waller, Patten, and Carnwath LJJ) and [2009] EWHC 637 (Comm), [2009] 2 Lloyd's Rep 72 (Blair J).

[6] *Global Process Systems Inc v Syarikat Takaful Malaysia Berhad (The Cendor MOPU)* [2011] UKSC 5; [2011] 1 Lloyd's Rep 560.

[7] The first instance judgment of Lloyd J was reported at [1980] 1 Lloyd's Rep 491. The High Court decision was affirmed by the Court of Appeal at [1982] 1 Lloyd's Rep 136 with speeches by Waller LJ and Donaldson LJ, O'Connor LJ agreeing with both.

they may not be objectively fortuitous but are fortuitous from the perspective of the insured, such as arson. The subject matter insured was a cargo of soya beans. The first shipment in a series had deteriorated and additional insurance was purchased against heat, sweat and spontaneous combustion ('HSSC') for the subsequent shipments, as follows:

> This insurance is to cover against the risks of heat sweat and spontaneous combustion only.

While most policies of marine insurance exclude inherent vice in addition to the statutory exclusion, it is worth noting that the insurance was, in a manner of speaking, the negative of a usual policy, in that it was designed to cover the carve-out of inherent vice which is not covered by a regular policy by virtue of the statutory exclusion, and of course any similar provision in the policy. The policy in this case was designed to cover risks also encompassing inherent vice namely, heat, sweat and spontaneous combustion. An additional argument of failure to disclose the condition of the first cargo arose but was summarily dismissed by Lloyd J at first instance. Upon appeal, the only remaining issue was the construction of the words quoted above, and whether they prevented the insurance from covering an inherent vice, which necessitated a definition of that concept. The House of Lords held that the words 'inherent vice' referred to the peril, or risk, by which the loss was caused and not to the loss itself. The definition provided was offered by Lord Diplock who stated that:

> This phrase (generally shortened to 'inherent vice') where it is used in s. 55(2)(c) refers to a peril by which a loss is proximately caused; it is not descriptive of the loss itself. It means the risk of deterioration of the goods shipped as a result of their natural behaviour in the ordinary course of the contemplated voyage without the intervention of any fortuitous external accident or casualty. Prima facie, this risk is excluded from a policy of marine insurance unless the policy otherwise provides, either expressly or by necessary implication.[8]

The House of Lords went on to conclude that the question whether particular kinds of inherent vice were covered under a particular policy was a question of construction of that policy. On the facts being considered, 'heat, sweat and spontaneous combustion' were all covered under the policy.

In *The Cendor MOPU*, a jack-up oil rig was to be transported from Galveston in Texas to Malaysia. It was placed on a barge and instead of detaching the legs, they were left attached and sticking up a 100 metres into the air. Although the arrangement was, perhaps reluctantly, approved by surveyors, it was an obviously risky one and indeed off the coast of South Africa, one of the legs came off, soon followed by the other two. The weather conditions were reasonably good and there was no signal event such as lightning or a storm or particularly bad swell that immediately caused the legs to come off. A key factor contributing to the loss was metal fatigue. Upon inspection in South Africa, subtle cracks had been discovered

---

[8] [1983] 1 Lloyd's Rep 122, at p 126.

and an attempt had been made at repairing them, which in the end did not prevent the loss from occurring.

At first instance, Blair J held that the loss had been caused by the inherent vice of the rig. The judge also found, as a matter of fact, that the loss was not inevitable.[9] This decision was appealed on the issue of inherent vice, but not on the judge's findings as regards inevitability. In contrast to the lower court's decision, the Court of Appeal held that the loss had not been caused by inherent vice but had resulted from an insured peril in the form of a leg-breaking wave, the occurrence of which was a fortuity.[10] The policy was on all risks terms, namely the Institute Cargo Clauses (A) 1982 and therefore proof of a fortuity was essentially sufficient to put the claimants in a position to recover. At the Supreme Court, the central issue was the meaning of the inherent vice exclusion.

II. FORTUITY AND INEVITABILITY

In *Soya v White*, the fact that the policy was said to cover heat and sweat meant that the relevant question raised was whether it also covered heat and sweat caused by the soya beans' own inherent propensity to overheat and ultimately to spontaneously combust. On the wording of the policy, this would certainly be covered, but at the same time it was clear that any inevitable damage could not be covered, because insurance does not cover inevitabilities. In *Soya v White*, this translated neatly to the difference between a moisture content of over 15 per cent upon shipment, when heat damage would become inevitable. A moisture content below 12 per cent was safe; therefore with the moisture content of 13 per cent, in the range between 12 and 14 per cent, damage could either happen or not happen. These numbers probably made the issue seem deceptively simple and perhaps obscured the potential for delicate borderline cases. In other cases, discerning when damage is 'inevitable' is not quite so obvious. In the context of the facts of *The Cendor MOPU*, just how much fatigue cracking was necessary for the leg to fall off spontaneously, without the impact of a leg-breaking wave? And to what extent must a leg-breaking wave be considered completely inevitable, so that it was not a fortuity but a certainty that the first leg should fall off in the course of the voyage? These issues were not before the Supreme Court because Blair J at first instance had concluded as a matter of fact that the loss, although very likely, had not been inevitable.

---

[9] For case comments on the first instance judgment see K Georgiou, 'Inherent Vice' (2009) 9 (5) *Shipping & Trade Law*, 6–8; and D Turner, C Dixon 'All Risks Insurance' (2009) 21 (8) *Insurance Law Monthly*, 10–12.

[10] For a summary and analysis of the judgment of the Court of Appeal, see J Lavelle, 'Marine Insurance – Inherent Vice' (2010) 10 (1) *Shipping & Trade Law* 6–8; and D Turner, C Dixon, 'Marine Insurance: All risks insurance' (2010) 22 (5) *Insurance Law Monthly* 7–8. The Supreme Court judgment is similarly reviewed by A Bugra, 'Inherent Vice and Perils of the Seas: Supreme Court finalises their Scope' (2011) 11 (2) *Shipping & Trade Law* 1–5; and R Merkin, 'Perils of the seas, inherent vice and causation' (2011) 23 (3) *Insurance Law Monthly* 1–5.

The policy in *Soya v White* did not cover the inevitable; not by virtue of some intricate interpretation but simply because insurance never covers the inevitable.[11] An element of fortuity is regarded as a conceptual limit on any policy under the law of England and Wales.[12] However, taking for a moment a practical – rather than a legal – perspective, it may be said that inherent vice carries with it an element of inevitability. It is known that potatoes rot, rabbit flesh rots, citrus fruits rot, tobacco rots and all other perishables rot. This *is* inevitable and is likely to have historically been the very reason for the exclusion of inherent vice from a marine policy. By way of illustration, in *Soya v White*, Lloyd J noted at first instance that the policy would not have covered the loss if the temperature rose above 15 degrees, because the loss would then have been entirely foreseeable.[13] The cargo of soya beans would spontaneously combust and therefore the damage at that temperature or more was inevitable. This serves as an illustration of a situation where there is no element of fortuity present in insurance for cargoes, beyond the point where they must inevitably be destroyed, and the only insurance that could make sense was one that did not cover them beyond that point. According to Blair J at first instance in *The Cendor MOPU*, that policy did not cover the inevitable either, and the wider question was whether metal fatigue in combination with waves of ordinary stature created a certainty where insurance required there to be only an uncertainty.

As a further issue, Donaldson LJ in *Soya v White* expressed preference for the term 'known certainty' rather than 'inevitability'. The judge stated that 'in practical terms there is as much a risk if the inevitability of a loss is not known as if the loss itself may or may not occur'.[14] The judge suggested that known certainty 'of the loss or of the particular extent of the loss' should be used instead of the concept of inevitability. Accordingly, where the certainty of loss is known to the assured but not the insurer, the insurer would be able to raise a defence of fraud or non-disclosure, so that the claim would fail. Where both parties are aware that the loss is a certainty, then it is highly unlikely that the insurer would provide cover. Where, however, the certainty of loss is not known to either party, then should the policy respond?

On the facts of *Soya v White*, it was common ground between the parties that were the soya beans shipped with a moisture content below or above a certain point, then the microbiological activity that would lead to heating would not occur in the first instance, or would be bound to occur in the second. As such there was a grey area between the points where it was unknown whether such activity would or would not occur; and it was in this grey area that a risk existed. Other cases may not, however, be as straightforward. For example, what if the assured and insurer did not know that the loss, which had ultimately occurred, had been inevitable? Where the inevitability is proved with hindsight, would it be acceptable for the insurers to not be liable, even though they had accepted a premium for the insurance? Without

---

[11] Life insurance does cover the inevitable: but it would not do so if it were a matter of certainty when the covered life would end.

[12] M Clarke, *Law of Insurance Contracts*, 4th edn, service issue 24 (London, Informa, 2012), at 17–3 and 3A.

[13] [1980] 1 Lloyd's Rep 491, at p 504.

[14] [1982] 1 Lloyd's Rep 136, at p 149.

specific reference to Donaldson LJ's comments on the matter, Lord Mance in *The Cendor MOPU* stated that 'if neither party knows, then inevitability resulting from inherent characteristics of the goods will, in the absence of express provision, bar recovery on the grounds of inherent vice.'[15] It could be inferred from this statement that Lord Mance rejected the test proposed by Donaldson LJ in *Soya v White*. Lord Mance questioned whether inevitability resulting from outside causes would prevent recovery, referring to such situations as 'an open question', but noted that the issue did not require examination in the context of the case.

III. BURDEN OF PROOF

A critical question is where the burden of proof lies as regards proving inherent vice, and how that burden may be affected, if at all, where the policy is extended to provide appropriate cover as regards the particular vice of the subject matter insured. It will be seen that the matter of what exactly must be proved has been the issue of some controversy.

A. 'All Risks' Cover

It is first necessary, however, to comment on the nature of policies that cover 'all risks', for example, those incorporating the 1982 or 2009 ICC(A). In such cases, previous case law has been understood as showing that the insured's hurdle is a low one. In *British & Foreign Marine Insurance v Gaunt*,[16] the claimant was the buyer of a portion of a clip of wool produced in Patagonia, to be delivered in bales to the port of Punta Arenas in Chile, and then shipped to Europe. The claimant was also the assignee of three policies of marine insurance, whereby the wool in question was insured during the transit from the sheep's back in the interior to Punta Arenas. The bales were badly damaged by water and it was proved at the trial that this damage arose during the transit to Punta Arenas. Consequently, the claimant brought an action against the defendant insurers in respect of a partial loss by damage. By the time the dispute reached the House of Lords, the questions raised by the appeal were (1) whether the damage was due to a risk covered by the policies, or, in other words, whether it was due to a casualty; and (2) whether the wool was removed from the scope of the policies on the ground that it was not specifically insured to be carried as deck cargo; the latter question being outside the scope of the discussion here.

In construing the policies which covered 'all risks', Lord Birkenhead emphasised that

these words cannot, of course, be held to cover all damage however caused, for such damage as is inevitable from ordinary wear and tear and inevitable depreciation is not

---

[15] [2011] UKSC 5; [2011] 1 Lloyd's Rep 560, at [51].
[16] *British & Foreign Marine Insurance Co v Gaunt* [1921] 2 AC 41.

within the policies... Damage, in other words, if it is to be covered by policies such as these, must be due to some fortuitous circumstance or casualty.[17]

Accordingly, under such policies, the insured must still establish his case. As asserted by Lord Birkenhead, the claimant insured

> must show that the loss comes within the terms of his policies; but where all risks are covered by the policy and not merely risks of a specified class or classes, the (claimant) discharges his special onus when he has proved that the loss was caused by some event covered by the general expression, and he is not bound to go further and prove the exact nature of the accident or casualty which, in fact, occasioned his loss.[18]

Lord Sumner also gave judgment in this case, providing the following, often quoted interpretation of the term all risks

> There are, of course, limits to 'all risks'. There are risks and risks insured against. Accordingly the expression does not cover inherent vice or mere wear and tear or British capture. It covers a risk, not a certainty; it is something which happens to the subject-matter from without, not the natural behaviour of that subject-matter, being what it is, in the circumstances under which it is carried ... Finally the description 'all risks' does not alter the general law; only risks are covered which it is lawful to cover, and the onus of proof remains where it would have been on a policy against ordinary sea perils.[19]

Lord Sumner continued, however, to note how the 'quasi-universality' of the description affects the onus of proof in one way, stating that

> The claimant insured against and averring a loss by fire must prove loss by fire, which involves proving that it is not by something else. When he avers loss by some risk coming within 'all risks', as used in this policy, *he need only give evidence reasonably showing that the loss was due to a casualty, not to a certainty or to inherent vice or to wear and tear.* That is easily done. I do not think he has to go further and pick out one of the multitude of risks covered, so as to show exactly how his loss was caused. If he did so, he would not bring it any the more within the policy.[20] (emphasis added)

Lord Sumner further concluded that 'if the casualty was a fortuity, it needed not to be a calamity'. In light of both judgments, it is apparent that, under an 'all risks' policy, the insured need only establish that the loss was due to some accident or casualty, and the exact nature of that casualty does not need to be proved. That being said, it is arguably unclear whether Lord Sumner also places the burden of proving that the loss under an all risks policy was *not* due to inherent vice on the insured. Even though uncertain, it is submitted that the judgment did not have such an effect.

---

[17] [1921] 2 AC 41, at pp 46–47.
[18] [1921] 2 AC 41, at p 47.
[19] [1921] 2 AC 41, at p 57.
[20] [1921] 2 AC 41, at p 58.

B. The Evolving Nature of the Burden

In the more recent case of *Soya v White*, Lloyd J was much more definitive on the matter, holding that 'the burden of proving inherent vice undoubtedly rests on the defendants'.[21] In that case, Lloyd J held that the defendant underwriters had proved that inherent vice was a cause in the sense that without moisture, the damage could not have occurred at all, but they had not succeeded in proving that inherent vice was the cause, the proximate cause, or one of the proximate causes. At the Court of Appeal, Donaldson LJ reiterated that the burden of proving inherent vice lay on the defendant underwriter, while providing that 'the burden of disproving inevitability might lie on the plaintiff'.[22] As the only issue on appeal to the House of Lords was the construction of the words in the HSSC policy, no comment on the burden of proof was given.

Subsequently, the case of *TM Noten BV v Harding* came before the courts. In that case, water contained in leather gloves shipped from Calcutta to Rotterdam during the monsoon season had condensed on the inside of the packaging and dripped back onto the leather gloves, causing them to arrive in a mouldy condition. The gloves had been covered on an all risks basis. At first instance, Phillips J had found that the damage was from an external source, as the water had left the gloves before it fell back onto them.[23] That decision was however overruled by the Court of Appeal,[24] who held that because the water had emanated from the gloves in the first place, the loss was caused by inherent vice.[25] While competing theories of causation were considered, the issue of where the burden of proof lay was not explicitly dealt with in either of the judgments. Perhaps this is because, as a general rule, it was understood that the burden of proving an exclusion to cover lay with the underwriter. Even so, it can be said that the law took an unexpected turn following the decision in *Mayban General Assurance BHD v Alstom Power Plants Ltd*.[26]

In *Mayban*, the cargo in question was a transformer which, just like the jack-up rig in *The Cendor MOPU* was afflicted by metal fatigue. The policy incorporated the ICC(A)1982 providing all risks cover with certain exclusions, including an express exclusion for loss or damage caused by inherent vice. The judge directed himself that such a policy only required the insured to show that the loss had happened through some fortuity. In particular, it was held that 'in order to recover under the

---

[21] [1980] 1 Lloyd's Rep 491, at p 505.

[22] [1982] 1 Lloyd's Rep 136, at p 144. The fact that the policy in this dispute specifically covered a risk that was described as the 'most obvious example of inherent vice' (at p 140) is a matter which will be dealt with below.

[23] [1989] 2 Lloyd's Rep 527. This decision can be said to be in line with a number of earlier authorities that dealt with moisture and condensation damage to cargoes. These cases, including in particular, *Bowring v Amsterdam London Insurance Co Ltd*, are discussed by Dunt in *Marine Cargo Insurance* (London, Informa, 2009), at [8.25]–[8.27].

[24] [1990] 2 Lloyd's Rep 283, Glidewell and Bingham LJJ, and Sir David Croom-Johnson.

[25] The Court of Appeal made reference in their decision (at p 288) to a case on analogous facts before the District Court of Rotterdam, where it was also held that the cause of the damage was inherent vice – *Bantle & Preiss BV v NV Schadeverzekering Maatschappil UAP-Nederland* (9 February 1990). The Dutch decision was unsuccessfully appealed – *Hof's-Gravenhage* (19 September 1992) S&S 1993, 17.

[26] [2004] 2 Lloyd's Rep 609, Moore-Bick J.

policy the insured must prove that the loss was caused by an accident or casualty of some kind'; as insurers accept the risk but not the certainty of loss. In addition, 'although the insured must prove a loss by an accident of some kind, it is not necessary for him to go further and establish the exact nature of the accident by which it occurred.'[27] There is no controversy here, as the words used clearly mirror the judgment in *Gaunt*. Moore-Bick J also provided that an all risks policy

> does not cover the insured against loss due to wear and tear or the inherent vice of the thing insured, whether that loss was bound to occur or was fortuitous in the sense that its occurrence depended on the particular circumstances to which the goods happened to be exposed in the course of the voyage.[28]

This statement correctly reflects the principle that loss or damage as a result of inherent vice is not inevitable; yet, even though the experience of loss may be fortuitous, it is not covered by the policy.

Satisfied that the damage was caused by the prolonged working of the transformer's joints brought about by the motion of the vessel in which it was carried, it fell to Moore-Bick J to determine the proximate cause of the loss. Based on evidence of previous successful shipments of similar kinds of transformers, it was held that the damage suffered was not inevitable, but that did not mean that the damage was proximately caused by an external fortuitous event. Further, even though it was common ground that the immediate cause of the damage was the violent movement of the vessel due to the actions of the wind and sea, the judge was not convinced that they were the real cause of the loss. Moore-Bick J referred, it is submitted erroneously, to the 'competing causes' of perils of the sea and inherent vice, as being 'to a large extent opposite sides of the same coin.'[29] He stated

> If the conditions encountered by the vessel were more severe than could reasonably have been expected, it is likely that the loss will have been caused by perils of the sea... If, however, the conditions encountered by the vessel were no more severe than could reasonably have been expected, the conclusion *must* be that the real cause of the loss was the inherent inability of the goods to withstand the ordinary incidents of the voyage.[30] (emphasis added)

It is submitted that the reasoning of Moore-Bick J regarding the cause of the loss was such as to turn inherent vice into a default outcome. If the conditions of the voyage were no worse than could reasonably be expected, and there was no other apparent cause of loss, that must mean, said Moore-Bick J, that the loss had been occasioned by an inherent vice of the subject matter insured. Unfortunately for the claimants, the judge concluded that the conditions encountered by the vessel on the relevant passage were neither extreme nor unusual in the sense that they were encountered often enough for mariners to regard them as a normal hazard.[31]

---

[27] [2004] 2 Lloyd's Rep 609, at p 611.
[28] [2004] 2 Lloyd's Rep 609, at p 611.
[29] [2004] 2 Lloyd's Rep 609, at p 614.
[30] [2004] 2 Lloyd's Rep 609, at p 614.
[31] [2004] 2 Lloyd's Rep 609, at p 615.

He made it clear that 'conditions or events which are well known to occur from time to time but which are nonetheless relatively uncommon may well properly be regarded as ordinary incidents of the voyage.'[32]

As a consequence, it is argued that the judgment had the effect of reversing the burden of proof. As noted above, exclusions to cover such as inherent vice, must usually be proven by the insurer. However in *Mayban*, the failure of the insured to demonstrate that any extraordinary event had occurred led the judge to the conclusion that the loss must have been caused by inherent vice, since there was no other cause of loss in evidence. Naturally, the burden of proof does initially rest on the insured; however, the onus is not to demonstrate that the voyage contained some extraordinary event, but to demonstrate that the loss took place through some fortuitous event. This set the scene for the same issues as they arose in *The Cendor MOPU*, thirty years on from *Soya v White*.

C. Burden of Proof and *The Cendor MOPU*

At first instance, Blair J first confirmed that the claimants were

> only required to show that the cause of the loss was accidental, or to put it another way, that the loss was not inevitable. Once the claimants discharge that burden, the burden is then on the insurer to make out the exclusion relied on.[33]

It was also reiterated that damage may be caused by inherent vice without it being inevitable, so it was therefore not an answer to a plea based on inherent vice that the loss was fortuitous. Blair J explicitly provided that 'the burden is however on the defendant insurer to make out the exclusion.'[34]

Ms Blanchard, counsel for the claimant cargo owners,[35] was also of the opinion that the effect of the decision in *Mayban* was 'to reverse the burden of proof, by taking the burden of proof off the insurer to prove inherent vice and requiring the insured to prove extraordinary weather,' thus significantly reducing the scope of cover afforded for perils of the sea in a cargo policy.[36] As the claimants had accepted that the weather experienced during the voyage was within the range that could reasonably be contemplated, their attempts to persuade the court that inherent vice did not follow from the lack of extraordinary weather was understandable. Blair J agreed with Ms Blanchard to the extent that if the *Mayban* decision had 'created a rule of evidence that, absent exceptional weather being shown to have occurred, the loss must be attributed to inherent vice, such a submission would be contrary to authority, and wrong.'[37] Nonetheless, Blair J held that this was a mistaken analysis

---

[32] [2004] 2 Lloyd's Rep 609, at p 616.

[33] [2009] EWHC 637 (Comm); [2009] 2 Lloyd's Rep 72, at [3].

[34] [2009] EWHC 637 (Comm); [2009] 2 Lloyd's Rep 72, at [90].

[35] Incidentally, Ms Blanchard was also an editor of *Arnould's Law of Marine Insurance and Average*, 17th edn (Sweet & Maxwell, 2008).

[36] [2009] EWHC 637 (Comm); [2009] 2 Lloyd's Rep 72, at [99].

[37] [2009] EWHC 637 (Comm); [2009] 2 Lloyd's Rep 72, at [101].

of the decision. Blair J ultimately held that the defendant insurers had proved that the proximate cause of the loss was the fact that the legs were not capable of withstanding the normal incidents of the insured voyage, including the weather to be reasonably expected. As such, the loss was due to inherent vice and thereby excluded from the policy.

On appeal, *The Cendor MOPU* allowed the Court of Appeal to re-examine the correct test to be applied in such cases, with particular focus on the relationship between perils of the sea and inherent vice.[38] After an extensive review of the authorities, Waller LJ, delivering the leading judgment, held that 'where one has an accident at sea such as occurred here, the burden is on the underwriter to establish inherent vice as the proximate cause.'[39] As regards the appropriate test, the judge reasoned

> Even if the question to be considered is – Was the cause an inability to withstand the ordinary incidents of the voyage? – the answer cannot be found by reference to what might be reasonably foreseeable as the ordinary incidents of that voyage, but by reference to wind or wave which, it would be the common understanding, would be bound to occur as the ordinary incidents on any normal voyage of the kind being undertaken. This is not equating inherent vice with certainty but it is recognising that an insurer would not cover damage to cargo flowing from the motion of a vessel in such seas, even if it was not certain to occur.[40]

As a result, Waller LJ was persuaded that a narrower test than that accepted by Moore-Bick J in *Mayban*, as applied by Blair J in the lower court, was the correct test.[41] This led to the conclusion that 'a leg breaking wave, not bound to occur in the way that it did on any normal voyage round the Cape of Good Hope, caused the starboard leg to break off.' The high probability of this happening was not known to the insured, and that was a risk against which the claimants insured. The insurers appealed.

The central issue before the Supreme Court was the meaning of the exclusion of inherent vice, both in the contract in question and in section 55(2)(c) of the 1906 Act. At the outset, Lord Saville repeated that it was common ground between the parties that it was for the insurers to prove that the loss was proximately caused by inherent vice.[42] In this regard, the insurers submitted that it was not enough to negative inherent vice to have some external fortuity. The external fortuity had to intervene so that it negated causation of the loss by the unfitness of the goods which existed on shipment. As the sea conditions were within the range that could

---

[38] In a comparable position to inherent vice, the interpretation of 'perils of the seas' is the subject of some controversy, which has led to a great deal of judgments on the matter. While relevant in determining the concept of inherent vice, a detailed analysis of the term 'perils of the seas' is outside the scope of this chapter. Readers are instead directed to H Bennett's article, 'Fortuity in the Law of Marine Insurance' [2007] *LMCLQ* 315, and the cases discussed therein.

[39] [2009] EWCA Civ 1398; [2010] 1 Lloyd's Rep 243, at [59].

[40] [2009] EWCA Civ 1398; [2010] 1 Lloyd's Rep 243, at [62].

[41] As a consequence, the decision in *Mayban* was overruled and the judgment at first instance was reversed.

[42] [2011] UKSC 5; [2011] 1 Lloyd's Rep 560, at [20].

reasonably have been contemplated for the voyage, there had been no intervention of any fortuitous external accident or casualty, so that the loss had been proximately caused by inherent vice.[43] In doing so, it could be said that the defendants were attempting to prove inherent vice by disproving the occurrence of any intervening act. Lord Saville held that the authorities relied upon by the insurers established that

> where the only fortuity operating on the goods comes from the goods themselves, the proximate cause of the loss can properly be said to be the inherent vice or nature of the subject matter insured and so (in absence of provisions to the contrary) falls outside the cover.

Lord Saville confirmed, however, that these cases did not provide authority for the proposition put forward by the insurers; the only case that did so, was the decision in *Mayban*, which, in the judge's opinion was 'wrongly decided'.[44]

Lord Saville agreed with the assured's submission that the effect of applying the test adopted at first instance would be to reduce much of the purpose of cargo insurance, for the cover would then only extend to loss or damage caused by perils of the seas that were exceptional, unforeseen or unforeseeable, and not otherwise. This would go far to frustrate the very purpose of all risks cargo insurance, which is to provide an indemnity in respect of loss or damage caused by, among other things, all perils of the seas.[45] As to the test applied at first instance, Lord Saville observed

> Where in my view the judge erred was in giving the phrase inherent vice or nature of the subject-matter insured too wide a meaning and, as the other side of the coin, giving the risk of perils of the seas too narrow a meaning, by in effect including in the former and excluding from the latter external fortuities that were unexceptional or which were foreseen or foreseeable; and then answering the question of fact on this erroneous basis. All or virtually all goods are susceptible to loss or damage from the fortuities of the weather on a voyage; this does not mean that such loss or damage arises from the nature of the goods; it arises from the fact that the goods have encountered one of the perils of the seas.[46]

To determine the proximate cause of the loss, the judge held that the question was one of fact, to be decided on common sense principles. Such principles, when applied to the present case, provided that the proximate cause of the loss was not inherent vice but an external fortuitous accident or casualty of the seas.

D. The Current Legal Position

It is argued in *Colinvaux* that following *The Cendor MOPU*, it is unclear where the burden of proof rests. Where it may have been previously argued that the burden of

---

[43] [2011] UKSC 5; [2011] 1 Lloyd's Rep 560, at [25].
[44] [2011] UKSC 5; [2011] 1 Lloyd's Rep 560, at [31]–[34].
[45] [2011] UKSC 5; [2011] 1 Lloyd's Rep 560, at [35].
[46] [2011] UKSC 5; [2011] 1 Lloyd's Rep 560, at [46].

proof rests on the insurer to demonstrate that inherent vice is the proximate cause, as it is an excluded peril, it is stated that 'it appears from *Global Process Systems* that as long as there is a peril of the seas then there is recovery.'[47] The following example is provided

> If there is a storm at sea, and the cargo on its arrival is found to have depreciated by reason of its perishable nature, the assured cannot recover simply because he cannot show that the loss was proximately caused by perils of the seas. But if the cargo is unfit for the voyage and is damaged by perils of the seas, the assured can recover. There is no need for the insurers to prove inherent vice, and there is no situation in which the assured will lose cover for a loss caused by perils of the seas even if the goods are at the same time affected by inherent vice. It would thus seem that inherent vice does not have to be proved at all.[48]

The correct interpretation of the Supreme Court's decision is thus of critical importance. It appears that where the insured can show that the loss was caused by some fortuity, then inherent vice cannot be an additional cause of the loss and the inquiry is concluded. *Colinvaux* expressly refers to perils of the seas as the relevant fortuity, although the judgment may have a wider application to all risks insured against. As a result of the decision, it would seem that perils of the seas and inherent vice can never be concurrent causes of loss, as they are alternative and mutually exclusive. If that is true, then it can also be argued that where the insured cannot discharge his burden of proving a fortuity, then the cause of loss must be inherent vice. Unlike the strict test applied in *Mayban* however, proving a fortuity seems to be a much lower burden following *The Cendor MOPU* judgment.

It may therefore be observed, following *The Cendor MOPU*, that the pendulum has simply swung in the other direction. Both judgments do not require inherent vice to be proved, but require the existence of a fortuity to disprove inherent vice. The only difference is that proving the fortuity appears to be much easier following the later decision. So, inherent vice is still a default outcome but it is only likely to result in a limited number of cases now that it is more straightforward for the assured to show a fortuity. Accordingly, if the facts of *Mayban* were reconsidered, the courts are likely to hold that the damage was caused by perils of the seas and not by the inherent vice of the transformer. The damage suffered by the transformer was not inevitable, nor was it an ordinary consequence of the wind and waves. Thus, the insured would be able to claim on the policy.

To sum up, if the comments provided in *Colinvaux* are an accurate summation of the effect of the decision, and, as a consequence, the current law, then the burden is simply on the insured to show a fortuity. Once proved, the policy should respond. If that burden is not discharged, however, there is still no need for the insurer to prove inherent vice, as the vice has already been established by the failure of the insured to demonstrate a fortuity. The issue that follows is whether this approach to inherent vice is appropriate.

---

[47] Colinvaux (2011), at [B-0646].
[48] Colinvaux (2011), at [B-0646].

In the alternative, if the burden of proving inherent vice as an exclusion to cover still rests with the insurer, then only express wording to the contrary included in such policies should shift that burden to the insured. Even then, as illustrated by Merkin in *Marine Insurance Legislation*, the insurer is still required to show that the loss was caused by an excepted peril

> It is permissible for the underwriters to seek to reverse the burden of proof by express wording to the effect that the assured must disprove any allegation by the underwriters that the loss was proximately caused by an excepted cause. However, in order to benefit from this type of clause, the underwriters must produce *prima facie* evidence demonstrating that the loss was caused by an excepted peril, and only then is the assured required to rebut that evidence (*Spinney's (1948) Ltd v Royal Insurance Co* [1980] 1 Lloyd's Rep 406).[49]

IV. THE ROLE OF CAUSATION

When considering the correct approach to inherent vice, it is necessary to briefly examine the part played by causation. The definition of inherent vice provided by Lord Diplock in *Soya v White* gives a prominent role to causation.[50] This is likely to be a result of section 55(1) of the Marine Insurance Act 1906 which provides:

> Subject to the provisions of this Act, and unless the policy otherwise provides, the insurer is liable for any loss proximately caused by a peril insured against, but, subject as aforesaid, he is not liable for any loss which is not proximately caused by a peril insured against.

When determining the proximate cause of the loss, it is clear from *Leyland Shipping Co Ltd v Norwich Union Fire Insurance Society Ltd*[51] that the last cause in time is not necessarily the proximate cause. Rather, the real or dominant cause needs to be determined, and the court is directed to apply the common sense of a business or seafaring man when doing so.[52] As expressed by Lord Saville in *The Cendor MOPU*, the proximate cause is that which is 'proximate in efficiency'.[53]

If it is determined that there are two or more concurrent causes of the loss, then the outcome will generally differ where one of the causes is a peril that is expressly excluded, as compared to the situation where one of the causes is simply not covered. To elaborate, where one of the causes is a peril insured against and the other cause is a peril that is simply not covered by the policy, but nor is it excluded by the policy, the insurer should satisfy the claim.[54] Yet, where one of the causes is a peril insured against and the other cause is a peril which is expressly excluded, the excluded peril takes priority and the policy does not respond. This principle emerges from *Wayne Tank & Pump Co Ltd v Employers*

---

[49] Merkin, *Marine Insurance Legislation,* 4th edn (London, Lloyd's List Group, 2010) at 75.

[50] Donaldson LJ, in the Court of Appeal, did not address causation but instead gave a definition of inherent vice that did not require examination of the relevant cause of loss.

[51] [1918] AC 350.

[52] See *TM Noten v Harding* [1990] 2 Lloyd's Rep 283.

[53] [2011] UKSC 5; [2011] 1 Lloyd's Rep 560, at [19].

[54] See *The Miss Jay Jay* [1987] 1 Lloyd's Rep 32.

Liability Assurance Corp Ltd,[55] and was approved by the Supreme Court in *The Cendor MOPU*. As a result, the determination of whether there is a single cause of loss or competing causes of loss may be essential for the assured's recovery.[56] For the sake of completeness, where none of the causes are perils insured against, then the insured cannot recover, for he is not insured against those perils.

In *The Cendor MOPU*, therefore, the courts sought to establish the proximate cause of the loss. At first instance, Blair J held that the proximate cause of the loss was the fact that the legs were not capable of withstanding the normal incidents of the insured voyage, including the weather reasonably to be expected. The Court of Appeal were of a different opinion, concluding that the proximate cause of the loss was an insured peril in the form of the occurrence of a 'leg breaking wave'. By the time the case reached the Supreme Court, the two remaining candidates for the proximate cause of loss were perils of the seas and inherent vice. Referring to the cases cited by the insurers, Lord Saville pointed out that *Noten v Harding* was a case in which it was determined that there was no operating external cause of loss at all.[57] The facts established in *Noten* were that only internal causes of loss were active, and there was no causation competition between external and internal causes. Lord Saville further commented that *Noten v Harding* did

> not provide authority for the proposition that inherent vice or nature of the subject matter insured is established by showing that the goods in question were not capable of withstanding the normal incidents of the insured voyage, including the weather reasonably to be expected. What they do establish is that where the only fortuity operating on the goods comes from the goods themselves, the proximate cause of the loss can properly be said to be the inherent vice or nature of the subject matter insured and so (in the absence of provisions to the contrary) falls outside the cover.[58]

Noten v Harding,[59] on its facts, therefore cannot necessarily assist with the resolution of a case where there is more than one active cause of loss.

A situation where a chain of events may be characterised as a single event involving no external factors is to be contrasted with a situation where there are two discernible, independent causes of loss. According to Lord Saville,

> what Lord Diplock was saying, as the assured submitted, was that where goods deteriorated, not because they had been subjected to some external fortuitous accident or casualty, but because of their natural behaviour in the ordinary course of the voyage,

---

[55] [1973] 2 Lloyd's Rep 237. See also *The Miss Jay Jay* [1987] 1 Lloyd's Rep 283. The principles arising from *Wayne Tank & Pump* and *Leyland Shipping* have arguably never been satisfactorily united.

[56] That being said, where there are two causes, an insurer may agree to pay half of the loss. Also, the doctrine of proximate cause is 'merely a rule of construction', which may be ousted by express agreement, in that the policy will only responded if a peril insured against is a sole and direct cause of the loss, or a policy may expressly exclude liability for a loss if it is in any way caused or contributed to by a peril that is expressly excluded. See further Merkin, *Marine Insurance Legislation* (London, Lloyd's List Group, 4th edn, 2010), at p 74.

[57] [2011] UKSC 5; [2011] 1 Lloyd's Rep 560, at [31].

[58] [2011] UKSC 5; [2011] 1 Lloyd's Rep 560, at [31].

[59] The same goes for the other case discussed by Lord Saville, *Nelson Marketing International Inc v Royal & Sun Alliance Insurance Co of Canada* (2006) 57 BCLR (4th) 27 from the British Columbia Court of Appeal.

then such deterioration amounted to inherent vice or nature of the subject matter insured.[60]

Lord Saville thus disapproved of Blair J's application at first instance of Lord Diplock's definition as meaning that an element of causation was intrinsic in the definition of inherent vice. The question in future cases, therefore, becomes whether on the facts, and not in law, there is a single process of destruction at hand, or two or more processes of destruction are implicated in the loss of the subject matter insured. On the facts of *The Cendor MOPU*, the defendant insurers were not able to prove that the metal fatigue, ie inherent vice of the rig, was an independently effective cause of the loss without the additional leg breaking wave, the occurrence of which was a fortuity. Once the leg-breaking wave was established, then there was a loss caused by perils of the seas and inherent vice could not enter the picture. As a result, the Supreme Court came to the conclusion that there was a single cause of loss, which was a peril insured against.

It is worth noting that the Supreme Court was also of the opinion that both the statutory and contractual exclusions of inherent vice had the same meaning. Lord Mance, in particular, stated that 'there seems to me some oddity in treating clause 4.4 as leading to a fundamentally different result from that which would have applied had section 55(2)(c) alone been in question.'[61] Accordingly, for insurers to get around the decision, a future contractual exclusion would require wording that overcomes section 55(2)(c) of the Marine Insurance Act.

V. A NEGATIVE BURDEN OF PROOF

Commenting again on the burden of proof under an all risks policy, if it is simply for the insured to prove a fortuity, does the opportunity even arise for the insurer to raise the exception of inherent vice? It appears not, with the result that inherent vice will only ever be the proximate cause of the loss where the insured cannot establish a fortuity. Even though the burden placed on the insured is a low one, it seems that the burden rests with the insured alone, and that the insurer can simply sit back and wait to see whether the insured establishes their case.

It is submitted that a different approach for cases involving all risks insurance is preferable. First, the insured must prove that there has been some fortuity or accident, and that the loss in question was not inevitable. Then, the burden should shift to the insurer who may raise any applicable exclusions or exceptions to cover. If the intention of the Supreme Court in *The Cendor MOPU* was to give precedence to perils of the seas over inherent vice, then this can be achieved by placing a higher burden on the insurer, rather than the default outcome outlined above. Accordingly, the insurer should prove that the vice was in operation, although, in itself, this is not enough to prevent the policy from responding. The insurer should also prove that the inherent vice was an independently effective or efficient cause of the loss;

---

[60] [2011] UKSC 5; [2011] 1 Lloyd's Rep 560, at [45].
[61] [2011] UKSC 5; [2011] 1 Lloyd's Rep 560, at [88].

in legal terms, perhaps the sole cause of the loss. It is argued that the burden on the insurer should be a positive one, and not a negative one. Inherent vice should not be established by proving that there were no other causes of loss in operation; inherent vice should not be treated as a statement of when there are no perils of the seas. As mentioned above, such an approach would have a similar effect to that of the decision in *Mayban*. Nor should it be upon the insurer to disprove all other causes of loss to discharge his burden.

Even so, it seems that the comments provided in *Colinvaux* are not without merit given the latest decision in *European Group Ltd and others v Chartis Insurance UK Ltd*,[62] where loss caused by fatigue stress cracking was once again brought before the High Court, although this time in relation to tubes in economiser blocks which were installed in a waste recycling plant. In this case, the dispute was between two insurers, rather than an insured and their insurer. It was common ground between the parties that the fatigue cracking was caused by resonant vibration, which was also agreed to be a fortuity that was covered by both of the insurance policies in question. The real issue for the court to decide was whether the cracking had occurred before or after delivery of the cargo at destination, as this would determine whether the claimant insurers or the defendant insurer would be liable for the loss. Popplewell J found, as a matter of fact, that the cracking had been caused during transit from Romania to England and therefore before delivery, so that the marine policy provided the appropriate cover.[63] Even so, the defendant insurer, who was the subscribing insurer under the marine policy, argued that inherent vice was an additional proximate cause to that of resonant vibration, and as a result, the policy should not respond by virtue of the inherent vice exclusion. The defendant's submission was rejected by the judge for two reasons.

First, the judge observed that the condition of the economiser blocks when they left the factory was such that 'they could reasonably be expected to survive the transportation to Lakeside, if properly packed,[64] and perform in service at the site,

---

[62] [2012] EWHC 1245 (QB), Popplewell J. Upheld on appeal, *ACE European Group Ltd and Others v Chartis Insurance UK Ltd* [2013] EWCA Civ 224.

[63] The policy in this case contained a so-called 50/50 clause providing that in case of difficulties in the attribution of the damage to the maritime voyage, the loss would be split between the insurers. The clause mitigates the effect of the rule on the burden of proof enunciated in *Rhesa Shipping Co SA v Edmunds (The Popi M)* [1985] 1 WLR 948 that where there are two competing explanations pleaded, but further explanations may be possible, the court is not entitled to limit the choice to the pleaded explanations. According to subsequent cases, where on the facts there are only a limited number of explanations, the court is not required to look beyond them – see *Fosse Motor Engineers Limited v Condé Nast and National Magazine Distributors Limited* [2008] EWHC 2037 (TCC, *Milton Keynes v Nulty* [2011] EWHC 2847 (TCC).

[64] Popplewell J also found that the fatigue cracking would not have occurred during transit had the cargo been adequately packed. Even so, the marine policy contained an express provision whereby the underwriters had agreed that they would not use the insufficiency or unsuitability of the packing as a defence to a claim where the packing had been carried out by a party other than the Assured, and the insufficiency or unsuitability arose entirely without the Assured's privity or knowledge – which was the case here – as the manufacture (and therefore the packing) of the economiser blocks had been sub-contracted to a company based in Romania. The provision is set out in the judgment at [136]. The effect of this clause is to set the case aside from earlier cases that considered insufficiency of packing as a form of inherent vice. The ICC(A) 2009 also deal with insufficiency of packing (when carried out by the Assured) and inherent vice separately, although both causes of loss are set out as exclusions to cover.

without fatigue cracking.' Accordingly, there was nothing in the inherent condition or design of the economisers which could be described as a proximate cause of the loss.[65] As a consequence must it be proved by the assured, or disproved by the insurer, that the cargo was in such a condition that it could reasonably be expected to survive the relevant transit *if properly packed*? Is proper packing now the 'other side of the coin' to inherent vice? Or does the judgment simply treat insufficient packing as an extension of inherent vice, rather than a stand alone concern? Alternatively, is the emphasis on packing only in issue on the facts of the case? On first glance, it may be assumed that the facts here are similar to those in *The Cendor MOPU*. However, the calculated probabilities of the fatigue cracking occurring for each cargo during their respective transit are substantially different. In *The Cendor MOPU*, it was noted that the rig was 'very lucky' to have survived the first leg of the journey, and that the failure of the legs was very probable, although not inevitable. By contrast, in the present case it was common ground between the experts that the fatigue cracking 'could not have occurred' during the journey had the packing not been missing. If the packing of the economiser tubes had been carried out by the assured, rather than a sub-contractor, it is unlikely that the marine policy would have covered the loss. Nor would the other policy cover the loss, as it only attached to equipment once it was on site. As such, the insured would be left without cover. Given the clear-cut finding of the judge that the loss was caused by resonant vibrations that would not have occurred if there had been adequate packing, the burden of proof as regards inherent vice was not discussed any further.

Subsequently, Popplewell J held that

> it is clear from the authorities that where it is established that a proximate cause of the loss is a fortuity occurring during the period of cover, there is no room for inherent vice to be treated as another proximate cause of the loss.[66]

The judge relied on the judgments of *Soya v White* and *The Cendor MOPU* as authority for his decision, concluding that there was 'no room *as a matter of law* for inherent vice to be an additional proximate cause.' (emphasis added)[67] As explained below, the Supreme Court in *The Cendor MOPU* only dealt with the issue of multiple causes of loss briefly, as they did not consider that there was more than one proximate cause of loss on the facts of the case. Nonetheless, it seems that Popplewell J has extracted a general principle of law from the decision. Popplewell J seems to be of the opinion that as long as a fortuity is established as a proximate cause of the loss, then inherent vice cannot also be a concurrent proximate cause. This argument appears to align with that found in *Colinvaux*. Such an outcome would severely narrow the exclusion of inherent vice, and would render it futile for the insurers to try to establish the exclusion where some fortuity is also in operation.

---

[65] [2012] EWHC 1245 (QB), at [135]–[137].
[66] [2012] EWHC 1245 (QB), at [138].
[67] [2012] EWHC 1245 (QB), at [139].

VI. MULTIPLE CAUSES OF LOSS INCLUDING INHERENT VICE

In spite of the above, it appears that the Supreme Court judgment in *The Cendor MOPU* leaves open the question of whether there can be two independently effective or efficient causes of loss – one of which being inherent vice – and the appropriate resolution in such cases. It is necessary to reiterate that the Supreme Court made clear that the facts of the case did not result in a situation where there were competing causes of loss. Nonetheless, there are some interesting comments obiter.

In *The Cendor MOPU*, Lord Mance considered at length the Court of Appeal judgment in *The Miss Jay Jay*, and the 'weighing exercise' that the decision suggested in respect of cases where two causes of loss were equal, or at least nearly equal, in their efficiency in bringing bout the damage.[68] The judge found it difficult to apply the weighing exercise to Lord Diplock's formulation of inherent vice in *Soya v White*, holding that 'anything that would otherwise count as a fortuitous external accident or casualty will suffice to prevent the loss being attributed to inherent vice.'[69] It is provided in *Colinvaux* that Lord Mance overrules the analogous judgment of the Court of Appeal to the effect that perils of the seas and lack of seaworthiness could be concurrent causes: if there was a peril of the seas, then for causation purposes seaworthiness was to be disregarded.[70]

Later in his judgment, Lord Mance is non-committal on the issue of whether both inherent vice and perils of the seas can be competing causes of loss, although it could readily be inferred that he questions whether such a situation is even possible. He does however raise the question, without answering it, whether in such a case the approach in *Wayne Tank* is applicable, contrasting situations where a combination of causes leads to a loss against situations where there are two independent causes of loss.[71] Lord Saville was also of the opinion that the case was not one in which 'it could be concluded that there was more than one proximate case of the loss,'[72] and Lord Collins held that the proximate cause of the loss 'was the result of a fortuity, and not the susceptibility of the legs to crack as a result of metal fatigue,'[73] thus implying that he too did not believe that there were competing causes of loss in this case. Neither of the latter two judges expressly or impliedly deals with the question of whether it is possible for there to be competing causes of loss where the inherent vice of cargo is in play.

Lord Clarke's judgment, however, appears to go further. The judge first confirmed 'it is common ground that, if the loss was proximately caused by inherent vice, the insurers are not liable even if the loss was also proximately caused by a peril insured against.'[74] However, he later gives the follow understanding of Lord Diplock's definition of inherent vice

---

[68] [2011] UKSC 5; [2011] 1 Lloyd's Rep 560, at [75]–[81], [88].
[69] [2011] UKSC 5; [2011] 1 Lloyd's Rep 560, at [80].
[70] See fn 47, Colinvaux (2011), at [B-0646].
[71] [2011] UKSC 5; [2011] 1 Lloyd's Rep 560, at [88].
[72] [2011] UKSC 5; [2011] 1 Lloyd's Rep 560, at [47].
[73] [2011] UKSC 5; [2011] 1 Lloyd's Rep 560, at [97].
[74] [2011] UKSC 5; [2011] 1 Lloyd's Rep 560, at [99].

the natural meaning to be given to Lord Diplock's definition is that, if there is an 'intervention of any fortuitous external accident or casualty' the law treats the loss as caused by that fortuitous external accident or casualty and not by inherent vice... As I see it, by in effect invoking the statutory definition of perils of the seas, he was defining 'inherent vice' *in opposition to perils of the seas, thereby avoiding any overlap between the insured risk and the excluded risk.* Thus where, as here, a proximate cause of the loss was perils of the seas, there was no room for the conclusion that the loss was caused by inherent vice.[75] (emphasis added)

Respectfully, attention is drawn to the words 'without the *intervention* of any fortuitous external accident or casualty' in Lord Diplock's formulation (see page 211 above). Where there are two (or more) concurrent causes, it is arguable that there has not been any intervention by the separate peril that would allow for the loss caused by the inherent vice to be considered as insignificant. That being said, the authors of *Colinvaux*, in light of the judgment in *The Cendor MOPU*, refer to inherent vice and seaworthiness as 'two key exceptions', where the rules relating to concurrent causes have no part to play.[76] Later in *The Cendor MOPU* judgment, Lord Clarke states

> The sole question in a case where loss or damage is caused by a combination of the physical condition of the insured goods and conditions of the sea encountered in the course of the insured adventure is whether the loss or damage is proximately caused, at least in part, by perils of the seas (or, more generally, any fortuitous external accident or casualty). If that question is answered in the affirmative, it follows that there was no inherent vice, thereby avoiding the causation issues that arise where there are multiple causes of loss, one of which is an insured risk and one of which is an uninsured or excluded risk.[77]

It is submitted, respectfully, that the learned judge has gone too far in his conclusions. In a situation where inherent vice of the cargo has contributed, to a limited extent, to the loss suffered but a separate peril is found to be the proximate cause of the loss, then it is perhaps correct to say that the inherent vice should not preclude the insured from recovery. In light of the dominant cause of the loss being the separate peril, that peril should be considered the sole proximate cause of the loss.

If, however, the inherent vice and the separate peril are capable of being concurrent causes of the loss, should Lord Clarke's interpretation of Lord Diplock's definition be applied with the result that the assured can still recover? It would appear, in light of *The Cendor MOPU*, that where the loss is caused by a combination of inherent vice and 'at least in part' by perils of the seas, the proximate cause of the loss should always be taken to be the peril insured against. This, it is submitted, renders the principle in *Wayne Tank* inapplicable to cases involving inherent vice.

[75] [2011] UKSC 5; [2011] 1 Lloyd's Rep 560, at [111].
[76] Colinvaux (2011), at [B-0593].
[77] [2011] UKSC 5; [2011] 1 Lloyd's Rep 560, at [137].

VII. INHERENT VICE AS A PERIL INSURED AGAINST

Where, however, a policy *specifically covers* losses that would otherwise be excluded by section 55(2)(c) of the Marine Insurance Act, such as inherent vice, it is questionable whether the burden of proof is reversed. Generally, under an all risks policy (discussed above), it is enough for the insured to show that an accident or casualty has occurred.[78] Once the insured has proved his loss, the burden should then shift to the underwriters to demonstrate that the peril proximately causing the loss was uninsured or that some other defence exists.[79] In contrast, where a policy provides an express list of perils that are insured against, it is usually the insured who must show that the accident or casualty was caused by one or more of the listed perils.[80] Thus, where a policy specifically *includes* inherent vice, should it not be for the claimant to establish that the loss was occasioned by the vice so covered?

In *Soya v White*, even though the cargo of soya beans was insured against 'heat, sweat and spontaneous combustion', it was nevertheless held by Lloyd J that the burden of proving inherent vice 'undoubtedly' lay with the defendant insurer.[81] It is submitted, on the facts being considered, that this analysis was wrong. Yet, as noted above, Donaldson LJ too held that the burden lay on the defendant, although he provided that 'the burden of disproving inevitability might lie on the plaintiff'.[82] A rule of general application, it is submitted, may be drawn from the latter part of Donaldson LJ's finding, which also aligns with Lord Sumner's judgment in *Gaunt*. Namely, it is the claimant's duty to disprove inevitability as part of the burden of proving that the accident or casualty fell within the scope of the policy; this is so, in spite of whether the cover provided is written on an 'all risks' or a specific perils basis, as insurance covers risks and not certainties. Nevertheless, this provides no answer to the question in hand.

The decision of Wright J in *Bowring v Amsterdam London Insurance Co Ltd*[83] should also be considered. In that case, consignments of ground nuts imported from China to Rotterdam and Hamburg were found, upon discharge, to be damaged by heating and sweat. The relevant policies covered against 'sweating and/or heating when resulting from an external cause', which put the onus on the assured to show that the loss was caused by an external source.

Furthermore, in *Overseas Commodities Ltd v Style*,[84] policies insuring a consignment of tins of pork from France to England included within the scope of cover inherent vice and hidden defect, thus expressly contracting out of section 55(2)(c) of the Marine Insurance Act. The relevant clause read

---

[78] See above. *British and Foreign Marine Insurance Co v Gaunt* [1921] 2 AC 41.

[79] *Munro, Brice & Co v War Risks Association Ltd* [1918] 2 KB 78.

[80] See, for example, *Rhesa Shipping v Edmunds (The Popi M)* [1985] 2 All ER 712; *Lamb Head Shipping Co Ltd v Jennings (The Marel)* [1994] 1 Lloyd's Rep 624; *North Star Shipping Ltd v Sphere Drake Insurance Plc* [2005] 2 Lloyd's Rep 76.

[81] [1980] 1 Lloyd's Rep 491, at p 505.

[82] [1982] 1 Lloyd's Rep 136, at p 144.

[83] (1930) 36 Ll L Rep 309.

[84] [1958] 1 Lloyd's Rep 546.

> All risks of whatsoever nature and/or kind. Average irrespective of percentage. Including blowing of tins. Including inherent vice and hidden defect. Condemnation by authorities to take place within three months of the date of arrival in final warehouse in the United Kingdom but not exceeding five months in all from the date of manufacture.

In view of the departure from the normal form of cover, McNair J held, obiter, that it was not unreasonable to suppose that the underwriters would seek to limit the extension within certain bounds. As a result, in construing the wording of the policy, he imported a qualification to the cover of inherent vice and hidden defect as only applying where condemnation of the cargo by customs authorities on the grounds of unfitness for human consumption took place.[85] The judge elaborated on his conclusion as follows

> Furthermore, having regard to the peculiar nature of the subject-matter – namely, a pasteurized and not wholly sterilized pig product – it seems inconceivable that the underwriters should, with their eyes open, have accepted liability for loss by inherent vice developing at any time in the future, since such a product must inevitably, if not consumed within a limited period, suffer loss from inherent vice, for, being perishable, it necessarily contains the seeds of its own ultimate destruction.[86]

McNair J also added that had the solving of this question been material for the judgment, he would have accepted the defendant's submission that if the insured claimed for a loss by inherent vice or hidden defect, he would also have to show condemnation by the authorities within the limits provided by the policy. Although an interesting point on the scope of the inherent vice provision, can it be taken from this judgment that the burden of proving inherent vice laid with the claimant? It is submitted that it can.

To conclude on this point, it is advised that for future disputes concerning insurance that *includes* cover for loss or damage caused by inherent vice, it is the insured's burden to prove that the accident or casualty was occasioned by inherent vice, and that the relevant vice was not inevitable. Subsequently, it will be for the insurer to raise any exceptions, limitations, exclusions or defences that may be available to him.

VIII. ON USAGE – THE CONCEPT OF INHERENT VICE

Their lordships in *The Cendor MOPU* devote a fair amount of attention to expressions similar to 'inherent vice' such as unseaworthiness, latent defect and ordinary wear and tear. All of these expressions are otherwise more closely associated with and applicable to ships, whereas inherent vice (or proper vice) has been a concept applied mainly, if not quite exclusively to cargo. This usage gives rise to the following observations. First, ought there to be uniformity of concepts, or rather a clear distinction between that which is being carried and the vehicle

---

[85] [1958] 1 Lloyd's Rep 560.
[86] [1958] 1 Lloyd's Rep 560.

that is carrying it, with the possibility of variations in the law applicable to each? Secondly, there is an obvious and correct distinction between an originally existing (latent) defect and a process of deterioration inherent to initially sound goods; but even so it is arguable, as a matter of practice, that the concept of latent defect is only relevant to cargo insurance, insofar as the subject matter is a non-perishable cargo. Finally, it is argued that the clear dissimilarity of the cover provided merit that the terms 'ordinary wear and tear' be used exclusively for hull insurance, and 'inherent vice' for cargo insurance. The following questions then arise: to what extent are these concepts distinct, and to what extent are they interchangeable? To some extent usage must of course overlap, as yachts are sometimes stowed upon the deck of ships and an oil rig with some limited capacity of locomotion may also be transported as cargo upon a barge, but the essential question is this: is there a valid scope for differentiation or can these concepts safely be commingled and merged with inherent vice? These questions find their clearest expression in the discussions of unseaworthiness found in sections 39 and 40 of the Marine Insurance Act 1906.

Section 40(1) of the Act provides that in a policy on goods or other moveables, there is no implied warranty that the goods or moveables are seaworthy. This does not only mean, as remarked by Lord Saville, that

> Under the 1906 Act therefore, the fact that the goods are not reasonably fit in all respects to encounter the ordinary perils of the seas of the adventure insured does not automatically deprive the assured of cover. There is no equivalent to the provisions relating to time policies, where loss or damage attributable to unseaworthiness at the outset known to the assured is excluded.[87]

It also means that cargo is not subject to the doctrine of stages which applies to voyage policies on ships by virtue of section 39(3). This doctrine is common to the law of carriage of goods by sea and that of marine insurance and specifies that the ship must be ready to encounter the vicissitudes of the particular stage of the voyage upon which she is about to embark. Nor do the cargo clauses contain any reference to the doctrine of stages. In its place, the cargo clauses apply their provisions on the adequacy of packaging.[88] Cargo clauses also apply the time policy principle of seaworthiness rather than the voyage policy warranty.

There is no particular reason for there being no 'warranty of seaworthiness' in relation to goods. On the contrary, this state of affairs is the default position and the warranty of seaworthiness is the exception. It comes about as a result of seaworthiness being a necessary condition of the ship in order for the insurance to operate. In *Koebel v Saunders*, the case that tried the proposition of the seaworthiness warranty for goods, Willes J said that

---

[87] At [41].

[88] Institute Cargo Clauses, cl 4.3. Both the 1982 and the 2009 sets of cargo clauses also waive the warranty of seaworthiness of the ship and carrying equipment (in clause 5) and introduce in its place an exclusion based on the time policy approach, that is, where the ship was unseaworthy or unfit to carry the goods and where she set to sea and the insured was privy to the unseaworthiness, the insurance does not respond.

nothing can be more distinct than the rule of insurance law, that it is a warranty or condition that the vessel shall be seaworthy at the time she sets out on her voyage.[89]

He went on to explain why the warranty of seaworthiness was not in that case introduced equally for goods as suggested by the insurers.

That is the distinction between an insurance on ship and an insurance on goods. Suppose a cargo of cotton shipped at New Orleans,—I am assuming a state of things which it is to be hoped may soon return,[90]—for this country in such a damp state as to be liable to spontaneous ignition, so that she could not continue her voyage without a strong probability that she would catch fire, but either the dampness was unknown or its probable consequences not foreseen; and suppose the vessel caught fire in the course of the voyage from some cause altogether remote from the condition of the cargo. That would be a case in which,—fraud or misrepresentation or concealment apart,—the underwriters would be clearly liable, unless we are to introduce the new implied warranty which is attempted to be set up here. I for one will not consent to lend myself to the introduction of a novelty the consequences of which it is difficult to foresee.[91]

Accordingly, the court declined to introduce a warranty of seaworthiness for goods. There has thus for quite some time been a well-recognised difference between ships and goods in this regard, even under the old form of policy which was otherwise applied equally to both. It is arguably apposite that such difference be maintained in modern times when the policies tend to be separate and distinct. As noted by the Supreme Court, the use of the concept of inherent vice should not be such as to introduce a warranty of seaworthiness for cargo by the back door.[92] Hull cases such as *The Miss Jay Jay*[93] and cargo cases such as *Soya v White* therefore arguably do not need to be reconciled into a single coherent doctrine. It is indeed historically wrong to assimilate the concepts of inherent vice and unseaworthiness. Not only does one pertain to cargoes and one to ships; but in addition, the former refers to perishables and the latter to the compliance of a ship with the doctrine of stages.

Following the quote from the speech of Lord Saville above, he goes on to point out that there is no equivalent for cargo in the Marine Insurance Act to section 39(5), which provides that a ship must be seaworthy at the start of the voyage and if she is not and the owner is privy to the unseaworthiness in question the insurer is not liable for a resulting loss. This would be surprising as section 39(5) applies to time policies only and it is very nearly unthinkable that a cargo policy would be a time policy, given that most cargo is intended to be shipped from point A to point B. The better comparison is with a voyage policy on ships – all cargo policies are voyage policies – as a time policy makes no sense whatsoever in the cargo context, except in the case of Norwegian Explorer vodka which must cross the equator a minimum number of times before it may be drunk. The appropriate comparison is therefore between a voyage policy for ships and a voyage policy

[89] *Koebel v Saunders* (1864) 144 ER 29.
[90] This judgment was given in 1864, during the American Civil War.
[91] *Koebel v Saunders* (1864) 144 ER 29.
[92] Lord Mance politely calls such an approach an 'oddity' at [57].
[93] *JJ Lloyd Instruments v Northern Star Insurance Co (The Miss Jay Jay)* [1987] 1 Lloyd's Rep 32.

for cargo. For the latter, there is as noted no implied warranty that the goods are seaworthy. All in all, there is thus – for the purpose of seaworthiness – a clear distinction in the regimes enshrined in the Act and in existing policies between hull and cargo insurance.

The judgment of the Supreme Court, while recognising the distinction between cargo and hulls on this point, on other points does not make a neat distinction, for instance in Lord Mance's treatment of ordinary wear and tear. Ordinary wear and tear occurs together with inherent vice among the concepts in section 55(2)(c). It has been suggested that they are one and the same or even that inherent vice is a sub-species of wear and tear;[94] however, it is submitted that ordinary wear and tear would generally denote the effect on hulls resulting from their being the active participant in the carriage of cargo – that is, their use – as opposed to the cargo which is passively shipped.[95] Inherent vice instead would be a concept applicable to the cargo. While this may be too simplistic, the words of Lord Mance are not necessarily apposite as a definition either

> ordinary wear and tear and ordinary leakage and breakage would thus cover loss or damage resulting from the normal vicissitudes of use in the case of a vessel, or of handling and carriage in the case of cargo, while inherent vice would cover inherent characteristics of or defects in a hull or cargo leading to it causing loss or damage to itself – in each case without any fortuitous external accident or casualty.[96]

In other words, without regard to whether the hull or cargo is at issue, wear and tear is said to be from usage, while inherent vice is from the characteristics of the thing. While it seems essentially correct that ordinary wear and tear is a process whereas inherent vice is a characteristic, inherent vice in some contexts arguably will also connote the process of destruction of the cargo as a result of that characteristic. The further distinction between inherent vice and inherent frailty, espoused by *Arnould* until the 16th edition (but no longer present in the 17th) further illustrates this; the frailty of eggs is an initial (and constantly present) characteristic, whereas inherent vice is a characteristic whose presence and importance will increase over time through the process of deterioration. A discussion of this issue was initiated but not carried through in the Court of Appeal.[97]

Oddly, there is no well-entrenched definition of inherent vice in historic case law: Clarke[98] cites two cases. The first is *Blower v Great Western Railway*[99] wherein a bullock that was part of a cargo of cattle managed to escape and it was deemed that its own efforts to do so had been crucial and that the railway carriage had been perfectly adequate, so that the railway was not at fault. The second case mentioned

---

[94] See Bennett, the article referred to in n 38 above, at p 336.
[95] The Australian case of *JSM Management Pty Ltd v QBE Insurance (Australia) Ltd* [2011] VSC 339 provides a review of the lexical definitions and case law and an extensive discussion of wear and tear where notably it is concluded that wear and tear means the same as 'ordinary' or 'normal' wear and tear and that wear and tear results from ordinary usage.
[96] At [81].
[97] At [23].
[98] Op cit fn 12, para 17.3A1 in fn 130.
[99] (1872) LR 7 CP 655.

by Clarke[100] is *Kendall v The London and South Western Railway Company*[101] which relies for the definition of inherent vice on *Blower* and is resolved on the burden of proof. These cases supply not so much a definition of inherent vice as examples of its usage, and the court in *Kendall* applies the Sherlock Holmes rule expressly disavowed by the House of Lords in *The Popi M*.[102] Merkin[103] refers to further cases, including the slave trade cases from the eighteenth century *Gregson v Gilbert*[104] and *Tatham v Hodgson*.[105] It will be recalled with dismay that the propensity to jump overboard and commit suicide was discussed as an inherent vice in the slave trade cases. The raison d'être for each of these cases must surely be that they are the borderline instance, the hard cases and therefore not suitable matter from which to extract a definition.

Historically, inherent vice is a concept that has been used for perishable cargoes. By way of example, another case from the twentieth century dealt with a large shipment of cigarettes from Glasgow to Baghdad that arrived so badly afflicted with mould that not one cigarette was useable. In *ED Sassoon v Yorkshire*,[106] the issue seemed to be whether on the evidence, the cigarettes had had such a moisture content upon shipment that destruction by mould – or in other words, loss by inherent vice – was inevitable. The first cases of inherent vice where the cargo was something other than a perishable have occurred within the thirty years since *Soya v White* made the concept more useable. The first is *Mayban General Insurance Bhd v Alstom Power Plants Ltd*[107] and the second is *The Cendor MOPU* itself. There had historically been a small number of cases where the concept was applied to the ship itself, however the category was usually reserved for the cargo which of course by its nature was usually perishable, consisting of foodstuffs, leather, tobacco (to name a few cargoes that have been the subject of case law).

Although Lord Mance did not, in his own words, intend to attempt a definition in the text quoted above, there is with respect, arguably a case for disregarding entirely his words on the distinction between ordinary wear and tear and inherent vice and the proposition that both concepts are equally applicable to hulls as well as cargo; first, because there is traditionally and for still valid reasons a distinction between how cargo and hulls are treated in the context of a marine policy, and secondly, because the law of cargo insurance is closely connected to the law of carriage of goods by sea and to the law of trade, whereas hull insurance is not.

These distinctions were present even in historical marine insurance which applied the same policy to ship and goods and *a fortiori* has validity today when different policy terms are applied to each. With that in mind, merging the definitions of unseaworthiness, latent defect, ordinary wear and tear and inherent

---

[100] See fn 98.
[101] (1871–72) LR 7 Ex 373.
[102] *Rhesa Shipping Co SA v Edmunds (The Popi M)* [1985] 1 WLR 948. See on burden of proof above.
[103] *Marine Insurance Legislation* at the commentary to s 55(2)(c).
[104] (1783) 3 Doug KB 232.
[105] (1796) 6 TR 656.
[106] (1923) 16 Ll L Rep 129.
[107] [2004] 2 Lloyd's Rep 609, Moore-Bick J.

vice risks raising the issue addressed in *The Cendor MOPU* all over again but in a different guise: namely when one has to determine whether some loss or damage is from characteristics or usage. This means therefore that *The Miss Jay Jay* and *Soya v White* arguably do not need to be reconciled into a single coherent doctrine. This distinction between cargo and hulls is thus arguably to some degree lost in the Supreme Court judgment in *The Cendor MOPU*; quite naturally, given that the subject matter of the insurance was a cargo with great resemblance to a hull or piece of machinery. However, by virtue of this homogenisation or assimilation of concepts, the concept of inherent vice itself could potentially change in scope and be disjoined from that related concept of satisfactory quality[108] in the Sale of Goods Act 1979 and also from the innumerable cases resulting from the railway litigations of the late nineteenth and early twentieth centuries that make up an important basis for carriage law and indirectly also for cargo insurance.

CONCLUDING REMARKS

This chapter ends not with a bang, but a whimper. The scope of the concept of inherent vice – carefully defined in *Soya v White* and the subject of several major cases during the twentieth century, not to mention several cases in the 30 years following *Soya v White* – is simply not terribly important any more, following the judgment of the Supreme Court in *The Cendor MOPU*. Only where there is no other discernible cause of loss, and inherent vice therefore is the only proximate cause of loss, does it become necessary to go through the exercise of determining whether the loss falls – to use the facts of *Soya v White* – at 15 per cent or above, so that it is inevitable or within the 12–14 per cent of moisture content where the loss may, but will not necessarily happen. This will be a purely factual and evidentiary assessment, such as that seen in *ED Sassoon v Yorkshire Insurance* and will be of little interest to marine insurance lawyers. If damage is so likely that it can easily be foreseen – as indeed it was in the case of *The Cendor MOPU*, where the surveyor's advice was to fold down or detach the legs before the towage – insurers must take their chances and set an appropriate premium to counter that risk. This limited scope for the effects of inherent vice is entirely logical; in modern times of post containerisation, and in particular post refrigeration, many cargoes need in practice no longer be treated as perishables.

---

[108] Or, historically, merchantable quality.

11

Thirty Years of Europeanisation of Conflict of Laws and Still all at Sea?

YVONNE BAATZ

I. INTRODUCTION

ALTHOUGH THERE HAS been a revolution in English law on the conflict of laws over the last thirty years, largely due to the European regulation of this area of the law, the thesis of this chapter is that there are still significant challenges to be faced in the next thirty years. Three key challenges will be discussed here: First whether a neutral choice of jurisdiction which has no connection with the dispute should be permitted; secondly whether such a choice can bind a third party and thirdly which tribunal should determine whether a valid choice has been made. It is important that these issues are addressed so that the European Union does not lose the undoubted economic benefits of its world class centres of litigation, both court and arbitration, to other competitors outside the European Union. This is especially important in times of economic recession. Although many of the points made in this chapter are applicable to commercial disputes in general, this chapter will focus specifically on maritime disputes in the carriage of goods by sea, for which England is so highly regarded and which bring such great economic rewards.

The three challenges lie at the heart of the role of the jurisdiction agreement in the field of carriage of goods by sea. This chapter will consider the approach to those three challenges taken by the English common law rules; the rules agreed by the Member States of the European Union in Council Regulation (EC) 44/2001 of 22 December 2000 on Jurisdiction and the Recognition and Enforcement of Judgments in Civil and Commercial Matters ('the EC Jurisdiction Regulation') and the Regulation (EU) No 1215/2012 of the European Parliament and of the Council of 12 December 2012 on jurisdiction and the recognition and enforcement of judgments in civil and commercial matters (recast) ('the Recast Regulation'); and the approach of various international conventions relevant to carriage of goods by sea culminating in the Convention on Contracts for the International Carriage of Goods Wholly or Partly by Sea and signed in Rotterdam in September 2009 ('the Rotterdam Rules'). Until agreement on those three issues can be reached there cannot be a European solution, let alone an international solution, to jurisdiction issues in carriage of goods by sea.

A. The Conflicts Revolution over the Last Thirty Years

The revolution has been brought about principally, but not exclusively, as a result of the Europeanisation of the field of conflict of laws. When the European Economic Community was set up it was perceived that free movement of judgments within the Community was very important for the economic success of the EEC, so that parties would feel confident to trade throughout the area. In order to have free movement of judgments it was necessary to have rules as to when each of the Contracting States would have jurisdiction in an international dispute.[1] Therefore the original six members of the EEC agreed the EC Convention on Jurisdiction and the Enforcement of Judgments in Civil and Commercial Matters 1968 ('the EC Jurisdiction Convention'). It was negotiated without any input from the United Kingdom and it is hardly surprising therefore that it was a very different system from that comprised by the common law rules in England. In 1978 the United Kingdom acceded to the EC Jurisdiction Convention. Although it negotiated certain important amendments when it acceded, so as to introduce a more generous approach to jurisdiction clauses in commercial contracts,[2] particularly commercial insurance contracts such as those relating to marine, aviation and transport,[3] nevertheless one might regard those amendments as tinkering on the edges rather than fundamentally changing the model. This was also true of the changes made by the EC Jurisdiction Regulation[4] which subsequently replaced the EC Jurisdiction Convention.

However, the Europeanisation of the rules on international jurisdiction and recognition and enforcement of judgments only went so far. The rules in the European provisions only apply in certain situations, generally based on the defendant's domicile, and Article 4 provides that each EU Member State should continue to apply its own national law where the defendant is domiciled in a non EU Member State, subject to some exceptions. This lead to a two-track system in

---

[1] The aim of the EC Jurisdiction Regulation is also to enable the free movement of judgments of the courts of any EU Member State so that it is possible to enforce such judgments quickly and efficiently in any other EU Member State (Recital 17), subject to limited exceptions, and thus ensure 'the sound operation of the internal market'(Recital 1). It is therefore necessary to provide when the courts of an EU Member State have jurisdiction in an international dispute (Recital 2) and ensure that the risk of parallel proceedings is minimised (Recital 15).

[2] Art 17(c) of the EC Jurisdiction Convention, now replaced by Art 23(1)(c) of the EC Jurisdiction Regulation.

[3] Art 12 of the EC Jurisdiction Convention, now replaced by Arts 13 and 14 of the EC Jurisdiction Regulation.

[4] The EC Jurisdiction Regulation entered into force in the United Kingdom on 1 March 2002 and replaced the latest Accession Convention to the EC Jurisdiction Convention. For current purposes the EC Jurisdiction Regulation, the EC Jurisdiction Convention, the EFTA Convention on Jurisdiction and the Enforcement of Judgments in Civil and Commercial Matters, 1988 ('the Lugano Convention') and the revised Lugano Convention 2007 are treated as identical, unless expressly stated otherwise.

most EU Member States[5] immediately creating further complexity. Even where the European rules apply, there are some significant gaps which need to be filled by national law. Some amendments have been made to eliminate the need to apply national law.[6] However, in some situations national law is still very important and, as we shall see the national law of the various EU Member States may be very different, so that on some issues there is no harmony at all.

Since 1968 the number of States applying these rules has increased dramatically from the original six EEC Contracting States in 1968 to twenty eight Member States of the European Union with a much more varied landscape in terms of the sophistication of their legal systems, increased scope for differences as to national law and a greater variety in the international conventions to which those States are parties.

Although the EC Jurisdiction Regulation has been described by the European Parliament as 'one of the most successful pieces of EU legislation'[7] as it promotes certainty and predictability and avoids parallel proceedings, nevertheless it was acknowledged that it needed modernisation. An excellent review of the Regulation was carried out by Heidelberg University,[8] followed by a detailed consultation. An Impact Assessment stated,

> The revision of Regulation Brussels I pursues two general objectives. First, it should facilitate cross-border litigation and the free circulation of judgments and cut unnecessary red tape in line with the principle of mutual recognition. This will make it easier and less time-consuming for European citizens and companies to litigate in another Member State if that is required for solving their disputes. Second, the revision should also help to create the necessary legal environment for the European economy to recover. In order to achieve this, the revised Regulation should further reduce the cost of litigation and enhance legal certainty for cross-border transactions.[9]

The Recast Regulation[10] will apply from 10 January 2015. The changes made by that Regulation and the solutions proposed by the European Parliament[11] in September 2010 and the European Commission in December 2010[12] before the

---

[5] Some Member States, such as Italy, sought to avoid this dual system by providing that the European Rules would apply no matter where the defendant was domiciled. For a discussion of whether the European rules should be extended see L Gillies, 'Creation of Subsidiary Jurisdiction Rules in the Recast of Brussels I: Back to the Drawing Board?' [2012] *Journal of Private International Law* 489.

[6] For example, the test for when a court is seised under Arts 27 to 29 of the EC Jurisdiction Regulation was inserted in a new Art 30 of that Regulation as the test had previously been left to national law under the EC Jurisdiction Convention (Case 56/79 *Zelger v Salinitri* [1980] ECR 89) with divergent approaches amongst the Contracting States creating a bumpy playing field.

[7] 2009/2140 (INI) dated 7 September 2010, Recital A.

[8] B Hess, T Pfeiffer and P Schlosser 'The Brussels I - Regulation (EC) No 44/2001 The Heidelberg Report on the Application of Regulation Brussels I in 25 Member States' (Study JLS/C4/2005/03), C.H. Beck, Hart, Nomos, 2008 (the Heidelberg Report). On 21 April 2009 the European Commission adopted a Report COM (2009) 174 and a Green Paper COM (2009) 175 inviting consultation by 30 June 2009.

[9] EU: SEC(2010) 1547 Celex No. 510SC1547 para1.5 Commission Staff Working Paper Impact Assessment Accompanying document to the Proposal for a Regulation of the European Parliament and of the Council on jurisdiction and the recognition and enforcement of judgments in civil and commercial matters (Recast) {COM(2010) 748 final} {SEC(2010) 1548 final}.

[10] OJ 20 December 2012, L 351/1.

[11] 2009/2140 (INI) dated 7 September 2010.

[12] COM (2010) 748. See A Briggs, 'The Brussels I *bis* Regulation Appears on the Horizon' [2011] LMCLQ 157 for a discussion of those proposals.

Recast Regulation was agreed by the European Parliament and the Council will be considered.

Following the harmonisation of the rules as to when a court of an EU Member State had jurisdiction, the rules as to how such a court should determine what law governs a contract were also harmonised in the Convention on the Law Applicable to Contractual Obligations of 1980 ('the Rome Convention').[13] If, however, the contract was concluded as from 17 December 2009, Regulation (EC) No. 593/2008 on the law applicable to contractual obligations (Rome I)[14] now applies. Where the obligation in question is non contractual Regulation (EC) No 864/2007 on the law applicable to non-contractual obligations (Rome II) will apply where the events giving rise to damage occurred after 11 January 2009.[15] Unlike the rules on jurisdiction, the rules on applicable law apply whenever the court of an EU Member State has to determine the applicable law, whether it is the law of an EU Member State or not. The aim is that it should not matter which court within the European Union has jurisdiction as in theory every court would apply the same rules to determine the applicable law and this would 'improve the predictability of the outcome of litigation.'[16] Furthermore the scope of the applicable law so determined is wider than it was and the line between substance and procedure is drawn in a different place than under the previous English law.[17] There are, however, areas which are excluded from the scope of the Rome Convention, Rome I and Rome II and where national law, with its differences of approach in different States and therefore lack of harmony, will still be important.

Further Europeanisation has taken place as a result of several other Regulations on conflict of laws and related procedural matters, such as Council Regulation (EC) No 1346/2000 of 29 May 2000 on insolvency proceedings, Regulation 861/2007 creating a European Small Claims Procedure; Regulation 805/2004 establishing a European enforcement order for uncontested claims and Regulation 1896/2006 creating a European Order for Payment Procedure.

On the wider international scene the European Union has competence to agree international conventions on private international law on behalf of the EU Member States.[18] It has therefore taken part in the negotiation of new international conventions on private international law, such as the 2005 Hague Convention

---

[13] Section 2 of the Contracts (Applicable Law) Act 1990 gives the force of law to the Rome Convention, as amended by subsequent Accession Conventions, with the exception of Arts 7(1) and 10(1)(e). It came into force on 1 April 1991 and still applies to contracts concluded before 17 December 2009.

[14] Rome I came into force on 17 December 2009 in all EU Member States, except Denmark and applies to contracts concluded as from 17 December 2009 (Art 28 as amended). The United Kingdom opted in to Rome I.

[15] Case C-412/10 *Homawoo v GMF Assurance SA & Ors.* [2011] ECR 0 applied in *VTB Capital PLC v Nutritek International Corp* [2013] UKSC 5.

[16] See Recital 6 of Rome I and Rome II.

[17] See Art 12 of Rome I and Art 15 of Rome II. Thus the assessment of damages would now be determined by the applicable law as opposed to the law of the forum (eg *Harding v Wealands* [2007] 2 AC 1).

[18] Opinion 1/03 of 7 February 2006 on the competence of the Community to conclude the revised Lugano Convention on jurisdiction and the recognition and enforcement of judgments in civil and commercial matters.'

on Choice of Court Agreements, which it has signed,[19] and Chapter 15 of the Rotterdam Rules on jurisdiction. It has no competence in relation to arbitration and therefore did not negotiate chapter 16 of the Rotterdam Rules on arbitration.

At the same time as the European rules on jurisdiction were being developed the English common law rules were taking a new direction of their own introducing discretion, which was diametrically opposed to the thinking behind the new European rules which value certainty and predictability so that it is easy for a defendant domiciled in an EU Member State to know where it can be sued. The doctrine of *forum non conveniens*, developed in Scottish law, was borrowed by the English and has become a much vaunted part of English national law.[20] So much so, that when the European Court of Justice limited its application in the controversial decision of *Owusu v Jackson*[21] the English were outraged.[22] The decision causes difficulties in drawing the line between those situations where *forum non conveniens* applies and those where the EC Jurisdiction Regulation does not permit this.[23] The Recast Regulation seeks to address the difficulties *Owusu* gave rise to by introducing discretion where there are already proceedings before the courts of a non EU Member State.[24]

The development of *forum non conveniens* also saw the rise of the anti-suit injunction. The clash of that remedy with the concept of mutual trust in the European rules lead to its rejection by the European Court of Justice to restrain breaches of a jurisdiction or arbitration agreement by commencing or pursuing court proceedings in the courts of another EU Member State.[25] That development

---

[19] See fn 172.

[20] See eg *Spiliada Maritime Corp. v Cansulex Ltd (The Spiliada)* [1987] AC 460; *VTB Capital plc v Nutritek* [2013] UKSC 5; [2013] 2 WLR 398 and *Alliance Bank JSC v Aquanta Corp* [2012] EWCA 1588; [2013] 1 All ER (Comm) 819 [83]–[118].

[21] *Owusu v Jackson (t/a Villa Holidays Bal Inn Villas)* (C-281/02) [2005] ECR I-1383; [2005] 1 Lloyd's Rep 452.

[22] E Peel, 'Forum Non Conveniens *and European Ideals*' [2005] LMCLQ 363 and A Briggs, 'Forum Non Conveniens *and Ideal Europeans*', [2005] LMCLQ 378; A Briggs, 'The Death of Harrods: Forum Non Conveniens *and the European Court*', (2005) 121 LQR 535 and Briggs and Rees, *Civil Jurisdiction and Judgments*, 5th edn. (Informa: 2009), at paras 2.256–2.258.

[23] The English court has held that *forum non conveniens* does apply where the defendant is domiciled in an EU Member State but the parties have chosen the courts of a non EU Member State - *Winnetka Trading Corporation v Julius Baer International Ltd* [2008] EWHC 3146 (Ch); [2009] 2 All ER (Comm) 735; land is situate in a non EU Member State or there is an equivalent situation to Art 22 – *Lucasfilm v Ainsworth* [2011] UKSC 39; [2012] AC 208 and *Ferrexpo AG v Gilson Investments Ltd* [2012] EWHC 721 (Comm); [2012] 1 Lloyd's Rep 588 (dispute regarding ownership of shares in a Ukrainian mining company); or there are proceedings in another non EU Member State - *Catalyst Investment Group Limited v Max Lewinsohn* [2009] EWHC 1964 (Ch); [2010] Ch 218; not followed in *JKN v JCN* [2010] EWHC 843; [2011] 1 FLR 826 and *Goshawk Dedicated Ltd v Life Receivables Irl Ltd* [2009] IESC 7; [2009] ILPr 26.

[24] See Recitals 23 and 24 and Arts 33 and 34. Although Recital 24 states that the court of an EU Member State may consider whether the court of a non EU Member State has exclusive jurisdiction in circumstances where a court of an EU Member State would have exclusive jurisdiction, this does not give sufficient protection to an exclusive jurisdiction clause in favour of a non EU Member State as Arts 33 and 34 only apply where the non EU Member State was first seised. This does not give the jurisdiction clause any weight where the EU Member State was first seised.

[25] See Case C-159/02 *Turner v Grovit* [2004] E.C.R. I-3565; [2005] 1 A.C. 101 (ECJ); Case C-116/02 *Erich Gasser GmbH v MISAT SRL* [2003] E.C.R. I-14693; [2005] Q.B. 1; and Case C-185/07 *Allianz SpA (formerly Riunione Adriatica di Sicurta SpA) v West Tankers Inc (The Front Comor)* [2009] 1 AC 1138; [2009] 1 Lloyd's Rep 413.

has given rise to the possibility of parallel proceedings in more than one EU Member State and therefore potential difficulties on recognition and enforcement of judgments.

In other ways, however, the English common law rules and the European rules have influenced each other's development, such as the approval by the European Court of Justice of the declaration of non-liability in *The Maciej Rataj*,[26] which has lead to increased use of this remedy by the English courts. This has in itself given rise to some problems discussed below.

B. The Challenges Facing Us

The European Union has very popular centres of litigation. One of them is London. Choice of such a centre has major economic benefits for the centre concerned. It is a huge invisible export supporting directly the legal professions, expert witnesses, and all the additional services they require.[27] This has resulted in the development of English law into a very sophisticated system which is often the applicable law of choice. This too has very clear economic benefits. For example, it attracts students to our Universities[28] from all over the world to study our law and this has led to the success of centres such as the Institute of Maritime Law at the University of Southampton.

In a Business Survey conducted by the Oxford Institute of European and Comparative Law and the Oxford Centre for Socio-Legal-Studies in 2008[29] of 100 European businesses engaging in cross-border transactions in Europe in eight focal Member States of the EU (France, Germany, Italy, Netherlands, Poland, Spain, UK and Belgium), with a minority of businesses from other European countries, English law and English jurisdiction were the most popular choices in cross border transactions.[30] 31 per cent thought that England has the most favourable

---

[26] Case C-406/92 *The Tatry (sub nom. The Maciej Rataj)* [1994] ECR I-5439; [1995] 1 Lloyd's Rep 302.

[27] Such as short hand writers, hotels for witnesses from all over the world, taxis etc.

[28] See E Davies, Made in Britain, Abacus, 2012, at pp 213–15 ('education is one of our national economic strengths' and 'we can be proud of our universities'); 244 ('universities are the economic sector of which we can be most proud'; 250–51 ('First is the importance of good universities. Not only are they a large service exporter in their own right, but they also have a significant role in the creation of intellectual property, often for our manufacturing industries. In almost all the smartest and most lucrative parts of the economy university research seems to have played an important role. Britain happens to be very lucky in being endowed with a disproportionately large share of the world's best universities, and if you forced me to tell you of which British export industry I am most proud, I would probably nominate our university sector. If the rule is that we build the best possible economy using the resources we have at hand, the universities seem like one of the most useful, particularly as the demand for higher education is growing very rapidly around the world. It is hard to beat places that combine pure research, applied research and teaching as centres of value creation in the modern world. They represent their own mini-clusters, and have the power to spawn major industrial clusters around them too. In terms of both regional and industrial policy, their role cannot be overstated.' See also the Times Education Supplement 20.7.2012 'The higher education sector is the powerhouse within the British education export brand.' 'Just how much ['British-style' schools] are worth to the UK economy is hard to pin down, but analysts have estimated that the figure for education overall, including universities, is somewhere between £7 billion and £15 billion a year.'

[29] See the website of the Institute of European and Comparative Law www.iecl.ox.ac.uk/ under research.

[30] *Ibid* pp 14 and 26 respectively.

civil justice system, followed by Germany.[31] Variations in European civil justice systems could deter companies from doing business in certain jurisdictions,[32] as they have a financial impact on business.[33] The factors which were most important in choosing jurisdiction were quality of judges and courts, fairness of the outcomes, corruption (presumably lack thereof), predictability of the outcomes, speed of dispute resolution, and contract law, in that order.

A significant proportion of the international litigation commenced before the English courts is due to the fact that the parties included an exclusive English jurisdiction clause in their contract.[34] Thus, for example, international sale of goods contracts, bank loans, insurance and reinsurance contracts, charterparties, and bills of lading are all commonly on standard form contracts which contain English jurisdiction clauses. The parties could provide for court jurisdiction or arbitration in London.[35]

There are also world class centres of arbitration within the European Union such as London[36] and Paris,[37] to give but two examples. It takes many years to develop the good reputation of such centres. The economic benefits brought by such centres are significant.[38] Traditionally in the maritime field there has been competition from New York arbitration,[39] but in recent years the competition has grown with new centres such as Singapore and Dubai. Both of these centres have poured resources into building and promoting themselves.[40]

English court jurisdiction clauses and London arbitration clauses have come under attack where parties have commenced proceedings in the courts of another

---

[31] *Ibid* p 34. See also p 35.

[32] *Ibid* p 40. See also R Fentiman, *International Commercial Litigation* (Oxford University Press, 2010) para 2.02.

[33] *Ibid* p 41.

[34] See the paper by K Siig at the Tripartite Colloquium organised by the Institute of Maritime Law with the Scandinavian Institute of Maritime Law, University of Oslo and the Tulane Maritime Law Center, Tulane University, in October 2010 for the economic arguments in favour of party autonomy in relation to choice of forum and choice of law.

[35] In the Study carried out by the Oxford Institute of European and Comparative Law and the Oxford Centre for Socio-Legal-Studies in 2008 of 100 European businesses (see fn 29) 63% preferred arbitration to court proceedings in cross border transactions. The main reason given for this was confidentiality but speed was also important. Arbitration results in ancillary applications to the courts eg for a freezing injunction or arrest or an appeal from the arbitration award, although the right to appeal is severely limited. Statistics of such applications were given by VV Veeder in his Donald O'May lecture in November 2011. It is important that a system of arbitration has a good supervisory court system which does not interfere too much but which can put things right if they have gone wrong. This balance has been achieved in the Arbitration Act 1996.

[36] For example, the London Maritime Arbitrators Association (LMAA); the London Court of Arbitration; the Grain and Feed Trade Association (GAFTA). Statistics were given by VV Veeder in his Donald O'May lecture in November 2011.

[37] For example, the International Chamber of Commerce.

[38] Supporting arbitrators, the legal profession, expert witnesses, shorthand writers, the use of facilities such as hotels, taxis etc.

[39] London arbitration may be preferred to New York arbitration as the successful party will usually recover their legal costs, or at least a good proportion of them in London. London arbitration awards are confidential and cannot be reported unless the parties consent, in which case they are sometimes reported in Lloyd's Maritime Law Newsletter, whereas in New York they are published.

[40] See R Merkin and J Hjalmarsson, *Singapore Arbitration Legislation Annotated* (Informa, 2009).

EU Member State. This is due to differences of approach within the EU Member States as to when a choice of forum is valid; whether it can be for a neutral forum; whether, if the choice is valid as between the original parties, it binds a third party such as a consignee or indorsee of a bill of lading, assignee, subrogated insurer or a liability insurer in a direct action; and which tribunal should decide whether the arbitration clause is valid.

II. THE ENGLISH COMMON LAW RULES

A. Court Jurisdiction

i. Neutral Choice

Where there is a jurisdiction agreement in a commercial contract, such as a bill of lading, and none of the parties are domiciled in a Member State of the European Union, the English court applies its national law to determine whether it will accept jurisdiction.[41] Party autonomy is an important principle and a neutral choice is permissible. Although the English courts will apply the principle of *forum non conveniens* and therefore have a discretion, they will usually decide that if the parties have chosen a particular court, that is the appropriate court to determine the dispute, unless there is good cause not to.[42] So, for example, the English Court of Appeal in *OT Africa Line Ltd v Magic Sportswear Corp*[43] applying its common law rules,[44] upheld an exclusive English jurisdiction clause in a bill of lading, although the Canadian court had jurisdiction pursuant to its national legislation.[45]

---

[41] Arts 4 and 23(3) of the EC Jurisdiction Regulation.

[42] *Donohue v Armco* [2001] UKHL 64; [2002] 1 Lloyd's Rep 425. This exception will apply where there are multiple proceedings between multiple parties, in this case New York, some of whom are not bound by the English jurisdiction agreement. See also *Royal Bank of Scotland plc v Highland Financial Partners LP* [2012] EWHC 1278 (Comm); [2012] 2 CLC 109 under appeal where an anti-suit injunction was refused as the claimant did not come with clean hands.

[43] [2005] EWCA Civ 710; [2005] 2 Lloyd's Rep 170. See also *Horn Linie GmbH & Co v Panamericana Formas E Impresos SA, Ace Seguros SA (The Hornbay)* [2006] EWHC 373 (Comm); [2006] 2 Lloyd's Rep 44.

[44] See Y Baatz, 'An English jurisdiction clause does battle with Canadian legislation similar to the Hamburg Rules', [2006] LMCLQ 143 at p 148 *et seq.* where it was argued that the English court has no discretion to stay proceedings where Art 23(1) of the EC Jurisdiction Regulation applies because one of the parties is domiciled in an EU Member State (a view accepted in *Skype Technologies S.A. v Joltid Ltd.* [2009] EWHC 2783 (Ch)), and should not have applied its common law rules on *forum non conveniens* in this case. However, the decision is correct on the application of those rules. *OT Africa* was followed in *Horn Linie GmbH & Co v Panamericana Formas E Impresos S.A., Ace Seguros S.A. (The Hornbay)* [2006] EWHC 373 (Comm); [2006] 2 Lloyd's Rep 44. There the proceedings were between German shipowners and a Colombian consignee with an English jurisdiction clause and again Art 23(1) would apply. If the claim was between ACE, the subrogated insurers and Maritrans, the carrier's agent in Colombia, assuming both parties were domiciled in a non Member State, Art 23(3) would apply, and then the English court could decline jurisdiction.

[45] Section 46 of the Canadian Marine Liability Act 2001 is a similar jurisdiction provision to Art 21 of the UN Convention on the Carriage of Goods by Sea 1978 ('the Hamburg Rules'), except that the Canadian legislation is more favourable to the cargo claimant as it permits an action to be brought if the defendant has *a* place of business, branch or agency in Canada, rather than *the* principal place of business or the habitual residence of the carrier provided for by the Hamburg Rules. The rationale

Furthermore the Court of Appeal upheld anti-suit injunctions to restrain the shippers and their insurers from pursuing the Canadian proceedings.[46]

Article 25 of the Recast Regulation introduces a significant change as it provides that regardless of the domicile of the parties, where the court of an EU Member State is chosen it shall have jurisdiction, unless the agreement is null and void as to its substantive validity under the law of that Member State. Thus the English court would no longer have a discretion whether to stay English proceedings, but must exercise its jurisdiction when chosen.[47] This has the merit that an exclusive English court jurisdiction clause will be given effect to no matter where the parties to the agreement are domiciled. However, the disadvantage is that the English court will no longer be able to find that there is good cause not to give effect to the jurisdiction clause, for example, where there are multiple proceedings between multiple parties elsewhere. Furthermore the jurisdiction clause must now satisfy the formalities required in Article 25(1) of the Recast Regulation.

Where a bill of lading incorporates the terms of a charterparty, the jurisdiction clause in the charterparty will only be incorporated if there is specific reference to it, as opposed to general words of incorporation. This is clear from the many decisions on whether charterparty arbitration clauses are incorporated into a bill of lading, which apply equally to court jurisdiction clauses.[48] In the recent decision of Gloster J. in *YM Mars Tankers Ltd v Shield Petroleum Co (Nigeria) Ltd (The YM Saturn)* [49] it was held that a bill of lading which expressly incorporated the 'law and arbitration' clause of the charterparty, incorporated the 'law and litigation' clause, clause 41 of the Shelltime form, which provides for disputes to be subject to the jurisdiction of the English court in the time charterparty, with a right to elect for London arbitration. The judge considered that it was clear that the 'law and arbitration' clause referred to in the bill of lading clearly should be construed as meaning the 'law and litigation' clause in the charterparty. This decision does make life very difficult for a third party who sees specific reference to arbitration in the bill of lading but is in fact bound by a court jurisdiction clause in the charterparty, which it may never have seen. These issues will be explored further below in relation to arbitration clauses.

ii. Third Parties

Where English law applies, the third party named in a bill of lading as the consignee or the lawful holder of a transferable bill of lading will also be

---

for section 46 included giving Canadian importers and exporters the right to pursue cargo claims in Canada and an attack on what was perceived to be a monopoly of the British courts over such claims.

[46] The Canadian court ultimately stayed the shippers' action in Canada - *OT Africa Line Ltd v Magic Sportswear Corp* [2007] 1 Lloyd's Rep 85.

[47] Although Arts 33 and 34 of the Recast Regulation do permit a discretion to stay proceedings in the court of a Member State if there is lis pendens or a related action in a third State, those provisions only apply where the jurisdiction in the EU Member State court is based on Art 4 or on Arts 7,8,or 9 of the Recast Regulation and not on an exclusive jurisdiction agreement under Art 25.

[48] *Siboti K/S v BP France S.A.* [2003] EWHC 1278; [2003] 2 Lloyd's Rep 364. For incorporation of arbitration clauses see pp 247 and 248 below.

[49] [2012] EWHC 2652.

bound by the jurisdiction clause in the contract,[50] as will the subrogated cargo insurer.[51]

iii. Who Decides?

The English court will determine the validity of an English jurisdiction clause even if proceedings have already been commenced in the court of a non EU Member State.[52] This is clear from *OT Africa Line Ltd v Magic Sportswear Corp*[53] and is illustrated in the recent decision of Gloster J. in *YM Mars Tankers Ltd v Shield Petroleum Co (Nigeria) Ltd (The YM Saturn)*[54] where the cargo receiver was held bound by an English jurisdiction clause incorporated into the bill of lading from the charterparty.

Similarly where the English court has to consider a foreign jurisdiction clause this would be upheld unless there is strong cause not to,[55] for example, where there are multiple proceedings between multiple parties.[56] However, in *The Morviken*[57] the House of Lords held a jurisdiction clause void where it would have resulted in a carrier enjoying lower limits of liability than those mandatorily imposed by the Hague-Visby Rules.[58]

---

[50] Pursuant to the Carriage of Goods by Sea Act 1992. See eg *YM Mars Tankers Ltd v Shield Petroleum Co (Nigeria) Ltd* [2012] EWHC 2652 and fn 73.

[51] See fn 81.

[52] See, eg *OT Africa Line Ltd v Magic Sportswear Corp* [2005] EWCA Civ 710; [2005] 2 Lloyd's Rep 170.

[53] [2005] EWCA 710; [2005] 2 Lloyd's Rep 170. See also *Horn Linie GmbH & Co v Panamericana Formas E Impresos SA, Ace Seguros SA (The Hornbay)* [2006] EWHC 373 (Comm); [2006] 2 Lloyd's Rep 44.

[54] [2012] EWHC 2652.

[55] See, eg *Aratra Potato Co Ltd v Egyptian Navigation Co (The El Amria)* [1981] 2 Lloyd's Rep 119. See also *Hamed el Chiaty & Co. v Thomas Cook Group Ltd (The Nile Rhapsody)* [1994] 1 Lloyd's Rep 382; *American International Specialty Lines v Abbott Laboratories* [2002] EWHC 2714 (Comm); [2003] 1 Lloyd's Rep 267 and *Import Export Metro Ltd v Compania Sud Americana de Vapores S.A.* [2003] 1 Lloyd's Rep 405.

[56] See, eg *Citi-March Ltd v Neptune Orient Lines Ltd* [1997] 1 Lloyd's Rep 72; *The MC Pearl* [1997] 1 Lloyd's Rep 566; *obiter Konkola Copper Mines Plc v Coromin* [2006] EWCA Civ 5; [2006] 1 Lloyd's Rep 410 and R Asariotis, Y Baatz and N Gaskell et al., *Bills of Lading: Law and Contracts* (London, LLP, 2000), paras 20.213 to 20.219.

[57] *The Hollandia sub nom The Morviken* [1983] 1 AC 565; [1983] 1 Lloyd's Rep 1. Where the EC Jurisdiction Regulation rules do not apply, *The Hollandia* is still good law; see, eg *Baghlaf Al Zafer Factory Co v Pakistan National Shipping Co* [1998] 2 Lloyd's Rep 229; *Sideridraulic Systems SpA v BBC Chartering & Logistic GmbH & Co KG (The BBC Greenland)* [2011] EWHC 3106 (Comm); [2012] 1 Lloyd's Rep 230 [29] and [30]; and R Asariotis, Y Baatz and N Gaskell *Bills of Lading: Law and Contracts* (LLP 2000) paras 20.74, 20.202, 20.220.

[58] The International Convention for the Unification of Certain Rules of Law Relating to Bills of Lading signed at Brussels on 25 August 1924 as amended by the Protocol signed at Brussels on 23 February 1968 and by the Protocol signed at Brussels on 21 December 1979. *The Hollandia sub nom The Morviken* [1983] 1 AC 565; [1983] 1 Lloyd's Rep 1 can only apply if the Hague-Visby Rules apply compulsorily: see *Hellenic Steel Co v Svolamar Shipping Co Ltd (The Komninos S)* [1991] 1 Lloyd's Rep 370; *Trafigura Beheer BV v Mediterranean Shipping Co SA (The MSC Amsterdam)* [2007] EWCA Civ 794; [2007] 2 Lloyd's Rep 622 and *Sideridraulic Systems SpA v BBC Chartering & Logistic GmbH & Co KG (The BBC Greenland)* [2011] EWHC 3106 (Comm); [2012] 1 Lloyd's Rep 230.

B. Arbitration

i. Neutral choice

Arbitration in London is again a popular choice of dispute resolution in maritime contracts.[59] The United Kingdom is a party to the New York Convention on the Recognition and Enforcement of Foreign Arbitral Awards 1958 ('the New York Convention') and it gives effect to its international obligations under that convention in the Arbitration Act 1996. Sections 5 and 6 of the Arbitration Act 1996 set out the formalities that have to be complied with for there to be a valid arbitration agreement. The parties may choose a neutral place of arbitration.[60]

English law is relatively liberal as to whether a bill of lading incorporates the arbitration clause of the charterparty pursuant to which it is issued. Although general words of incorporation will not successfully incorporate an arbitration clause,[61] words of incorporation that specifically refer to the arbitration clause will, even if it is necessary to manipulate the wording of the charterparty clause.[62] For example, in *The Nerano*[63] the charterparty clause referred 'all disputes arising out of this charterparty' to arbitration. The Court of Appeal determined that the parties made clear their intention by the specific words that the arbitration clause was to be incorporated into the bill and added the words 'and under any bill of lading issued hereunder' to the charterparty clause.

Even if the bill of lading does not specify which of several charterparties is incorporated into the bill of lading, the court will determine which is the relevant charterparty.[64] Where there are two or more potentially relevant charters, the courts are very reluctant to hold that the contract is void for uncertainty, as this does not give effect to the obvious intention of the parties that the terms of a charter are to be incorporated.[65] Although it is a question of construction in each case, the general rule is that the head charter, to which the shipowner is party, is incorporated.[66] However, the position may well be different where the head

---

[59] The London Maritime Arbitrators Association (LMAA).

[60] Section 3 of the Arbitration Act 1996.

[61] *Skips A/S Nordheim v Syrian Petroleum Company (The Varenna)* [1983] 2 Lloyd's Rep 592.

[62] *Daval Aciers d'Usinor et de Sacilor v Armare S.R.L. (The Nerano)* [1996] 1 Lloyd's Rep 1; *The Delos* [2001] 1 Lloyd's Rep 703 and *Welex AG v Rosa Maritime Ltd (The Epsilon Rosa)(No.2)* [2003] EWCA Civ 938; [2003] 2 Lloyd's Rep 509. See also M. Ozdel, Presumptions on the Law Governing the Incorporation of Forum Selection Clauses: Should the Putative Applicable Law Lead the Way? [2011] JBL 357, which also considers the differences between English and US law. On US law see R Force and M Davies, Forum Selection Clauses in International Maritime Contracts, in M Davies (ed) *Jurisdiction and Forum Selection in International Maritime Law Essays in Honor of Robert Force* (Kluwer Law International 2005).

[63] *Ibid.*

[64] *Pacific Molasses Co and United Molasses Trading Co v Entre Rios Compania Naviera SA (The San Nicholas)* [1976] 1 Lloyd's Rep 8 and *Bangladesh Chemical Industries Corp v Henry Stephens Shipping Co and Tex-Bilan Shipping Co (The SLS Everest)* [1981] 2 Lloyd's Rep 389.

[65] *The San Nicholas* [1976] 1 Lloyd's Rep 8 and *K/S A/S Seateam & Co v Iraq National Oil Co. (The Sevonia Team)* [1983] 2 Lloyd's Rep 640 and Bills of Lading (Aikens, Lord and Bools), 2006, paragraph 7.104.

[66] *The San Nicholas* [1976] 1 Lloyd's Rep 8 at 11 per Lord Denning; *The Sevonia Team* [1983] 2 Lloyd's Rep 640 at 644 per Lloyd J.; *Partenreederei M/S Heidberg v Grosvenor Grain & Feed Co Ltd (The*

charterparty is a time charterparty, on the basis of the presumed unlikelihood of the parties wishing to incorporate the terms of a time charter which are different in kind.

Thus in *Kallang Shipping SA v Axa Assurances Senegal and Comptoir Commercial Mandiaye Ndiaye (The Kallang)*[67] Jonathan Hirst QC sitting as a Deputy Judge of the High Court considered bills of lading which expressly provided that all terms and conditions, liberties and exceptions of the Charter Party dated 1 February 2005 'including the Law and Arbitration Clauses' were incorporated. There were two charterparties dated 1 February 2005, a time and a voyage charterparty, both of which provided for London arbitration but in different terms. The bills of lading also provided that freight was payable as per the charterparty. It was held that this was a reference to the voyage charterparty and that the terms of the voyage charter are 'more naturally germane to a bill of lading' and therefore the intention was to incorporate the terms of the voyage charter, including its arbitration clause.[68]

This will be the case even if the carrier has not seen the charterparty. In *National Navigation Co v Endesa Generacion SA (The Wadi Sudr)*[69] the shipowner, which was also the carrier, had not seen the charterparty when it commenced proceedings in England against Endesa, the named consignee under the bill of lading. The bill of lading was in the Congenbill form which incorporates the 'Law and Arbitration clause' of the 'charterparty dated as overleaf,' but no date was given. There were three charterparties: a head time charter, a sub time charter and a voyage charterparty between the subtime charterers, Morgan Stanley Capital Group and Endesa's co-subsidiary, Carboex S.A. The day the owners' solicitor was instructed he asked for a copy of the voyage charterparty. Despite repeated requests the charterparty was not disclosed until a court order was made that it be disclosed over eight months later. Gloster J. thought that the voyage charterparty was incorporated,[70] but even if the head charterparty were the relevant charterparty, as both head and voyage charterparties provided for London arbitration, the bill of lading also so provided.[71] In the meantime the Spanish court held that no arbitration clause was incorporated into the bill of lading and that the owners had waived their right to rely on the arbitration clause by commencing the English court proceedings. The Court of Appeal held that the arbitrators were bound to recognise the Spanish judgment on the validity of the arbitration clause as a result of the common law doctrine of res judicata.[72]

Heidberg) [1994] 2 Lloyd's Rep 287 'such authorities do no more than indicate guidelines for ascertaining the intentions of the parties' per Judge Diamond QC at 311.

[67] [2008] EWHC 2761 (Comm); [2009] 1 Lloyd's Rep 1245.
[68] [64].
[69] [2009] EWHC 196 (Comm); [2009] 1 Lloyd's Rep 666 which was appealed ([2009] EWCA Civ 1397; [2010] 2 All ER (Comm) 1243), but not on this point.
[70] *Ibid* [111].
[71] *Ibid* [112].
[72] See pp 264 and 265.

ii. Third Parties

Under English law a third party consignee or indorsee of the bill of lading will also be bound by the arbitration clause in a bill of lading. Thus in *Welex AG v Rosa Maritime Ltd (The Epsilon Rosa) (No 2)*[73] the Court of Appeal held that the consignee of the bill of lading was bound by the arbitration clause incorporated in the bill of lading from the charterparty evidenced by the fixture recap telex.

In recent years the business practice of drawing up a formal charterparty signed by both parties has become very sloppy and this is frequently not done. The Court of Appeal considered the practice of concluding a charterparty in *Golden Ocean Group Ltd v Salgoacar Mining Industries Pvt Ltd*[74] in a different context. In that case the issue was whether a guarantee of a charterparty satisfied section 4 of the Statute of Frauds and was therefore enforceable. Tomlinson L.J. giving the judgment of the court stated,

> The conclusion of commercial contracts, particularly charterparties, by an exchange of emails, once telexes or faxes, in which the terms agreed early on are not repeated verbatim later in the exchanges, is entirely commonplace. It causes no difficulty whatever in the parties knowing at exactly what point they have undertaken a binding obligation and upon what terms. As Mr Young pointed out, it is often a matter of happenstance, or, metaphorically, the pressing of a button, whether a sequence of emails manifests itself in a single document as a thread or string of emails or in a series of individual documents... I can see no objection in principle to reference to a sequence of negotiating emails or other documents of the sort which is commonplace in ship chartering and ship sale and purchase. Whether the pattern of contract negotiation and formation habitually adopted in other areas of commercial life presents difficulty in adoption of the same approach must await examination when the problem arises. Nothing I have said is intended to discourage the obviously sensible practice of incorporating a guarantee either in a readily identifiable self-standing document or otherwise providing for it as part of the terms of a formally executed document. The Statute must however, if possible, be construed in a manner which accommodates accepted contemporary business practice. The present case is not concerned with prescribing best or prudent practice. It is concerned with ensuring, so far as is possible, that the adoption of usual and accepted practice cannot be used as a vehicle for injustice by permitting parties to break promises which are supported by consideration and upon which reliance has been placed.[75]

Although the decision that the guarantee was enforceable is clearly correct on its merits, we need to consider how the terms of a charterparty which has never been drawn up can affect a bill of lading holder.

---

[73] [2003] EWCA Civ 938; [2003] 2 Lloyd's Rep 509. See also *National Navigation Co v Endesa Generacion SA (The Wadi Sudr)* [2009] EWHC 196 (Comm); [2009] 1 Lloyd's Rep 666 and fn 69. In that case the Spanish consignee of the bill of lading in the Congenbill form, was held by Gloster J. to be bound by the arbitration clause incorporated from the charterparty. The Spanish court held that the arbitration clause was not valid.

[74] [2012] EWCA Civ 265; [2012] 1 Lloyd's Rep 542.

[75] [22].

In *The Heidberg*[76] Judge Diamond QC considered which charterparty arbitration clause had been incorporated in a bill of lading where the latter document provided for the arbitration clause of an unidentified charterparty to be incorporated in the bill. At the time the bill of lading was issued there were two potential charterparties containing arbitration clauses: the first in time was a contract of affreightment on the Synacomex form which contained a Paris arbitration clause. The second agreement in time was an oral one concluded by telephone and evidenced in writing by a fixture 'recap telex' between brokers the same day. A formal charterparty was not signed by the charterers until some two years later. The fixture 'recap telex' failed accurately to record the agreement between the parties which was for a charterparty in an amended Synacomex 90 form and contained the Centrocon arbitration clause which provided for arbitration in London according to English law. The 'recap telex' provided erroneously that the charterparty was in the Synacomex form. The wording of both arbitration clauses in the two charterparties was wide enough to apply to the bill of lading without manipulation. Judge Diamond QC held that the English court was bound by the Brussels Convention to recognise a decision of the French court that the Centrocon clause was not incorporated in the bill of lading;[77] that English law should determine whether the clause was incorporated in the bill and that if English law were to be applied, the clause incorporated in the bill was the Paris arbitration clause. The judge held that the bill of lading did not incorporate a charter agreed orally. The bill of lading referred to a charterparty which had been reduced to writing. His reasons for this conclusion include the need for terms incorporated by reference to be readily ascertainable. Extensive investigation as to the undocumented contractual arrangements of third parties would introduce considerable uncertainty.

However, in *Welex AG v Rosa Maritime Ltd (The Epsilon Rosa) (No 2)*[78] the Court of Appeal held that a bill of lading in the Congenbill form incorporated the charterparty arbitration clause, even though the charterparty had been concluded by a fixture recap telex which referred to a standard form charterparty and clearly stated 'London arbitration.' The drawn up charterparty was subsequently executed but on the date the bill of lading was issued there was no executed charterparty as it had not been signed on behalf of charterers by that time. Tuckey L.J., giving the judgment of the court, agreed with the decision in *The Heidberg* but distinguished it. He suggested that the courts are more willing to incorporate terms into bills of lading than in some other contractual contexts as the carrier wishes to ensure that its rights and obligations are back to back under both the charterparty and the bill of lading, as both contracts cover the same voyage by the same carrier.[79]

[76] [1994] 2 Lloyd's Rep 287.
[77] For further discussion of this point see pp 264 and 265 below.
[78] [2003] EWCA Civ 938; [2003] 2 Lloyd's Rep 509. See also *National Navigation Co v Endesa Generacion SA (The Wadi Sudr)* [2009] EWHC 196 (Comm); [2009] 1 Lloyd's Rep 666 which was appealed ([2009] EWCA Civ 1397; [2010] 2 All ER (Comm) 1243), but not on this point, where the Spanish consignee of the bill of lading also in the Congenbill form was also held to be bound by the arbitration clause incorporated from the charterparty. The Spanish court held that the arbitration clause was not valid.
[79] *Ibid* [25].

What is not clear is whether if the charterparty were never drawn up, or was evidenced by an exchange of emails as in *Golden Ocean Group Ltd v Salgoacar Mining Industries Pvt Ltd*[80] rather than one fixture recap telex, a bill of lading could still effectively incorporate the arbitration clause from the charterparty which has undoubtedly been concluded and bind a third party.

A subrogated cargo insurer would also be bound by the London arbitration clause in the bill of lading.[81] Furthermore if the shipper, consignee, indorsee or their subrogated insurer commences or threatens to commence proceedings elsewhere in breach of the arbitration agreement, the other party to the agreement may apply to the English court for an anti-suit injunction to restrain the first party from commencing or pursuing the proceedings elsewhere, provided the proceedings are in a court of a State which is neither an EU Member State nor Lugano Contracting State.[82]

Thus in *Kallang Shipping SA v Axa Assurances Senegal, Comptoir Commercial Mandiaye Ndiaye and Axa France Assurance SA (The Kallang)*[83] Gloster J. upheld an order by Cooke J. granting an anti-suit injunction sought by Kallang Shipping SA Panama to restrain the defendants from continuing, instigating or commencing

---

[80] [2012] EWCA Civ 265; [2012] 1 Lloyd's Rep 542.

[81] *Schiffahrtsgesellschaft Detlev von Appen GmbH v Voest Alpine Intertrading GmbH (The Jay Bola)* [1997] 2 Lloyd's Rep 279 per Hobhouse L.J. at pp 286-5; *Navigation Maritime Bulgare v Rustal Trading Ltd (The Ivan Zagubanski)* [2002] 1 Lloyd's Rep 106 [52] and [54]; *Kallang Shipping SA v Axa Assurances Senegal (The Kallang)* [2006] EWHC 2825, [2007] 1 Lloyd's Rep 160; *Starlight Shipping Co v Tai Ping Insurance Co Ltd* [2007] EWHC 1893 (Comm); [2008] 1 Lloyd's Rep 230 and *Niagara Maritime SA v Tianjin Iron & Steel Group Co. Ltd* [2011] EWHC 3035 (Comm). At first instance in *The Front Comor* [2005] EWHC 454 (Comm); [2005] 2 Lloyd's Rep 257 [32] and [33] Colman J. considered the issue of which law is applicable to determine whether the subrogated insurers are bound by the arbitration clause. The insurers contended that their right to pursue the subrogated claim was a matter of Italian law and that law must also determine whether the arbitration agreement was binding on the insurers. The owners, however, contended that whether the arbitration agreement was binding on the insurers fell to be determined by the law of the arbitration agreement itself ie English law. Colman J concluded that under Italian law the insurers were entitled to enforce the insured charterer's right of action in delict against the owners. However, the issue whether the scope of the arbitration agreement covered the claim in tort was to be determined by reference to the proper construction of the arbitration agreement in accordance with English law. Furthermore by reference to English law, as the governing law of the arbitration agreement, the insurers' duty to refer their claim to arbitration was 'an inseparable component of the subject-matter transferred to the insurers.' ([33]). Colman J. also found, after considering the expert evidence on Italian law, that if Italian law were applicable, the result would be the same.

[82] *Kallang Shipping SA v Axa Assurances Senegal (The Kallang)* [2006] EWHC 2825, [2007] 1 Lloyd's Rep 160 (Senegal); *Sotrade Denizcilik Sanayi Ve Ticaret AS v Amadou LO (The Duden)* [2008] EWHC 2762 (Comm); [2009] 1 Lloyd's Rep 145 (Senegal); *Noble Assurance Co. v Gerling-Konzern General Insurance Co* [2007] EWHC 253 (Comm), [2007] 1 CLC 85; *C v D* [2007] EWHC 1541 (Comm), [2007] 2 All ER (Comm) 557; *Markel International Co Ltd v Craft (The Norseman)* [2006] EWHC 3150 (Comm), [2007] Lloyd's Rep I.R. 403; *Starlight Shipping Co v Tai Ping Insurance Co Ltd* [2007] EWHC 1893 (Comm); [2008] 1 Lloyd's Rep 230 (China); *Midgulf International Ltd v Groupe Chimiche Tunisien* [2010] EWCA Civ 66; [2010] 2 Lloyd's Rep 411 (Tunisia); *Royal Bank of Scotland plc v Hicks* [2011] EWHC 287 (Ch) (Texas, United States of America, where the defendant sought punitive damages) ; *AES Ust-Kamenogorsk Hydropower Plant LLP v Ust-Kamenogorsk Hydropower Plant JSC* [2011] EWCA Civ 647 (Kazakhstan); and *Niagara Maritime SA v Tianjin Iron & Steel Group Co Ltd* [2011] EWHC 3035 (Comm) (China). For the position where the proceedings are in the court of an EU Member State or a Lugano Contracting State see pp 263 and 264.

[83] [2006] EWHC 2825 (Comm); [2007] 1 Lloyd's Rep 160. *Cf* the decision of Gloster J. in *YM Mars Tankers Ltd v Shield Petroleum Co Nigeria Ltd (The YM Saturn)* [2012] EWHC 2652 which involved a court jurisdiction clause in the charterparty which was incorporated into the bill of lading and where the vessel was arrested in Nigeria. She also granted an anti-suit injunction.

proceedings against the claimants other than in London arbitration. The defendants were the receiver of the cargo of rice from Montevideo under fourteen bills of lading; their cargo underwriter, Axa Senegal; and Axa France who it was alleged was, if not the parent company of Axa Senegal, at least in the same group of companies and was directing and controlling Axa Senegal's conduct of the litigation. The bills of lading incorporated a charterparty containing an English law and London arbitration clause. Axa Senegal demanded a guarantee for cargo allegedly short delivered. It contended that it was not bound by the arbitration clause. The claimants' P&I Club, American Protection and Indemnity Club, offered to put up a letter of undertaking as security, subject to English law and London arbitration being agreed. That offer was rejected and the receiver and Axa Senegal insisted on a bank guarantee with Senegalese jurisdiction not only for resolution of any disputes under the guarantee but also in relation to the cargo. The claimant argued that the anti-suit injunction granted by Cooke J. should be upheld as although it accepted that the arrest of the vessel in Dakar for the purposes of obtaining security was not a breach of the arbitration clause, nevertheless the receiver and the cargo underwriter sought to invoke the jurisdiction of the Senegalese court not merely to obtain security for their claim, but also to ensure that the substance of the cargo claim was litigated in Senegal and to circumvent or frustrate the London arbitration clause. It was 'necessary to look at the wider picture with the result that the Court should ask itself the question whether, in acting in the way that it did, the Defendants were attempting to render the London arbitration clause meaningless.'[84] It was further submitted by the claimant that the attempt to obtain Senegalese jurisdiction was to put pressure on the claimant to settle the dispute disadvantageously as if the defendants were successful in obtaining Senegalese jurisdiction over the cargo claim, the likelihood was that the claimant, or their P&I Club would pay up, 'since the relatively modest amount of the claim could not justify the expense of disputing it in Senegalese proceedings as opposed to the relatively modest costs of a London arbitration.'[85] Gloster J. accepted this argument and an argument that the defendants' conduct amounted to a breach of implied terms of the arbitration clause, and held that Cooke J. was entitled to grant an anti-suit injunction.

Moreover, where the common law rules apply, a party to an exclusive jurisdiction agreement which has been breached may be able to recover damages for breach of contract[86] or for the tort of procuring a breach of contract.[87] In *Kallang Shipping*

---

[84] [17].

[85] [18]. The voyage sub charterparty incorporated into the bill of lading (See *Kallang Shipping SA v Axa Assurances Senegal and Comptoir Commercial Mandiaye Ndiaye (The Kallang)* [2008] EWHC 2761 (Comm); [2009] 1 Lloyd's Rep 124 [64]) contained a Small Claims Procedure Clause providing, 'If the amount claimed is less than $US50,000, then the arbitration shall be conducted by a sole arbitrator and be conducted in accordance with "The London Maritime Arbitrators' Association Small Claims Procedure FALCA (fast and low cost arbitration)".'

[86] *Union Discount Co. v Zoller* [2002] 1 WLR 1517; *Donohue v Armco Inc* [2001] UKHL 64; [2002] 1 Lloyd's Rep 425 at [36], [48] and [75]. See also *West Tankers Inc v Allianz SpA* [2012] EWHC 854 (Comm) discussed below at p 265 concerning the situation where the court proceedings are in an EU Member State.

[87] See Morison J in *Horn Linie GmbH & Co v Panamericana Formas E Impresos S.A., Ace Seguros S.A. (The Hornbay)* [2006] EWHC 373 (Comm); [2006] 2 Lloyd's Rep 44 at [26]. See also *The Kallang* [2008] EWHC 2761 (Comm); [2009] 1 Lloyd's Rep 124.

SA Panama v Axa Assurances Senegal and Comptoir Commercial Mandiaye Ndiaye (The Kallang)[88] Jonathan Hirst QC sitting as a Deputy Judge of the High Court granted Kallang Shipping SA damages of US$130,350 against Axa Senegal, the cargo underwriters, as their conduct, knowledge and intent was such as to make it liable for the accessory tort of procuring the receiver's breach of the contract to arbitrate all disputes in London. An alternative claim for causing loss by unlawful means did not add anything and was not pursued.[89] A further claim that the cargo underwriters unlawfully conspired with the receivers to injure the owners ie a conspiracy involving no acts or means which were unlawful with the object of causing deliberate damage to the Owners without any just cause, also added nothing and the judge was not satisfied that the receiver was involved in any conspiracy as the cargo underwriters took over the running of the claim.[90] The judge found that the ship would have been arrested but could and should have been released from arrest ten days earlier on the provision of adequate security had the arrest not been used as a means of defeating the arbitration clause. The cargo underwriters were therefore liable for ten days of delay during which the ship was under arrest after she should have been released and the owners lost the use of their ship.[91] The shipowner brought evidence in relation to numerous ships which was accepted by the judge that Axa Senegal did not accept that charterparty arbitration clauses can be incorporated in bill of lading contracts and bind receivers and their cargo underwriters; it was Axa Senegal's standard practice to try and secure a Senegalese guarantee triggered by Senegalese jurisdiction, whatever the bill of lading provided; it is very difficult to provide a Senegalese bank guarantee and may be practically impossible to do so on terms acceptable to Axa Senegal and that Axa Senegal acted without the involvement of the receiver.

iii. Who Decides?

Where arbitration proceedings are commenced by one party and the other party does not consider it is bound by an arbitration agreement in the contract, the respondent should object to the jurisdiction of the arbitration tribunal before it contests the merits of the matter.[92] The arbitration tribunal may rule on its own substantive jurisdiction.[93] In other words the arbitrators may decide, for example, whether there is a valid arbitration clause, and, if there is, whether it is wide enough in scope to cover the dispute which has arisen. The party wishing to enforce the London arbitration clause may also seek a declaration from the English court that there is a valid arbitration clause.[94] If the court of another country has already given judgment that there is not

---

[88] [2008] EWHC 2761 (Comm); [2009] 1 Lloyd's Rep 124.
[89] [94].
[90] [96].
[91] [99].
[92] Section 31 of the Arbitration Act 1996.
[93] Section 30 of the Arbitration Act 1996.
[94] For the role of the court to determine whether an arbitration clause binds a party see *Dallah Real Estate & Tourism Holding Co v Pakistan* [2010] UKSC 46; [2011] 1 A.C. 763; *TTMI Sarl v Statoil ASA* [2011] EWHC 1150 (Comm); [2011] 2 All ER (Comm) 647; [2011] 2 Lloyd's Rep 220; and *Excalibur Ventures LLC v Texas Keystone Inc* [2011] EWHC 1624 (Comm); [2011] 2 Lloyd's Rep 289.

a valid arbitration agreement the English court or London arbitration tribunal would be bound to recognise that decision due to the common law on res judicata.[95]

Where a party to an arbitration clause, which provides for arbitration in England or abroad,[96] commences proceedings in the English court, the court is obliged to stay the court proceedings if the other party applies for a stay, unless satisfied that the arbitration agreement is null and void, inoperative, or incapable of being performed.[97]

III. THE EUROPEAN POSITION

A. Court Jurisdiction

i. Neutral Choice

Party autonomy is a well recognised principle in the EC Jurisdiction Regulation.[98] Where a jurisdiction agreement has been concluded between parties, at least one of whom is domiciled in an EU Member State,[99] and the court of an EU Member State has been chosen, Article 23(1) of the EC Jurisdiction Regulation provides that the court chosen shall have jurisdiction, provided that actual or deemed consent to the jurisdiction agreement can be demonstrated. The interpretation of the formalities that must be satisfied in order to establish an exclusive jurisdiction clause under Article 23(1)(a), (b) or (c) of the EC Jurisdiction Regulation has led to some complex, time consuming and costly litigation in relation to bills of lading. This is particularly, although not exclusively, the case where a party relies on a trade usage of which the parties are or ought to have been aware within Article 23(1) (c). In *Trasporti Castelletti Spedizioni Internazionali SpA v Hugo Trumpy SpA*[100] the European Court of Justice held that the original parties to a bill of lading contract may choose a neutral forum. There is no requirement of any link between the relationship in dispute and the court chosen.

Party choice of jurisdiction is further subject to the restriction that if there is another international convention which a Member State was party to when the EC Jurisdiction Regulation came into force and which 'in relation to particular matters, govern[s] jurisdiction or the recognition or enforcement of judgments' that other

---

[95] See page 264.

[96] Sections 9–11 apply even if the seat of the arbitration is outside England and Wales or Northern Ireland or no seat has been designated or determined (s 2(2)(a)).

[97] Section 9(4) of the Arbitration Act 1996. *Halki Shipping Corp v Sopex Oils Ltd* [1998] 1 Lloyd's Rep 465; *Exfin Shipping (India) Ltd Mumbai v Tolani Shipping Co Ltd Mumbai* [2006] EWHC 1090 (Comm.); [2006] 2 Lloyd's Rep 389 and *Joint Stock Company Aeroflot Russian Airlines v Berezovsky* [2012] EWHC 1610.

[98] Recital 14 of the EC Jurisdiction Regulation. This is subject to a number of exceptions for policy reasons, such as consumer, insurance (but not marine insurance) and employment contracts, (Sections 3–5) where there may be unequal bargaining power. See SEC (2010) 1547 para 2.3.1.3 on the extent to which jurisdiction agreements are used in commercial contracts.

[99] Art 25 of the Recast Regulation will apply these rules no matter where the parties are domiciled. See page 245.

[100] Case C-159/97 *Trasporti Castelletti Spedizioni Internazionali SpA v Hugo Trumpy SpA* [1999] I L Pr 492 [50].

convention will prevail over the EC Jurisdiction Regulation, if it conflicts with it.[101] Such conventions[102] of great significance in relation to carriage of goods by sea, include the International Convention for the Unification of Certain Rules Relating to the Arrest of Seagoing Ships of 1952 (the 'Arrest Convention'), the International Convention on the Arrest of Ships 1999 (the '1999 Arrest Convention'),[103] the International Convention for the Unification of Certain Rules Concerning Civil Jurisdiction in Matters of Collision 1952 ('the Collision Convention'), and the UN Convention on the Carriage of Goods by Sea 1978 (the 'Hamburg Rules'), but probably not the Hague-Visby Rules.[104] The 2005 Hague Convention on Choice of Court Agreements,[105] signed by the European Union, even if it comes into force,[106] does not apply to the carriage of goods.[107]

The approach of those conventions to jurisdiction clauses varies significantly. The Arrest Convention 1952 refers to the domestic law of the State in which the vessel has been arrested which may recognise the priority of a jurisdiction or arbitration clause. The Collision Convention[108] and the Arrest Convention 1999[109] which has been ratified by some EU Member States, gives priority to jurisdiction and arbitration clauses; whereas the Hamburg Rules, which contain provisions on both jurisdiction and arbitration, [110] provide that the cargo claimant can choose from a number of different fora including the court chosen, so that the jurisdiction clause is reduced to a mere option. Of the EU Member States, Austria, the Czech Republic, Hungary and Romania have ratified the Hamburg Rules. Austria, the Czech Republic and Hungary are landlocked and are not therefore notable maritime States. Of the

---

[101] See Art 71 of the EC Jurisdiction Regulation which is discussed in some detail in Baatz, Y, 'Forum selection in Contracts for the Carriage of Goods by Sea:– the European Dimension' [2011] LMCLQ 208, and in particular pages 217 to 224.

[102] Whether the conventions on tonnage limitation fall within Art 71 is considered by M Tsimplis, 'The effect of European regulations on the jurisdiction and applicable law for limitation of liability proceedings' [2011] LMCLQ 307.

[103] Entered into force on 14 September 2011. The States parties are Albania, Algeria, Benin, Bulgaria, Ecuador, Estonia, Latvia, Liberia, Spain, and Syria.

[104] See Y Baatz, 'Forum selection in Contracts for the Carriage of Goods by Sea:– the European Dimension' [2011] LMCLQ 208 at pages 218 to 220.

[105] See fn 171.

[106] See fn 172.

[107] See fn 173.

[108] Art 2 provides that, 'The provisions of Art 1 [specifying the courts with jurisdiction] shall not in any way prejudice the right of the parties to bring an action in respect of a collision before a Court they have chosen by agreement or to refer it to arbitration.'

[109] Art 7(1) provides that 'the Courts of the State in which an arrest has been effected or security provided to obtain the release of the ship shall have jurisdiction to determine the case upon its merits, unless the parties validly agree or have validly agreed to submit the dispute to a Court of another State which accepts jurisdiction, or to arbitration.'

[110] Arts 21 and 22. Many of the other transport conventions in relation to the carriage of goods by air, road and rail, but not inland waterways, also restrict the effect of exclusive court or arbitration agreements. R Herber 'Jurisdiction and Arbitration - Should the New Convention Contain Rules on these Subjects?' [2002] LMCLQ 405 for a comparison of the provisions of those conventions. See, eg the decision of the European Court of Justice in Case C-533/08 *TNT Express Nederland BV v Axa Versicherung AG* considering Art 71 of the EC Jurisdiction Regulation and Art 31 of the Convention on the Contract for the International Carriage of Goods by Road 1956 (CMR). The CMR has been acceded to by more than 50 States, including all the Member States of the European Union.

other EU Member States some have incorporated the jurisdictional provisions of the Hamburg Rules into their national law, such as Denmark, Finland, and Sweden. [111] In the latter case, it would not be possible to override Article 23 of the EC Jurisdiction Regulation.

ii. Third Parties

The EC Jurisdiction Regulation does not provide whether third parties should be bound by a jurisdiction clause which binds the carrier and the shipper. The matter is currently governed by the applicable national law of each EU Member State. Transferees of the contract of carriage of goods by sea will be bound by the jurisdiction clause 'if the latter succeeded to the rights and obligations of the shipper under the applicable national law when he acquired the bill of lading'.[112] As we have already seen the position under English national law is that the third party can succeed to the rights and obligations of the shipper. This is not, however, the position in all the EU Member States[113] and as soon as national law is applicable there is no harmony.

The Heidelberg Review of the EC Jurisdiction Regulation recommended that a third party bill of lading holder should be bound by a clear jurisdiction clause.[114] Although the Parliament Resolution[115] which followed considered that there should be an express provision to deal with third party bill of lading holders, it would only be binding if stringent conditions were satisfied and the choice was

[111] Although the Hamburg Rules did not achieve the international support hoped for by its promoters, some states which did not ratify them, such as the Nordic countries, have introduced similar national legislation on jurisdiction. See, for example, s 46 of the Canadian Marine Liability Act 2001 set out at fn 45 and considered in *OT Africa Line Ltd v Magic Sportswear Corp* [2005] EWCA 710; [2005] 2 Lloyd's Rep 170 discussed at pp 244 and 245. On the Nordic position see, eg P Wetterstein, 'Jurisdiction and Conflict of Laws under the New Rules on Carriage of Goods by Sea' in H Honka (ed) *New Carriage of Goods by Sea: the Nordic Approach Including Comparisons with Some Other Jurisdictions* (Institute of Maritime and Commercial Law Abo Akademi University Abo, 1997); T Falkanger, H J Bull and L Brautaset *Scandinavian Maritime Law The Norwegian Perspective*, 3rd edn (Universitetsforlaget, 2011) paras 1.51, 1.52, 1.56 and 14.31 on the Maritime Code of 1994 '...the liability system in the Hague-Visby Rules is modified using those provisions of the Hamburg Rules which can be incorporated into the Scandinavian countries' maritime codes without conflicting with their obligations as Hague-Visby states.' (para 14.31); H Honka Ch 7 'Jurisdiction and EC Law: Loss of or Damage to Goods' in M Davies (ed) *Jurisdiction and Forum Selection in International Maritime Law Essays in Honor of Robert Force* (Kluwer Law International, 2005).
[112] Case-387/98 *Coreck Maritime GmbH v Handelsveem BV* [2000] ECR 1-09337; Case C-159/97 *Trasporti Castelletti Spedizioni Internazionali SpA v Hugo Trumpy SpA* [1999] I L Pr 492. *O.T. Africa Line Ltd v Hijazy* [2001] 1 Lloyd's Rep 76 paras 65 to 68. Under English law the 'lawful holder' of a transferable bill of lading does have transferred to it the rights and liabilities under the bill of lading pursuant to ss 2(1) and 3 of the Carriage of Goods by Sea Act 1992. See also Case C-543/10 *Refcomp SpA v Axa Corporate Solutions Assurance SA* [34] to [36] where the European Court of Justice referred to bills of lading but distinguished the position from a jurisdiction clause in a contract between the manufacturer of goods and a buyer which does not bind a sub buyer as there is no contractual link between them.
[113] See the Heidelberg Report (see fn 8) paras 265–70 on the differences that exist in some of the EU Member States. See also F Berlingieri, A Review of Some Recent Analyses of the Rotterdam Rules, 2009 Il Diritto Marittimo pp 1028 and 1029.
[114] The Heidelberg Report paras 269–70.
[115] See also Recital O and Art 13.

limited to one of five places linked with the dispute. The European Parliament also considered that it should further be provided that, in all other cases, the third party may bring an action before the court otherwise competent under the Regulation if it appears that holding that party to the chosen forum would be blatantly unfair. This proposal was a major departure from the current position as it would not permit a neutral choice to bind a third party.

It appears that the Resolution proposal sought to align the provisions of the EC Jurisdiction Regulation with the provisions on jurisdiction in volume contracts[116] for third parties in the Rotterdam Rules, which are criticised below, not least because they do not permit a neutral choice to bind a third party.[117] In the subsequent European Commission Proposals and the Recast Regulation these proposals were abandoned.

The problem of third parties is also reflected in the Rome Convention, Rome I and Rome II. Article 1(2)(d) of Rome I and Article 1(2)(c) of Rome II exclude from the scope of those Regulations 'obligations arising under bills of exchange, cheques and promissory notes and other negotiable instruments to the extent that the obligations under such other negotiable instruments arise out of their negotiable character'.[118] It was not clear under the Rome Convention whether this exclusion included bills of lading[119] but Recital 9 of Rome I clarifies that the exclusion covers obligations under 'bills of lading to the extent that the obligations under the bill of lading arise out of its negotiable character.' There is no such Recital in Rome II. However, Recital 7 of Rome II provides that the substantive scope and the provisions of Rome II should be consistent with the EC Jurisdiction Regulation, the Rome Convention and Rome I[120] and Recital 7 of Rome I is in similar terms. It is clear that Rome I applies to the obligations between the original parties to the contract, the carrier and the shipper as the obligations under the bill of lading between the original parties to the bill of lading do not 'arise out of its negotiable character.' For example, where the shipper, who is not the charterer, sues the carrier on a bill of lading contract dated 1 October 2010, Rome I applies. What is not clear is whether the exclusion should be given a wide interpretation[121] and the bill of lading is not covered by Rome I in all cases where the bill comes into the hands of a third party or there should be a narrower interpretation so that only proprietary obligations are excluded.[122] In the case of the wider interpretation,

---

[116] Defined in Art 1(2) of the Rotterdam Rules.

[117] Y Baatz, 'Jurisdiction clauses in Bills of Lading - Rotterdam Rules by the Back Door in Europe? [2010] STL.

[118] Art 1(2)(c) of the Rome Convention.

[119] R Asariotis, Y Baatz and N Gaskell, *Bills of Lading: Law and Contracts*, LLP, 2000. paras 19.7 and 19.8 where it is argued that, as a bill of lading is not a negotiable instrument, bills of lading are covered by the Rome Convention.

[120] 'the instruments dealing with the law applicable to contractual obligations.'

[121] See the view of H Boonk, [2011] LMCLQ 227 at pages 231 to 232.

[122] See the view of Professor Erik Rosaeg that bills of lading are only excluded where the issue is a proprietary one as opposed to a contractual one – see his paper at the Colloquium on Maritime Conflict of Laws held at Southampton, 2010. In the Giuliano Lagarde Report No C 282/11 it is stated that 'certain Member States of the Community regard these obligations [arising from bills of exchange, cheques, promissory notes] as non-contractual.'

where the bill of lading is negotiable as it is an order bill[123] or a bearer bill, Rome I will not apply as the obligations under it 'arise out of their negotiable character.' Where, however, the bill of lading is a straight bill of lading as it is made out to a named consignee, the bill of lading is not negotiable although it may well be transferred by the shipper (who may be the seller) to the consignee (who may be the buyer)[124] in exchange for payment where the sale contract or the letter of credit so requires. Moreover, the terms of the straight bill of lading may well require it to be presented to the carrier in order to obtain delivery of the cargo.[125] Do the obligations of the carrier to the named consignee under the bill of lading arise out of its negotiable character? It might seem odd if Rome I does not apply to some third parties but does to others. If Rome I does not apply, the courts of the EU Member States would apply their differing national laws.

Furthermore the effectiveness of an assignment or subrogation of a claim against third parties and the priority of the assigned or subrogated claim over a right of another person are to be reviewed within two[126] and others within five[127] years of the adoption of Rome I.

In Rome II, as in Rome I, obligations arising under bills of lading to the extent that the obligations arise out of their negotiable character are excluded from the scope of Rome II.[128] Party autonomy is recognised in Rome II, although conditions are imposed on the choice to protect weaker parties.[129] Thus the parties may choose to submit non-contractual obligations to the law of their choice in two situations: first where an agreement is concluded after the event giving rise to the damage[130] or secondly where all the parties are pursuing a commercial activity, by an agreement freely negotiated before the event giving rise to the damage occurred.[131] In either case the choice must be express or demonstrated with reasonable certainty. It is important to note that the choice shall not prejudice the rights of third parties. So

[123] In *Parsons Corporation v C.V. Scheepvaartonderneming 'Happy Ranger' (The Happy Ranger)* [2002] 2 Lloyd's Rep 357 the Court of Appeal held that the bill of lading issued was a document of title within Art I (b) of the Hague-Visby Rules as, although only a named consignee appeared in the consignee box, the printed words on the front of the bill referred to delivery of the goods to the 'consignee or to his or their assigns.' Read together this made the bill of lading transferable and not a straight bill of lading.

[124] In *Welex A.G. v Rosa Maritime Ltd (The Epsilon Rosa)* – see fn 73 – Steel J and the Court of Appeal applied the Rome Convention to the contract between the carrier and the consignee.

[125] In *J.I. MacWilliam Co Inc v Mediterranean Shipping Co S.A. (The Rafaela S)* [2005] 1 Lloyd's Rep 347 the House of Lords held that a straight bill of lading is a 'similar document of title' and therefore the Hague-Visby Rules apply to it. The bill of lading in that case provided: 'IN WITNESS whereof the number of Original Bills of Lading stated above [viz three] all of this tenor and date, has been signed, one of which being accomplished, the others to stand void. One of the Bills of Lading must be surrendered duly endorsed in exchange for the goods or delivery order.' However, Rix L J in the Court of Appeal, at [145] and Lords Bingham and Steyn in the House of Lords, at [20] and [45] stated *obiter* that a straight bill of lading would be a document of title even if it contained no express provision requiring surrender. See also *Peer Voss v APL Co Pte Ltd* [2002] 2 Lloyd's Rep 707 Singapore Court of Appeal.

[126] Art 27(2).

[127] The law applicable to insurance contracts and Art 6 in particular as regards consumer protection – Art 27(1).

[128] The combined effect of Art 1(2)(c) and Recital 7 of Rome II and Recital 9 of Rome I.

[129] Recital 31 and Art 14.

[130] Art 14(1)(a).

[131] Art 14(1)(b). Compare the Rotterdam Rules considered below at pages 270–74.

once again there is some doubt as to whether such a choice of law in a bill of lading would bind the third party bill of lading holder.

Article 19 of Rome II deals with subrogation. Where the insured has a non-contractual claim against the debtor, and the insurer has a duty to satisfy the insured, or has in fact satisfied the insured, the law which governs the insurer's duty to satisfy the insured, ie the law applicable to the insurance contract, shall determine whether, and the extent to which, the insured is entitled to exercise against the debtor the rights which the insured had against the debtor under the law governing their relationship. Article 18 deals with a direct action against an insurer and gives effect to the diverging views in Europe by allowing a direct action to be brought against a liability insurer either if the law applicable to the non-contractual obligation or the law applicable to the insurance contract so provides. Thus although under English law the claimant is treated as standing in the shoes of the insured and is thus bound by the jurisdiction clause in the insurance contract, in other jurisdictions the direct action would not be characterised as contractual but as non-contractual.[132]

iii. Who Decides?

Where the claimant commences proceedings in a court other than that agreed by the parties, the defendant who wishes to contest the jurisdiction of that court must take steps to do so within what may be relatively short time limits. The European Court of Justice held in the controversial decision of *Erich Gasser GmbH v MISAT SRL*[133] that any court other than the court first seised, even if allegedly chosen, must stay its proceedings until the court first seised has established its jurisdiction. This has lead to 'torpedo actions' in which a recalcitrant debtor seises a court first which is very slow so that considerable time elapses before that court ever considers the jurisdiction issue. If the court first seised then decides that it must stay its proceedings because the parties have chosen the courts of another EU Member State, much time may, deliberately or otherwise, have been wasted in a court which should never have been seised in the first place. Furthermore the European Court of Justice rejected any exception to their decision, even if there is excessive delay by the court first seised.

This decision has been criticised as it does not give adequate weight to the parties' choice of jurisdiction. The last thing that a claimant wants is litigation about where to litigate, especially where there is a clear jurisdiction clause.[134] It is

---

[132] See J Hjalmarsson, 'Direct Claims against Marine Insurers in the English Legal System' [2010] APLR 18, 269 and V Ulfbeck, 'Direct Actions Against the Insurer in a Maritime Setting: the European Perspective' [2011] LMCLQ 293.

[133] Case C-116/02 [2003] ECR I-14693; [2005] QB 1. It is now clear as a result of this decision and Case C-159/02 *Turner v Grovit* [2004] ECR I--3565; [2005] 1 AC 101; [2004] 2 Lloyd's Rep 169 that the English court cannot grant an anti-suit injunction to restrain a party from pursuing proceedings in another EU Member State in breach of an English jurisdiction agreement. However, it can still do so where the other proceedings are in a non EU Member State – see page 245.

[134] This is amply illustrated in *JP Morgan Europe Ltd v Primacom AG.* [2005] EWHC 508 (Comm); [2005] 2 Lloyd's Rep 665. Noted R Swallow and R Hornshaw, 'Jurisdiction Clauses in Loan Agreements:

costly[135] and time consuming and distracts from the main issue ie. determination of the substance of the matter. It may make a case very difficult to settle because which jurisdiction will determine the dispute may have a significant impact on the outcome of the substantive issues. The whole point of including a jurisdiction clause in your contract is to avoid these problems. As a result of *Gasser* parties who have chosen a jurisdiction clause may nevertheless find themselves embroiled in lengthy litigation in the wrong jurisdiction before they can get back on track in the right jurisdiction. Ironically clogging up the courts of slow jurisdictions with trials on the issue of jurisdiction will simply make them slower and confounds the reason for choosing the English courts partly on the grounds that they are speedy, as it makes the quick jurisdiction subject to the speed of the court first seised. The pace of the litigation is subject to the weakest link.

The danger of *Gasser* was that parties might start searching for a jurisdiction which is outside the scope of the EC Jurisdiction Regulation and is not therefore subject to the *Gasser* problem. Why should a Singapore claimant continue to choose English High Court jurisdiction, or indeed that of any EU Member State, if it knows that the agreement will only be effective provided that, if the other party is domiciled in a Member State, it does not seise another court first. Turning elsewhere could have dire economic consequences for England.

It is therefore to be welcomed that the Recast Regulation reverses *Gasser* by strengthening the principle of party autonomy. Following the Heidelberg Review of the EC Jurisdiction Regulation[136] and extensive consultation, proposals were made to amend the Regulation by permitting the court chosen to determine the validity of a jurisdiction clause.[137] The Recast Regulation has accepted those proposals and it is now clear that the lis pendens provisions are subject to Article 31(2) which provides that where a court has been chosen in accordance with Article 25, any court of another Member State shall stay its proceedings until such time as the court seised on the basis of the agreement declares that it has no jurisdiction under the agreement.[138] Where the court chosen has established that it has jurisdiction, any court of another Member State shall decline jurisdiction in favour of that court.[139] Recital 22 clarifies

---

practical Considerations for Lenders' Bankers Law Vol. 1 number 2 18, Y Baatz, *English Jurisdiction Clauses - a matter of Choice in Europe?*, Shipping and Transport Lawyer International, Volume 6(1) pp 8-11 and N Sifakis, (2006) 12 JIML 307. In *Primacom* the debtor brought proceedings in breach of the English jurisdiction clause purely to buy time and was unable to give any reason for the invalidity of the clause.

[135] 'It is not uncommon for each party's costs in relation to a jurisdiction application to substantially exceed £10000, and not unknown for costs to exceed £100000.' See page 57 the Report on the application of the Brussels 1 Regulation in the UK (England and Wales) submitted by the British Institute of International and Comparative Law in 2006 as part of the European Commission Study JLS/C4/2005/03.
[136] The Heidelberg Report (see fn 8) paras 265–70; 378–407; summarised at 715–22.
[137] See Recital N and Art 13 of the EU Parliament Resolution 2009/2140 (INI) dated 7 September 2010 and Art 32(2) of the revised Brussels I proposed by the European Commission which has been neither deleted nor amended in the Draft Report of the Committee on Legal Affairs dated 28.6.2011 (2010/0383 (COD)). See A Briggs, '*The Brussels I bis Regulation Appears on the Horizon*' [2011] LMCLQ 157 for a discussion of the European Commission proposals.
[138] See Recital 22 and Arts 29(1) and Art 31(2).
[139] Art 31(3).

that the designated court 'has priority to decide on the validity of the agreement and on the extent to which the agreement applies to the dispute pending before it', even if it is second seised and even if the other court has not already decided on the stay of proceedings. Where, however, there is a conflict as to whether both courts have been chosen, then the court first seised will determine the validity of the jurisdiction clause.

This solution is similar to that adopted by Article 6 of the 2005 Hague Convention on Choice of Court Agreements,[140] an initiative of the Hague Conference on Private International Law, an intergovernmental organisation whose members include all EU Member States. That Convention has been signed by the European Union. However, even if the Convention comes into force,[141] it does not apply to the carriage of goods.[142]

The risk of the solution adopted by the Recast Regulation was outlined by Advocate General Leger in his Opinion in *Gasser*. He thought that such a solution might encourage delaying tactics by an unscrupulous party by alleging the existence of an agreement and bringing an action before the court allegedly designated in order deliberately to delay judgment until that court had declared that it had no jurisdiction.[143] This is a risk but presumably a lesser one than that which *Gasser* gave rise to, as the party would need to point to a jurisdiction agreement.

An alternative solution outlined by Advocate General Léger in his Opinion in *Gasser* has fortunately been rejected. Bound as he was by the wording of the EC Jurisdiction Convention, he proposed that a court second seised which has exclusive jurisdiction under an agreement could, by way of derogation from Article 21 on *lis pendens*, give judgment in the case, without waiting for a declaration from the court first seised that it has no jurisdiction where there is no room for doubt as to the jurisdiction of the court second seised.[144] He was not overly concerned that irreconcilable decisions would result from both courts proceeding simultaneously, as both courts should apply the same criteria to determine whether the clause is valid ie those set out in Article 23 of the EC Jurisdiction Regulation or Article 17 of the Conventions, and no others. This was in fact the result in *Primacom*,[145] but it may be rather optimistic and does not deal with the point that the party who has agreed to a jurisdiction agreement should not have to incur the cost of pursuing proceedings in two or more jurisdictions, even if it is only the cost in one set of proceedings of contesting jurisdiction.[146] It is in effect, however, similar to the position at common law.[147] It has the merit that the court chosen has every incentive to proceed apace. However, it defers the problems until after a judgment

---

[140] See fn 171.

[141] See fn 172.

[142] See fn 173.

[143] Para 74.

[144] This raises the issue of standard of proof. The Privy Council confirmed the good arguable case test in *Bols Distilleries v Superior Yacht Services Limited* [2006] UKPC 45.

[145] See fn 134.

[146] See fn 135. It may be possible to recover such costs or at least part of them from the court which declines jurisdiction or by way of damages from the court which has jurisdiction under the jurisdiction clause.

[147] Without the same criteria being applied to determine the validity of the jurisdiction clause.

has been obtained. The party who has commenced proceedings in breach of the jurisdiction clause, probably for negative declaratory relief, is most likely to have commenced proceedings in the courts of the State where it is domiciled and that is the State where it is most likely to have assets and where the claimant in the court chosen most needs to be able to enforce.

It is not surprising that a further solution, proposed by the UK Government in *Gasser*, was rejected. This was that the court second seised could examine the jurisdiction of the court first seised where the proceedings were commenced in the court first seised in bad faith to block proceedings in the court second seised, or if the court first seised has not determined its own jurisdiction within a reasonable time. What is reasonable in all the circumstances in the opinion of one court may differ somewhat from the opinion of another court. Even once the issue has been decided it may be subject to appeal or appeals.

Under the provisions on recognition and enforcement of judgments in the Recast Regulation it is not permissible for the court of an EU Member State requested to recognise a judgment of another EU Member State to review the jurisdiction of the latter court to give that judgment.[148] Thus the recognising court cannot refuse to recognise a judgment on the ground that there was an exclusive jurisdiction agreement in favour of the court of a State other than that of the court which has given the judgment which is to be recognised. In other words by the time the recognition stage has been reached jurisdiction is no longer an issue.

However, the decision of the court of an EU Member State that it does not have jurisdiction because there is a valid jurisdiction agreement in favour of a Lugano Member State court is binding on any other EU Member State court. In *Gothaer Allgemeine Versicherung AG v Samskip GmbH*[149] the Court of Justice of the European Union held that where the Belgian court had dismissed actions on the ground that the bill of lading contained a jurisdiction clause providing that any dispute arising thereunder was to be decided by the Icelandic courts according to Icelandic law the German Court was not only bound by the decision that the Belgian court did not have jurisdiction, but also by the reason for that decision which was that there was a valid Icelandic jurisdiction clause.

B. Arbitration

i. Neutral Choice

Within the European Union the EU Member States may apply different rules as to the validity of an arbitration clause, even though the EU Member States are parties to the New York Convention. A neutral choice of the place of arbitration in carriage of goods by sea is permitted under English law but such a choice will not be binding in all EU Member States. For example, where an EU Member State has ratified the

---

[148] Art 35(3), except as provided in Art 35(1) in the case of insurance, consumer contracts, or exclusive jurisdiction under Art 22.
[149] Case C-456/11.

Hamburg Rules, such as Austria, the Czech Republic, Hungary and Romania, or even where they have not, but have adopted similar rules in their national legislation, such as the Nordic countries,[150] the cargo claimant can choose the place of arbitration from a list of places linked with the carriage of goods, or the place chosen.

ii. Third Parties

In some EU Member States the rules as to whether the arbitration clause is incorporated at all are stricter than under English law.[151] Even if the clause is incorporated, the rules as to whether it binds a third party, such as the transferee of the transport document, subrogated insurer, or liability insurer in a direct action may differ. Difficulties may arise as a result of the different approaches in the EU Member States.

iii. Who Decides?

In *Allianz SpA (formerly Riunione Adriatica di Sicurta SpA) v West Tankers Inc (The Front Comor)*[152] the European Court of Justice held that if a party commences court proceedings in an EU Member State, the English court cannot grant an anti-suit injunction to restrain the respondent in the English arbitration from pursuing those court proceedings. There must be mutual trust between the EU Member States and the court of the EU Member State must be trusted to come to its own correct determination as to whether there is a valid arbitration clause. If there is such a clause, all the EU Member States are parties to the New York Convention and therefore each EU Member State would be obliged to stay its court proceedings in favour of arbitration. In *The Front Comor* the European Court of Justice rejected the argument that as arbitration proceedings fall outside the scope of the EC Jurisdiction Regulation, as they are excluded by Article 1(2)(d),[153] the judgment of another EU Member State in relation to the validity of the arbitration agreement was also not within the EC Jurisdiction Regulation and therefore for the English court to grant an anti-suit injunction was not inconsistent with the EC Jurisdiction Regulation. The court held that as the Italian court in that case was seised of a substantive dispute for damages in a tort claim as a result of the *Front Comor* hitting the Italian

---

[150] See, eg paras 1.54 and 14.31 of T Falkanger, HJ Bull and L Brautaset, *Scandinavian Maritime Law, The Norwegian Perspective*, 3rd edn, 2011 Universitetsforlaget.

[151] See, eg *National Navigation Co v Endesa Generacion SA (The Wadi Sudr)* [2009] EWCA Civ 1397; [2010] 2 All ER (Comm) 1243 discussed at p 248.

[152] Case C185/07 *Allianz SpA (formerly Riunione Adriatica Di Sicurta SpA) v West Tankers Inc (The Front Comor)* [2009] 1 AC 1138; [2009] 1 Lloyd's Rep 413 applied in *Youell v La Réunion Aérienne* [2009] EWCA Civ 175; [2009] 1 Lloyd's Rep 586. See Y Baatz and A Sandiforth, 'A Setback for Arbitration' [2009] 9 STL.

[153] Case C-190/89, *Marc Rich & Co. A.G. v Societa Italiana P.A. (The Atlantic Emperor)* [1992] 1 Lloyd's Rep 342; *The Heidberg* [1994] 2 Lloyd's Rep 287 at pp 298–303; *Toepfer International GmbH v Société Cargill France* [1998] 1 Lloyd's Rep 379; Case C-391/95 *Van Uden Maritime BV v Kommanditgesellschaft in Firma Deco-Line* [1999] All ER (EC) 258 ECJ; *Navigation Maritime Bulgare v Rustal Trading Ltd (The Ivan Zagubanski)* [2002] 1 Lloyd's Rep 106 and *Through Transport Mutual Insurance Association (Eurasia) Ltd v New India Assurance Co Ltd (The Hari Bhum)* [2004] EWCA (Civ) 1598; [2005] 1 Lloyd's Rep 67; *A v B* [2006] EWHC 2006 (Comm), [2007] 1 Lloyd's Rep 237.

claimants' jetty in Syracuse, and the Italian court had jurisdiction to decide the substantive claim under Article 5(3) of the EC Jurisdiction Regulation, unless there was a valid arbitration agreement, the issue as to whether there was a valid arbitration clause was a preliminary issue to the substantive claim which fell within the EC Jurisdiction Regulation. Therefore it was inconsistent with the Regulation for the English court to grant an anti-suit injunction restraining the Italian claimant from pursuing proceedings within the EC Jurisdiction Regulation in Italy.

The unfortunate result of the decision of the European Court of Justice in *The Front Comor* is that there may be, and indeed were in *The Front Comor*, parallel arbitration proceedings in one EU Member State and court proceedings in another EU Member State. There is no mechanism to prevent parallel proceedings with the consequent duplication of costs; risk of conflicting decisions, both as to whether there is a binding arbitration agreement and on the substance of the dispute; and complex questions on recognition and enforcement.[154] If the other party is determined to pursue proceedings in its own court for its own advantage,[155] there remains uncertainty as to whether the foreign court judgment can be refused recognition in the English courts and this may ultimately depend on timing. In *The Front Comor*[156] once the arbitration award had been made, but before any decision of the Italian court on jurisdiction, the Court of Appeal upheld the decision of Field J. that the English court had jurisdiction to grant leave to enforce the award[157] and to enter judgment in terms of the award.[158] The arbitrators held that the shipowners had no liability whatsoever in contract, tort or otherwise to the jetty owners or their subrogated insurers, and if this were wrong, that any liability was limited under the Convention on Limitation of Liability for Maritime Claims 1976.

The case of *The Wadi Sudr*[159] may be contrasted with *The Front Comor* as in that case the Spanish court gave their judgment that no arbitration clause was incorporated into the bill of lading and that the shipowners had waived their right to rely on the arbitration clause by commencing the English court proceedings, before either the London arbitration tribunal or English court could consider jurisdiction and the Court of Appeal held that the arbitrators were bound by the Spanish judgment.

It will be important to obtain the award of the arbitrators and enter judgment in terms of the award or a declaration from the English court, as quickly as possible on the validity of the arbitration clause, and in any event before the judgment of the

---

[154] See also *National Navigation Co v Endesa Generacion SA (The Wadi Sudr)* [2009] EWCA Civ 1397; [2010] 2 All ER (Comm) 1243 noted in Y Baatz, 'A Jurisdiction Race in the Dark' [2010] LMCLQ 364.

[155] In the case of *The Wadi Sudr*, because Spanish law imposed absolute liability rather than an obligation to exercise due diligence under English law. In the case of *The Front Comor* the Italian insurers may have preferred the Italian court's interpretation of the exception of navigational error.

[156] *West Tankers Inc v Allianz SpA* [2012] EWCA Civ 27; [2012] 2 All ER (Comm) 113 [35] – [39]; [2011] EWHC 829 (Comm); [2011] 2 All ER (Comm) 1. The Court of Appeal approved *African Fertilizers and Chemicals NIG Ltd v B D Shipsnavo GmbH & Co Reederei KG* [2011] EWHC 2452 (Comm); [2011] 2 Lloyd's Rep 531 which is under appeal. See also *Sovarex SA v Romero Alvarez SA* [2011] EWHC 1661 (Comm); [2012] 1 All ER (Comm) 207.

[157] Pursuant to s 66(1) of the Arbitration Act 1996.

[158] Pursuant to s 66(2) of the Arbitration Act 1996.

[159] [2009] EWCA Civ 1397; [2010] 2 All ER (Comm) 1243 noted in Y Baatz, 'A Jurisdiction Race in the Dark' [2010] LMCLQ 364.

court of the other EU Member State. This may give a defence to recognition of any subsequent judgment of the other EU Member State court under Article 34(3) of the EC Jurisdiction Regulation. In *The Wadi Sudr* Waller L.J. indicated *obiter* that he thought this would be the position,[160] but the point is controversial.[161]

In the latest twist of *The Front Comor* litigation Flaux J. held[162] that the arbitration tribunal were not deprived, by reason of European law, of the jurisdiction to award equitable damages for breach of the obligation to arbitrate. The damages claimed were for legal fees and expenses reasonably incurred in connection with the Italian proceedings and for an indemnity against an award made against the shipowners in the Italian proceedings which is greater than the liability of the shipowners as established in the London arbitration. Commenting on *The Wadi Sudr* Flaux J. stated in *The Front Comor*,[163]

> …The Regulation simply does not apply to arbitration or arbitral tribunals. The reason why the arbitrators were bound to recognise the Spanish judgment was nothing to do with any principle of European law derived from the Regulation but because of the English common law doctrine of res judicata.'

It is important that a party who chooses London arbitration can rely on its disputes being determined by the arbitrators supported by the English court and will not land up in the courts of a completely different country. This is not just a matter of protecting London arbitration, but arbitration in any chosen EU Member State. Although the Advocate General and the European Court of Justice in *The Front Comor* were not swayed in their decision by commercial practicalities, arbitration anywhere in the European Union will be under pressure as a result of competition from other centres of arbitration such as New York, Bermuda and Singapore, and must consider how best to maintain their competitive edge.

Originally it was intended that there should also be European legislation to deal with arbitration but that has never materialised.[164] The Heidelberg Review

---

[160] *Ibid* [63]. This was also the view, *obiter*, of Judge Diamond Q.C. in *Partenreederei M/S Heidberg v Grosvenor Grain and Feed Co. Ltd (The Heidberg)* [1994] 2 Lloyd's Rep 287 at 301 to 302 where he distinguishes between the position when the judgment of the foreign court is given before (the facts of the case he had to decide) and after the English court appoints an arbitrator.

[161] See Briggs and Rees, *Civil Jurisdiction and Judgments Act*, 5th edition, 2009, paras 7.23 and 8.14; Dicey, Morris and Collins, *The Conflict of Laws*, 15th edn, 2012, 14-206 to 14.213 and Hans Van Houtte, 'Why not include Arbitration in The Brussels Jurisdiction Regulation?' (2005) Arbitration International, Vol. 21, No. 4 509 at 514 and 520 where it was proposed that a new fifth ground be added to Art 33 to refuse recognition or enforcement of a judgment which is irreconcilable with an arbitral award. The position does not appear to be uniform throughout the EU Member States – see, eg B Hess, T Pfeiffer and P Schlosser 'The Brussels I -- Regulation (EC) No 44/2001 The Heidelberg Report on the Application of Regulation Brussels I in 25 Member States' (Study JLS/C4/2005/03), CH Beck, Hart, Nomos, 2008 ('the Heidelberg Report') para 127 which states that 'the recognition of judgments of other Member States that were given despite an arbitration agreement is widely accepted in case law and legal doctrine' and the Report from the Commission to the European Parliament COM(2009) 174 final dated 21 April 2009 para 3.7. See also J Lavelle, 'Declarations of validity: a cunning vehicle for non-recognition of a foreign judgment in a post-Front Comor era?' [2010] Arbitration Monthly.

[162] *West Tankers Inc v Allianz SpA* [2012] EWHC 854 (Comm); [2012] 2 All ER (Comm) 395; [2012] 2 Lloyd's Rep 103. For a history of this litigation see paras [4]–[16].

[163] [67].

[164] See the Heidelberg Review para 105 and the Schlosser Report.

proposed two possible alternative solutions. First the deletion of Article 1(2)(d) of the EC Jurisdiction Regulation. This would bring arbitration within the scope of the Regulation. Such an amendment was suggested by Advocate General Kokott in her opinion in *The Front Comor*. The New York Convention would prevail over the Regulation as a result of Article 71 of the Regulation. This would mean that if the English court has been requested to declare, or has already given a judgment, that an arbitration clause is valid and binds the subrogated insurer, and it was the court first seised, the court second seised would be obliged to stay its proceedings under Article 27 of the Regulation. Alternatively if the English court had already given a judgment that the arbitration clause was valid and binding, that judgment would have to be recognised and enforced in any other EU Member State.

The second solution was to insert new provisions in the Regulation to deal with the interface between arbitration and the Regulation including specific provisions: first that the courts of the Member State in which the arbitration takes place have exclusive jurisdiction in relation to ancillary proceedings in support of the arbitration; secondly requiring a court of a Member State to stay its proceedings if its jurisdiction is contested due to an arbitration clause where the court of the Member State designated in the arbitration agreement is seised in relation to the binding nature of the arbitration agreement and thirdly a new recital recognizing the parties' choice as to the place of arbitration, but providing default provisions if no such choice is made.[165]

The European Commission preferred the second solution and proposed amendments to the Regulation[166] to 'enhance the effectiveness of arbitration agreements in Europe, prevent parallel court and arbitration proceedings, and eliminate the incentive for abusive litigation tactics.'[167] Article 29(4) of the revised Regulation provided that where the jurisdiction of the courts of a Member State is contested because there is an arbitration agreement providing for arbitration in another Member State, the court shall stay its proceedings where the courts of the Member State where the seat of the arbitration is located or the arbitration tribunal have been seised of proceedings to determine, as their main object or as an incidental question, the existence, validity or effects of that arbitration agreement. The risk is that a party alleges an arbitration agreement and it is found that there is not one.[168]

In a draft report of the Committee on Legal Affairs this revision was deleted and in the draft European Parliament Legislative Resolution[169] Article 1(2)(d) was amended so that the Regulation did not cover '(d) arbitration, including judicial procedures ruling on the validity or extent of arbitral competence as a principal

[165] See clause 6 of the LMAA Rules.
[166] COM (2010) 748. See A Briggs, *'The Brussels I bis Regulation Appears on the Horizon'* [2011] LMCLQ 157 for a discussion of those proposals.
[167] COM (2010) 748 Explanatory Memorandum para 3.1.4.
[168] *Claxton Engineering Services Ltd v TXM Olaj-Es Gazkutato KFT (No 2)* [2011] EWHC 345; [2011] 1 Lloyd's Rep 510 where an injunction was granted to restrain arbitration proceedings in Hungary where the English court had already given a judgment, after finding that there was no Hungarian arbitration clause but an exclusive English jurisdiction clause.
[169] Dated 28 June 2011 (2010/0383 (COD)).

issue or as an incidental or preliminary question.'[170] This raised the question whether the English court could grant an anti-suit injunction to restrain the respondent in the London arbitration proceedings from pursuing proceedings in the courts of another EU Member State on the preliminary issue of whether there is a valid arbitration clause. This would no longer be inconsistent with the EC Jurisdiction Regulation as for the EU Member State to consider whether there is a London arbitration clause falls outside the scope of the EC Jurisdiction Regulation.

Article 1(2)(d) of the Recast Regulation simply excludes arbitration from the scope of the Regulation and Article 73 provides that the Regulation shall not affect the application of the New York Convention. Recital 12 states that a ruling by the court of a Member State as to whether or not an arbitration agreement is null and void, inoperative or incapable of being performed should not be subject to the rules of recognition and enforcement laid down in the Regulation, regardless of whether the court decided on this as a principal issue or as an incidental question. The decision of *The Front Comor* has therefore been reversed. Neither an English court judgment nor the Italian court judgment as to the validity of the arbitration agreement would be a Regulation judgment. However, if the court of an EU Member State decides that there is not a valid arbitration clause and proceeds to a substantive judgment on the merits, Recital 12 further states that that judgment will not be precluded from being recognised or enforced under the Regulation. This should not prejudice the competence of the courts of the Member States to decide on the recognition and enforcement of arbitral awards in accordance with the New York Convention which takes precedence over the Recast Regulation. Therefore the London arbitration award should be able to be enforced in Italy under the New York Convention.

IV. THE INTERNATIONAL POSITION

A. The Background

There is no global convention that governs jurisdiction, recognition and enforcement of judgments or which law is applicable. The Hague Conference on Private International Law started work in 1992 on a draft convention on the international jurisdiction of courts and the recognition and enforcement of their judgments abroad. It failed to achieve its goals. More recently there have been efforts to revive the project. It was possible to salvage a more limited convention dealing with jurisdiction agreements: the 2005 Hague Convention on Choice of Court Agreements.[171] That Convention recognises freedom to choose court jurisdiction. It has never come into force. However, even if it does so,[172] it does not apply to the

---

[170] See also the amended Recital 11.

[171] On 30 June 2005 the Final Act of the Twentieth Session of the Hague Conference on Private International Law was signed including the Convention on Choice of Court agreements. The text of the Convention is available from http://www.hcch.net/index_en.php?act=conventions.text&cid=98.

[172] Two ratifications or accessions are required - Art 31. As at July 2013, Mexico had acceded to the Convention on 26 September 2007, the United States of America had signed on 19 January 2009 and

carriage of goods.[173] The reason[174] for this is firstly that some States which give effect to the Hague Rules would not agree to a convention which permitted a carrier to escape the liability those rules impose mandatorily by choosing the jurisdiction of another State[175] and secondly that the details of the draft Rotterdam Rules were still being finalised.

It is accepted internationally that there should be some limit on the freedom of contract in the carriage of goods by sea in transport documents, other than charterparties, as regards the minimum obligations imposed on the carrier. The major reason for this is to protect the rights of third parties such as the consignee under a straight bill of lading[176] or the transferee of a transferable bill of lading. Thus if such a party sues the carrier it knows that the carrier will have minimum obligations which it cannot contract out of. If all States agreed to be bound by the same rules as to substantive liability it might be said that there was no need for any provisions on jurisdiction or arbitration as any court or arbitration tribunal chosen would apply the same rules. Unfortunately as there is no international uniformity on substantive law, it may be argued that there needs to be some provision which prevents a party intentionally providing for a jurisdiction so that it may avoid the rules.

Some, however, go further than that and argue that even where the substantive liability has been agreed between States, there should be limits on the freedom to contract as to jurisdiction or the place of arbitration in order to protect the rights of the cargo interests. For example, it has been suggested that it is usually the carrier that has the upper hand as far as choice of jurisdiction is concerned as standard form transport documents are drafted by the carrier and therefore frequently contain a choice of the jurisdiction where the carrier has its principal place of business.[177] This is not always the case as some shippers have stronger bargaining power than carriers.[178] Either party may prefer to use its local courts. Therefore some have argued that a new international convention should strike a better balance between the interests of the carrier and the cargo interests. There are, however, good reasons for choosing the principal place of business of the carrier as there is usually only one contractual carrier, but there may be many cargo interests located in different States, with the risk of multiple proceedings arising out of the same facts. Where

---

the European Community, now replaced by the European Union, signed on 1 April 2009 (but this does not bind Denmark).

[173] Art 2(2)(f) excludes the carriage of passengers and goods and Art 2(2)(g) excludes marine pollution, limitation of liability for maritime claims, general average and emergency towage and salvage. The Convention does apply to contracts of insurance and reinsurance that relate to such matters (Art 17).

[174] M Dogauchi and T Hartley 'Explanatory Report Preliminary Draft Convention on Exclusive Choice of Court Agreements' (preliminary document No 26 of December 2004) available from http://www.hcch.net/index_en.php?act=publications.details&pid=3512&dtid=35.

[175] See p 246.

[176] *J.I. MacWilliam Co Inc v Mediterranean Shipping Co S.A. (The Rafaela S)* [2005] 1 Lloyd's Rep 347.

[177] See, eg R Herber 'Jurisdiction and Arbitration - Should the New Convention Contain Rules on these Subjects?' [2002] LMCLQ 405 at p 406 where it is suggested that the shipper has no power to negotiate the jurisdiction clause.

[178] For example, the US Ocean Liner Service Agreements – see DR Thomas (gen ed), *The Carriage of Goods by Sea under the Rotterdam Rules*, Lloyd's List, 2010, paras 1.81 to 1.84.

there is multimodal transport the number of possible locations that could be connected with the claim are also multiplied. The cargo interests usually have the protection of being able to obtain security for their claim by arresting the carrier's ship and therefore being able to enforce any judgment or award swiftly. In practice it will usually be the cargo interests' subrogated insurers who pursue any claims against the carrier. It is doubtful that they are in need of consumer protection.[179]

There is no international harmony on which rules apply compulsorily to transport documents for the carriage of goods by sea. Some States still give effect to the Hague Rules[180] (most notably the United States of America by its US Carriage of Goods by Sea Act 1936 but this Act applies the Rules to both inward and outward shipments). Other States give effect to the Hague-Visby Rules (including most EU Member States), and yet other States (including a few EU Member States), give effect to the Hamburg Rules. National legislation which gives effect to a set of Rules may provide for some local variation or a combination of more than one set of Rules. In a final bid for international unity, the United Nations Commission on International Trade Law produced the Rotterdam Rules.[181] They are not yet in force.[182]

Furthermore the approach taken to jurisdiction and arbitration clauses in the maritime conventions varies significantly.[183] Neither the Hague nor the Hague-Visby Rules contain any specific provisions on jurisdiction or arbitration. The Hamburg Rules contain provisions on both jurisdiction and arbitration, as do many of the other transport conventions in relation to the carriage of goods by air, road and rail, but not inland waterways.[184] Such provisions restrict the effect of exclusive court or arbitration agreements. Although the Hamburg Rules have not achieved the international support that had been hoped for, some states which did not ratify them, such as Canada and the Nordic countries, have introduced similar national legislation on jurisdiction.[185]

The international position is therefore fragmented and confused. There is no international harmony as to which rules apply when and no coordinated approach

---

[179] Under English law the subrogated cargo insurers would be bound by the jurisdiction or arbitration clause in the bill of lading contract – see fn 81 However, see F Berlingieri, in A von Ziegler et al, *The Rotterdam Rules 2008*, 2010, Wolters Kluwer at 22 where he states that the subrogated insurer would not be bound by the jurisdiction or arbitration clause under Art 66(a) or 75(2)(b) of the Rotterdam Rules.

[180] The International Convention for the Unification of Certain Rules of Law Relating to Bills of Lading (Brussels 25 August 1924).

[181] See generally Y Baatz et al, *The Rotterdam Rules: A Practical Annotation*, Informa, 2009; D R Thomas (ed), *A New Convention for the Carriage of Goods by Sea – The Rotterdam Rules*, Lawtext Publishing Limited, 2009; gen. ed. DR Thomas, *The Carriage of Goods by Sea under the Rotterdam Rules*, Lloyd's List, 2010; A Diamond, 'The Rotterdam Rules' [2009] LMCLQ 445; M Sturley et al, *The Rotterdam Rules*, 2010, Sweet & Maxwell and A von Ziegler et al, *The Rotterdam Rules 2008*, 2010, Wolters Kluwer.

[182] As at 26 February 2013 the Rotterdam Rules have been signed by Armenia, Cameroon, Congo, the Democratic Republic of Congo, Denmark, France, Gabon, Ghana, Greece, Guinea, Luxembourg, Madagascar, Mali, Netherlands, Niger, Nigeria, Norway, Poland, Senegal, Spain, Sweden, Switzerland, Togo and the United States of America. Only Spain and Togo have ratified.

[183] See page 255.

[184] R Herber 'Jurisdiction and Arbitration - Should the New Convention Contain Rules on these Subjects?' [2002] LMCLQ 405 for a comparison of the provisions of those conventions.

[185] See fn 111.

between conventions on our three challenges. We will now turn to the most recent convention, the Rotterdam Rules, to consider its provisions on jurisdiction and arbitration in more detail.

B. The Rotterdam Rules

i. Opt In

The Rotterdam Rules did not originally provide for jurisdiction and arbitration. As the reports of the UNCITRAL Transport Law Working Group (Working Group III) show, there were diametrically opposed views as to whether all or any exclusive choice of court clauses should be recognised and whether, if they were recognised, they should bind third parties, and on what conditions.[186] There were also strong views in favour of arbitration agreements provided that arbitration would not be allowed to circumvent the bases of jurisdiction in the Convention, and other views against all arbitration.[187]

It was decided at the twentieth session of Working Group III in October 2007 that the provisions on jurisdiction and arbitration would not apply unless a State specifically chose them. It was hoped that this would encourage States to ratify the Rotterdam Rules, and to do so quickly.[188] Therefore the provisions of Chapter 14 on Jurisdiction and Chapter 15 on Arbitration will only bind Contracting States that declare in accordance with Article 91 that they will be bound by each of them.[189] Such declarations may be made[190] or withdrawn at any time.[191] So a State may ratify the Rotterdam Rules and not opt in to either of the chapters on jurisdiction and arbitration or may opt in to either or both of them.[192] The problem with this is that it creates further diversity when one of the key reasons for a new convention was to seek to achieve international harmonisation.[193]

---

[186] Reports of Working Group III on its fourteenth session A/CN 9/572 paras 130–34; fifteenth session A/CN 9/576 paras 156-68; sixteenth working session A/CN 9/591 paras 20–25; and eighteenth session A/CN 9/616 paras 245-60. All UNCITRAL working group reports are available from http://www.uncitral.org/uncitral/en/commission/working_groups/3Transport.html.

[187] *Ibid* fourteenth session paras 151 to 157; fifteenth session paras 176 to 179; sixteenth working session paras 85 to 103; eighteenth session paras 267 to 279.

[188] *Ibid* twentieth session A/CN 9/642 paras 202 to 05; 216 to18.

[189] Arts 74 and 78 respectively. Pursuant to Art 93(3) any reference to 'Contracting States' applies equally to a regional economic integration organisation but Art 93(1) which provides that a regional economic integration organisation may sign, ratify, accept, approve or accede to this Convention does not mention making a declaration within Art 91.

[190] Art 91(1). A declaration will take effect at the same time as the Convention enters into force in a Contracting State, but if the declaration is made after such entry into force it will take effect six months after the notification of the declaration is received by the depositary (Art 91(4)).

[191] Art 91(5). A declaration may be withdrawn and the withdrawal would be effective six months after notification of withdrawal is received by the depositary.

[192] A proposal that the ability to opt into the chapter on arbitration should be tied to opting into the chapter on jurisdiction was rejected. See the Report of Working Group III on its twentieth session A/CN 9/642 para 217.

[193] See W Tetley, Ch 12 'Some General Criticisms of the Rotterdam Rules', *A New Convention for the Carriage of Goods by Sea – The Rotterdam Rules*, p 286.

The Rotterdam Rules distinguish between those contracts to which the parties are deemed to be in need of mandatory protection and those contracts called volume contracts.[194] The parties to volume contracts have greater, although still limited, freedom to agree court jurisdiction or arbitration agreements, in certain circumstances. Those circumstances differ as between the carrier and the shipper and as between the carrier and a third party.

ii. Court Jurisdiction

An exclusive jurisdiction clause will only be binding if:

1. as between the shipper and the carrier it is in a volume contract; the parties agree on exclusive court jurisdiction; the volume contract clearly states the names and addresses of the parties and either (i) it is individually negotiated or (ii) contains a prominent statement that there is an exclusive choice of court agreement and specifies the sections of the volume contract containing that agreement, and clearly designates the courts of one Contracting State or one or more specific courts of one Contracting State;[195] or

2. as between the carrier and a third party, but not a maritime performing party, it is in a volume contract and it satisfies the requirements of Article 67(1) set out in the previous paragraph and satisfies the requirements of Article 67(2) which are:

   (a) the court chosen is in the same place as the domicile[196] of the carrier;[197] the contractual place of receipt; the contractual place of delivery; the port where the goods are initially loaded on a ship or the port where the goods are finally discharged from a ship;

   (b) that agreement is contained in the transport document or electronic transport record;

   (c) that person is given timely and adequate notice[198] of the court where the action shall be brought and that the jurisdiction of that court is exclusive; and the law of the court seized recognises that that person may be bound by the exclusive choice of court agreement[199]; or

---

[194] A volume contract is defined in Art 1(2) as a 'contract of carriage that provides for the carriage of a specified quantity of goods in a series of shipments during an agreed period of time. The specification of the quantity may include a minimum, a maximum or a certain range'. See Y Baatz et al, *The Rotterdam Rules: A Practical Annotation*, Informa, 2009 para 1-04; R Asariotis 'UNCITRAL Draft Convention on Contracts for the Carriage of Goods Wholly or Partly by Sea: Mandatory Rules and Freedom of Contract' in A Antapassis, L Athanassiou and E Rosaeg (eds) *Competition and Regulation in Shipping and Shipping Related Industries* (Martinus Nijhoff 2009); A Diamond, 'The Rotterdam Rules' [2009] LMCLQ 445; D R Thomas, Ch 3 'An Analysis of the Liability Regime of Carriers and Maritime Performing Parties', *A New Convention for the Carriage of Goods by Sea – The Rotterdam Rules*, Lawtext Publishing, pp 52 and 84–88; Gen ed. D R Thomas, *The Carriage of Goods by Sea under the Rotterdam Rules*, Lloyd's List, 2010, paras 1.77 to 1.108; M Sturley et al, *The Rotterdam Rules*, 2010, Sweet & Maxwell and A von Ziegler et al, *The Rotterdam Rules 2008*, 2010, Wolters Kluwer.

[195] Art 67(1)(a),(b).

[196] Defined in Art 1(29).

[197] The principal place of business of the carrier is often chosen in standard form contracts eg Conlinebill. This falls within the definition of domicile in Art 1(29)(a)(iii).

[198] Any agreement and notice under this art must be in writing (Art 3).

[199] Under English law the 'lawful holder' of a transferable bill of lading does have transferred to it the

3. as between the parties to the dispute the clause is concluded after the dispute has arisen.[200]

In all three cases the exclusive jurisdiction provision will be overridden if the parties vary their agreement by making a new agreement under Article 72(1) or submit to the jurisdiction of the court of another Contracting State under Article 72(2), or another court has jurisdiction by virtue of an international convention under Article 70(b). Where there is an exclusive court jurisdiction agreement the carrier can commence proceedings first by seeking a declaration of non-liability in the court chosen.[201]

Where there is no such exclusive jurisdiction agreement Article 66 provides that the claimant can choose to sue the carrier in a number of places including in a competent court or courts of a Contracting State agreed between the shipper and the carrier for the purpose of deciding claims against the carrier that may arise under the Rotterdam Rules.[202]

iii. Arbitration

The key question in the Rotterdam Rules is where arbitration will take place. To a large extent mirroring the provisions on court jurisdiction, Chapter 15 again draws a distinction between volume contracts which satisfy certain requirements and other contracts. Thus the choice of where the arbitration will take place is binding for disputes 'between the parties to the agreement' where the agreement is a volume contract which satisfies the same requirements under Article 75(3) as for a jurisdiction agreement under Article 67(1)(a) (with necessary amendments to reflect that this is an arbitration agreement rather than a court jurisdiction clause), but does not need to provide for a place of arbitration in a Contracting State as required by Article 67(1)(b). That choice will also be binding on 'a person who is not a party to the volume contract,' provided it satisfies the requirements in Article 75(3) and additionally satisfies Article 75(4). This latter provision sets out the same requirements as for a jurisdiction agreement (with necessary amendments), save for the requirement that the applicable law permits that person to be bound by the arbitration agreement,[203] rather than the law of the forum which applies to court

---

rights and liabilities under the bill of lading pursuant to ss 2(1) and 3 of the Carriage of Goods by Sea Act 1992.

[200] Art 72(1).

[201] Art 71(2) is against actions for declaration of non-liability but begins 'Except when there is an exclusive choice of court agreement that is binding pursuant to articles 67 or 72'.

[202] Compare Art 21(1) of the Hamburg Rules. Unlike Art 21(1)(b) of the Hamburg Rules, the Rotterdam Rules do not provide for the place where the contract was made.

[203] Art 75(4)(d). *Raffeisen Zentralbank Osterreich AG v Five Star General Trading LLC (The Mount I)* [2001] EWCA Civ 68; [2001] 1 Lloyd's Rep 597 in relation to an assignment; *Schiffahrtsgesellschaft Detlev von Appen GmbH v Voest Alpine Intertrading GmbH (The Jay Bola)* [1997] 2 Lloyd's Rep 279 per Hobhouse LJ at pp 286-5 (arbitration clause in time and voyage charterpaties bound subrogated insurers); *Through Transport Mutual Insurance Association (Eurasia) Ltd v New India Assurance Co Ltd (The Hari Bhum)* [2004] EWCA Civ 1598; [2005] 1 Lloyd's Rep 67 (CA) noted J Harris 'Arbitration

jurisdiction clauses.[204] Any term of an arbitration clause that is inconsistent with these provisions is void.[205]

The parties may agree to resolve a dispute by arbitration in any place after a dispute has arisen.[206]

If, however, the contract is not a volume contract, or, if it is, but the requirements of Article 75(3) and/or (4) are not satisfied, and the parties have not entered into an arbitration agreement after a dispute has arisen, the cargo claimant is still bound to arbitrate but can choose to arbitrate in any of the six places listed in Article 75(2) ie the place chosen in the arbitration agreement; or in a State where the carrier is domiciled, or the contractual place of receipt or delivery of the goods is located, or the port where the goods are initially loaded on or finally discharged from a ship is located.

I have argued elsewhere that the arbitration provisions are very unappealing.[207] A neutral place chosen by the parties for the expertise of the arbitrators in maritime matters, would be infinitely preferable to arbitration in the place of receipt of the goods, if that is an inland place to which a container has been carried after the sea leg, where there is no experience of arbitration and no knowledge of the complex Rotterdam Rules. Chester Hooper has written that 'the arbitration provisions are meant to prevent the parties from using an arbitration clause to circumvent the jurisdiction chapter.'[208]

Clauses and the Restraint of Proceedings in Another Member State of the European Union' [2005] LMCLQ 159 and *The Front Comor* [2005] EWHC 454; [2005] 2 Lloyd's Rep 257 in relation to an insurer exercising its subrogated right to sue where there was a claim in tort which was held to fall within the charterparty arbitration clause. *The Front Comor* subsequently went to the House of Lords and the European Court of Justice (Case C185/07 *Allianz SpA (formerly Riunione Adriatica Di Sicurta SpA) v West Tankers Inc (The Front Comor)* (see pp 263–66) but not on the point whether a subrogated insurer is bound by an arbitration agreement.

[204] Art 67(2)(d).

[205] Art 75(5).

[206] Art 77. Compare Hamburg Rules Art 22(6).

[207] See Y Baatz et al, *The Rotterdam Rules: A Practical Annotation*, Informa, 2009, pp 237–39. See also F Berlingieri, A Review of Some Recent Analyses of the Rotterdam Rules, 2009 Il Diritto Marittimo pp 1028 and 1029 agreeing with those criticisms.

[208] A von Ziegler et al, *The Rotterdam Rules 2008*, 2010, Wolters Kluwer at p 323. Chester Hooper further states at p 326, 'The choices offered by the Rotterdam Rules Art 75(2) will probably convince carriers not to include arbitration clauses in their form transport documents or electronic records. Such an agreement would allow the cargo side to commence arbitration against the carrier in a place that might not have an established arbitration procedure. Cargo claimants could choose a place of arbitration that would be inconvenient for the carrier or would place the carrier at a disadvantage. By choosing an inconvenient place for the carrier to arbitrate, the cargo claimant might apply settlement pressure on the carrier. This pressure would, ironically, be similar to the pressure now applied by some carriers when choosing a forum in which to litigate or arbitrate. The Rotterdam Rules should, of course, provide the same substantive law in all its contracting states, but the procedure may change. Carriers would probably feel more comfortable in allowing cargo interests to sue in a court whose results may be more predictable than would be obtained by the unknown procedure of an unfamiliar arbitration forum.' See also M Sturley *et al, The Rotterdam Rules*, Sweet & Maxwell, 2010 paras 12.071–12.074 and 12.079 and 12.080 where it is stated that if Chapter 15 of the Rotterdam Rules has the effect of ensuring that carriers do not include arbitration clauses in bills of lading subject to the regime, it will be a success. In this author's view such an attitude is contrary to the spirit of the New York Convention.

iv. Criticisms of the Rotterdam Rules

The two chapters on jurisdiction and arbitration in the Rotterdam Rules do not provide the solution on jurisdiction and arbitration for carriage of goods by sea. First it is unlikely that there will be international harmony as States have to opt in to those chapters which are extremely controversial. Indeed it is likely that there will be further diversity. Secondly where the States have all agreed on the same rules to determine liability it is unnecessary to have specific rules as between those States restricting party choice, provided a real choice has been made. Thirdly the provisions in the Rotterdam Rules on jurisdiction and arbitration are much more restrictive and complex than the position under the English common law rules, Article 23 of the EC Jurisdiction Regulation or the Arbitration Act 1996. None of those systems provides for consumer protection in contracts for the carriage of goods by sea. Nor do they make any distinction between volume and other contracts, a distinction which is difficult to justify, as the safeguards put in place for volume contracts would be more than sufficient for all contracts to which the Rotterdam Rules apply, both for the original parties and for third parties who take the benefit of that contract. Thus the two chapters have failed to provide a satisfactory balance between the interests of the carrier and the cargo interests, especially where the substantive rules are much more cargo friendly as they shift the balance of risk between the carrier and the shipper.[209] A neutral choice of forum cannot bind a third party. Jurisdiction should not be imposed on the carrier as this could have a detrimental economic impact on those jurisdictions if carriers preferred not to trade to such places at the risk of litigation with unpredictable results which could be a significant factor in assessing the profitability of certain trades.[210] Fourthly the Rotterdam Rules fail to resolve the central issue whether a third party will be bound by the jurisdiction agreement as the law of the court seized must recognise that that person may be bound by the exclusive choice of court agreement or the applicable law permit that person to be bound by the arbitration agreement. In summary these provisions are likely to lead to major differences of approach by Contracting States and therefore do not provide international harmony. This is a fatal flaw of Chapters 14 and 15 of the Rotterdam Rules on jurisdiction and arbitration

CONCLUSION

This chapter has considered the differing approaches of the common law; the European rules; and existing international conventions, including the Rotterdam Rules, to three critical issues affecting jurisdiction in maritime disputes: whether a neutral choice of jurisdiction which has no connection with the dispute should be permitted; whether such a choice can bind a third party and which tribunal should determine whether a valid choice has been made.

[209] Eg as the limits of liability are higher, the seaworthiness obligation is continuous, the elimination of the defence of navigational fault etc.
[210] See fns 32 and 33.

By its very nature shipping is frequently an international business which may involve many different jurisdictions. By trading its vessel to different jurisdictions should a carrier be obliged to submit to the jurisdiction of the courts in the places to which it trades or be obliged to hold any arbitration in such places? The Rotterdam Rules would go even further and would impose on the carrier jurisdiction or arbitration in an inland place, which may have no expertise in maritime matters and be very unsophisticated in legal matters in general, or, even worse, corrupt. Alternatively should the parties be entitled to provide for a contractual choice of a place which is highly regarded for its expertise and integrity?

For this author the answer is clear. Commercial certainty is of great importance in contracts for the carriage of goods by sea. Provided that the parties have chosen a jurisdiction or arbitration clause, that choice should be given effect to as this is part of the price for the contract. A neutral choice should therefore be allowed. The test for whether such a clause is binding should be clear and simple so that money is not wasted on arguing about where a dispute should be determined rather than on the merits of the dispute itself. We should therefore focus on that test. Once it has been satisfied then the clause should bind a third party who wishes to rely on the other terms of the contract. We should avoid variations of national law with the risk of conflicting decisions on jurisdiction and then on the merits of the dispute. The tribunal allegedly chosen should decide whether there is a valid clause.

Whereas the English common law rules are fiercely protective of English jurisdiction clauses, whether for court or arbitration, and will grant an anti-suit injunction to restrain a breach of such a clause in a court outside the European Union, there is currently no such protection within the European Union. The Recast Regulation is welcome to give greater protection for a choice of the court of an EU Member State. Such a choice brings economic benefits not only to contracting parties, but also brings significant wealth into the European Union. In times of recession such benefits need to be protected, indeed celebrated, rather than squandered. As Recital 4 of the Recast Regulation states, 'Certain differences between national rules governing jurisdiction and recognition of judgments hamper the sound operation of the internal market.'

Although some strides have been made towards unification in the Recast Regulation, nevertheless significant differences between national laws on jurisdiction in the field of carriage of goods by sea amongst the EU Member States remain, and even more so on the world scene. Recent attempts on an international level to harmonise the position on choice of jurisdiction or arbitration should be strongly resisted and the European Union and other States should not opt in to either of the Chapters on jurisdiction or arbitration in the Rotterdam Rules. Significant challenges therefore remain.

Index

Page reference in **bold** refer to information found in tables.

arbitration:
 arbitration agreements, 253–4
 neutral choice, 247–8
 third parties, 249
breach of contract, 137n24
court jurisdiction:
 jurisdiction clauses, 246
 neutral choice, 244–5
 third parties, 245–6
discretion, 241
environment:
 Declaration of the United Nations
  Conference on the Human
  Environment, 113
 duty to protect, 95–7
  shipping, 96
 global protection strategy, 100–2
 ship breaking, 120–4
 shipping and, 97–100
  carbon emissions, 124–5
  environmental standards, 110
  ship breaking, 120–4
 sustainable development, 102–6
EUNAVFOR, 10, 15, 15n76
 Operation Atlanta, 15
  establishment, 15
  objectives, 15
  remit, 15
European Association for Forwarding,
 Transport, Logistic and Customs Services
 (CLECAT), 177–8
European Court of Justice, 33–4
European Union, 237, 240
 arbitration, 243, 262–3
 civil justice systems, 243
 conflict of laws, 237–40
  arbitration, 262–3
  court jurisdiction, 254–62
  variation in civil justice systems, 243
 court jurisdiction:
  European Court of Justice, 259–62
  neutral choice, 254–6
  third parties, 256–9
 European regulation, 237
 Europeanisation, 238
  EC Jurisdiction Convention, 238
  EC Jurisdiction Regulation, 238–9
  harmonisation of rules, 240

Recast Regulation, 239
EUNAVFOR, 10, 15, 15n76
harmonisation:
 contract law, 240
 jurisdiction, 238–40
 solvency proceedings, 240
litigation, 242
Marine Strategy Framework Directive,
 100–2
multimodal transport, 172–4
 feasibility of uniform liability regime,
  173
 transport integrators' liability, 173
private international law, 240–1
Rome Convention, 240
solvency proceedings, 240
transport law:
 inadequacies, 172–3
exclusive economic zones, 5, 67, 87, 111
 designation, 108n64
 freedom of navigation, 23–4

flag states, 116–7
 coastal state interests versus, 106–12
 financial issues of re-flagging, 118
 flags of convenience, 117
 'genuine link' requirement, 119–20
 impact of globalisation, 118
 prosecution of mariners, 32
 rule of exclusive jurisdiction (UNCLOS),
  25
foreign ports:
 administrative proceedings, 31
 penal proceedings, 31
fortuity and inevitability, 212–3, 216–7, 218,
 219
 external fortuitous accident, 220
forum non conveniens, 241–2
freedom of fishing:
 freedom of navigation distinguished, 25,
  31, 39–40
 right to fish, 39
freedom of navigation, 23–6
 compliance with international standards
  and rules, 28–9
 concepts:
  absolutism, 26–35
  relativism, 35–41